K 1231/1703 A1

AK/10   R

Psychological and Behavioral Aspects of Physical Disability

A MANUAL FOR HEALTH PRACTITIONERS

Contributors

ROBERT D. BOYD, Ph.D., Professor of Medical Psychology and Head of Psychology Section, Crippled Children's Division, The Oregon Health Sciences University, Portland, OR 97201.

ANN M. GARNER, Ph.D., Professor of Medical Psychology, Director of Clinical Training in Psychology, Crippled Children's Division, The Oregon Health Sciences University, Portland, OR 97201.

RUSSELL H. JACKSON, Ph.D., Associate Professor of Medical Psychology, Crippled Children's Division, The Oregon Health Sciences University, Portland, OR 97201.

JAMES E. LINDEMANN, Ph.D., Professor of Medical Psychology, Crippled Children's Division, The Oregon Health Sciences University, Portland, OR 97201.

JOSEPH D. MATARAZZO, Ph.D., Professor and Chairman, Department of Medical Psychology, The Oregon Health Sciences University, Portland, OR 97201.

VICTOR D. MENASHE, M.D., Professor of Pediatrics, Director, Crippled Children's Division, The Oregon Health Sciences University, Portland, OR 97201.

MAURINE B. OTOS, M.S., State Coordinator of Programs and Services for Deaf/Blind Children, Department of Education, Salem, OR 97403.

MARY ELLEN STANGER, M.D., Assistant Professor of Pediatrics, Crippled Children's Division, The Oregon Health Sciences University, Portland, OR 97201.

LEIF G. TERDAL, Ph.D., Professor of Medical Psychology, Crippled Children's Division, The Oregon Health Sciences University, Portland, OR 97201.

NORTON B. YOUNG, Ph.D., Professor of Audiology in Pediatrics, Crippled Children's Division, The Oregon Health Sciences University, Portland, OR 97201.

Psychological and Behavioral Aspects of Physical Disability

A MANUAL FOR HEALTH PRACTITIONERS

JAMES E. LINDEMANN
The Oregon Health Sciences University
Portland, Oregon

With contributions from
ROBERT D. BOYD, ANN M. GARNER,
RUSSELL H. JACKSON, MAURINE B. OTOS,
MARY ELLEN STANGER, LEIF G. TERDAL,
and NORTON B. YOUNG

Medical Consultant: VICTOR D. MENASHE, M.D.

PLENUM PRESS • NEW YORK AND LONDON

Library of Congress Cataloging in Publication Data

Lindeman, James Earl, 1927-
  Psychological and behavioral aspects of physical disability.

  Includes bibliographies and index.
  1. Physically handicapped—Psychology. 2. Physically handicapped—Rehabilitation—Psychological aspects. I. Title. [DNLM: 1. Handicapped—Psychology. 2. Counseling. 3. Chronic disease—Psychology. 4. Chronic disease—Rehabilitation. WM 55 L743p]
  RD798.L56   616   81-17885
  ISBN 0-306-40776-0   AACR2

© 1981 Plenum Press, New York
A Division of Plenum Publishing Corporation
233 Spring Street, New York, N.Y. 10013

All rights reserved

No part of this book may be reproduced stored in a retrieval system, or transmitted in any form or by any means, electronic, mechanical, photocopying, microfilming, recording, or otherwise, without written permission from the Publisher

Printed in the United States of America

To Our Patients

Foreword

A relationship between the disciplines of psychology and medicine is evident in writings from the beginnings of recorded history. This interaction was characterized in some epochs by mutual interest and support, only to be followed by periods of relative disinterest. During the past century there have been several formal attempts to acknowledge this interdependence and to revive and codify on a more permanent basis the working relationships between practitioners and scientists from both psychology and medicine. These twentieth-century waves of interest, which have also come and gone, have been identified by such names as psychosomatic medicine and rehabilitation psychology. For a variety of reasons, notably the lack of a sufficient knowledge base in either discipline, the desired partnership has not come to full flower. This state of affairs seems to be changing as we enter the last two decades of the twentieth century.

In the *American Psychologist* in September, 1980, I reviewed recent developments in psychology and in medicine and in federal and private funding patterns, which give evidence of revitalizing this partnership between these two disciplines and their relevant subspecialties. For example, after six decades of spectacular biomedical scientific advances which have all but eradicated such life-threatening diseases as poliomyelitis and tuberculosis, leaders in medicine, the behavioral sciences, and other segments of society reached a consensus during the 1970s that the *behavior* of the individual is one of today's unexplored frontiers for modern medical practice and related good health care. This country is asking medicine and psychology to define and target health services and to deploy their resources in ways better suited to assist the millions of individuals who today are afflicted with *chronic* disease and dysfunction. This contrasts with the emphasis on acute disease which constituted the major focus of medicine a generation ago.

From the perspective of scholarship only, the present volume exemplifies the contributions of modern psychologists in transporting relevant psychological, social, and behavioral concepts to many areas of medicine. It represents an initial organization of the empirical, clinical, scientific, and theoretical knowledge which they and their colleagues from medicine and allied disciplines have amassed during the past two decades. There is also a more personal perspective.

The recent history of The Oregon Health Sciences University (formerly University of Oregon School of Medicine) mirrors the developments which have taken place in major medical centers. The rapid and extensive post–World War II expansion added thousands of full-time faculty members to this country's medical schools, and the numbers of pediatricians, psychologists, and other clinically trained specialists in our school increased considerably after 1955. For example, the personnel of the Department of Medical Psychology increased from one individual in 1957 to 41 psychologists on the current full-time faculty. Six of the clinical psychologists in this group have primary teaching and patient care responsibilities in the Crippled Children's Division of our Health Sciences University. This division is the agency which extends services to the children, adolescents, and young adults of Oregon who are crippled or who suffer from diseases which may lead to crippling. It also includes a university-affiliated program for interdisciplinary training in developmental disability. Since helping to recruit the first faculty psychologist in 1963, I have watched with pride as five additional psychologists joined this pioneer in the professionally challenging and rewarding application of their clinical, teaching, and research skills as members of a multidisciplinary team using its collective skills in the service of the patient–client.

The present volume is but one index of the singular success of this marriage among representatives of psychology, medicine, and a variety of allied professional fields (dentistry, hearing and speech specialties, social work, and others). Although many have learned relatively recently that the behavior of the individual was a critical variable in the treatment and rehabilitation of our patients, my colleagues at the Crippled Children's Division were aware of this and were utilizing such knowledge a decade earlier. Whereas many of us have recently learned that the behavior of our patients plays a crucial role in such conditions as lung cancer, obesity, and diet-related cardiovascular dysfunction, our colleagues at the Crippled Children's Division have long known that the difference in the therapeutic outcome with two patients each afflicted with hemophilia, for example, depended upon the behavioral motivation of each patient and the familial and societal supports available to him or her.

In the present volume, James Lindemann, a psychologist–specialist in clinical and counseling psychology, has asked his medical, psychological, and other colleagues to join together and to place between the covers of a single volume the experience they have gained over the years of assessing, teaching, and counseling patients (and their families) with the disorders described in each chapter heading. The result is a product which combines, on the one hand, the clinical skills which the clinician–authors have honed in years of working with patients and the scholar's perspective achieved in those same years as they wrestled with the task of transmitting this knowledge to students in psychology, medicine, nursing, and a dozen other health-related fields.

I learned a great deal from reading this book and commend it to practicing professionals, to teachers, and to the students in the various health disciplines. The volume brings together the major concepts in each subject area, relates them to the most recent findings, and brings them to life with the spice of clinical wisdom. The seasoned practitioner will find new insights and perspectives, and the newcomer will find an invaluable organization of the field.

JOSEPH D. MATARAZZO

Portland, Oregon

Preface

This book is a guide for those engaged in work with persons who have serious physically disabling conditions. Its contents are directed toward the interests and needs of the practicing counselor, psychologist, social worker, special educator, physician, physical therapist, occupational therapist, nurse, or student preparing for work in these and other health-related fields. It is intended for use in applied settings and contains, in addition to information about psychological and social characteristics and problems, "how-to" suggestions for evaluation and intervention. There is an underlying assumption that the effectiveness of any procedure (e.g., interview, testing, therapy, teaching) will be closely related to the quality of the relationship between the helping person and the patient/client/student. The reader will note continuing emphasis, therefore, on relating to the person rather than to the disease stereotype. Methods are stressed which serve to reduce the obscuring effects of poorly articulated speech, limited hearing or vision, social pressure to avoid reference to the disability, or lack of knowledge of the implications of the disability. Given this stress on the quality of the relationship, the book then has the bias that changing what the patient *does* is at least as important as changing how he/she feels about it.

This is not a "mental illness" book, nor a "mental health" book. It attempts to address the life decisions and behavioral problems that arise when a serious disability is present. It assumes that the helping person is in a consulting relationship to the patient, his family, and the significant others in his life. Where mental health or mental illness concepts are relevant (e.g., depression, suicide) they are discussed, with appropriate suggestions. They are not the focus. The focus is on helping individuals to make those decisions, acquire those skills, and to seek those experiences which will permit them most fully to enjoy the competencies and satisfactions of human existence. The concern is with living effectively with the disability, rather than "curing" it. In this respect, the thrust of the volume is in the developing tradition of behavioral medicine and health as defined by Matarazzo (1980) and Schwartz and Weiss (1978).

Because understanding the developmental process is important to the total understanding of the individual with a lifelong physical disability, many of the chapters devote considerable attention to the impact of the disability on child and family. This is not, however, primarily a book about children; the reader will find coverage of vocation, sex and marital relations, and other aspects of adult social adjustment.

Chapter 1 covers some matters of general importance in working with most physically disabled persons. It touches on the stigma of, and the process of adjustment to, physical disability. Some characteristics and problems found in many physically disabled persons are described, with suggestions for coping with them or for developing strengths which will obviate them. Some methods are described for enhancing the relationship of the health professional with the "disabled" person, as well as handling problems of mental illness (including suicidal ideation) which may be encountered. The current concepts of normalization and mainstreaming are discussed, and some important milestones in the transition to adult independence are enumerated. This brief chapter is not intended to replace general reference works on counseling physically disabled persons. It does attempt to include concepts which appear to be particularly relevant or which have not been presented elsewhere.

Chapters 2 through 14 follow a common format. Each begins with a brief section entitled "The Physical Disability," a description of important points about the disability, its etiology, diagnosis, and treatment, sufficient to provide a frame of reference for the nonmedical health professional. This is followed by a more detailed exposition of "Common Psychological Characteristics and Problems," which describes response patterns and behavioral or personality traits frequently associated with the disability. "Evaluating Persons with (the Disability)" describes interview approaches, with mention of unique problems or special areas which require attention. If there are unusual problems in psychological testing, appropriate tests and methods are described, with suggestions for their interpretation with this population. "Intervention Methods" includes long-term management in the interdisciplinary team context, as well as individual and group psychotherapy and behavioral, social and family-oriented interventions. In general, this section will emphasize prophylactic approaches to dealing with life stresses rather than treatment of psychological abnormalities. "Trends and Needs" gives a very brief projection of current directions in the field, as well as mention of significant needs for research and development. Finally, the reader will find sources of further information, including organizations, books, or other materials of interest to the professional, the patient, or his family.

The orientation is notably eclectic, reflecting the varied backgrounds of the authors and a consciously catholic approach to literature review so that the findings of many disciplines are represented. A consistent attempt has been made to include concepts from divergent viewpoints such as traditional dynamic, relationship therapy, behavior modification, and biofeedback. The contributors have in addition drawn upon their extensive clinical backgrounds to provide anecdotal examples and subjective observations to enliven the text. The experience of preparing this book has been enriching to this group of colleagues, and it is offered in the hope that the reader's experience will be similar.

JAMES E. LINDEMANN

Portland, Oregon

REFERENCES

Matarazzo, J. D. Behavioral health and behavioral medicine. *American Psychologist*, 1980, *35*, 807–817.

Schwartz, G. E., & Weiss, S. M. Behavioral medicine revisited: An amended definition. *Journal of Behavioral Medicine*, 1978, *1*, 249–251.

Acknowledgments

Much of the life and many of the insights in this book flow from the rich contribution of feelings and ideas provided by our patients in the Crippled Children's Division of The Oregon Health Sciences University. The principal author wishes to acknowledge, also, his debt to many vocational rehabilitation clients and counselors who have shared with him.

Each chapter contributor, with the skill of an independent expert, has had the grace to accept a common format, to meet deadlines, and to work in genuine collaboration so as to produce a cohesive and useful volume. Special thanks are extended to Ann M. Garner, who, in addition to her own chapter on diabetes, has provided a thorough reading and thoughtful critique of each of the other chapters, adding significantly to the clarity and scholarship through her editorial wisdom.

Victor D. Menashe added perceptive medical authority to the contents. Joseph D. Matarazzo provided initial encouragement as well as a generous foreword. Both gave helpful administrative encouragement and support to the project.

We could never fully identify the many contributions of our colleagues in the Crippled Children's Division, The Oregon Health Sciences University and the Oregon professional community. Those who gave of their expertise by chapter review or special consultation were: Timothy Carmody, Leland Cross, Phyllis Donohue, Douglas Golden, William Guyer, Susan Hanks, John Keiter, Doug Kinney, Stephen LaFranchi, Elaine Lis, David Macfarlane, Ellen Magenis, Margaret McGill, Ray Meyers, Lois Mock, Rodney Pelson, Diane Plumridge, Gerald Prescott, and Sue Underwood.

Joanie Livermore added her own touch to the effectiveness of the illustrations. Typing assistance was provided by Don LaBare, Karen Guthreau, and Adrienne Weller. Margaret Haworth performed the heroic task of preparing the final manuscript.

The principal author could not have managed without the help of his wife, Sally Lindemann, who happily combines the role of supportive helpmate with that of constructive professional critic.

Contents

Foreword by *Joseph D. Matarazzo* vii

Chapter 1 General Considerations for Evaluating and Counseling the Physically Handicapped 1

The Stigma of Disability 1
The Process of Adjustment to Disability 3
Psychological Characteristics and Problems Commonly Associated with Disability 5
Helping Relationships with the Physically Disabled 10
Suggestions about Process 11
Labeling, Normalization, and Mainstreaming 14
Milestones 15
References 18

Chapter 2 Hemophilia 21

The Physical Disability 21
  Definition and Incidence 21
  Manifestations 22
  Treatment 23
Common Psychological Characteristics and Problems 24
  Introduction 24
  The Family 25
  Intelligence—Schooling 26

xvii

Emotional Adjustment	27
Vocation	29
Evaluating Persons with Hemophilia	29
Intervention Methods	30
Trends and Needs	34
Appendix: Sources of Information	35
References	36

Chapter 3 Diabetes Mellitus ... 39

Ann M. Garner

The Physical Disability	40
Classification	40
Prevalence	40
Genetic Factors	41
Clinical Characteristics	42
Treatment	43
General Effect on Physical Development	44
Common Psychological Characteristics and Problems	46
General Consequences of Chronic Conditions	46
Psychological Characteristics Unique to Diabetes	50
Evaluating Diabetic Patients	54
Evaluating the General Level of Cognitive Functioning	56
Evaluating the Patient's Emotional Status	57
Evaluating the Patient's Adaptive Behavior	58
Intervention Methods	58
Trends and Needs	61
Management and Self-Care	61
Clinical and Laboratory Research	62
Appendix: Sources of Information	63
References	64

Chapter 4 Other Genetic Disorders ... 69

Russell H. Jackson

Genetic Disorders	69
Mechanisms of Inheritance	70
Autosomal and X-Linked Recessive Disorders	71
Autosomal Dominant Disorders	72

CONTENTS xix

    Chromosomal Abnormalities 72
    Genetic Counseling 73
  Phenylketonuria 74
    The Physical Disability 74
    Common Psychological Characteristics and Problems 78
    Evaluating Persons with Phenylketonuria 79
    Intervention Methods 82
  Turner's Syndrome 82
    The Physical Disability 82
    Common Psychological Characteristics and Problems 85
    Evaluating Persons with Turner's Syndrome 87
    Intervention Methods 89
  Klinefelter's Syndrome 90
    The Physical Disability 90
    Common Psychological Characteristics and Problems 92
    Evaluating Persons with Klinefelter's Syndrome 93
    Intervention Methods 94
  Huntington's Disease 95
    The Physical Disability 95
    Common Psychological Characteristics and Problems 99
    Evaluating Persons with Huntington's Disease 105
    Intervention Methods 107
  Trends and Needs 109
  Appendix: Sources of Information 110
  References 110

Chapter 5 Cerebral Palsy 117

The Physical Disability 117
  Definition 117
  Incidence 118
  Motor 120
  Speech 121
  Hearing 121
  Vision 122
  Intelligence 122
  Seizures 122
Common Psychological Characteristics and Problems 123
  Family 123
  Intellectual and Emotional Functioning 125

Speech	126
Self-Concept	127
Social and Work Adjustment	128
Evaluating Persons with Cerebral Palsy	129
Interview	129
Psychological Testing	131
Intervention Methods	136
The Family	136
Realistic Expectations, Self-Appraisal, Self-Concept	136
Identity and Competence	138
Employment and Vocational Counseling	139
Behavior Modification	140
Trends and Needs	142
Appendix: Sources of Information	142
References	143

Chapter 6 Epilepsy 147
Leif G. Terdal

The Physical Disability	148
Classification of Epileptic Seizures	148
Prevalence	151
Etiology	152
Current Treatment Procedures	153
Common Psychological Characteristics and Problems	162
Impact of Seizures	162
Misperceptions or Fears Associated with the Diagnosis of Epilepsy	163
Epilepsy and Predicaments	164
Employment	165
Epilepsy and Intellectual Impairment	166
Epilepsy and Personality Disorders	167
Evaluation of Individuals with Epilepsy	168
Impact of Epilepsy on the Adjustment of a Child	168
Specialized Assessment for Evaluation of Seizure-Related Transient Mental Deficits	171
Intellectual and Cognitive Assessment of Individuals with Epilepsy	172
Specialized Neuropsychological Assessment	173
Assessment of Issues Pertaining to Epilepsy and Employment	173

CONTENTS xxi

Intervention Methods 174
Trends and Needs 175
Appendix: Sources of Information 176
References 176

Chapter 7 Mental Retardation 179
Leif G. Terdal

The Physical Disability 180
   Definition 180
   Levels of Mental Retardation 180
   Mental Retardation as "Reversible" 181
   Prevalence 182
   Etiology 182
Common Psychological Characteristics and Problems 189
   Impact of Diagnosis 189
   Altered Feedback 191
   Peer Relations 192
   Adult Adjustment 192
Evaluating Persons with Mental Retardation 193
   Recurring Assessment Questions. Infancy, School Years,
   Adult Years 193
   Types of Assessment Instruments 194
   Selection of Assessment Procedure 202
   Special Considerations 206
Intervention Methods 207
   Intervention: A Framework 207
   Interdisciplinary Care 210
   Residential Treatment 211
Trends and Needs 212
Appendix: Sources of Information 212
References 213

Chapter 8 Spinal Cord Injury 217

The Physical Disability 217
   Incidence 217
   Acute Care 218
   Rehabilitation Care 219
Common Psychological Characteristics and Problems 221
   Stages of Reaction 221

Personality Patterns 223
Social and Sexual Adjustment 224
Evaluating Persons with Spinal Cord Injury 227
Interview 227
Psychological Testing 228
Intervention Methods 231
Early Stages 231
The Family 232
Independence 232
Psychotherapy 233
Sex and Marital Counseling 234
Vocation 235
Trends and Needs 236
Appendix: Sources of Information 238
References 239

Chapter 9 Myelomeningocele (Spina Bifida) 243

James E. Lindemann and Robert D. Boyd

The Physical Disability 243
Definition 243
Incidence and Etiology 245
The Decision to Treat 245
Associated Problems 246
Common Psychological Characteristics and Problems 248
Family Impact 248
Intelligence and Schooling 250
Emotional Adjustment 252
Vocation 255
Evaluating Persons with Myelomeningocele 256
Evaluation of the Environment 256
Evaluation of the Person 258
Intervention Methods 261
Intervention Goals 261
Intervention with Parents 261
Intervention with School Personnel 263
Direct Intervention with the Myelomeningocele Patient ... 266
Trends and Needs 268
Training of Professional Care Personnel 268
Appendix: Sources of Information 268
References 269

CONTENTS

Chapter 10 Progressive Muscle Disorders 273
James E. Lindemann and Mary Ellen Stanger

- The Physical Disability 273
  - Diagnostic Methods 274
  - The Anterior Horn Cell or Lower Motor Neuron 276
- Common Psychological Characteristics and Problems 285
  - Childhood Onset 287
  - Adolescent and Early Adult Onset 290
  - Adult Onset 291
- Evaluation of Patients with Progressive Muscle Disorder 293
  - Interview 293
  - Psychological Testing 294
- Intervention Methods 296
- Trends and Needs 298
- Appendix: Sources of Information 299
- References 299

Chapter 11 Congenital Heart Defects 301

- The Physical Disability 301
  - Definition and Incidence 301
  - Associated Conditions 304
  - Manifestations 305
  - Diagnosis and Treatment 305
- Common Psychological Characteristics and Problems 306
  - Emotional 306
  - Cognitive 309
- Evaluating Persons with Congenital Heart Defect 310
- Intervention Methods 311
- Trends and Needs 313
- Appendix: Sources of Information 314
- References 314

Chapter 12 Coronary Heart Disease 317

- The Physical Disability 317
  - Definition and Incidence 317
  - Risk Factors 318
  - Diagnosis 319
  - Treatment 320

Common Psychological Characteristics and Problems 321
   Type A Personality 321
   Post-Coronary 323
Evaluating Persons with Coronary Heart Disease 326
Intervention Methods 327
Trends and Needs 331
Appendix: Sources of Information 331
References 332

Chapter 13 Visual Handicaps 335

Robert D. Boyd and Maurine B. Otos

Physical Disability 335
   Overview 335
   Incidence and Causation 335
   Definition of Blindness 338
Common Psychological Characteristics and Problems 341
   Parent-Child Interactions 341
   Early Development and Learning 342
   Development of Communication Skills 345
   Psychological and Behavioral Reactions to Blindness 346
Evaluating the Blind 354
   Parental and Environmental Evaluation 354
   Evaluation of Development and Intelligence 356
   Evaluation of Personality 359
Intervention Methods 361
   Medical Intervention 361
   Parent Training and Child Training 362
   Training the Blind Person 363
   Rehabilitative and Therapeutic Intervention 366
Trends and Needs 369
Appendix: Sources of Information 369
References 371

Chapter 14 Hearing Disorders 375

Robert D. Boyd and Norton B. Young

The Physical Disability 375
   Definition and Incidence 375

CONTENTS

Principal Causes and Medical Treatments
for Hearing Loss 377
Problems in Identifying Hearing Impairment 384
Hearing Aid Amplification 385
Common Psychological Characteristics and Problems 386
   Overview 386
   Family Effects 386
   Individual Effects 388
Evaluating the Hearing-Impaired Person 392
   General Problem: Communication 392
   Evaluating Cognitive Ability 393
   Measurement of Personality 395
   Evaluation Interview 396
Intervention Methods 399
   The Multidiscipline Approach 399
   Intervention with the Family 400
   Educational Methods 403
   Personal Counseling 404
Trends and Needs 406
   Electrical Stimulation of the Auditory Nerve 406
   Electrophysiological Audiometry 406
   Regional Resource Centers 407
   Public Attitude 407
   Preventive Procedures 408
Appendix: Sources of Information 408
References 409

Index 413

1

General Considerations for Evaluating and Counseling the Physically Handicapped

THE STIGMA OF DISABILITY

In this era of social causes and consciousness-raising, there remains a curious void in the crusade of the disabled. Only occasionally is there a note of militancy, and virtually nothing about pride. "Help the Disabled" and "Hire the Handicapped" do little to deemphasize the dependent role of people who need special assistance. The powerful connotations of the sick role appear to grip us all, normal and disabled alike.

The implications of the sick role have been outlined by Parsons (1964) as follows: (1) it is beyond the power of the person to overcome the affliction, and therefore he cannot be held responsible; (2) it carries with it exemption from normal role and task obligations; (3) the role is *conditionally* legitimated in that the person must recognize it as undesirable; and (4) the person must seek help. Thus, the person is defined as needing help and put in a position of dependency on people who are not ill. Further, there is emphasis on insulating the "normal" from the "sick," as though the role might be motivationally contagious.

The presumption of dependency and helplessness seems to operate, at almost an unconscious level, in the attitudes of both the normal and the disabled. To this presumption must be added the problems of social interaction and stigmatization which are faced by the visibly handicapped. The visibly handicapped may move awkwardly, speak strangely, or be unattractive in appearance from the viewpoint of traditional standards. Davis (1961) describes the experience of the visibly handicapped in casual social interactions. They report a pronounced "stickiness" in interactional flow, with the disability either the focal point of the interaction or conspicuously avoided. They frequently receive fictional acceptance consisting of polite social amenities in which the " . . . interaction is kept starved at a bare subsistence level of sociability" (Davis, 1961, p. 127). He notes that there is no ready-made symbolic shorthand as there has been historically for stereotyped minority groups. Thus, the visibly handicapped person must explore the possibilities of a relationship with each new acquaintance, not knowing whether to expect enlightened acceptance or prejudiced pigeon-holing.

This stereotypy in reaction and interaction is companion to a concept which Wright (1960) has called *spread*. This is the common conviction that people who are inferior in some areas must be inadequate in others. People have difficulty in integrating a mixture of positive and negative attributes (Could Hitler possibly have been kind to animals? Could Albert Schweitzer have had bad thoughts?). They tend to feel that negative effects should have negative causes; disability and unattractive appearance, therefore, are equated with emotional instability and intellectual limitation, with neither rhyme nor reason. This phenomenon of spread may lead to curiously paradoxical perceptions of disabled persons. Those with visible handicaps may be seen as more emotionally maladjusted than, in fact, they are. Those with serious disabilities which are not visible (e.g., diabetes, heart condition) may be assumed to be emotionally healthy, with subsequent surprise should they prove to have significant emotional problems related to their disability.

Weinberg and Santana (1978) suggest that disabled stereotypes are maintained by the media. They rated 290 comic book characters and found that 63 were presented as physically deformed. Every one of the physically deformed persons was clearly characterized as good or evil. None was neutral. Of those with deformities, 57% were portrayed as evil, in contrast to 20% evil among those without deformities.

Abroms and Kodera (1979) asked college students to rank the acceptability to them of various disabling conditions. Their results are presented in Table I. The organizing principle which they discerned from the ratings was that organic impairments typically responsive to medical intervention were rated generally most acceptable, followed by sensorimotor impairments, with psychoeducational or functional impairments typically not responsive to medical intervention rated least acceptable.

TABLE I
Overall Rankings of Disabling Conditions[a]

Rank	Disability	Mean rank	SD
1	Ulcer	3.20	3.270
2	Asthma	3.45	2.368
3	Diabetes	3.71	2.418
4	Arthritis	4.86	2.739
5	Learning disability	6.36	3.139
6	Speech defect	6.50	3.150
7	Deafness	8.51	3.231
8	Epilepsy	8.72	3.245
9	Tuberculosis	8.79	3.329
10	Amputee	9.46	3.769
11	Blindness	9.74	2.949
12	Cancer	10.77	3.619
13	Mental illness	11.46	3.249
14	Cerebral palsy	12.17	2.544
15	Mental retardation	12.37	2.679

[a] Adapted from Abroms and Kodera, 1979.

THE PROCESS OF ADJUSTMENT TO DISABILITY

There appear to be certain commonalities in the response of afflicted persons and their families to the occurrence of serious physical disability. Stages of reaction have been described repeatedly in the literature of trauma (e.g., Kübler-Ross, 1969). These are more sharply defined in the case of traumatic injury or other disability which may appear suddenly (e.g., heart attack). Describing such responses to spinal cord injury, Weller and Miller (1977) characterize these as shock, denial, anger, depression, and acceptance or adjustment. This author prefers to use the term *adaptation* for the final phase; this term more readily lends itself to the interpretation that this phase may vary markedly from positive to negative in nature.

Shock may be physical or psychological, depending upon the nature of the disability. It is a massive protective mechanism which is usually relatively short in duration.

Denial is often more prolonged and is used to protect the individual from the implications of severe disability which may be devastating in the short run to the self-concept and emotional stability of patient and family. It is a helpful mechanism if it is slowly relinquished as accommodation is made to the changes required and possibilities permitted by the particular disability. It becomes maladaptive if it interferes significantly with necessary treatment or rehabilitation procedures. Premature attempts to combat denial will ordinarily evoke defensiveness and, if successful, may destroy the hope that is necessary for motivation. Although unrealistic beliefs should not be positively reinforced, neither should they be confronted unless the issue is critical or the patient is ready to change.

Anger may parallel denial or follow it. It is a response to physical and psychological hurt, the perceived unfairness of the injury, and the fact that the person is being forced by circumstances to make significant changes in the way he/she looks at self and life. Anger may be impunitive, directed at the fates or God. It may also be directed at family or at professional staff. It is important that it be viewed as part of a process and not as a personal attack. Ordinarily it should be tolerated and not reinforced. If anger becomes excessively disruptive, it may require personal counseling beyond the supportive contacts provided by the various disciplines who would ordinarily be providing service to a traumatically injured individual.

Depression may occur at any point in the process. It may reflect perception of what the patient sees as a hopeless and unrewarding life ahead. It may reflect guilt about the patient's role in the trauma which resulted in the injury. It may reflect guilt about expressions of anger, especially if they have been irrational. Depression will require supportive counseling from regular staff and should prompt consideration of the need for referral for more formal psychotherapy, as well as alertness to the possible threat of suicide.

As has been suggested, *adaptation* to physical disability may vary from optimal, positive self-actualizing to negative, embittered retreat. This will usually reflect both the inner resources which the patient originally possessed and the treatment which has been received.

In the case of developmental disabilities and other chronic impairments, patient and family are generally spared acute physical trauma, and the patient frequently does not have to alter an established adjustment. Nevertheless, Kessler (1977) describes the advent of a chronic disability within a family in much the same terms as have been used in describing response to traumatic injury. Under the *diagnostic phase* she subsumes the categories of shock, denial, anger and depression. These generally describe the reaction of the family to the fact of the diagnosis. Kessler's *adaptive phase* then covers the considerable period of time in which patient and family learn to function in terms of the patient's developmental progress and within any limits which are posed by the disability. It is this author's observation that the families of chronically disabled persons, while frequently protective (sometimes too much so), at the same time often have a perspective developed over time which makes their relationship to the patient and the disability less intense than is the case with the traumatically injured.

Moos and Tsu (1977, p 12–15) have reconceptualized the adjustment process as the acquisition and use of seven major types of coping skills. The first category includes skills based on *denying or minimizing the seriousness* of the illness, using defense mechanisms as previously described here. A second set of coping skills consists of *seeking relevant information*, learning about the disability. A third is requesting reassurance and emotional support from family, friends and professionals. The fourth is learning specific illness-related procedures, such as infusion of blood products or use of wheelchairs. The fifth involves setting concrete limited goals, breaking large overwhelming problems into small manageable parts. Number six is rehearsing alternative outcomes to prepare for difficulties and allay anxiety. Finally, the seventh coping skill is finding a general purpose or pattern of meaning, setting a direction and putting things in perspective. This conceptualization of adaptation as skills acquisition has the useful effect of suggesting the patient's role as one of very active participation in the process.

PSYCHOLOGICAL CHARACTERISTICS AND PROBLEMS COMMONLY ASSOCIATED WITH DISABILITY

There are problems commonly faced by parents and those who seek to nurture others which become magnified in the case of the handicapped. These are problems generally subsumed under such headings as dependence–independence and protection–overprotection. Most parents can describe the delicate decisions involved in allowing children to expand horizons, grow, make their own decisions, and make their own mistakes. Most of us, having experienced adolescence, can describe the difficulty in exerting just enough aggressiveness to be our own person without either feeling like a controlled extension of our parents or outraging their values, expectations or limits (which frequently seem from our peer perspective to be outrageous from the start).

In the case of the seriously physically disabled this already difficult developmental process is additionally burdened with problems of *ignorance, expedience, psychological self-protection,* and *unsophisticated benevolence.* These will be briefly discussed here in a developmental context, although it should be pointed out that they similarly affect the adult disabled, either in adjustment to a new disability or as residuals of the developmental process. There are over-protected fifty-year-olds as well as five-year-olds.

Ignorance should not be overlooked as a basis for psychological problems of the disabled. Many parents, teachers, and others (e.g., employers) really do not know how much to expect from the disabled person. Should we include the child in family walks, dragging foot and all? (Probably yes.) Could the patient mow a lawn? (If it is a question, probably yes.) Should this mildly retarded person be put in an English literature course just to get as much as possible out of the class contact? (Probably no.) With a special raised seat at the assembly line could this employee be expected to meet regular production standards? (Probably yes.) Kessler (1977) has pointed out that conservative overprotection is usually the easiest and safest approach. This becomes doubly true when the decision makers lack technical information of a medical or psychological nature and to a triple degree when they already feel guilty about the disabling condition. Regular evaluation and counsel from knowledgeable professionals can be invaluable in helping to set appropriate goals and expectations. Contact with disabled persons and their families who have already successfully coped with the problem at hand can also be enormously helpful. Finally, parents, teachers, and others need to know that to be mildly protective of a disabled person can be much more destructive than to be mildly demanding.

Expedience contributes greatly to the overprotection and underemployment of the disabled. The author has heard literally hundreds of times, "They could dress themselves, but it would take an hour and we just don't get up that early." Consequently, they almost never dress themselves to get the practice that would reduce the time requirement to one half hour. The author has met the family whose child could do the lunch dishes if they were plastic but to whom it is more important to eat from china. Persons with manual dexterity problems can be so embarrassed by their untidy eating that they refuse to practice enough to improve their skills. The technique of setting easily attained short-term goals that lead to long-term skills can often be useful in coping with these problems.

Psychological self-protection may cause significant problems in the adjustment of the physically disabled. Many come to enjoy being "special" and this, in fact, may be a plausible social role. It is when this attitude is translated into "You can't expect as much from me" or "You shouldn't criticize poor me" that it begins to retard optimal growth and effectiveness. It should be noted that in some persons this use of the disability can be consciously manipulative. More often, and more sadly, the person themselves and to resist the temptation to overrate them in relation to other criteria. It is not to dash hope, but to temper it with occasional demurrers, such as: "Well, you're sure going to give it a good try."; "Even if you can't be a radio announcer, you may be able to work in the station"; "Sure you can try, but, you know, even if you don't make it, there are plenty of people with good jobs who didn't go to college." Small but consistent hints from the significant people in a person's life can be enough to promote more realistic self-appraisal. It is most traumatic later when the cocoon of protection has been invisible and the self-concept is dashed against the reality of unexpected failure. Let us hasten to say that there are instances that are opposite to those exemplified: there are college-bright disabled persons whose experiences have led them to devalue themselves and who need help in raising their aspirations.

Persons with serious physical disabilities frequently have strong feelings about identification and interaction with other handicapped persons. The extremes vary from those whose only peer contacts and only identification is with other handicapped persons to those who eschew any contact with any handicapped person, sometimes maintaining a posture of moral superiority in so doing. Goldman (1978) suggests that many disabled incorporate the notion that the "beautiful body means a beautiful person" and maintain this prejudice against themselves and others. In the author's experience, those seriously handicapped persons do best who move back and forth between activities and identification with the handicapped and similar activities and identification with people at large. Socially isolated persons may have little choice but to begin to develop relationship skills with other handicapped persons. They may then need help in expanding their horizons. This may come in the form of individual or group counseling. Ideally, the handicapped adolescent (or adult) would have opportunity to participate at some time in a therapy or personal growth group with persons of a similar age from the general population. The seriously handicapped person who avoids any contact or identification with other handicapped persons may be doing so from a solid basis of self-awareness but more likely is denying self-doubt, fear, or anger which might be resolved in interaction with other handicapped persons, with subsequently increased inner comfort.

Blandness in the lives of the physically disabled is a problem which has received little notice or attention. Kessler (1977) has observed that boredom may provoke misbehavior in some handicapped children and that life should have some novelty. Similarly, Goldman (1978) advocates programming risk (and novelty) into the lives of the adult disabled. Choice of the safe and conservative seems to permeate the thinking of disabled and normal alike. Haring and Myerson (1979) report that even among presumably liberated college students, 46% disapprove of "a crippled woman's" use of contraceptives, although only 11% disapproved of their general use. Much progress is needed toward the attitude that the disabled are as entitled as anyone else to seek gratification, as well as to be eccentric, have bad taste, look foolish, or make mistakes.

HELPING RELATIONSHIPS WITH THE PHYSICALLY DISABLED

Much of the mystique and anticipated difficulty in working with the disabled fades away as the helping person is able to relate to the person inside the skin of each disabled individual. When the clutter of stereotype, real but surmountable communication problems, or special physical requirements is breached, it is reassuring to find that the psychological problems, and the means for their amelioration, are not very different from those of others.

A certain amount of experience and consciousness-raising is helpful in developing the capacity to establish meaningful and facilitative relationships with disabled clients. Spencer (1979, p. 193) has said, "The most experienced and knowledgeable rehabilitation professional may be subjected to unexpected or unrecognized perceptual biases." He refers to such influences as the immobility of the paralyzed person, with reduced body language and other nonverbal cues, and aversive responses to avoid self-identification with strange motor functions or absence of limbs.

Leviton (1970) examined three of the problem areas most often brought up by professional and client subjects. These were (a) personal involvement and emotional neutrality, (b) hope and reality, and (c) independence and dependence. The latter two have been discussed earlier in this chapter, with conclusions that may be summarized as follows: (1) Unrealistic hopes should not be specifically endorsed (do not lie to the patient), but it is not necessary to confront these aspirations if they do not interfere with progress toward realistic goals. (2) It is better to err in the direction of expecting or demanding slightly too much independence than to err in the opposite direction.

With regard to personal involvement and emotional neutrality, it is significant that of 20 patients studied by Leviton (1970, p 234) not one favored emotional neutrality. The professionals were divided. This appears to underscore the importance of the relationship to the patient. In her discussion, Leviton makes the useful observation that "warmth–coldness" is one continuum and that it may be independent of objectivity. Objectivity is probably a necessary state of mind for the professional, but it is not required that one explicitly argue each difference of perception or judgment with the patient. It is possible to empathize with and accurately reflect a passionate desire to walk again, without sharing the patient's view of the likelihood of that occurrence. It is frequently necessary to hear and recognize such preemptive feelings before it is possible to turn to the planning of the next immediately feasible steps toward a satisfying life.

SUGGESTIONS ABOUT PROCESS

In initial contacts with clients/patients, the author has found it extremely useful, in most instances, to state explicitly "the contract." This usually consists of a statement of the reasons that have been given for requesting the service (evaluation, counseling, etc.) plus a very brief description of the procedures to be carried out, time that will be required, and, if appropriate, the nature of the information or result that is anticipated. It is particularly useful to state these in the presence of others who may have escorted the client for the appointment, especially if they were the ones who initiated the referral. This public sharing of the problem (e.g., "Mom said she was worried about the amount of time you spend in your room and the fact that your grades are going down"), if tactfully done, may be very useful in promoting discussion of problems with significant others. Although some families do this easily, others are very much in need of help toward such discussion. One should insist, wherever possible, that referring persons be willing to acknowledge the fact of and the reasons for their referral.

Although communication is at best an uncertain process, there are some fairly tangible obstacles which may be avoided. Many physically disabled clients speak indistinctly, reflecting problems of articulation, phonation, etc. In ordinary discourse, it may be considered the socially desirable thing to nod or assent to a phrase which is only half understood, rather than to embarrass the patient and oneself by saying that you did not understand it. It is more professionally appropriate and ultimately a source of strength to the relationship to point out that the patient is sometimes difficult to understand and that you, the professional, desiring to understand him fully, will persevere until you do so, so long as the patient is willing to do the same.

Davis (1961) points out that, to go anywhere, a relationship must take the disability into account. Thus it is in the professional–patient encounter. It is important, at some point, to note explicitly that the client has a disability and to discuss it. With some clients this is easy. Others may come from settings in which the disability is never mentioned and may, at first, be quite uncomfortable. The desensitization of the client regarding such discussion may be a useful by-product of a professional encounter. The author has often found it useful to ask clients to describe their disability as if they were doing so to a new friend in whom they wished to confide. The terminology chosen and characteristics described often reveal areas of insight or ignorance of which the professional would not otherwise be aware.

In dealing with adolescents and adults, the author, a psychologist, has made it a policy, with extremely rare exceptions, not to administer psychological tests without a preceding interview.

In providing information to a client and/or the family, one should let the facts speak for themselves. Ability statements can be given in graphic or statistical form which places them in reference to familiar groups. Achievement scores can be given in grade levels. Predictions can be given as generalities: "People who have that degree of difficulty usually . . . " Job requirements can be read from occupational information sourcebooks. Pains should be taken to explain all of the findings and concepts so that they are understood, but the inferences, the judgments about the meaning for *this* person, should be left whenever possible in his/her hands.

Ordinarily, most of the psychosocial assistance provided to physically disabled persons should be supportive, aimed at making decisions, facilitating development, and coping with life problems. These problems may be caused by the disability or, more frequently, be ordinary life problems that have been made more complicated or difficult by the disability. Disabled persons also have their proportionate share of mental illness problems, and this share may be increased by the additional stresses they experience. Thus, there are times when it is appropriate and necessary to think in traditional mental health–illness concepts and to seek services provided by fully qualified mental health professionals. Suggested criteria for mental health referral are presented in Table II. They may be applied to persons at large, as well as to those with physical disability.

In working closely with any population, including the physically disabled, the professional will at times become aware of thoughts of suicide and, at other times, will wish to learn if such ideas might be held by his patient. The significant relationship reported between suicide and physical illness (Dorpat, Anderson, & Ripley, 1968) suggests the wisdom of this policy. Litman (unpublished) has suggested that the most tactful

TABLE II
Suggested Criteria for Mental Health Referral

Mental health referral *may* be made
  When a person has:
  1. Adjustment problems—family, work, other interpersonal, or
  2. Undue anxiety or preoccupation, or
  3. Immaturity, poor judgment, poor impulse control (if motivated for help).

Mental health referral *should* be made
  When person has:
  1. Depression—as evidenced by some combination of (a) depressed mood, (b) apathy, loss of interest, (c) sleep disturbance or (d) appetite disturbance, or
  2. Psychotic symptoms—delusional beliefs, hallucinations or disorganized thinking, or
  3. Adjustment, anxiety, or impulse problems of long standing resulting in serious life problems.

Mental health referral *must* be made
  When there is clear and present danger to self or others.

and informative technique is to approach the suicidal motivation gradually through a series of questions which move from the general to the more specific. An adaptation of his suggested approach is as follows: Talking rather seriously and sincerely (not casually, socially) one might ask the patient questions such as "How have things been going in your life? How is your mood, your outlook? Do things look hopeful for you?" If the patient gives negative or pessimistic responses, you might follow with another series, such as "Do you ever feel way down in the dumps? Ever ask yourself if it's all worth it? Ever think about just giving up?" If answers to these are affirmative, then you might ask, "Did you get to a point where you actually thought about killing yourself? About suicide?" And, finally, "When you thought about it, did you think about how you'd do it? Do you still think about it sometimes?"

Appropriate handling of the person who is potentially suicidal should correspond to the imminence and seriousness of the threat. It may include notification of relatives, referral for psychotherapy or psychotropic medication, or arrangement for hospitalization. An imminently suicidal person should not be left alone. Where there is a continuing possibility of suicide, in addition to professional care, it is suggested: (1) that the patient be engaged as much as possible in activities, without long periods of isolation; (2) that family, friends, and treating professionals reach out to discuss with the patient those things that are important to him/her, including suicide if that is a preoccupation; and (3) that access to means of self-destruction, including quantities of prescription drugs, be controlled.

LABELING, NORMALIZATION, AND MAINSTREAMING

It is fashionable today to oppose labeling (and normative measurement) and to favor normalization and mainstreaming. The many cogent reasons for doing so are well known and will not be reiterated here. There are, however, some reasons for not disposing of the baby with the bath water in the case of labeling, and some reasons for tempering our enthusiasm for normalization and mainstreaming.

Hobbs (1975, p. 3), while acknolwedging that labeling may stigmatize, also notes that "categorization is necessary to open doors . . . to write legislation . . . to design service programs, to evaluate outcomes." Similarly, Gordon (1979) says "Labels do not solve problems, they merely indicate them," and he further observes that classification should serve to increase freedom of choice and range of options. Labeling does not have to be mislabeling, stereotyping and prejudice. To fail to notice that a person differs from others is to fail to see the strengths that can be developed and the deficits that should be accommodated. To be content with the truism that each individual is unique is to run to the real risk that, while basking in our idealism, we will fail to provide in a practical way those supports which can be critical to the needs of persons with certain classes of disability. Those who are cynical rather than idealistic may also be happy with this position, since it is less costly in both effort and funds.

Zigler and Muenchow (1979) caution that the mandate of Public Law 94–142 (1975) to educate handicapped children in the "least restrictive environment" may be interpreted by fiscally pressed school districts as the "least expensive." They point to the requirement of sufficient numbers of adequately trained teachers to make mainstreaming work. They also report mixed findings when the academic outcome of mainstreaming mentally retarded students is evaluated.

Goldman (1978) states that normalization involves not only physical integration into the mainstream but also becoming a valued member of the community. Parish, Ohlsen, and Parish (1978) report findings that should raise concern about the reception of handicapped children in the classroom. They asked grade school children to apply negative and positive adjectives and found significant differences among four groups, with "normal" rated most positive, "physically handicapped" next, "learning disabled" next and "emotionally disturbed" most negative.

They speculate that negative attitudes toward handicapped children might seriously interfere with the educational environment.

An adult corollary of the mainstreaming concept is the reasoning that results in sheltered employment and residential settings that are routinely and almost uniformly set up to be transitional rather than long-term in nature. While this acts as a beneficial prod to those with the capacity to make the transition, it has negative results for those who have the capacity to be only partially productive or partially independent. These are typically transferred out of such facilities after a few years, with resultant disruption and, sometimes, total loss of productivity.

Mainstreaming and normalization require a great deal of individual attention, awareness in the interpersonal environment, and, frequently, parallel or partial support services to be effective. They should not be a "sink or swim" experiment. Handicapped persons need to be challenged, and they need to achieve self-evaluation which is ultimately related to realistic standards. They also frequently require very specific physical and psychological support systems, and these should not be sacrificed to the latest theoretical or political shibboleth.

MILESTONES

There are certain areas of activity which, in the experience of the author, warrant mention because of their special significance in the progress of physically disabled persons toward a competent and satisfying adult adjustment. These areas are (a) development of common independence and self-help skills, (b) learning to drive a car, (c) vocation, and (d) sexual activity.

The importance of the relationship between maximized self-help skills and function as a competent adult would seem to be self-evident. Amazingly, that importance frequently needs to be spelled out for patients, family, and others. Interest is commonly expressed in the development of beginning vocational skills during the early teen years. It is appropriate and necessary at that time to encourage explicit efforts to develop the following prevocational skills:

1. Self-care. Dress and toilet self. Eat independently. Eat in a public place (restaurant). Choose one's own diet. Learn to cook, do laundry, manage money.
2. Self-responsibility. Be alone for extended hours during the day. Stay away from home overnight—with relatives, with friends, at camp.

3. Mobility. Go about the neighborhood alone. Ride a bus or other public transportation. Drive a car.
4. Social. Use appropriate verbal social behavior—hello, good-bye, please, and thank you. Give eye contact. Accept supervision, orders, criticism. Relate with peers as peers.
5. Work skills. Initiate responsibility for appropriate chores. Take outside employment, if feasible.

The author has sometimes labeled these as tasks for those from age 12 to 16, although it is clear that their development should begin earlier. It should also be noted that they are skills which frequently may need to be relearned by an adult who has incurred a disability or learned for the first time by an adult who has experienced overprotection and underdemand. They are skills which ordinarily can be developed within home, family, social, and recreational spheres, and which do not require an employment setting.

Driving a car seems to occupy a special place in the motivation and independence of disabled persons. It has the obvious advantages of personal freedom. It also appears to be a symbol of adulthood and perhaps of belonging in our motorized society. It is a subject of excitement for adolescents and consternation for their parents. When it is appropriately achieved, it frequently signals a spurt in progress toward such lauded goals as social independence and vocational preparation, as well as progress toward such equally necessary but mildly tarnished goals as pizza, beer, and sex.

Driving a car requires strength, coordination, appropriate reaction time, and judgment. It also requires consideration of special problems such as seizures or impaired vision. Bardach (1970) reports much greater difficulty in learning to drive on the part of left hemiplegics than right hemiplegics, suggesting that verbally mediated skills are not nearly as important as perceptual-motor and integrating skills.

When a disabled person shows general delay in intellectual, motor, or social maturation, it is often appropriate to delay the teaching of driving skills, despite the chagrin of the 16-year-old. Nevertheless it should ultimately be viewed as an important and highly desirable attainment if and when it can be achieved. Marginal cases warrant instruction and, eventually, the experience of sitting behind the wheel of an appropriately equipped vehicle with a patient teacher in the middle of a large field, with sufficient opportunity to demonstrate to oneself and others one's ability or inability to carry out the required functions.

Vocation or career is here defined as a set of activities which require a specified set of competencies, are carried out on a regular basis, and bestow upon their possessor a defined role or status. Regular or partial employment is one of the most common and effective ways of achieving these goals, although vocations or careers may be built around social or recreational roles (the bridge player, the American Legionnaire, the artist). One's identity in our society is commonly tied directly to such a role. In addition, such activities provide the framework (schedule, setting) for a large part of daily life. Finally, there is the relationship between financial self-sufficiency and personal independence. The importance of vocation as a milestone in the progress of the physically disabled person cannot be denied.

In considering vocational goals for disabled persons, the author has found it useful to set minimum requirements for competitive employment. These are represented in Table III.

It should be pointed out that the criteria in Table III are suggested as *minimum*, below which competitive employment is probably impossible. Meeting these criteria, however, does not mean with any certainty that the person will, in fact, achieve employment.

In addition to the minimum requirements mentioned above, there are certain behaviors which are important in achieving and maintaining employment. Table IV is a listing of such behaviors which was originally prepared for its applicability to mentally retarded persons and employment but which appears to have more general utility.

TABLE III
Minimum Requirements for Competitive Employment

Assumes effective hearing or vision.

Level A
  Intellectually below average but capable of self-care and self-responsibility (travel to work, eat away from home, social relations).
  Motor ability in upper limbs.
  Job examples—assembly work, janitorial work, food service

Level B
  Intelligence in average range.
  Effective speech.
  No assumptions about motor ability.
  Job examples—selling, human services, telephone answering service.

Level C
  Intelligence in superior range.
  No assumptions about speech or motor ability.
  Job examples—accounting, technical law.

TABLE IV
Critical Social–Vocational Behaviors[a]

1. Acknowledge communication received.
2. Come on time.
3. Dress appropriately.
4. Know when a job is done.
5. Recognize own limitations regarding advancement and/or duties within competency.
6. Give notice of inability to report for work or carry out duties.
7. Accept supervision, including criticism.
8. Know how to quit a job.

[a] Acknowledgement is made of Leif Terdal, Ph.D., for his assistance in compiling this list.

Interest in and, especially, attainment of an active sexual life is frequently a hallmark of achievement with the physically disabled. It suggests the absence of preoccupation with the disease and the limiting aspects of the disability. It suggests that the person feels worthy of attention and love. It suggests interest directed outward—toward another person. Interest in sex is manifested fairly quickly by those who have been sexually active prior to disability, but it is often postponed (or even relinquished) by those who have never been sexually active. Goldman (1978) points out that disabled adults share responsibility for this in that they frequently acquiesce in the requirement that they be sexless. At the same time, Glass and Padrone (1978) note that one effect of normalization and mainstreaming is that the handicapped are insisting on their right to sexuality. I would join strongly in the insistence on the right to sexual activity, while being conservative about the right to parenthood, wishing to maintain some minimum criteria that would safeguard the right of children to have adequate parenting.

Nigro (1976) has pointed out that many disabled persons lack the social skills to form peer relationships which can become sexual relationships. She calls for improvement in the basic social skills, as well as the promotion of opportunities for sexual experience. She observes that parents frequently do not stop relating to disabled adults as children. Opportunity for sexual expression is something which should be accommodated by parents, by planners of activity and residence programs, and, most especially, by the physically disabled themselves.

REFERENCES

Abroms, K. I., & Kodera, T. L. Acceptance hierarchy of handicaps: Validation of Kirk's statement, "Special Education often begins where medicine stops." *Journal of Learning Disabilities*, 1979, *12*(1), 15–20.

Bardach, J. L. Psychological considerations in the driving skills of the handicapped person. *Psychological Aspects of Disability,* 1979, *17:*(1), 10–13.
Davis, F. Deviance disavowal: The management of strained interaction by the visibly handicapped. *Social Problems,* 1961, *9*(2), 120–132.
Dorpat, T. L., Anderson, W. F., & Ripley, H. S. The relationship of physical illness to suicide. In H. L. P. Resnik (Ed.), *Suicidal behaviors: Diagnosis and management.* Boston: Little, Brown, 1968.
Glass, D. D., & Padrone, F. J. Sexual adjustment in the handicapped. *Journal of Rehabilitation,* 1978, *44*(1), 43–47.
Goldman, F. Environmental barriers to sociosexual integration: The insider's perspectives. *Rehabilitation Literature,* 1978, *39*(6–7), 185–189.
Gordon, N. Labels—an advantage or disadvantage. *Developmental Medicine and Child Neurology,* 1979, *21*(1), 106–108.
Haring, M., & Myerson, L. Attitudes of college students toward sexual behavior of disabled persons. *Archives of Physical Medicine and Rehabilitation,* 1979, *60,* 257–260.
Hobbs, N. *The futures of children.* San Francisco: Jossey-Bass, 1975.
Kessler, J. W. Parenting the handicapped child. *Pediatric Annals,* 1977, *6,* 654–661.
Kübler-Ross, E. *On death and dying.* New York: Macmillan, 1969.
Leviton, G. L. Professional–client relations in a rehabilitation hospital setting. In National Conference on the Psychological Aspects of Disability, *Rehabilitation Psychology.* Washington: American Psychological Association, 1970.
Litman, R. E. Management of acutely suicidal patients in medical practice. Unpublished paper. Los Angeles Suicide Prevention Center.
Moos, R. H., & Tsu, V. D. The crisis of physical illness: An overview. In R. H. Moos (Ed.), *Coping with physical illness.* New York: Plenum Press, 1977.
Nigro, G. Some observations on personal relationships and sexual relationships among lifelong disabled Americans. Rehabilitation Literature, 1976, *37,* 328–330, 334.
Parish, T. S., Ohlsen, R. L., & Parish, J. G. A look at mainstreaming in light of children's attitudes toward the handicapped. *Perceptual and Motor Skills,* 1978, *46,* 1019–1021.
Parsons, T. *Social structure and personality.* Glencoe, Ill.: The Free Press, 1964.
Public Law 94–142. Education for all handicapped children act. November 29, 1975.
Spencer, W. A. Is anybody listening. *Archives of Physical Medicine and Rehabilitation,* 1979, *60*(5), 191–199.
Weinberg, N., & Santana, R. Comic books: Champions of the disabled stereotype. *Rehabiliation Literature,* 1978, *39*(11–12), 327–331.
Weller, D. J., & Miller, P. M. Emotional reactions of patient, family and staff in acute-care period of spinal cord injury: 1. *Social Work in Health Care,* 1977, *2*(4), 369–377.
Wright, B. *Physical disability—a psychological approach.* New York: Harper & Row, 1960.
Zigler, E., & Muenchow, S. Mainstreaming: The proof is in the implementation. *American Psychologist,* 1979, *34*(10), 993–996.

2

Hemophilia

Hemophilia is a disease so surrounded by mystique and misunderstanding that it may be difficult to achieve an accurate perception of its physical manifestations. It was described in the Talmud thousands of years ago. Its association with royalty gave it prominence, and its relative infrequency promoted the development of second-hand superstition-tinged "knowledge," without benefit of empirical observation. A proper understanding of its transmission awaited the discovery of genetic principles, and adequate control depended upon the development of modern blood technology. A full knowledge of its psychophysiology lies in the future. Misinformation persists in the thinking of the general public, as well as that of many health professionals and even of hemophilia sufferers themselves.

THE PHYSICAL DISABILITY

Definition and Incidence

About one of every 4,000 males is born with hemophilia. There are an estimated 25,000 Americans with moderate or severe hemophilia (Petit & Klein, 1976). When all the hemophilias with all degrees of severity are combined, the prevalence may be 100,000. In each case, there is a factor inactivated in the blood which causes a delay in forming a clot adequate to stop bleeding. Patients with less than 1% of normal activity of the clotting factor are considered to be "severe," those with 1–5% "moderate," and those who have symptoms but are above 5% in activity "mild."

Hemophilia A (Factor VIII Deficiency) is sometimes called Classic Hemophilia and Hemophilia B (Factor IX Deficiency) is sometimes called Christmas Disease. Together they account for about 85% of all cases. They are X-chromosome-linked traits carried by a recessive gene. Thus, they are sex-linked, carried by females and afflicting males. On the average, half the daughters of a carrier mother will be carriers and half her sons will have hemophilia.

VonWillebrand's disease accounts for approximately 10% of bleeding disorders (Weiss, 1978). It is transmitted by a dominant gene and thus may be acquired by both men and women.

About one third of all cases of hemophilia show no family history of the disease. The first occurrence is apparently attributable to chance mutation. Thereafter, however, it is transmitted in accordance with the genetic principles previously described.

Manifestations

Hemophilia manifests itself primarily by bruises and bleeding into muscles and joints, often from mild injuries which are unnoticed or unremembered. These bleeds produce chronic and sometimes severe pain. This pain and the orthopedic deformity that may result from repeated bleeds in the same joint are the primary physical manifestations of hemophilia. Repeated bleeds, especially if not treated promptly, cause swelling and eventually may result in permanent immobilization of the joint, which may become a focal point of the disability insofar as impairment of function is concerned. Time lost from school or work and difficulties in the development of self-image due to restricted activities are primary causes of psychological problems.

It is important to note that profuse external bleeding is not here listed as a primary problem of hemophilia. Acute care for a severe external lesion is as critical for a normal person as it is for one with hemophilia and not much different in nature. Only the long-term healing and treatment differ, and these do not usually require emergency priority. Emergency priority is indicated in those rare cases when the hemophilia patient has head trauma or bleeding into his abdominal cavity. When employers, educators, parents, and others have a full appreciation of these facts it is usually much more feasible for the hemophilic person to enjoy a wide range of activities. The "handle with kid gloves" stereotype of hemophilia lingers from the past, when less was known about the disease and, most importantly, when modern blood products had not been developed.

Treatment

Blood products used in the treatment of hemophilia are made from plasma and essentially replace the deficient clotting factor in the blood. The products most frequently used are concentrates which require only ordinary refrigeration for storage, allowing mobility and facilitating home treatment. Cryoprecipitate, also commonly used, requires storage at subfreezing temperatures. Factor replacement promotes clotting, reduces pain, and minimizes long-term orthopedic damage. Availability of prompt treatment significantly reduces downtime and makes it prudently possible for most hemophilic patients to engage in a very broad array of activities, approaching that which would be considered normal. Factor replacement also allows for a wide range of dental and surgical procedures, including reconstructive orthopedic surgery such as hip or knee replacement (Gilbert, 1977). The greatest limitation in factor replacement therapy is cost. About $4,000 to $6,000 is spent annually in a case of severe hemophilia, when blood products are used only in response to bleeding episodes (Petit & Klein, 1976). The cost is estimated at $22,000 per annum for prophylactic treatment.

Boone (1976) and Wincott (1977) have described the comprehensive care model of hemophilia treatment. They point out the necessity of a team approach to the many facets of the disease. Wincott goes on to observe that medical personnel and hospitals with little experience in dealing with hemophilia may perpetuate fear and ignorance detrimental to the patient and his family. Quality of care is most effectively assured by seeking professionals who are experienced with the disease and who work in a team setting. Recent federal funding to establish regional treatment centers has helped to make this approach more generally available. Major medical centers and state crippled children's services are also important sources of such care.

Lack of sophistication of medical personnel in remote or underserved areas has meant that, in the past, the patient and his family have frequently been in situations where they were more conversant with the details of symptomatology and treatment than the attending professionals. Agle and Mattsson (1976) point out that some parents incorporate an attitude of superiority toward physicians and other personnel. A mother known to the author proudly recounts the episode in which she impulsively blurted to her son's physician, "Oh, doctor, Johnny's much too sick for me to leave him in the hospital." She smilingly acknowledges her tactlessness, but makes it clear that she really meant it. While this attitude may be interpretable as part of the psychological defense against the recurrent distresses of the illness, this should not obscure the fact that in many situations the patient and his family may be the best consultants available and their knowledge and views should be solicited. The patient will, of course, be the only source of information about the presence of, or changes in, subjective pain. The patient is incorporated as a full member of the team when treatment is working optimally in a comprehensive care center.

This team concept has been logically extended through programs of home care or home infusion. Initiated by Rabiner (Rabiner & Telfer, 1970), the method has been rapidly put into use throughout the country. The patient and/or members of his family are instructed in techniques of blood concentrate reconstitution, venipuncture, and infusion. Written guidelines are provided and, usually, medical advice is made available on a 24-hour basis. Careful selection, training, and follow-up are required. The method provides obvious benefits in availability and promptness of care. For most patients, it also provides great advantages in terms of mobility, normalization of function, independence, and self-reliance, which quickly translate into psychosocial gains. These will be discussed further in the "Intervention Methods" section of this chapter.

COMMON PSYCHOLOGICAL CHARACTERISTICS AND PROBLEMS

Introduction

There are commonalities about hemophilic persons which have become stereotypes in the professional and scientific literature, notably the overprotected passive and the risk-taking rebel. These concepts have a certain validity in that they do frequently characterize those who are presenting problems. But it should be noted that these descriptions have been based primarily on patients who have come to the attention of pathology-oriented mental health professionals. Before reviewing the problem areas, it seems appropriate to remind ourselves that the majority of hemophilic people have a satisfactory psychosocial adjustment and creditable records of educational and vocational achievement. It is also important to note that the characteristics and problems described are products of the past and, while currently descriptive of many hemophilic persons, will almost certainly change with the continued use of blood products and home treatment.

In the classic study by Mattsson and Gross (1966) of 35 hemophilic boys and young adults, 8 showed poor adjustment (3 passive, 5 rebels), but 27 showed satisfactory to optimum adjustment. Agle and Mattsson (1976) observed no increased frequency of severe psychiatric disorders, although they do note a higher rate of adjustment problems. Steinhausen (1976) contrasted 50 German hemophilic boys with controls and found no significant difference in neuroticism, specifically concluding that hemophilia *per se* does not lead to personality disorder. In a similar study (Steinhausen, 1975), he found hemophilic adults to be slightly more depressed and less dominant than controls, attributing the effect to those whose illness had produced severe physical handicap. While Katz (1970, pp. 20–21) details the problems of education, we also learn that 60% attended regular high school and 23% received education beyond the high school level. From a survey of 290 hemophilia patients in Michigan, Mould (1977) tells us that 68% are currently employed and only 1.4% have never been employed.

In the normal course of events, the hemophilic boy starts to comprehend the relationship between trauma, bleeding, and treatment at age six or seven and thus begins to assume some of the responsibility for his own risks. Thereafter, he typically accumulates considerable knowledge, which in many cases is put to positive use. It is common for hemophilic boys to give science reports to their classes about their genetic disorder and to be active educators of those whom they meet. An extension of this is the patient who becomes the "professional hemophiliac." Even this need not be a negative adjustment. Most workers in the field, including the present author, know patients who can be perfectly charming about themselves and their disease, in the manner of one who makes an engaging conversation piece of the fact that he has six toes. It is when the disease role is used as a demand to be special in all aspects of life and dominate all interactions that this adjustment becomes pathological.

The Family

Central to the development, the strengths, and the problems of the hemophilic person is the family. The mother is the genetic transmitter and may translate this into conscious or unconscious psychological or moral guilt. Her feelings are often fueled by memories of the life of a father, uncle, or brother who likely had a bad time of it in the days of nonexistent or inadequate treatment. How the mother has been able to handle her early exposure to bleeders will have a profound effect on her anxiety, protectiveness or, sometimes, her rejection. Extremes in the experience of the author include the mother whose son grew up wearing a football helmet in a padded room and one who said of her troubled young adult son, "They told me he wouldn't live past fourteen," as if it were a broken promise.

Hurt (1976, p. 118) has said, "The role assumed by the father is the most important factor in determining the hemophilic boy's emotional adjustment." The most destructive influence occurs when the father perceives the child as a threat to his own image, blames the wife, and rejects the child. A less destructive, but also negative relationship is one in which a father joins a mother in being anxious and oversolicitous. The optimal relationship appears to be a team effort in which both parents provide care, with one (often the mother) being solicitous as appropriate to the circumstances, while the other (often the father) adopts a slightly daring "why not" attitude toward the boy's participation in sports and other activities, providing a role model and a liberating influence. In some instances these roles may be exchanged, with the father as the primary support figure while the mother is the role-expander.

The stress on the family cannot be minimized. There are real protections that must be provided, real worries to experience, and real disruptions when treatment must be carried out. Hospitalization means enforced separation for a young child. Worried parents and frightened children fall easily into the trap of passive inactivity rather than ego-developing assertion. Those patients who do rebel against restraint frequently indulge in imprudent risk-taking to make their point, seeking soccer games, motorcycles and sometimes barroom brawls.

Siblings may resent the extra attention and time spent with their brother. This resentment is understandably increased if the patient uses his illness for privilege or protection. "You can't hit me, I have hemophilia" is a tempting mechanism for a seven-year-old. The whole family (including the patient) may consciously or unconsciously resent the interrupted vacation or the cancelled party. A negative self-image is easily developed.

Intelligence—Schooling

The intelligence level of groups of hemophilic persons has consistently been found to be significantly above average (Olch, 1971; Weise, 1968). Typical are the results of Olch (1971), in which she found an IQ range of 61 to 152, with a mean of 109. It is tempting to interpret increased intellectual ability as genetically determined, although it should be noted that enforced sedentariness may have led to development of skills useful in taking IQ tests. The encouraging news of high intelligence is, unfortunately, tempered by that regarding school achievement. Katz (1970, p. 124) mentions "some evidence that hemophiliacs tend to be at least one and a half to two years behind in grade level." An unpublished study of 38 elementary and secondary school boys at the Hemophilia Treatment Center of the Crippled Children's Division, University of Oregon Health Sciences Center, revealed that 20 of the 38 were at least one grade behind. Katz (1970) goes on to point out the extremely high relationship between school successes and personal and vocational adjustment.

Poor school achievement is generally attributed to enforced absences due to bleeds with associated treatment and pain. Taylor (1968) mentions an average of 27 days of absence per school year, and 35 students studied at the Oregon Hemophilia Treatment Center in 1976 had an average of 33.2 days absent per annum. Absences typically range from a half-day to a few days in length. Because absences are intermittent and because hemophilia is usually not a visible handicap, teachers may not be alert to developing problems until the student has fallen seriously behind in his classwork. Most schools have policies requiring an absence of several weeks before assignment of a home teacher and, thus, the hemophilic student usually does not qualify for this assistance. In the past, numerous parents have surrendered to the pressures of repeated absence and have accepted the arrangement of full-time home tutoring. The result is usually a less enriched curriculum and frequently a disaster in terms of social development, academic motivation and overall achievement.

Emotional Adjustment

Hurt (1976, p. 117) lists some psychological manifestations shown by hemophilic persons as: "(1) A low self-esteem and limited self-confidence; (2) a delay in masculine identification; (3) a failure to accept the realities of hemophilia; and (4) a general prolonged immaturity." Jonas (1977) remarks on the depression and pessimistic expectation of hemophilic young adults and the potential for adult drug abuse in passive dependent personalities (especially those with long experience with pain medication). He sees early realistic pain medication as a key to reduction of later drug abuse. Jonas also notes instances of counterphobic risk-taking. Henderson (1977) conceptualizes hemophilic adjustment on a continuum from "internalized-passive" to "externalized-active" and finds most of the problems at the extremes in the previously noted rebellion or excessive passive dependence.

The mechanism of denial is prominent in persons with hemophilia. Historically, this was probably appropriate when life span was an uncertainty and the renewed experience of pain a certainty. Agle and Mattsson (1976) point out the need to use some denial in a positive way, allowing some risk-taking. They also, however, mention the value of verbal expression of anxiety, anger, and sadness. As with the professional patient role, the judicious use of denial appears to be appropriate and necessary, while its extreme may so distort perceptions and judgments as to divorce the patient from reality.

The literature on hemophilia regularly mentions an observed relationship between a sense of psychological well-being and the absence of bleeds. In an early clinical study, Agle (1964) described reports of increased "spontaneous" bleeds following periods of emotional stress or of anticipation. He reported an improved clinical state in patients who changed from passiveness to more aggressive independence and even noted clinical regression in a patient who reverted to his previous passive adjustment. Steinhausen (1975) reports a correlation between neuroticism and increased bleeding risks during emotional stress. More tangible indications of this relationship are seen: Lucas (1965) describes a relationship between psychiatric state and bleeding during dental surgery and the possibility of control of bleeding through hypnotic relaxation; and Agle, Ratnoff, and Wasman (1967) describe "spontaneous" ecchymoses (bruises) produced by hypnotic suggestion. This relationship between emotional factors and incidence of bleeds is a hypothesis to which most professional workers in the field subscribe, although no one has yet produced an adequate explanation as to how it is mediated.

The adult hemophilic person frequently must make a painful decision: Should he attempt to finance the high cost of his medical care through employment, or should he seek assistance through social agencies? The continued need for expensive care places a burden upon achieving an individual adjustment and an even greater burden upon a marital adjustment. Many hemophilic persons have satisfying marriages. Their achievement is possible through a resolution of the financial dilemma, as well as successfully coming to grips with the questions regarding parenthood which are raised by the genetic nature of the disease.

Hemophilic patients who are now adult have had imposed upon them an additional ironic adjustment problem. Development of blood products and home treatment has confronted them with the challenge to normalize their lives to accommodate the wider range of activity now prudently possible. This represents the removal of a psychological defense after personality traits and mechanisms have been ingrained. They lose their rationale for cautiousness, for passiveness, for being special, and thus suffer a new crisis of identity. This crisis in itself constitutes a cause for depression in some and may require intensive psychotherapy for its resolution.

Vocation

Jones (1974) has described the ideal conditions of employment as follows:

> The haemophiliac would enjoy the work; the employer would know of the haemophilia and have accurate and up-to-date information about the employee's disorder; there would be an arrangement to provide cover for the haemophiliac's work during his absence; facilities for efficient and speedy treatment should be near the place of employment; the job should not involve work likely to put heavy strain on joints and musculature, and should be in a warm dry environment if the haemophiliac has chronic arthritis; the job should allow movement and not confine the haemophiliac to long periods of sitting or standing in one position; the rates of pay and conditions of service should be the same as those for non-affected employees.

Actually, most persons with hemophilia work under less than ideal conditions. As a group, they are underemployed, and the principal contributors to this appear to be: (1) erroneous stereotypes held by employers, personnel officers, industrial physicians, and insurance carriers; (2) negative self-concept and poor social adaptation as secondary products of the illness; and (3) realistic problems posed by some necessary restrictions in job choice and by absence due to bleeds. Mould (1977) reported that a higher proportion of the unemployed were unskilled and semi-skilled workers, and the employed tended to be white collar workers or technical craftsmen. In observing the relationship between employment and adjustment, Katz (1970) observed that unemployed hemophilic persons with low severity of disease were inactive, socially withdrawn, likely to be unmarried, undereducated, and had gloomy and pessimistic views of life. The fact that their emotional adjustment did not equal that of persons with high severity of disease who were employed suggests the powerful influence of employment on overall adjustment and life satisfaction.

For most hemophilic persons, it is preferable to have a job which does not require vigorous physical activity, especially repeated use of the same musculature or joints. However, hemophilic persons successfully hold a wide variety of jobs which require mobility, manual dexterity, and the use of many kinds of machinery.

EVALUATING PERSONS WITH HEMOPHILIA

A satisfactory evaluation interview of a person with hemophilia is best carried out by an interviewer who has some background of knowledge about the disease and, preferably, experience in the field. As is apparent from the description of the disability and the characteristics of hemophilic persons, the disease and associated treatment have powerful direct effects on psychosocial adjustment and many more subtle influences on family and peer interaction, education, and vocation. In addition, the interviewee may well turn out to be an articulate person with above-average intelligence and a slightly superior attitude about his knowledge of his disability. Ordinarily, this attitude will give way if the interviewer has reasonable sophistication about the disease and relates to the person rather than to the illness. Occasionally, the interviewer may be subjected to efforts at outright deception by the professional patient who blatantly uses his illness for secondary gain.

The hemophilic person does not usually pose special problems in psychological testing, for the kinds of orthopedic problems incurred rarely interfere with the dexterity needed for testing, and sensory problems are ordinarily no different from those found in the normal population.

In following the early development of the hemophilic child, adaptive behavior measures such as the Boyd Developmental Progress Scale (Boyd, 1974) or the Vineland Social Maturity Scale (Doll, 1965) may be useful. The Oregon Hemophilia Treatment Center has begun periodic evaluations using the Child Behavior Checklist devised by Achenbach (1979). Its measures of competencies in activities and social and school performance are promising. School problems may require standard measurements of intelligence and achievement. Taylor (1968, p. 126) has given mean and standard deviation scores on MMPI scales for 33 juvenile and 31 adult hemophilic persons. Other standard personality tests are appropriate when psychodiagnostic evaluation of emotional adjustment is indicated, as in assessing stability and judgment as part of selecting appropriate patients and families for the responsibility of home treatment.

Vocational evaluation is especially appropriate for many hemophilic persons, who may need to tailor their career goals to some restrictions and who also may have developed denial mechanisms which lead them to unrealistic choices. General guidance is appropriate during school years, with intensive evaluation utilizing measures of intelligence, aptitude, personality, and vocational interest as the person begins to formulate specific goals and education training plans.

INTERVENTION METHODS

The earliest form of psychosocial intervention in hemophilia is the provision of support and information to the new parents of the hemophilic child. Confusion, fear, and guilt are best handled by open discussion with both parents conducted by a professional who has knowledge of the disease and skill in counseling. A relationship of trust between parents and care-providers is critical at this point. Agle and Mattsson (1976) also suggest referring young parents to more experienced parents for emotional support and advice.

Work with the hemophilic patient is best seen as a life-span process of relationship and supportive counseling, punctuated at times by intensive psychotherapy or crisis intervention. Ideally, this is provided by a stable staff in a treatment center, although factors of geography and mobility will frequently interfere with this. The hemophilic person will profit from help with problems arising from his illness and from help during ordinary stages of transition (e.g., adolescence), which may be made more difficult by the additional burden of the illness.

Parents usually need support and encouragement in allowing their child as wide a range of activities as possible, and this begins with participation in nursery school or kindergarten. If there is any question of intellectual ability or a special learning problem, this should be formally evaluated by a psychologist as the child approaches school age. School personnel (e.g., teacher, principal, nurse) may need assistance in the form of information about the disease and about the specific child. The principal of a large elementary school began by saying (seriously), "We can't afford to have a child bleed to death in the school." Over time, with information and consultation from knowledgeable professionals, he became extremely supportive and helpful toward his hemophilic student. Especially necessary may be support and encouragement to the school in allowing participation in activities which are not significantly more dangerous for hemophilic boys than for others but which may have been judged so by someone using an erroneous stereotype about the effects of the disease. Thus, Lindemann and Lovrien (1973) say, "Boys with hemophilia should take shop if it fits their pattern of interests. For example, they may run a bandsaw or learn auto mechanics. As with all persons, it is important that they learn safety measures and avoid bodily injury."

Schools are often insular and sovereign, and all the careful work of one year may need to be repeated the next year, when the child changes schools. Arrangements should be made between teachers and parents for a continuation of school assignments (as appropriate to the pain and debility of the child) during periods of school absence. Above all, every effort should be made to avoid a permanent home teacher arrangement.

A useful tool for informing school children (and, incidentally, their teachers) about hemophilia is the series of educational storybooks developed and distributed by Cutter Biological Laboratories (Friedlander, 1979). They relate the adventures of a boy named Harold who has hemophilia. They are written for children, designed to entertain and inform, and are accompanied by a coloring book. At the time of this writing (1980), three of a projected series of eight are available.

Home infusion has such important consequences that it warrants mention as a psychosocial intervention. It liberates families and patients to move about, take trips, go camping. It involves family members (often including fathers and siblings) in the treatment, removing the mystique and encouraging supportive relationships. It fosters independence. Boys as young as ten have learned to take responsibility for their own treatment.

Boutaugh and Patterson (1977) have described hemophilia camp, pointing out the value of this experience in leading to recognition of personal abilities in a peer group and also the (frequently rare) value of a period of separation from parents. Camp also encourages the appropriate physical activity recommended by Agle and Mattsson (1976). Camp participation is valuable both for younger boys and adolescents.

Peer interaction is recognized as important for the social development of adolescents. In some instances, assessment and counseling by a recreation therapist may be helpful in furthering peer contacts. Sex education may be very useful if offered by a professional who is experienced and comfortable in dealing with the topic. Groups for adolescents may be useful in developing social skills as well as in coping with some of the fears and anxieties.

Group approaches to psychological problems and psychosocial development have frequently been found to be helpful in working with hemophilic persons. Caldwell, Leveque, and Lane (1974) worked with groups consisting of hemophilic patients and their wives, describing a progression over eight months of weekly sessions from orientation to the disease (first five months) to a more profitable personal orientation. Waters (1977) works with families in a systems approach, seeking to promote flexibility in the family's attitudes to their hemophilic member, rather than stereotypy. Lamb (1977) questions group approaches focused on defenses and pathogenic emotional responses. He describes a broader psychosocial approach, involving parent education, parent–child communication, and child-rearing issues.

The Hemophilia Treatment Center of the University of Oregon Health Sciences Center has found it useful to provide individual stress-reduction sessions for selected adult patients, following the model described by LaBaw (1975). This recognizes the relationship between anxiety and bleed frequency, as well as the utility of relaxation and post-hypnotic suggestion.

During the early adolescent years, the hemophilic patient should be provided with appropriate information about career choices that may be available to him. This information should be based on some knowledge of his general abilities and school achievement. He should be encouraged to try part-time or summer jobs which are available to him and to develop work skills. If his career goals are not clear or appear to be inappropriate, he should receive vocational evaluation and career counseling from a qualified psychologist or rehabilitation counselor. Referral to the state vocational rehabilitation agencies for further counseling and assistance through training and placement services is often appropriate. Hemophilic clients may require special assistance in placement, especially in providing employers with authoritative information about the disease and with accurate medical information about the particular person. As we indicated in the descriptions of physical disability, safety precautions against being cut or hit by machinery or tools are approximately the same as required for others. Occasionally it may be necessary to allow the worker time to treat himself by self-infusion, and it would be convenient if a refrigerator were available for storage of blood products. Stuart, Forbes, Jones, Lane, Rizza, and Wilkes (1980) found that only a small number of employed hemophilic persons on home treatment actually self-administered concentrates while at work. Some returned home during work hours when self-infusion was necessary. Availability of a first aid room or other clean area will enhance both the promptness of treatment and the available work time of the hemophilic employee.

Stuart *et al.* (1980) report an apparent reduction in the unemployment rate of hemophilic persons in Great Britain during recent years. They refer to surveys published in 1977 which place this rate at 18% to 35% (comparable to Mould's (1977) employment rate of 68% in Michigan), while their more recent findings place the rate at 17.5% in Great Britain. Large numbers of the home treatment patients included in their study reported that the home program allowed them to return, continue, or increase the potential range of their work. In describing rehabilitation services, Marshall (1977, p. 465) says, "Few restrictions should be placed on the hemophiliac's occupational choices." That is a goal that can be achieved with the proper coordination of services. Hemophiliacs may be accountants, draftsmen or sales clerks; they may also be electronics technicians, machinists, or auto mechanics. There are a myriad of occupations they can handle.

As noted earlier, appropriate treatment of hemophilia includes realistic pain medication. If properly administered in the earlier years, this should help to minimize drug abuse in later years. Nevertheless, drug abuse is encountered and can represent a serious mental health problem, along with others, such as severe depression or suicidal ideation. In evaluating or counseling the hemophilic patient, it may become appropriate to probe for suicidal ideation as described in Chapter 1 under "Suggestions about Process." Memorable is the response of the articulate college student who, sensing the direction of the questions, volunteered, "Don't worry, Doc, I'm not going to commit suicide. I decided not to kill myself when I was thirteen years old. But that doesn't mean it's easy." In dealing with hemophilic persons, the author has observed the value of empathically acknowledging the reality of the pain that is suffered and, if possible, encouraging comment and discussion about it. This seems to enhance the relationship and to facilitate moving on to other meaningful material.

Chronic drug abuse, severe depression, suicidal ideation, thought disorder, or bizarre delusional beliefs require the attention of a fully qualified mental health professional and may necessitate intensive individual psychotherapy, psychotropic medication, or hospitalization, as any other serious emotional disturbances. Individual approaches more often include brief supportive counseling and, as Wincott (1977) has described, the anticipation of problems and pre-crisis counseling. This may include preparation for surgery, which may be traumatically threatening to patients, as well as being a troubling interruption of their daily lives.

In addition to providing group and individual personal counseling, the social worker may be especially valuable in helping the patient to cope with agencies such as social security and welfare or those which provide medical services. Financial counselors may be helpful with these and other matters relating to health insurance and financial assistance. While genetic counseling should be part of the life-span support system, the genetic counselor can play a particularly valuable role in premarital counseling with the hemophilic person and his fiancée.

TRENDS AND NEEDS

The most provocative, and possibly the most important, psychological problem in hemophilia is that of the relationship between the state of emotional well-being and the clinical severity of the disease. This relationship warrants investigation at both the psychophysiological and behavioral levels. Knowledge of the physiological events which relate symptoms such as interstitial bleeding and emotional stress would be of immense value in our understanding of ordinary human functioning as well as our understanding of hemophilia and other diseases. Discovery at the behavioral level of relationships between certain classes of human behavior (e.g., emotional, cognitive, interpersonal) and bleeding would be invaluable in prevention of physical symptoms and control of the disease. The first step in furthering our understanding in this area will probably be the more careful plotting of this relationship between behavior and symptoms.

Within the universe of hemophilic persons, there exist three major groups which warrant identification and comparative observation. These are: (1) those who grew well into their adult years with the relatively inadequate treatment and chronic invalid image of the past; (2) those who, sometime between early adolescence and young adulthood, came into the advantages of blood concentrates and home treatment, with the subsequent challenge to normalize their activities; and (3) those who have had relatively good treatment all of their lives. It may well be that, for some time, the approach to treatment, especially psychosocial treatment, may have to be tailored to the unique dynamics of each group. This may be subject to additional influences in the future if refined procedures for processing blood products should so reduce the cost that prophylactic treatment would be readily available to most patients, further intensifying the pressure to normalize and to abandon the sense of special identity so easy to maintain with this rather exclusive and exacting disease.

APPENDIX: SOURCES OF INFORMATION

General:

The National Hemophilia Foundation
25 West 39 St.
New York, NY 10018
(212) 869-9740

General information for the professional: *Comprehensive Management of Hemophilia*, Donna C. Boone (Ed.). Philadelphia: F. A. Davis Co., 1976.
Hemophilia in Children, Margaret W. Hilgartner (Ed.). Littleton, Mass.: Publishing Sciences Group, Inc., 1976.
Mental health information for the professional: *Mental Health Services in the Comprehensive Care of the Hemophiliac*, David P. Agle (Ed.). New York: National Hemophilia Foundation, 1977.
Information for the family: *Living with Haemophilia*, Peter Jones. Philadelphia: F. A. Davis Co., 1974.
Information for school children: *Harold's Secret: A Boy with Hemophilia*, Nan Friedlander, 1979. Cutter Laboratories, Fourth and Parker Sts., Berkeley, CA 94710.

REFERENCES

Achenbach, T. M. *Child behavior checklist and child behavior profile.* Bethesda, Md.: National Institutes of Mental Health, 1979.
Agle, D. P. Psychiatric studies of patients with hemophilia and related states. *Archives of Internal Medicine,* 1964, *144,* 76–82.
Agle, D. P., & Mattsson, A. Psychological complications of hemophilia. In M. W. Hilgartner (Ed.), *Hemophilia in children.* Littleton, Mass.: Publishing Sciences Group, 1976.
Agle, D. P., Ratnoff, O. D., & Wasman, M. Studies in autoerythrocyte sensitization: the inducement of purpuric lesions by hypnotic suggestion. *Psychosomatic Medicine,* 1967, *29*(5) 491–503.
Boone, D. C. *Comprehensive management of hemophilia.* Philadelphia: F. A. Davis, 1976.
Boutaugh, M., & Patterson, P. C. Summer camp for hemophiliacs. *American Journal of Nursing,* 1977, *77*(8), 1288–1291.
Boyd, R.D. *Boyd developmental progress scale.* San Bernardino, Calif.: Inland Counties Regional Center, 1974.
Caldwell, H. S., Leveque, K. L., & Lane, D. M. Group psychotherapy in the management of hemophilia. *Psychological Reports,* 1974, *35,* 339–342.
Doll, E. A. *Vineland social maturity scale.* Circle Pines, Minn.: American Guidance Service, 1965.
Friedlander, N. *Harold's secret. A boy with hemophilia.* Berkeley, Calif.: Cutter Laboratories, 1979.
Gilbert, M. S. Reconstructive surgery in the hemophiliac. *The Mount Sinai Journal of Medicine,* 1977, *44*(3), 374–388.
Henderson, D. B. Clinical presentations and problems in working with hemophilia. In N. U. Cairns (Chair), *Psychological approaches to hemophilia: Medical–psychological interface.* Symposium presented at the 85th Annual Convention of the American Psychological Association, San Francisco, 1977.
Hurt, C. H. Psychological and social aspects. In D. C. Boone (Ed.), *Comprehensive management of hemophilia.* Philadelphia: F. A. Davis, 1976.
Jonas, D. L. Psychiatric aspects of hemophilia. *The Mount Sinai Journal of Medicine,* 1977, *44*(3), 457–463.
Jones, P. J. *Living with haemophilia.* Philadelphia.: F. A. Davis, 1974.
Katz, A. H. *Hemophilia: A study in hope and reality.* Springfield, Ill.: Charles C Thomas, 1970.
LaBaw, W. D. Auto-hypnosis in hemophilia. *Haematologia,* 1975, *9,* 103–110.
Lamb, W. A. Therapeutic interventions with parents of hemophiliacs: Review and suggestions. In N. U. Cairns (Chair), *Psychological approaches to hemophilia: Medical–psychological interface.* Symposium presented at the 85th Annual Convention of the American Psychological Association, San Francisco, 1977.
Lindemann, J. E., & Lovrien, E. W. *The Schoolchild with hemophilia.* Portland: Oregon Chapter of the National Hemophilia Foundation, 1973.
Lucas, O. N. Dental extractions in the hemophiliac: Control of emotional factors by hypnosis. *American Journal of Clinical Hypnosis,* 1965, *7,* 301–307.
Marshall, F. N. Vocational rehabilitation and the hemophiliac. *The Mount Sinai Journal of Medicine,* 1977, *44*(3), 464–469.
Mattsson, A., & Gross, S. Adaptational and defensive behavior in young hemophiliacs and their parents. *American Journal of Psychiatry,* 1966, *122,* 1349–1356.
Mould, P. C. The impact of hemophilia upon employment. In D. P. Agle (Ed.), *Mental health services in the comprehensive care of the hemophiliac.* New York: National Hemophilia Foundation, 1977.

Olch, D. Effects of hemophilia upon intellectual growth and academic achievement. *Journal of Genetic Psychology*, 1971, *119*, 63–74.
Petit, C. R., & Klein, H. G. Hemophilia, hemophiliacs and the health care delivery system. DHEW Publication No. (NIH) 76-871. Bethesda, Md.: National Heart and Lung Institute, 1976.
Rabiner, S. F., & Telfer, M. C. Home transfusion for patients with hemophilia. *New England Journal of Medicine*, 1970, *283*, 1011–1015.
Steinhausen, H. A psycho-clinical investigation in adult hemophiliacs. *Journal of Psychosomatic Research*, 1975, *19*, 295–302.
Steinhausen, H. C. Hemophilia: Psychological study in chronic disease in juveniles. *Journal of Psychosomatic Research*, 1976, *20*, 461–467.
Stuart, J., Forbes, C., Jones, P., Lane, G., Rizza, C., & Wilkes, S. Improving prospects for employment of the hemophiliac. *British Medical Journal*, 1980, *280*, 1169–1172.
Taylor, C. Educational–vocational program. In S. L. Dietrich (Ed.), *Hemophilia: A total approach to treatment and rehabilitation*. Los Angeles: Orthopaedic Hospital, 1968.
Waters, D. Hemophilia and the family system. In D. Agle (Ed.), *Mental health services in the comprehensive care of the hemophiliac*. New York: National Hemophilia Foundation, 1977.
Weise, P. Psychological program. In S. Dietrich (Ed.) *Hemophilia: A total approach to treatment and rehabilitation*. Los Angleles: Orthopaedic Hospital, 1968.
Weiss, A. *Genetic counseling in the hemophilias*. Miami: Merieux Institute, 1978.
Wincott, E. Psychosocial aspects of hemophilia: Problems, prevention, treatment modalities, research, and future directions. *The Mount Sinai Journal of Medicine*, 1977, *44*,(3), 438–455.

3

Diabetes Mellitus

ANN M. GARNER

Over three hundred years ago, Thomas Willis, the English anatomist and physician, identified a disease characterized by "sweet urine" and attributed its etiology to "prolonged sorrow" (Willis, 1674). Both the symptom and its presumed antecedent remain today as constituents of the disorder called *diabetes mellitus*. During the intervening centuries, however, diabetes has been seen not as one disorder but as many clinical states; its interrelationships with emotional factors have become increasingly controversial; and—with the advent of the use of insulin—it has shifted from a fatal to a controllable condition.

Diabetes presents a special challenge to the practitioner. It is a chronic, lifelong condition with serious later complications. Its manifestations and therapy affect the basic bodily processes of eating, drinking, and excreting which for most persons have special emotional significance. Its control demands that the patients, or their families, assume the complex roles of dietitian, laboratory technician, physician, and nurse. The limitations it may impose provide a context within which the patient may develop dependence, rebel against authority, or succumb, figuratively or literally, to futility and depression. Its challenge lies in the opportunities it affords the practitioner to prevent or minimize these adverse reactions, while helping the patient to maintain the physiological and psychological balance necessary for normal growth and development.

The preparation of this chapter was supported in part by the Bureau of Community Health Services, Maternal and Child Health Services Project 920.

THE PHYSICAL DISABILITY

Classification

Diabetes mellitus is a heterogeneous chronic disorder of carbohydrate metabolism characterized by glucose intolerance resulting from inadequate pancreatic function. Its immediate distinguishing signs are elevated levels of sugar in the blood *(hyperglycemia)* and in the urine *(glycosuria)*. Until recently, it was common practice to distinguish two major forms of diabetes mellitus: juvenile (also called *brittle* or *insulin-dependent*) and *adult-onset*. As the terms imply, the juvenile type was thought to occur in childhood, while the adult type developed later, usually after the age of forty. In the juvenile type, the insulin-producing capacity of the beta cells of the islets of Langerhans gradually decreases and finally disappears completely, leaving the patient dependent upon injected insulin for life. In the adult-onset type, the patient may not be dependent upon injected insulin but may achieve control of hyperglycemia by diet or oral agents.

Recent research has established, however, that there are more than 30 distinct disorders involving glucose intolerance. The classification of diabetes mellitus into two types based partly upon age of onset does not adequately represent the heterogeneity of this group of disorders. Consequently, a new classification has been developed by the National Diabetes Data Group of the National Institutes of Health (1979) and endorsed by the American Diabetes Association (ADA) and by the World Health Organization. Diagnosis based on age of onset has been eliminated, and proneness or resistance to the development of ketosis (and hence dependence on insulin) has been used as a determinant.

What was formerly termed *juvenile diabetes* is now classified as a separate group and termed *insulin-dependent diabetes mellitus* (IDDM). The formerly designated adult-onset types, if they are not secondary to other conditions, constitute a second subclass called *non-insulin-dependent diabetes mellitus* (NIDDM). The latter group is further subdivided into *obese* NIDDM and *nonobese* NIDDM. Many other forms of glucose intolerance have been identified and are classified by the data group.

Prevalence

Diabetes mellitus constitutes a major health problem in the United States, although the heterogeneity of the disorders of glucose intolerance makes judgments of the frequency of diabetes mellitus uncertain. A reasonable prevalence estimate seems to be 2% of the total population, excluding the Pima Indians of Arizona, who have an unusually high occurrence rate, for reasons that are unknown. If diabetes mellitus occurs in 2% of the population, then there are about four million diabetic persons in the United States, of whom probably two to three million have been identified. Only about 5% of the diagnosed patients are children, although diabetes mellitus is the most common childhood endocrine disorder.

The incidence of diabetes in the United States has increased by over 50% between 1965 and 1973 (Ganda, 1977), and it appears to continue to increase. All these figures taken together suggest that there are approximately 10 million persons in this country who either have diabetes mellitus—identified or unidentified—or will develop the condition. There is no difference in incidence between boys and girls or between men and women up to age 45; after that, the rates for women are higher.

Genetic Factors

Both the insulin-dependent and the non-insulin-dependent forms of diabetes have a genetic basis, although the exact mechanism of transmission is not known. There are some families within the non-insulin-dependent category in which an autosomal dominant pattern of inheritance appears to be well established. The prevailing theory of genetic transmission, however, is that predisposition to diabetes mellitus is an autosomal recessive trait, that is, that it may be inherited and transmitted by persons of either sex. This theory is still open to question, since the actual occurrence of the disorder in families does not accord with the theoretical predictions. Indeed, diabetes has been termed the "geneticist's nightmare" because of the lack of a genetic marker or heritability index.

The fact that a tendency toward diabetes mellitus runs in families carries considerable clinical significance for the practitioner. As is the case with many other developmental disabilities, diabetic families may seek genetic counseling and information about family planning. Evidence that the condition is often recessive, implicating both sides of the family, is particularly helpful in easing the burden of guilt or responsibility which one parent may feel for the occurrence of the diabetes in the child. Information regarding probabilities of occurrence must be interpreted with great care, however. For example, the young parents of an only child who was diabetic once solemnly told the writer that they could now have three more children without fear of another diabetic child, since the occurrence rate was one in four. Furthermore, genetic propensities in diabetes mellitus, as in other conditions, work themselves out in interaction with environmental factors. In the NIDDM type, for example, weight gain and obesity probably interact with genetic susceptibility to produce the overt clinical signs. Emotional stress has also been thought to trigger the onset of the condition, as we shall see later.

Clinical Characteristics

The visible clinical manifestations of IDDM appear abruptly, with dramatic and often frightening suddenness. The young patient loses weight, complains of weakness and fatigue, and develops the telltale "three p's," *polydipsia* (excessive thirst), *polyphagia* (excessive hunger), and *polyuria* (excessive urination). The latter three symptoms, which are pathognomonic for diabetes mellitus, may be confusing to parents. Bed-wetting in a previously trained child, for example, may be one sign of insulin insufficiency; but it is often seen by parents as an indication of rebelliousness, anger, or emotional upset. One boy in a series of family studies (Garner & Thompson, 1978) developed polyuria and polydipsia on a cross-country automobile trip. His weary father at the steering wheel, forced to stop at ten-minute intervals for drinks or toileting, finally lost his temper at what he considered provocative behavior in his son. Only a stop at the hospital emergency room when the boy became comatose provided the medical information needed to interpret his behavior as symptomatic of unsuspected diabetes.

If, as in this case, the initial symptoms are misunderstood, the IDDM patient may develop the graver signs of drowsiness and coma which herald the development of ketoacidosis. Such an introduction to the disorder, involving emergency hospital procedures, understandably arouses anxiety in the young patient's family—an anxiety which may persist and complicate the care of the patient long after the emergency is over. For, if the onset of symptoms in IDDM is abrupt, the control and subsidence of symptoms are equally sudden, once appropriate medical measures are applied.

The non-insulin-dependent variety of diabetes, by contrast, develops slowly and insidiously. The patient may remain asymptomatic for decades, with no visible signs other than, in most instances, a gradually increasing weight gain. By the age of forty or so, 60 to 90% of these patients are obese. The relationship between diabetes mellitus and obesity is still controversial, some diabetologists arguing that obesity causes diabetes and others suggesting that diabetes causes obesity. In any case, hyperglycemia and glucose intolerance usually improve if the patient loses weight.

Treatment

Once the nature of the patient's disorder has been identified as a type of diabetes, the next step is the achievement of control of the condition. This is far from an easy task. Diabetes mellitus, especially the insulin-dependent type, is by its nature variable and somewhat unpredictable in its day-to-day course. Dietary factors, insulin levels, exercise, fatigue, illness, and emotional stress all interplay in a complex, ever changing, often seemingly capricious manner.

The goals of diabetic treatment are twofold: (1) The concentrations of sugar in blood and urine must be maintained within acceptable limits. What "acceptable" means will vary from patient to patient and from physician to physician. Too low blood sugar *(hypoglycemia)* may lead to irritability, shakiness, even unconsciousness and seizures. Too high blood sugar, on the other hand, may lead to acidosis, ketosis, and eventually to diabetic coma. Maintaining a balance between these extremes is a delicate matter. (2) The patient's general well-being must be fostered. This condition is indicated in young patients by normal physical growth, as shown by development in height and weight. In adult diabetic patients, particularly those who have had the disorder for some years, well-being is evaluated also in terms of freedom from the usual complications of diabetes, which are discussed below.

In order to maintain acceptable control, patients, or their care-givers, must regularly monitor urine sugar levels, insulin dosages, dietary intake, and exercise. Insulin-dependent patients usually spend some time in hospital, where these four factors are evaluated and balanced. During such hospitalization, patients usually attend classes regularly, to learn about their disorder, about diet calculations and exchanges, insulin measurement and injection, urine testing and exercise. Thereafter, it is assumed that patients will independently follow the regimen of urine testing four times daily, measured insulin injection two times daily, diet calculation and maintenance, and exercise monitoring. As in many other branches of health care, however, compliance does not always occur.

Individual differences among patients along many dimensions—age, duration, stress, economic status, physical constitution, general health—contribute to the achievement of diabetic control. Individual differences among physicians in prescribing treatment also exist. For example, the margin of blood or urine sugar tolerated varies, some physicians favoring a positive sugar level to offset possible insulin reactions, others arguing that such a procedure invites acidosis. Some minimize the monitoring of exercise, while others emphasize it (Vranic,

Horvath, & Wahren, 1979). A controversy has long raged over the relative desirability of rigorous versus relaxed control. Recently the American Diabetes Association accepted as official policy a relatively tight control over glucose levels (Cahill, 1976). The association's public statement of philosophy inspired replies from those favoring a looser control (Ingelfinger, 1977). The consequences of these new philosophies for psychological development are considered in a later section. Regardless of the psychosocial factors, however, the philosophies have evolved in the interest of preventing complications.

General Effect on Physical Development

The presence of a chronic disorder from early childhood throughout life always raises the question of the effect of the condition upon normal growth and development. In the case of insulin-dependent diabetes mellitus, effects upon such basic measures as height and weight seem minimal. If the diabetes is diagnosed before the growth spurt, the mean adult height achieved may be less than the average for both sexes; there is no difference in the height of persons diagnosed during the growth spurt. Except for a slight tendency toward overweight in diabetic girls during adolescence, there is no regular effect of the condition upon weight. Nor do diabetic children differ from their nondiabetic peers in frequency or types of infections.

Sexual maturation proceeds normally in the female adolescent diabetic patient, with menarche occurring at the usual age. However, the childbearing years may bring complications. Fertility is not decreased, and there is no increase in fetal loss in the first trimester. The spontaneous abortion rate is somewhat higher in the second trimester, however, and there are significant problems in the third trimester, when percentages of toxemia, of perinatal deaths, and of infants with lethal defects or obesity are higher for diabetic mothers than for the nondiabetic. The appearance of diabetes mellitus for the first time during pregnancy, with remission after delivery, has given rise to the diagnosis of a special type of diabetes named *gestational diabetes mellitus*. Some of these patients later develop established diabetes. Pregnant women whose diabetes antedated pregnancy, on the other hand, suffer few if any residual effects after delivery.

Boys with diabetes mellitus are considered to proceed normally through sexual maturity, but there is some evidence that diabetic men may have problems of impotence. Estimates of frequency range around 48% of men whose diabetes has lasted six years or more and whose age is over 50 years (Kolodny, 1974; Renshaw, 1975; Wabrek, 1979). A number of the physical complications related to diabetes may be responsible for the sexual dysfunction. However, such psychological factors as helplessness, depression, and anxiety over a lifelong chronic illness may well be the more important antecedents. Studies suggest that a pattern of sexual dysfunction may also develop in diabetic women (Kolodny, 1971), but the results are far from clear.

Although the developmental progress of diabetic patients thus seems generally normal, there are complications which can occur. A rather minor one is the cosmetic problem which arises after repeated injections of insulin. Fatty tissue at the site of the injections atrophies, so that the areas appear wasted. This condition, called *lipodystrophy*, is significant in its effect upon the patient's self-concept. It occurs more often in women than in men and usually undergoes remission in two to three years.

More serious complications are those which involve three particularly vulnerable systems of the body: the vascular, the visual, and the neural. Many of these complications are present in incipient form long before the diagnosis of diabetes is made, although they may not actually appear until many years after the onset of symptoms. This leads most diabetologists to consider complications as integral parts of the disease process. It is not surprising, therefore, to discover, as we noted above, that control of the diabetes does not seem to be related to frequency or severity of complications.

Vascular complications constitute the most common hazard for the diabetic patient. Cardiovascular disease, especially *coronary artery disease*, is probably the most frequent cause of death in the adult diabetic patient. *Retinopathy* is another exceedingly serious complication, appearing in insulin-dependent diabetes mellitus patients about ten years after the growth spurt (Knowles, 1971). Retinal hemorrhages and neovascularizations occur, usually leading eventually to visual impairment and blindness. Indeed, blindness is 10 to 28 times as frequent in diabetic patients as in the general population. *Renal disease* and failure are particular threats to the younger diabetic patient.

Neuropathy, particularly in the lower extremities, is observable in a small percentage of very young diabetic patients. In the adult patient, there may be motor weakness, decreased pain and vibratory sensitivity, and numbness or coldness. It is thought that some instances of sexual dysfunction and impotence in older diabetic males may result from peripheral neuropathy (Faerman, Glocer, Fox, Jadzinsky, & Rapaport, 1973).

The variety and seriousness of the complications in diabetes testify to the pervasiveness of this disorder in the human body. Diabetes is indeed a systemic condition, with an unremitting progression throughout the life of the patient. It is listed as the sixth leading cause of death in the United States. Clearly, so severe and debilitating a condition may have serious psychological and emotional effects upon the patients and their families, as we shall now see.

COMMON PSYCHOLOGICAL CHARACTERISTICS AND PROBLEMS

The practitioner seeking to understand, evaluate, and aid diabetic patients will discover two general classes of psychological characteristics which typify them: (1) those which represent the usual consequences of chronic illness, which appear in diabetes as in other lifelong disabling conditions; and (2) those which are unique to diabetes, because of the particular physiological and psychosocial processes involved in this disorder.

General Consequences of Chronic Conditions

Like all lifelong disabilities, diabetes has effects upon the patient's development at every stage of life. If the diabetic symptoms appear in infancy or early childhood, the entire family feels the effect. Hospitalization separates the child from the family in frightening circumstances, and the ensuing anxieties may retard or distort the nature of the bonding process between parent and child. Dietary and other therapeutic requirements alter the daily schedule of the entire family, with the danger that the child and the disease may become the center of attention and concern. The knowledge that they have produced a child who is less than perfect and whose care will require special skill, devotion, and economic resources for years, comes as a shock to the parents. The special attention which the diabetic child seems to require is often interpreted by brothers and sisters as evidence of unfair partiality and even, perhaps, of the desirability of illness or disability in winning parental affection.

Like other families, those with a diabetic child respond differently to the challenges of living with a chronic condition. In one study of parental response, for example, the mother of a nine-year-old was already concerned about the status of her grandchildren; the same mother considered diabetes the "worst thing" that ever happened to the family. In the same group, another mother seemed relatively, but realistically, unconcerned; she explained, "Some families with diabetes . . . go into a tizzy over it. We aren't like that" (Garner & Thompson, 1978, p. 222). Between these two extremes, there may be found in diabetic families examples of all the varieties of adjustive techniques described in Chapter One. One extensive study, for example (Koski, 1969), investigated the development of coping techniques throughout the first year after the diagnosis of the diabetes, comparing families whose children were in good control with those whose children were not. Although all families demonstrated initial shock and disorganization, those whose child was in good control were more open and expressive in their reactions, while the others were more likely to deny their feelings. As the year progressed, some families were able to put the diabetes in its appropriate perspective, emphasizing other aspects of the child's life while making the therapeutic regimen a part of the daily routine. Other families seemed helpless, depressed, and angry in the face of the disorder and its demands upon them. These differences were related, over the year, to the control of the diabetic condition. Similar findings are reported by others (Bruch, 1948; Frankel, 1975; Swift, Seidman, & Stein, 1967).

As in many clinical investigations, it is difficult in studies of this sort to distinguish between cause and effect. Poor control in the diabetic child, with its life-threatening significance, may well tax the coping abilities of the family. Good physiological control in the child, on the other hand, may demand of the parents less skill, devotion, patience, and tolerance for frustration.

One area which is a particularly sensitive indicator of the strain in the family of a chronically disabled child is that of the marital relationship. There is considerable, though conflicting, evidence that the presence of a handicapped child may contribute to the weakening of the parents' marriage. This phenomenon has been studied in families where the child is diabetic by Crain, Sussman, and Weil (1966). In a well-conceived comparison of parents of diabetic children and their siblings with parents of a matched group of controls, the diabetic couples achieved lower scores on four measures of marital functioning. Such findings are familiar to many clinicians working with diabetic families (Minuchin, 1974).

Adolescence presents special problems to the diabetic patient, as to all handicapped young persons. Strivings toward identity and self-definition, desires for independence and freedom from authority and restriction, and experimentation with styles of life complicate these years for all chronically disabled youths. For the diabetic adolescent, however, the common conflicts, frustrations, and challenges of the teens are in some ways exaggerated and distorted.

It has been thought that a basic conflict in the development of diabetes is that between a desire to attain and maintain dependence upon the parent and a desire to be free—a core problem for all adolescents. For a variety of historical reasons, however, the tug of the apron strings and the pull of the peer group are more evenly balanced for the diabetic teenager. Moreover, the physiological consequences of efforts to resolve this particular conflict may be grave or even fatal.

At the simple level of self-report, it would appear that diabetic adolescents see themselves as equal to, if not superior to, their nondiabetic peers in the achievement of independence in everyday matters (Partridge, Garner, Thompson, & Cherry, 1972). When a wider sampling of items is used and the results factor-analyzed (Sullivan, 1979), "dependence–independence" emerges as a conflict area for teenaged diabetic girls. Because this factor is significantly related to the attitude toward diabetes, a positive attitude toward diabetes is associated with independence.

Adolescents may alter diet, insulin, and exercise out of sheer curiosity about the possible effects, in a way similar to the testing of limits seen often in much younger children. At a more mature level, they may experiment with the therapy as part of assuming personal responsibility for their own bodies. Both reactions may be complicated by a view of the physician as one more unwelcome authority figure, whose instructions are to be challenged and opposed as part of becoming independent. Both may jeopardize the health and even the survival of the young patient.

If the diabetic symptoms occur after the developmental period, in young adulthood or middle life, the initial shock is complicated by vocational, marital, and parental demands. For many adults, the appearance of a chronic disabling condition carries with it the first definite implication of mortality. Depressive reactions may follow this realization. These reactions are intensified if the young adult discovers that plans for marriage or vocation must now be altered. Studies of diabetic teenagers have indicated (Davis, Shipp, & Pattishall, 1965) that most plan to marry and to have children; many contemplate college or professional school. These plans must often be changed or forsaken as the young patient faces rejection by employers, insurance companies, and motor vehicle departments and as he learns more about the genetic components of his disorder and rethinks prospective marriage and parenthood.

Most of the restrictions imposed upon diabetic patients are the product of ignorance or fear in the general population (Forsham, 1959; Partridge, 1967). The official recommendations of the American Diabetes Association on employment of diabetic persons make clear that patients under good control are perfectly satisfactory employment risks in a wide variety of occupations. Studies suggest that in performance and in absentee record the diabetic patient is comparable to the nondiabetic worker (American Diabetes Association, 1957). However, much remains to be done in the education of the general public regarding the acceptability of the diabetic patient in the many complex social roles of adulthood.

As in other chronic conditions, so in diabetes there are aspects of the disorder and its treatment which may cause the patient to feel different and thus influence the self-concept. Frequent trips to the bathroom; foregoing refreshments at social events; eating snacks at particular times of day; spells of dizziness; and, in the case of hypoglycemic reactions, the apparently paradoxical need for sugar identify the diabetic patient as somehow unusual. Indeed, in the case of adult patients, the shakiness, poor balance, and disorientation of impending hypoglycemia are often mistaken for alcoholic intoxication. How this uniqueness affects the development of such persons' self-concepts will depend partly on how they view their own bodies and partly on how others view them and their condition.

The body image which the diabetic patient develops is determined by information concerning the condition itself and by individual sensations and feelings. As we have seen, the young diabetic patient typically has an imperfect understanding of the nature of the condition and is subject to confusion and anxiety concerning it. One little girl, in hospital for initial regulation of her diabetes, overheard a reference to her disorder, which she misinterpreted as "die of betes." Her inconsolable crying and despair were expressions of her misguided conviction that she was about to die. Diabetic teenagers who had received extensive instruction about their condition revealed, through interview and drawing procedures, that they were still confused and inaccurate in their perceptions of their bodily functioning (Kaufman & Hersher, 1971). Their drawings of their own internal organs were strongly influenced by their private notions that they were deprived and somehow gravely damaged by the condition.

Despite these confusions, most diabetic young people who have been objectively studied seem to be able to identify the various internal states which characterize the disorder. They can distinguish poor diabetic control from "sickness," for example (Thompson, Garner, & Partridge, 1969); they relate dietary indiscretions to feelings of tiredness or weakness; and, like persons with other handicaps, they prefer their own familiar diabetes to most other conditions (Davis *et al.*, 1965).

Perhaps the most powerful determiner of self-concept is the reaction of others to the individual. Diabetes is one of the relatively invisible handicapping conditions; on casual acquaintance, the diabetic person neither looks nor acts differently from others. Indeed, there is evidence that the condition itself is ranked as among the most acceptable, as described in Chapter 1 (Abroms & Kodera, 1979). Nevertheless, studies of children and teenagers suggest that there is a lowering in self-esteem, a feeling of damage, and negative self-references (Richardson, Hastorf, & Dornbusch, 1964; Swift *et al.*, 1967). In one such study (Sullivan, 1979), over a hundred adolescent girls with diabetes completed a scale of self-esteem, along with a Diabetes Adjustment Scale and depression inventory. Girls with lower self-esteem scores also scored lower in total adjustment, had difficulty with peer relationships and family relationships, and had developed problems with dependence–independence issues. Their overall attitudes toward their diabetes were negative.

The same investigation provides information concerning another relatively common consequence of chronic disability: *depression*. The adolescent diabetic girls in Sullivan's study also completed an inventory which measures four areas of depressive behavior: (1) physiological indicators, (2) self-depreciation, (3) pessimism–suicide, and (4) indecisiveness. In this group, those with lower total adjustment scores, more dependence–independence conflicts, and negative attitudes toward their diabetes described themselves as more depressed on the inventory.

To the experienced clinician, of course, indications of depressive behavior always raise the question of the danger of self-injury or suicide. As we mentioned above, diabetic adolescents may, for a variety of reasons, alter or stop their therapeutic regimen. In this they endanger both their health and their survival. Occasional evidence (Rosen & Lidz, 1949) appears to indicate that a diabetic patient may purposefully disrupt the regimen as a means to hospitalization, which may then provide sanctuary from insupportable life situations. The practitioner working with the diabetic patient needs to be aware of the possibly tragic outcome of the interplay between individual conflict, diabetic state, and depressive or suicidal trends. Approaches in interviewing the potentially suicidal subject, as well as recommendations for care, have been included in the "Suggestions about Process" section of Chapter 1.

Psychological Characteristics Unique to Diabetes

Diabetes mellitus, as described above, is a disorder of carbohydrate metabolism which has pervasive effects throughout many systems of the body. Blood sugar levels may fluctuate widely, from hyperglycemia, which may lead to acidosis and diabetic coma, to hypoglycemia, which may lead to insulin reactions and also to coma. Neural tissue is particularly sensitive to glucose concentrations in the blood, and these fluctuations, therefore, may produce a variety of behavioral consequences. The basic physiological processes involved in diabetes, in other words, are related, in direct and indirect ways, to the unique psychological characteristics of the disorder.

Psychophysiological Factors. For many decades, a relationship has been suspected between stress and the physiological derangements of diabetes. Hinkle and his associates (Hinkle, Evans, & Wolf, 1951; Hinkle & Wolf, 1952; Hinkle, 1956) studied the life histories of diabetic patients and related significant life events to blood glucose concentrations. Other investigators have employed hypnotically or experimentally induced stress (VandenBergh, Sussman, & Titus, 1966; VandenBergh, Sussman, & Vaughan, 1967) in studies of carbohydrate metabolism. Blood glucose levels decrease during periods of induced stress for the diabetic patients but not for nondiabetic controls, although only a relatively small number of cases have been studied. Occasional clinical reports of individual patients identify episodes of acidosis which seem to be precipitated by stressful situations (Schless & VonLaveran-Stiebar, 1964). These basic observations, however, have stimulated further investigations of possible effects of stress upon the etiology of diabetes mellitus and upon its course.

The psychological factor most often implicated in the etiology of diabetic symptoms is personal loss. As we have seen, sorrow was thought to be involved in the disorder centuries ago. More recent writings continue this line of argument. In one study of adolescents (Stein & Charles, 1971), 69% of the diabetic group had suffered parental loss through separation, divorce, illness, or death, as compared with 19% of a nondiabetic control population with heritable blood diseases; the difference is statistically significant.

A significant question regarding etiology, however, is raised by investigators who believe that there is an underlying psychological conflict in biologically susceptible persons which renders them candidates for overt diabetic symptoms. Dunbar, for example (1943), in her classic studies of psychosomatic disorder, argued that the focal conflict in diabetes was a lifelong vacillation between dependence and independence, particularly in relation to the parents. Similar observations have been made by Alexander (1950), whose well-known studies of psychosomatic disorder included a formulation of the basic conflict in diabetes. He presents clinical evidence that glycosuria of diabetic patients increases as the patients' wishes to be cared for conflict with demands that they care for others.

Although much clinical evidence favoring this formulation has been adduced, controlled studies do not consistently support it (e.g., Crowell, 1953; Simonds, 1977). That there may be difficulty in achieving independence seems evident, but the difficulty could as well be the consequence as the cause of the diabetic symptomatology. A somewhat more convincing approach is that made by the use of the Schedule of Recent Events (Holmes & Rahe, 1967), in which patients rate the significant life events which have preceded the onset or exacerbation of diabetic symptoms. Indeed, studies of factors which may affect the course of diabetes mellitus are in general more productive than those which focus upon etiology. That the day-to-day fluctuations in glucose and metabolism may be responsive in part to environmental and personal events seems reasonable. It also seems reasonable, as argued by one writer (Kimball, 1971), that the individual differences in such fluctuations are related to the psychological vulnerability of the patient, such that the more vulnerable the person, in terms of the adequacy of coping skills, the more likely it is that major changes will be apparent in the physiological processes.

However, the results obtained in systematic studies of this relationship are conflicting. The clinical studies of Minuchin (1974), who monitored sugar levels in patients during therapeutic sessions, indicate a relationship between the discussion of stressful topics and physiological changes, as well as a relationship over longer periods of time. However, a careful study (Grant, Kyle, Teichman, & Mendels, 1974) in which adults filled out the Schedule of Recent Events at each visit to the physician revealed no relationship of recorded life events to the patients' overall physical condition. The interplay between physiological and environmental factors in determining both the etiology and the course of diabetes remains an elusive problem.

Patients' Responsibility for Care. Diabetic patients share with a few other developmentally disabled persons, such as those with hemophilia, the responsibility for monitoring and ministering to their bodily condition. This is a complex, never-ending process, involving the daily testing of urine, the measurement and injection of insulin or the daily administration of oral medications, the calculation and maintenance of diet, and the evaluation and control of physical exercise. In a sense, some of the skills of the nurse, the laboratory technician, the dietitian, and the physical therapist must be acquired by patients and then applied in their own behalf.

In the young patient, the responsibility for the regimen rests initially with the parents. There are many different reactions which parents show in this regard. Often it is the mother, for a variety of reasons, who performs the daily routines. In one family studied (Garner & Thompson,

1978), the father refused even to observe the insulin injections, saying he had a phobia of blood (although no blood is drawn in an insulin injection). In another family, the father regularly evaluated the urinary results and measured the appropriate insulin dosage—although with such anxiety that he referred to this daily event as the "moment of truth."

Parents differ from one another and from their physicians in the literalness with which they apply instructions regarding diet, exercise, and insulin. They also differ in the amount and accuracy of the information about diabetes which they possess. Studies using tests of diabetic information (Collier & Etzwiler, 1971; Etzwiler, 1962; Partridge et al., 1972) suggest that, despite attendance at diabetic classes, parents still retain misconceptions regarding acidosis, dietary control, genetic factors, and the general philosphy of care.

Young patients must ultimately assume responsibility for their own care, although the age at which this occurs and the efficiency, devotion and anxiety which it entails are all highly individual matters. Results from diabetic information tests administered to children suggest (Etzwiler, 1962; Garner & Thompson, 1974) that diabetic patients' store of information about the disorder increases systematically with age. Judging from these results alone, young patients between the ages of 12 and 15 are ready, on the average, to undertake the responsibility for their own care. When the young persons are asked directly about the matter (Garner & Thompson, 1974; Partridge et al., 1972), they identify ages 11 to 12 years as the appropriate time for assuming independent responsibility for insulin injections, urine testing, and dietary management.

Those in whom the disorder manifests itself during the adult years—usually the NIDDM types—learn the details of diabetic management directly, without lengthy intervention by parents or care-givers. Except for taking oral medication rather than insulin injections, these patients face the same tasks of monitoring urine, diet, and exercise as do the children. These older patients, however, are by no means immune from carelessness or misinformation or anxiety in monitoring their disorder, nor are they typically in good control.

In one study of 213 adult patients (Williams, Martin, Hogan, Watkins, & Ellis, 1967), 71% were rated as in poor or very poor control. Poor control in these patients was significantly correlated with age at onset of the disorder, those with early onset and thus longer duration being in poorer control. Tests of diabetic information revealed that these patients varied widely in their knowledge of diabetes. On questions involving practical situations which they might face as diabetic patients, these adults showed many gaps in their knowledge, particularly on items concerning insulin reactions, high urine sugars, and exercise. As has been found in other studies, however (Garner & Thompson, 1974; Ludvigsson, 1977), control of diabetes is not correlated with information about it. Apparently, an accurate store of information does not guarantee that the diabetes will be well controlled.

A more direct test of the factors related to control involves observation of the patient's performance of the tasks required in dealing with his condition. As part of the study described above, Watkins, Williams, Martin, Hogan, and Anderson (1967) obtained reports from observers who visited 60 adult diabetic patients in their homes. Management of the diabetes was evaluated by having the patients demonstrate their usual methods of insulin dosage, urine testing, meal planning, and foot care. Eighty per cent of the patients administered insulin unacceptably. Over half made errors in insulin dosage; the longer they had had the disorder, the more errors they made. Only one third tested their urine correctly; only one fourth used the results appropriately in determining diet and insulin dosage. Similarly discouraging results emerged in the other areas studied. Again, however, no correlation was obtained between observed management and control.

The demands made upon patients by these daily requirements are inconvenient, troublesome, and often painful. They may also contribute to the enduring personality structures and patterns of diabetic persons. Tight control and rigid scheduling, for example, may appeal to children, parents and adult patients who have already developed compulsive means of handling anxiety and may reinforce these techniques. There is some evidence (Bruch, 1948; Koski, 1969) that mothers' perfectionistic attitudes toward control are related to the child's behavior difficulties, while a more relaxed environment (Weil, 1967) may attenuate the emotional reactions. Adolescent rebellion against diabetic requirements is thought by some to be intensified by rigid preadolescent restrictions. On the other hand, self-care at any age may enhance one's feelings of adequacy and counteract the development of lowered self-esteem and attitudes of dependency (Swift *et al.*, 1967). A balance between realistic control of the diabetic condition and freedom and flexibility in coping with stress is desirable, but by no means easy to achieve.

EVALUATING DIABETIC PATIENTS

As with other groups, the instruments and approaches to evaluating diabetic patients are determined by the questions being asked. The initial approach, however, is the same no matter what the specific goal may be. An open-ended, partially structured interview (Kimball, 1971) most often begins the evaluation, allowing the practitioner to estimate the point at which the patient has arrived in development as well as to begin to establish a relationship that is different from a parental or medical one.

Perhaps the most important first requirement of the interviewer of the diabetic patient is information concerning diabetes in general. Persons who have lived and dealt with the disorder for many years, as we have seen, will have amassed a good deal of factual information about it and will also have acquired a good many skills in dealing with it. The practitioner who lacks the information, if not the skills, will be at a considerable disadvantage in maintaining a productive relationship with the diabetic patient.

Knowledge not only of general facts concerning diabetes, but also of characteristics specific to the patient is helpful in the initial interview. The interviewer needs to know the time of onset of the diabetes and its duration, since early onset and long duration are adverse factors often correlated with poor control and negative self-image (Swift *et al.*, 1967). The philosophy of treatment espoused by the patient's physician— whether "tight" or "loose" control—is also important in helping the practitioner evaluate the context within which the patient must deal with the diabetes. Particularly in the case of children. it is also important to understand the extent to which the patient has undertaken responsibility for the details for self-care.

Most diabetic patients have certain common areas of sensitivity about their disorder, which the interviewer will do well to know and respect. In one study of adult insulin-dependent patients (Sanders, Mills, Martin, & Horne, 1975), who had dealt with the disorder for at least five years, over half admitted to awareness of and concern over complications, particularly blindness and vascular difficulties. To these were added a fear of burdening family and friends, of becoming invalid and unable to manage one's own life, and of an early death. As mentioned above, the possibility of depressive reactions is always present, in children and adolescents as well as in adults. Indeed, some writers feel that overconcern with the physical details of diabetes may mask an underlying depression, as do hypochondriacal preoccupations in patients with many other disorders. The diabetes may serve as a target for depressive feelings, rather than the reverse.

A final consideration for the interviewer, unique to the diabetic patient, is the variety of behavioral manifestations of impending hypoglycemia or other physiological changes. Patients vary widely in the ways in which these changes are expressed. One little girl, for example, burst into tears and became distraught when her blood sugar reached dangerously low levels. Irritability, shakiness, tremors, inattentiveness, vagueness, and many other idiosyncratic reactions may presage the occurrence of an insulin reaction. Both patient and interviewer may be misled by these reactions, many of which resemble the behaviors observed during stress or anxiety.

There are three rather general questions which arise in the evaluation of diabetic patients, to which the initial interview may lead: What is the patient's general level of cognitive development or functioning? What is the patient's emotional status, particularly as it affects self-esteem and self-image? What is the nature of the patient's adaptation to the various tasks involved in achieving social maturity? Let us consider each of these questions briefly.

Evaluating the General Level of Cognitive Functioning

As we have seen, a commonly employed index of well-being for the diabetic child is the trend of general development. To the usual measures of height, weight, and freedom from illness and infection may be added measures of intellectual function. It was formerly thought (Joslin, 1937) that diabetic children were superior in intelligence to their nondiabetic peers. Recent evidence, based upon more representative samples, however, makes it clear that diabetic children do not differ, on the average, from nondiabetic children in intelligence test scores. The only exception to this finding appears to occur in groups of children whose diabetes is of very early onset; such children often score lower, on the average, than the norm (Ack & Weil, 1961).

Since the tracking of intellectual development is often undertaken in dealing with diabetic children, it is important that measures be employed which are well standardized and reliable. For very young children, the Bayley Scales of Infant Development provide adequate baseline information; later, the usual standard measures such as the Stanford–Binet Intelligence Scale and the Wechsler Intelligence Scale for Children—Revised are appropriate. As with all repeated testing, so here, the interval between tests must be long enough to circumvent the effects of practice.

A further question which may depend in part upon cognitive functioning is that of the child's readiness to assume responsibility for self-care in urine testing, insulin measurement and injection, and diet. As we have seen, child patients are able to specify the chronological ages at which they feel competent in these areas. However, an additional indicator of readiness may be the amount and accuracy of information about diabetes which the child possesses. Diabetes information tests are available in the research literature (Etzwiler, 1967; Garner & Thompson, 1974) and may prove helpful in appraising this variable.

Although the general level of cognitive functioning may not be as important in evaluating the adult patient, any change over time is significant. With the passage of time, and particularly with repeated episodes of hypoglycemia, coma or seizures, there is always the possibility of central nervous system changes which may be reflected through systematic decreases in intelligence test scores. The precise effects of changes in blood sugar levels upon the nervous system is still in question, although it is thought that low blood sugar may adversely affect concentration, memory, orientation, and possibly speech behavior. Support for such conclusions, however, comes from occasional case reports and studies with infrahuman animals rather than from controlled research on diabetic patients. The question is complicated by the fact that the behaviors described as indicators of central nervous system (CNS) malfunction occur also during emotional arousal (Bruhn, 1974).

As with the repeated evaluation of cognitive functioning in children, so in the adult it is essential to employ instruments which can be administered several times. The Wechsler Adult Intelligence Scale is a useful instrument, although it may be necessary to modify it for diabetic patients with visual handicaps.

Evaluating the Patient's Emotional Status

We have already seen that the earlier concept of the "diabetic personality" has not prevailed in recent years. Diabetic patients demonstrate a wide range of emotional reactions to their disorder, and they may share with other disabled patients the lowered self-esteem and tendency toward depression which handicap seems to foster. Practitioners wishing to evaluate these aspects of the young patient's behavior may find the sentence completion devised by Frankel (1975) useful. Sullivan's Diabetic Adjustment Scale (1979) is another promising technique, applicable to adolescent girls.

When conventional measures of personality and adjustment are applied to diabetic patients, commonly no unusual findings emerge. An early study of adolescent and young adult diabetic persons (Kubany, 1956) yielded no significant differences in Minnesota Multiphasic Personality Inventory (MMPI) scores when these were compared with control groups. Diabetic children and adolescents produced no differences in Rorschach content categories from those given by a comparison group (McCraw & Tuma, 1977). A group of adult diabetic patients gave responses to Cattell's Sixteen Personality Factor Questionnaire (Cattell's

16PF scale) which were within the normal range (Sanders *et al.*, 1975). In a study of adult patients whose diabetes was of very long duration, ranging from 25 to 48 years, however, one difference in MMPI scores emerged (Murawski, Chazan, Balodimos, & Ryan, 1970). This study compared a group of Quarter-Century Victory Medal winners, who had been free of vascular complications for over 25 years, with a comparable group which had not achieved this victory. The latter group had a significantly higher score on hypochondriasis. However, both groups fell within the normal MMPI limits on all scales.

Evaluating the Patient's Adaptive Behavior

The expectations of parents, friends, and spouses, as well as the general societal demands, are the same for diabetic patients as for nondiabetic persons. The diabetic child goes to regular school, for example; he closely resembles his nondiabetic peers in school achievement. As we have seen, plans for marriage, parenthood, and vocation are made by diabetic adults, although here societal restrictions complicate the situation.

The practitioner evaluating the patient's approach to the expectations of others may well find the interview the method of choice, supplemented in the case of vocational evaluation with the usual tests of interest and aptitude. However, the open-ended interview may well expose areas of social immaturity or confusion within which some form of intervention is desirable.

INTERVENTION METHODS

The general outline of a program of intervention which the practitioner dealing with diabetic patients might consider can be deduced from the foregoing pages. Many of the useful techniques are the same as those applicable to any early, chronic, lifelong disorder. Others are unique to the problems faced by the diabetic child or adult.

When the diagnosis has been IDDM, arising early in life, the first requirement is that of support for both parents and child. As in all lifelong systemic disorders, the impact of the diagnosis upon the family is severe. The stages through which families ordinarily progress in dealing with the initial situation have been outlined earlier; their occurrence in families with a diabetic child has been documented by Koski (1969) and others. The gradual incorporation of the information and its significance requires time and continuing interpretation by health care professionals. Perhaps the most important—and the most difficult—service which the practitioner can offer is that of continuing availability to the family during these early days. The professional will discover that information must be given repeatedly, misinterpretations corrected again and again, personal vulnerabilities weighed against the necessity for realistic acceptance. In their dealings with family and patient, health care workers always need to balance the handling of the diabetes with the achievement of normal social and emotional development in the patient.

Another source of early intervention is the formal program of instruction organized by physicians and hospital personnel who are responsible for the first regulation of the diabetes. Since the complex details of care for the diabetic child must first be handled by the parents, child and parents together attend formal classes, usually in the hospital or the clinic. These classes contribute more than the information regarding control of the diabetic condition, they provide a group of fellow-patients with whom the anxieties, uncertainties, successes, and failures of early efforts at care can be shared. They should be organized so as to permit, indeed to facilitate, this valuable interaction. Such group support is useful at all stages of the disorder, but it is invaluable at the beginning of the coping process, when the diabetes and its care are strange, bewildering, and even terrifying to the new patients and their families.

As our understanding of learning and teaching in general increases, new techniques of instructing diabetic patients and families develop. There are now available programmed curricula, textbooks, teaching machines (Collier & Etzwiler, 1971), and operant conditioning models (Warnberg, 1974) for use in some aspects of diabetic instruction. As in other forms of learning, however, the commonly accepted principles of readiness to learn, consequences of learning, and regular review still apply. Children may be too young and families too distraught to profit from formal instruction, for example. Increases in energy and feelings of well-being which will ensue when the disorder is in control may serve to reinforce dietary and exercise requirements. Regular review of information and practice is essential, often involving a return to the classroom for refresher sessions.

Professional services and support provided by diabetologists and their staff, and by practitioners who count some diabetic patients among their caseloads, are continuously supplemented by regular community contributions. Furthermore, because the diabetic child attends regular school, teachers and classmates there provide another sort of support system. How diabetic children are perceived in the classroom will depend heavily upon how well informed and how relaxed teachers are in regard to the disorder and its more public manifestations. The ADA provides a useful fact sheet written for teachers which aims to reduce fear and misunderstanding, while still guaranteeing the diabetic child the assistance needed should an emergency arise.

Other community resources include special diabetic camps, often sponsored by hospitals or clinics, where children with diabetes may develop skills of independent outdoor living in interchange with their diabetic peers. Attitudes toward the usefulness of such camps vary with individuals and with families. One especially self-sufficient 11-year-old diabetic boy, for example, scorned such camps and insisted upon attending "regular" camp where he was able to perform successfully. Other children, or their parents, prefer the familiar, partially sheltered environment of the diabetic camp and its trained medical staff. Many of the usual community or oganizational camps cannot take the responsibility for dealing with diabetic children and therefore exclude them from attendance.

The American Diabetes Association is a valuable source of information and materials for the practitioner dealing with diabetic patients. There are instructional aids (Travis, 1975), special cookbooks for children and adults, instructional sheets for babysitters, teachers, and the general public, and charts and posters. Many of these aids are available in Spanish as well as English, and a few have been published in braille. Local branches of the ADA are located in most large centers of population.

Intervention, counseling, or psychotherapy may become necessary at any stage in the life of the diabetic patient. The importance of early career counseling has already been stressed. Some of the biases and roadblocks confronting the job-seeking patient may be overcome through work with the local vocational rehabilitation service. If the demands of school, family, marriage, or job become excessive, individual psychotherapy may become advisable. This is particularly important if, as noted above, depressive attitudes or suicidal preoccupations develop. Such intervention will require the time and talents of trained health service personnel.

Family therapy has proved useful in instances where the interaction of family stress with diabetic symptomatology has exacerbated both, as in the structural family therapy of Minuchin (1974). A combination of family and individual therapy, with some emphasis on relaxation techniques, has been found effective in some cases (Bauer, Harper, & Kenny, 1974). For adolescents particularly, group therapy in which patients can share the demands, problems, and restrictions of diabetes have proved popular (Paulsen & Colle, 1969). It is important to remember, in this regard, that the diabetic patient, whether child, adolescent, or adult, is not a special type of person. These patients share the joys and sorrows, frustrations and disappointments, demands and achievements common to all human beings. The kind of intervention which may prove helpful will depend quite as much upon individual differences in these characteristics as upon a diagnosis of diabetes mellitus.

TRENDS AND NEEDS

The discovery and use of insulin in 1922 was heralded as a turning point in the control and treatment of diabetes. A disorder which had been fatal was now manageable; lives were prolonged and their quality immensely improved. But the availability of insulin is not a cure, nor is its use easy or without hazard. Many unsolved problems regarding diabetes remain, both in the practical area of management and self-care and in the field of clinical and laboratory research.

Management and Self-Care

As we have seen, the management of diabetes requires a lifelong commitment by patients to numerous procedures which interrupt and alter the course of their daily lives. Any developments which improve the precision of these procedures or ease the burden upon patients and families would be most welcome. Some improvements, though still in the experimental stage, hold promise for the future. Simple changes in the calibration of syringes and in the legibility of the scales are helping elderly or visually handicapped patients to increase the precision with which they administer their insulin. Experiments are under way in the construction of a device for the continuous delivery of insulin in response to continuously monitored blood sugar levels. Such a device would be worn by the diabetic patient, much as a pacemaker is worn by the cardiac patient. The technical problems involved in the miniaturization of such devices are great; production of a dependable mechanism for general use is probably years away.

As a somewhat simpler level, methods of monitoring blood sugar levels at home, rather than making periodic visits to the laboratory, are also being developed. Tapes providing immediate readouts of sugar levels of the blood, comparable to those long used by patients for urine testing, may soon be generally available.

While improvements in the handling of these practical details are important, it must be remembered that overemphasis upon the daily routines, at the expense of normal social and emotional growth, is to be avoided. Perhaps of equal significance is the fact that the relationship between control of blood sugar levels and the occurrence of later complications is still by no means clear, even though research on this and other topics continues.

Clinical and Laboratory Research

Research on the prevention of diabetes begins with the identification of patients and of those at risk for the disorder. Epidemiologists decry the fact that, of the predicted four million persons in this country with diabetes, from one-half million to one million are diabetic but remain undiagnosed (Knowles, 1971). Screening programs for identifying these persons, as well as the many others whose obesity or family history puts them at risk, are an immediate need. The results of this investigation should assist materially also in helping to unravel the complex question of genetic transmission, upon which active efforts at prevention depend.

Although laboratory studies of infrahuman animals have yielded information regarding the complications of long-term hyperglycemia, precise findings on human subjects are not available. Perhaps the ideal study would be a prospective one, based on random samples of subjects with a variety of hyperglycemic conditions (Knowles, 1971). Following such a group for two or three decades and collecting precise periodic measurements of control and of indicators of predicted complication would yield valuable information. Such studies, and others in this area, will be greatly assisted by the classifications of research subjects and recommendations for data collection now available from the National Diabetes Data Group (1979).

The recurring question of the interrelationship between emotional and psychosocial variables and the occurrence or exacerbation of diabetic symptoms needs to be answered. Again, prospective studies with carefully defined comparison groups will yield more valuable information than occasional case reports.

Perhaps the most dramatic of the contemporary research approaches are those, still largely restricted to infrahuman subjects, involving organ transplantation (Brown, 1980). Transplants of the total pancreas and of the islets of Langerhans are being studied. Here, as elsewhere, ethical considerations are of great importance; some clinicians feel that transplantation, if it ultimately proves possible, should be employed only as a life-saving procedure, rather than one which relieves the patient of the onerous daily tasks of self-care. Again, the practical solution to the problem of transplant is probably many years away.

It is clear that community organizations and governmental agenices are influencing the amount and direction of research on diabetes. The National Commission on Diabetes, authorized in 1974 upon the passage of the Diabetes Mellitus Research and Education Act (PL 93–354), has developed a long-range program to support research and to develop better treatment methods. The American Diabetes Association and the more recently organized Juvenile Diabetes Foundation stimulate and support research. The ADA publishes *Diabetes,* a journal devoted to the dissemination of research information. These organizations also strive toward better education of the public in the understanding of diabetes mellitus. Much remains to be done in eliminating public misconceptions of diabetes and in assisting teachers, employers, and the general public to accept the diabetic patient as an essentially normal and potentially contributing member of society.

Many decades ago, an early worker in the field of diabetes put forth a philosophy which is as true today as it was then:

> It is not enough to view the person with diabetes simply as a sort of living test tube, in which the proper mixture of diet, insulin, and activity, will always produce the proper degree of regulation, if no other illness is present. It is necessary to view him as a sentient, active member of his society, constantly interrelating with and adapting to his family, his associates, his job, and all of the complex events and situations of the world around him. It is essential to know that his adaptations to his daily life constantly influence the course of his illness. (Hinkle, 1952, p. 417)

APPENDIX: SOURCES OF INFORMATION

General: Sources of informational and educational materials:
American Diabetes Association, Inc.
2 Park Avenue
New York, NY 10016
Phone: (212) 683–7444

Juvenile Diabetes Foundation
23 East 26 Street
New York, NY 10010
Phone: (212) 889–7575

Cooperative research program:
University Group Diabetes Program
Division of Clinical Investigation
600 Wyndhurst Avenue
Baltimore, MD 21210
Phone: (301) 528–7860

General information for the professional: Fajans, S. S. (Ed.). *Diabetes Mellitus*. NIH–DHEW Publication #76–854. Bethesda, Md.: John E. Fogarty International Center for Advanced Study in the Health Sciences, 1976.

Ganda, O. P., & Soeldner, S. S. Genetic, acquired and related factors in the etiology of diabetes mellitus. *Archives of Internal Medicine*, 1977, *137*, 461–469.

Garner, A. M., & Thompson, C. W. Juvenile Diabetes. In P. R. Magrab (Ed.), *Psychological management of pediatric problems* (Vol. 1). Baltimore: University Park Press, 1978.

Information for the Patient: *You and Diabetes*. The Upjohn Company, Kalamazoo, Mich., 1977.

Travis, L. B. *An Instructional Aid on Juvenile Diabetes Mellitus*. Galveston, Texas: University of Texas Medical Branch, 1975.

REFERENCES

Abroms, K. I., & Kodera, T. L. Acceptance hierarchy of handicaps: Validation of Kirk's statement, "Special Education often begins where medicine stops." *Journal of Learning Disabilities*, 1979, *12*, 15–20.

Ack, M. I., & Weil, W. B., Jr. Intelligence of children with diabetes mellitus. *Pediatrics*, 1961, *28*, 764–770.

Alexander, F. *Psychosomatic medicine: Its principles and applications*. New York: W. W. Norton, 1950.

American Diabetes Association. Analysis of a survey concerning employment of diabetics in some major industries. *Diabetes*, 1957, *6*, 550–553.

Bauer, R., Harper, R., & Kenny, T. Treatment for uncontrolled juvenile diabetes. *Pediatric Psychology*, 1974, *2*, 2–3.

Brown, J. (Ed.). Proceedings of a conference on pancreas transplantation. *Diabetes*, 1980, *29*, 1–128(Supplement 1).

Bruch, H. Physiologic and psychologic interrelationships in diabetes in children. *Psychosomatic Medicine*, 1948, *11*, 200-210.

Bruhn, J. G. Psychological influences in diabetes mellitus. *Postgraduate Medicine*, 1974, *56*, 113–118.

Cahill, G. F., Jr., Etzwiler, D. D., & Freinkel, N. "Control" and diabetes. *New England Journal of Medicine*, 1976, *294*, 1004.

Collier, B. N., & Etzwiler, D. D. Comparative study of diabetes knowledge among juvenile diabetics and their parents. *Diabetes*, 1971, *20*, 51–57.

Crain, A. R., Sussman, M. B., & Weil, W. B., Jr. Effects of a diabetic child on marital integration and related measures of family functioning. *Journal of Health and Human Behavior*, 1966, *7*, 122–127.

Crowell, D. H. Personality and physical disease: A test of the Dunbar hypothesis applied to diabetes mellitus and rheumatic fever. *Genetic Psychology Monographs*, 1953, *48*, 117–153.

Davis, D. M., Shipp, J. C., & Pattishall, E. G. Attitudes of diabetic boys and girls toward diabetes. *Diabetes*, 1965, *14*, 106–109.

Dunbar, H. F. *Psychosomatic Diagnosis.* New York: Paul Hoeber, 1943.
Etzwiler, D. D. What the juvenile diabetic knows about his disease. *Pediatrics,* 1962, *29,* 135–141.
Faerman, I., Glocer, L., Fox, D., Jadzinsky, M. N., & Rapaport, M. Histological studies of the autonomic nervous fibers of the corpora cavernosa in impotent diabetics. *Excerpta Medica,* 1973. Proceedings of the 8th Congress of the International Diabetes Federation, Series #280. (Abstract)
Forsham, P. H. (Ed.). Current trends in research and clinical management of diabetes. *Annals of the New York Academy of Sciences,* 1959, *82,* 229–235.
Frankel, J. J. Juvenile diabetes—The look from within. In Z. Laron (Ed.), *Diabetes in juveniles: Medical and rehabilitation aspects. Modern problems in paediatrics* (Vol. 12). Basel: S. Karger, 1975.
Ganda, O. P., & Soeldner, S. S. Genetic, acquired and related factors in the etiology of diabetes mellitus. *Archives of Internal Medicine,* 1977, *137,* 461–469.
Garner, A. M., & Thompson, C. W. Factors in the management of juvenile diabetes. *Pediatric Psychology,* 1974, *2,* 6–7.
Garner, A. M., & Thompson, C. W. Juvenile diabetes. In P. R. Magrab (Ed.), *Psychological management of pediatric problems* (Vol. 1). Baltimore: University Park Press, 1978.
Grant, I., Kyle, G. C., Teichman, A., & Mendels, J. Recent life events and diabetes in adults. *Psychosomatic Medicine,* 1974, *36,* 121–128.
Hinkle, L. E. The influence of the patient's behavior and his reaction to his life situation upon the course of diabetes. *Diabetes,* 1956, *5,* 406–407.
Hinkle, L. E., & Wolf, S. The effect of stressful life situations on the concentration of blood glucose in diabetic and nondiabetic humans. *Diabetes,* 1952, *1,* 383–392.
Hinkle, L. E., Jr., Evans, F. M., & Wolf, S. III. Life history of three persons with labile diabetes, and relation of significant experiences in their lives to the onset and course of the disease. IV. Life history of three persons with relatively mild, stable diabetes and relation of significant experiences in their lives to the onset and course of the disease. *Psychosomatic Medicine,* 1951, *13,* 160–202.
Holmes, T. H., & Rahe, R. H. The social readjustment rating scale. *Journal of Psychosomatic Research,* 1967, *11,* 213–217.
Ingelfinger, F. J. Debates on diabetes. *New England Journal of Medicine,* 1977, *296,* 1228–1230.
Joslin, E. P. *The treatment of diabetes mellitus.* Philadelphia: Lea & Febiger, 1937.
Kaufman, R. B., & Hersher, B. Body-image changes in teenage diabetes. *Pediatrics,* 1971, *48,* 123–128.
Kimball, C. P. Emotional and psychosocial aspects of diabetes mellitus. *The Medical Clinics of North America,* 1971, *55,* 1007–1018.
Knowles, H. C., Jr. Diabetes mellitus in childhood and adolescence. In P. Felig & M. K. Bondy (Eds.), Symposium on Diabetes Mellitus. *The Medical Clinics of North America,* 1971, *55,* 975–987.
Kolodny, R. D. Sexual dysfunction in diabetic females. *Diabetes,* 1971, *20,* 557–559.
Kolodny, R. D., Kahn, C. B., Goldstein, H. H., & Barnett, D. M. Sexual dysfunction in diabetic men. *Diabetes,* 1974, *23,* 306–309.
Koski, M. L. The coping processes in childhood diabetes. *Acta Paediatrica Scandinavica,* 1969, *198,* 7–56. (Supplement)
Kubany, A. J., Dankowski, T. S., & Moses, C. The personality and intelligence of diabetics. *Diabetes,* 1956, *5,* 462–467.
Ludvigsson, J. Socio-psychological factors and metabolic control in juvenile diabetes. *Acta Paediatrica Scandinavica,* 1977, *66,* 431–437.

McCraw, R. K., & Tuma, J. M. Rorschach content categories of juvenile diabetics. *Psychological Reports*, 1977, *40*, 818.
Minuchin, S. *Families and family therapy.* Cambridge: Harvard University Press, 1974.
Murawski, B. J., Chazan, B. I., Balodimos, M. E., & Ryan, J. R. Personality patterns in patients with diabetes mellitus of long duration. *Diabetes*, 1970, *19*, 259–263.
National Diabetes Data Group. Classification and diagnosis of diabetes mellitus and other categories of glucose intolerance. *Diabetes*, 1979, *28*, 1039–1057.
Partridge, J. W. Employment of patients with diabetes. *Diabetes Bulletin*, 1967, *43*, 1, 3.
Partridge, J. W., Garner, A. M., Thompson, C. W., & Cherry, T. Attitudes of adolescents toward their diabetes. *American Journal of Diseases of Children*, 1972, *124*, 226–229.
Paulsen, E. P., & Colle, E. Diabetes mellitus. In L. E. Gardner (Ed.), *Endocrine and genetic diseases of childhood.* Philadelphia: Saunders, 1969, 808–823.
Renshaw, D. C. Impotence in diabetics. *Diseases of the Nervous System*, 1975, *36*, 369–371.
Richardson, S. A., Hastorf, A. H., & Dornbusch, S. M. Effects of physical disability on a child's description of himself. *Child Development*, 1964, *35*, 893–907.
Rosen, H., & Lidz, T. Emotional factors in the precipitation of recurrent diabetic acidosis. *Psychosomatic Medicine*, 1949, *11*, 211–215.
Sanders, K., Mills, J., Martin, F. I. R., & Horne, D. J. Emotional attitudes in adult insulin-dependent diabetics. *Journal of Psychosomatic Research*, 1975, *19*, 241–246.
Schless, G. L., & Von Laveran-Stiebar, R. Recurrent episodes of diabetic acidosis precipitated by emotional stress. *Diabetes*, 1964, *13*, 419–420.
Simonds, J. F. Psychiatric status of diabetic youth matched with a control group. *Diabetes*, 1977, *26*, 921–925.
Stein, S. P., & Charles, E. Emotional factors in juvenile diabetes mellitus: A study of early life experience of adolescent diabetics. *American Journal of Psychiatry*, 1971, *128*, 700–704.
Sullivan, B-J. Adjustment in diabetic adolescent girls: I. Development of the diabetic adjustment scale; II. Adjustment, self-esteem, and depression in diabetic adolescent girls. *Psychosomatic Medicine*, 1979, *41*, 119–138.
Swift, C. R., Seidman, F., & Stein, H. Adjustment problems in juvenile diabetes. *Psychosomatic Medicine*, 1967, *29*, 555–571.
Thompson, C. W., Garner, A. M., & Partridge, J. W. Sick? or diabetic? A research report. *Diabetes Bulletin*, 1969, *45*, 2–3.
Travis, L. B. *An instructional aid on juvenile diabetes mellitus.* Galveston: University of Texas Medical Branch, 1975.
VandenBergh, R. L., Sussman, K. E., & Titus, C. C. Effects of hypnotically induced acute emotional stress in carbohydrate and lipid metabolism in patients with diabetes mellitus. *Psychosomatic Medicine*, 1966, *28*, 383–390.
VandenBergh, R. L., Sussman, K. E., & Vaughan, G. D. Effects of combined physical-anticipatory stress on carbohydrate lipid metabolism in patients with diabetes mellitus. *Psychosomatics*, 1967, *8*, 16–19.
Vranic, M., Horvath, S., & Wahren, J. (Eds.). Proceedings of a conference on diabetes and exercise. *Diabetes*, 1979, *28*, 1–113. (Supplement)
Wabrek, A. J. Sexual dysfunction associated with diabetes mellitus. *Journal of Family Practice*, 1979, *8*, 735–740.
Warnberg, L. Psychological aspects of juvenile diabetes. *Pediatric Psychology*, 1974, *2*, 10–11.
Watkins, J. D., Williams, T. F., Martin, D. A., Hogan, M. D., & Anderson, E. A study of diabetic patients at home. *American Journal of Public Health*, 1967, *57*, 452–457.
Weil, W. B., Jr. Social patterns and diabetic glucosuria: A study of group behavior and diabetic management in summer camp. *American Journal of Diseases of Children*, 1967, *113*, 454–460.

Williams, T. F., Martin, D. A., Hogan, M. D., Watkins, J. D., & Ellis, E. V. The clinical picture of diabetic control, studied in four settings. *American Journal of Public Health,* 1967, *57,* 441–451.

Willis, T. *Practice of Physick. Treatise II. Pharmaceutice rationalis. I.* London: T. Ding, C. Harper, & J. Leigh, 1674. (Koski, M. L. The coping processes in childhood diabetes. *Acta Paediatrica Scandinavica,* 1969, *198,* 7–56, Supplement.)

4

Other Genetic Disorders

RUSSELL H. JACKSON

The four disorders to be discussed in this chapter (phenylketonuria, Turner's Syndrome, Klinefelter's Syndrome, and Huntington's Disease) were chosen because of their clinical interest, their frequency of occurrence, and their differing modes of inheritance. These four disorders also are representative of genetic conditions that differ in severity, ease of diagnosis, age of onset of symptoms, and impact on the family. Additionally, current issues in the field of genetic counseling and the psychological problems relating to genetic disease are discussed. Before discussion of the specific disorders, some more general information will be reviewed.

GENETIC DISORDERS

There are some 2,800 (McKusick, 1978) known genetic disorders. An estimated 6% of the United States population, amounting to over 12 million people, suffer from significant genetic disease (Commission for the Control of Huntington's Disease, 1977). Presently, the neurosciences and genetics are at the leading edge of biological science, and major breakthroughs into our understanding of the mechanisms of the human body and reproduction are becoming routine. It is now possible to diagnose approximately 100 serious genetic disorders during pregnancy by means of amniocentesis. Through effective screening programs and

---

The preparation of this chapter was supported in part by the Bureau of Community Health Services, Maternal and Child Health Services Project 920.

informed pediatricians, a high proportion of some disorders are diagnosed in the neonatal period (Down's Syndrome and phenylketonuria). Some genetic disorders which have a variable or mild expression may be diagnosed at some later time when clinical manifestations become of concern to the family, for example, short stature and lack of secondary sex characteristics as in Turner's Syndrome. Other genetic disorders manifest themselves primarily in adulthood (Huntington's Disease), at which point the diagnosis is made on the basis of clinical symptoms and a thorough family history. Sometimes a genetic disorder is discovered by serendipity; for example, Klinefelter's Syndrome can be diagnosed through an inquiry into the cause of sterility.

Mechanisms of Inheritance

Although human chromosomes were described many years ago, it was not until 1956 that the correct number of chromosomes was identified as 46 (23 pairs). Human cells contain 22 pairs of autosomes (chromosomes other than sex chromosomes) and one pair of sex chromosomes. One sex (X) chromosome plus 22 autosomes are inherited from the mother and one sex (X or Y) chromosome plus 22 autosomes are inherited from the father. The reproductive cell, that is, the sperm or ovum, each contains 23 unpaired chromosomes. By genetic notation, a normal female is designated as 46,XX and a normal male is designated as 46,XY.

The individual autosomes are numbered 1 to 22 according to specific criteria, such as size and shape. Technological advances in chromosomal staining and banding techniques (Hecht, Wyandt, & Magenis, 1974; Sanchez & Yunis, 1977) have enabled scientists to begin the process of mapping out sites on chromosomes to localize specific genes. These chromosomes can be carefully studied by examination of a karyotype, made by taking photographs of the chromosomes which are cut out and arranged by pairs on a sheet of paper according to size and banding pattern so that they are easy to study. Scientists are now learning that many individuals with various birth defects have associated chromosomal aberrations. Approximately 50% of spontaneous abortions are chromosomally abnormal (Sankaranarayanan, 1979).

Individual traits are determined by the genes located on the chromosomes (some 60,000–100,000 for each cell). During cell division, genes inherited from the father are matched with genes (alleles) having the same function from the mother. An exception is that the Y chromosome contains those genes that determine male sex characteristics.

Today we are becoming more and more sensitive to the fact that genes may be affected when subjected to viruses, chemicals or radiation

Other Genetic Disorders

from the external environment. These forces may occasionally be responsible for mutating genes and producing offspring by Mendelian recessive and dominant modes of inheritance.

Autosomal and X-Linked Recessive Disorders

An individual who inherits an autosomal recessive disorder must acquire a matched pair of defective genes, one from each parent. An individual having one defective gene and one normal gene would appear normal clinically but would be labeled as a carrier of the disease. These individuals will not manifest the disorder. Each child who is born to parents who are carriers will inherit one of the following genetic makeups as shown in Figure 1.

1. There will be a 25% chance to inherit two recessive genes and thus be affected by the disorder.
2. There will be a 25% chance to inherit two normal genes and not be affected by the disorder.
3. There will be a 50% chance to inherit one defective gene and be a carrier of the disorder, but not manifest it.

More than 1,100 genetic diseases are known to be inherited as autosomal recessives (McKusick, 1978). There appears to be a high degree of biochemical specificity characteristic of recessive disorders. In this chapter, phenylketonuria (PKU) will be discussed as an example of this mode of inheritance. Other examples of diseases transmitted by the

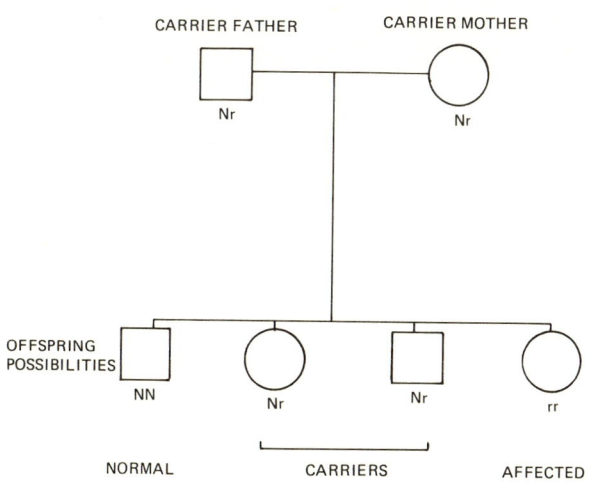

FIGURE 1. How recessive inheritance works. N = normal gene; r = recessive gene.

recessive mode are Tay–Sachs Disease (a fatal neurological disorder), galactosemia (an inability to metabolize milk sugar), and Wilson's Disease (an inability of the body to metabolize copper).

When the affected recessive genes are located on the X chromosome, the greatest impact is on the male. This is commonly called an X-linked recessive inheritance. When the gene comes from the female, there is a 50% chance that it will be expressed in the male because the male has only one X chromosome. There is no matched gene on the Y chromosome to counteract its effect. In most cases of X-linked disorder, it is the mother who passes on the defective gene to her sons. An affected father, on the other hand, will transmit the defective gene to all of his daughters, who will then be clinically normal but will be carriers. It will not be passed to any of his sons. On those rare occasions when the father has the defect and the mother is a carrier, females have a one in two chance of being affected.

There are about 200 disorders which are X-linked. Among the more commonly known ones are color blindness, Duchenne's muscular dystrophy (see Chapter 10), and hemophilia (see Chapter 2).

Autosomal Dominant Disorders

There are nearly 1,500 dominant gene disorders discovered to date (McKusick, 1978). However, scientists do not yet understand the underlying basic defect as they do in many of the recessive disorders. Traits inherited in the autosomal dominant pattern are expressed in the presence of one mutated gene, regardless of the nature of the matched gene. Each pregnancy of an affected individual represents a 50–50 chance of inheriting the abnormal gene and the disorder. However, dominant genes display their effects in varying degrees of severity from person to person in an unpredictable manner (variable expression). In an autosomal disorder, the parent is usually affected but it is possible for an affected child to have normal parents by acquiring the disorder by mutation (Kirkman, 1978).

A few examples of dominant disorders are Huntington's Disease (to be discussed in this chapter), *osteogenesis imperfecta* (characterized by brittle bones), *tuberous sclerosis* (brain tumors causing progressive mental deterioration), *achondroplasia* (dwarfism), and *myotonic dystrophy* (slow progressive atrophy of the muscles).

Chromosomal Abnormalities

Abnormal combinations of chromosomes occur without following the Mendelian genetic processes. Both parents may have normal chromosomes, but something goes awry in the cell division process of meiosis (the maturation of the sex cells by which each daughter nucleus receives half the number of chromosomes characteristic of the somatic cells) or mitosis (wherein the two daughter nuclei receive identical complements of the somatic chromosomes). An abnormal number of chromosomes (aneuploidy) is the result of two chromosomes' failing to separate and pass to the different daughter cells but remaining together in one of the daughter cells (nondisjunction). As a consequence, this cell has an extra chromosome, while its sister cell has a corresponding deficit. The cell with the extra chromosome is referred to as trisomic; Down's Syndrome (Trisomy 21) is the most familiar example. Translocation is another genetic accident by which an individual can have a normal configuration of 46 chromosomes, but a third number 21 chromosome is actually attached to the arm of another chromosome causing Down's Syndrome and other translocations. Multiple combinations of the X and Y chromosomes sometimes occur creating specific mechanisms of the most common sex chromosome abnormalities, for example, Turner's Syndrome and Klinefelter's Syndrome.

Genetic Counseling

When all genetic disorders are taken into account, as much as 10% of the population may at some point seek out or be referred to a genetic counselor (Kessler, 1979).

To understand how potent the threat of occurrence or diagnosis of a genetic disease can be, one must understand the basic psychological process involved. Health is usually experienced as coming from within, while illness is experienced as external to the individual.

> Genetic disorders, however, are experienced as consequences of internal "causes" and thus cannot be as readily projected outward. . . . Thus, genetic disorders are often experienced as intractable, unalterable and permanent; the diagnosis of a genetic disorder may seem like a sentence of doom. (Kessler, 1979, p. 24)

Traditionally, the task of the genetic counselor has been to provide information to the patient about the implications of the genetic factors involved. Recently, however, the emphasis has shifted, and the genetic counselor is now also likely to attend to the patient's feelings, to develop open communication about the problem with the patient, and to help him develop a plan of action.

A current definition of genetic counseling endorsed by the Ad Hoc Committee on Genetic Counseling of the American Society of Human Genetics (1975, p. 41) states:

Genetic counseling is a communication process which deals with the human problems associated with the occurrence, or the risk of occurrence, of a genetic disorder in a family. This process involves an attempt by one or more appropriately trained persons to help the individual or family: (1) comprehend the medical facts, including the diagnosis, the probable course of the disorder, and the available management; (2) appreciate the way heredity contributes to the disorder; (3) understand the options for dealing with the risk of occurrence; (4) choose the course of action that seems appropriate to them; (5) make the best of all possible adjustments to the disorder and/or the risk of occurrence of the disorder.

Achieving these five points may be accomplished through a single interview with the family. More likely, it will require additional sessions over time, in which the issues are worked through in a therapeutic sense. Coordination between the physician and other members of the health care team is essential to help the individual to make the optimal adjustment.

PHENYLKETONURIA[1]

The Physical Disability

Definition and Incidence. Phenylketonuria (PKU) is a group of inherited disorders of phenylalanine metabolism which occur in approximately 1 in 10,000 to 15,000 births (Kleinman, 1964). First described in 1934 (Folling, 1934), the classical form of PKU involves the absence or reduced activity of the liver enzyme phenylalanine hydroxylase which is needed to convert the essential amino acid phenylalanine (PA) to tyrosine. Comprising 90% of the cases (Hsia, 1967), the classical form of PKU results in toxic levels of phenylalanine (PA) and its by-products in the blood, brain, body tissues, and urine.

It is important to recognize the dramatic effects of PKU before the development of dietary treatment (Armstrong & Taylor, 1955; Bickel, Gerrard, & Hickmans, 1953). Untreated PKU results in mental retardation, with 96% of those untreated having IQs less than 60 and the majority functioning in the severely to profoundly retarded range (Baumeister, 1967; Knox, 1960). Studies of institutions for the mentally retarded indicated that 1 out of every 100 patients had PKU (Langdell, 1965). Although the precise mechanisms are still unknown (Menkes, 1967), toxic levels of PA are associated with severe seizures and other

---

[1] This section was prepared by Jeffrey B. Sosne, Psychologist, Good Samaritan Hospital, Portland, Oregon.

neurological abnormalities (Allen & Gibson, 1961; Kang, Kennedy, Gates, Burwash, & McKinnon, 1965). Perceptual motor difficulties (Hackney, Hanley, Davidson, & Lindsao, 1968), autistic features (Lowe, Tanaka, Seashore, Young, & Cohen, 1980) and psychiatric disturbances (Anderson, Siegel, & Bruhl, 1976) were also found.

Genetic Factors. PKU is an autosomal recessive disorder (see Figure 1), with approximately 1 out of 50 persons a carrier (Schild, 1979). Although carriers appear normal, laboratory identification procedures exist for use in diagnosis and genetic counseling (Cunningham & Day, 1969). Other less common or variant forms of PKU appear also to follow an autosomal recessive pattern of inheritance, although it is unclear whether these atypical forms represent an additional modifying allele to the recessive gene or an independent locus which has a modifying effect (Berman & Ford, 1970; Hsia, 1967).

Diagnosis. One of the most important advances in the early diagnosis of PKU has been the development of a safe, simple, and cost-effective screening test conducted within the first days of life (Schild, 1979). Although there exist some problems of misdiagnosis (Binder, Johnson, Saboe, & Krug-Wispe, 1979; Holtzman, Mellits, & Kallman, 1974), an inhibition assay procedure (Guthrie, 1961) has resulted in a dramatic reduction in undetected cases. PKU metabolic screening, which requires that a few drops of blood be taken from the infant 24 to 48 hours after the first protein feed, is mandatory in 44 states and most developed countries (Schild, 1979). This simple method of screening has allowed treatment to begin in early infancy before brain damage can occur.

Classification of PKU Severity and Variant Forms. It is important to realize that the type and severity of the enzyme deficiency varies with individuals (Anderson, Siegel, & Bruhl, 1976; Sutherland, Umbarger, & Berry, 1966). Although direct measurement of the enzyme activity is technically feasible through a liver biopsy, the type and severity of the disorder is usually and more easily described by the amount of PA found in the blood and the level of by-products identified in the urine. The results of blood and urine analysis are used to classify the severity and type of PKU. Normal individuals have PA levels of from 1–3 mg/100 ml of blood (Koch, Shaw, Acosta, Fischler, Schaffly, Wenz, & Wohlers, 1970). Individuals with classical, *untreated* PKU have PA levels of 20 mg/100 ml or greater, with an increase of PA by-products and reduced levels of tyrosine in the urine. Other individuals with milder (hyperphenylalaninemia) or variant forms of PKU have lower serum blood levels, 16 mg/100 ml or below (Hsia, Knox, Quinn, & Paine, 1958; Koch *et al.*, 1970).

Recognizing individual differences in the severity and type of PKU, researchers have presented classification systems in describing the degree and nature of enzyme deficiency (Berman & Ford, 1970; Hsia, 1967; Kennedy, Wertleki, Gales, Sperry, & Cass, 1967). The problem of classification, however, is quite difficult, because the level of PA and associated metabolites may vary according to the protein ingested and physical health at the time of testing. In addition, there is no consistent relationship between the level of PA intake, measures of PA in the body, and clinical manifestations of the disease. There are, for example, cases reported of individuals with abnormal levels of PA but average intelligence (Allen & Gibson, 1961; Knox, 1960), with the suggestion that some persons may be able to use PA more efficiently than others (Acosta, Wenz, & Williamson, 1977). Although it is true that a variant form of PKU has been identified which does not respond to traditional dietary treatment (Bartholome, Byrd, Kaufman, & Milstein, 1977; Smith, Clayton, & Wolff, 1975), classification systems have used a varied and confusing nomenclature and tend to offer little guidance to clinicians working with the majority of PKU children and their families.

Treatment. Once individuals are identified as having PKU, the primary treatment is dietary. The basic approach has remained essentially unchanged since its development in the early 1950s (Armstrong & Tyler, 1955; Bickel, Gerrard, & Hickmans, 1953). The objective is to lower the levels of PA in the blood and body tissues by reducing the amount of PA ingested. This is done through a low PA/protein diet (food protein contains approximately 2.5–5% PA) that supplies the person with sufficient levels of tyrosine, usable protein, and other nutrients necessary for adequate physical growth. During infancy, all nutrient needs are met by a synthetic, low PA formula. Lofenelac and Phenylfree (Mead–Johnson Laboratories) are the most commonly used and cost approximately $60 per month during the early stages of infancy. When the child begins eating solids, food containing high amounts of protein, and therefore PA (meats, poultry, eggs, milk, and cheese), are restricted or eliminated from the child's diet. Low PA foods (e.g., fruits, vegetables, and grains) become the mainstay of the child's diet and are supplemented by the formula to ensure adequate nutrition.

Parents, in consultation with an interdisciplinary team (physician, nutritionist, nurse, psychologist, occupational therapist), play the primary role in managing the PKU child's diet. This is particularly true in the early years when parents, working with the team, must be able to monitor the amount of PA ingested and ensure that there are adequate calories, protein, and other nutrients in the child's diet. It is vital that parents have a working knowledge of the disease, diet management, and monitoring procedures. The parents must collect food diaries, blood samples (heel or finger prick), and urine specimens (using filter paper) needed to measure the quality of diet control. Their role is particularly extensive in the early years, when regular monitoring is necessary (samples are taken daily until the PA blood levels are stabilized, weekly for the next month and then once or twice a month from that point on).

Although there is overall agreement as to the importance of beginning treatment within the first weeks of life, there is far less agreement regarding the most desirable level of dietary control. While it is generally accepted that PA levels of greater than 12 mg/100 ml are undesirable (Fuller & Shuman, 1971), clinicians differ as to the degree of optimal dietary control, with recommendations ranging from 4 to 10 mg/100 ml (Acosta & Elsas, 1975; Sutherland, Umbarger, & Berry, 1966). There is some indication that excessively restricted PA intake in early infancy may be contraindicated, with serious problems of PA deficiency and inadequate nutrition reported (Fisch, Solberg, & Borud, 1971; Rouse, 1966).

The question of when to terminate or relax the diet is quite controversial and has been the focus of an ongoing collaborative PKU project which began in 1967 (e.g., Williamson, Koch, & Berlow, 1979). It was initially believed that PKU was a childhood problem and that the diet was only needed until age 3–5, until the brain was developed (Vandeman, 1963). Although this may be true for some persons (Holtzman, Welcher, & Mellits, 1975; Kang, Sollee, & Gerald, 1970; Solomons, Keleske, & Opitz, 1966), data suggest that increased levels of PA following diet termination can result in deterioration in intellectual functioning and behavior (Koch, Fishler, Schild, & Ragsdale, 1964; Smith, Lobascher, Stevenson, Wolff, Schmidt, Gruber-Kaiser, & Bickel, 1978). Although changes in activity level, attention span, and school performance may be apparent, deterioration in intellectual functioning may be more gradual and not noticeable until months and even years after termination (Williamson, Koch, & Berlow, 1979). This recent evidence suggests that PKU may not be a childhood disease but one which requires monitoring, evaluation, and management throughout adolescence and perhaps for life (Berry, O'Grady, Perlmutter, & Bofinger, 1979; Hackney *et al.*, 1968). This is particularly true of children with a history of neurological problems (Wood, 1976).

It may, indeed, be the case that studies which have suggested that early termination is permissible may not have been extensive enough. Without sufficiently long follow-up to detect gradual changes in a person's functioning level, a gradual decline over the course of months and even years may not be detected. The question appears not to be one of diet termination *per se,* but rather what level of dietary control is needed during what stage of life. In each instance, an individual decision must be made weighing the desire for a more normalized diet and life style against the risks associated with increased PA levels associated with relaxation of diet control.

A relatively new area of research in PKU management may be particularly relevant to the question of dietary termination or relaxation. With the development and refinement of dietary procedures, PKU persons have been able to lead normal lives, and some, naturally, wish to raise children. Recent findings suggest, however, that abnormal levels of PA in pregnant women with PKU are likely to result in retarded fetal and infant development (Komrower, Saroharwalla, Coutts, & Ingham, 1979; Mabry, Denniston, & Caldwell, 1966). Although researchers have investigated the usefulness of renewed dietary management, in avoiding the adverse effects of maternal PKU on the fetus, these results have not been encouraging, and there is some indication that careful diet control may be required before the child is conceived (Buist, Lis, Tuerck, & Murphy, 1979; Komrower *et al.,* 1979). For this reason, it may be necessary for female patients to continue with the diet through childbearing years, with some women choosing to adopt or not to have children rather than risk having a retarded child. Regardless of the decision made, the identification of maternal PKU is yet another indication that PKU is a metabolic disease with effects beyond childhood.

Common Psychological Characteristics and Problems

Although careful dietary intervention can avoid retardation and other serious difficulties associated with untreated classical PKU, there is some question whether full intellectual potential can be achieved (Berman & Ford, 1970; Koch *et al.,* 1970; Smith & Wolff, 1974). Findings indicate that treated children are of essentially average ability but may show less intellectual potential than unaffected siblings and parents (Berman, Waisman, & Graham, 1966; Dobson, Kushida, Williamson, & Friedman, 1976). Learning difficulties (Leonard, Chase, & Childs, 1972), behavior problems (Stevenson, Hawcroft, Lubascher, Smith, Wolff, & Graham, 1979), perceptual–motor difficulties (Koff, Boyle, & Pueschel, 1977), and lowered self-esteem (Moen, Wilcox, & Burns, 1977) have been reported as common difficulties which may appear when there has been inadequate control or when the diet is relaxed. The most consistent finding is the wide *variability* across individuals (Baumeister, 1967; Beckner, Centerwall, & Holt, 1976; Berman, Waisman, & Graham, 1966; Frankenburg, Goldstein, & Olson, 1973). The abilities and difficulties of PKU children vary so greatly that it is difficult to predict what problems, if any, will arise for a given child.

Although the traditional focus is on the PKU child, it is important to recognize the great responsibility facing the parents of PKU children. In addition to learning the complexities of the disease, diet, and monitoring procedures, parents must learn how to prepare meals and integrate the child's diet into the family's eating patterns and schedule. Typical childhood problems of refusing foods or eating forbidden goodies have critical significance for the PKU child who refuses to drink the formula or who "sneaks" foods high in PA. Developmental transitions, from formula to baby foods to table foods, require modifications in the diet. Common childhood illnesses affect the child's willingness or ability to eat and therefore have particular significance. Everyday events, going to school, or eating at restaurants, can require special planning. It has been our experience that, although families vary in their ability to implement dietary recommendations and resolve everyday problems, all families describe difficulties at one or more stages in their child's development.

It is perhaps not surprising to find that parents report strong feelings of guilt, anger, frustration, and anxiety (Johnson, 1979; Schild, 1979). They are first told that their seemingly healthy child has a disease which will lead to retardation if not treated properly. Parents may feel guilty at having passed on a disease that will require a specialized diet for their youngster. They are then faced with the difficult task of understanding the disease, the diet, and monitoring procedures. The responsibility, and accompanying stress, can be considerable for the parent's ability to control the child's diet is directly related to their youngster's development. With the threat of retardation in the back of their minds, parents report negative feelings with every small failure in fulfilling the demands made on them. Everyday problems of behavior management can acquire special significance, and it is not uncommon to find problems in parent–child interaction and child-rearing (Johnson, 1979; Schild, 1979). The entire family is affected; siblings who receive less attention from their parents must often deal with feelings of jealousy and anger.

Evaluating Persons with Phenylketonuria

It is important to realize that families differ in their understanding and attitudes toward PKU and its treatment as well as in their ability to deal with the responsibilities and pressures associated with diet management. It is extremely important to evaluate each family on an individual basis and assess those factors which might affect implementation of clinic recommendations. Interviews and pencil-and-paper measures (Acosta, Fiedler, & Koch, 1968; Sibinga & Freidman, 1971) indicate that parents lack or distort information regarding the genetic, metabolic, and treatment aspects of PKU (Fisch, Conley, Eysenbach, & Chang, 1977; Keleske, Solomons, & Opitz, 1967; Wood, Friedman, & Steisel, 1967). This can have an important effect on their ability to carry out diet recommendations. The child's own understanding and attitudes toward his or her disease, particularly with school-age children, also play a role. Surveys also reveal important family differences in food preparation, planning, and mealtime interaction (Acosta *et al.*, 1968). Observations of parents with their children during mealtime and play situations (Steisel, Friedman, & Wood, 1967) provide information regarding those parenting skills needed for effective diet management.

It is important to obtain from parents their own impressions of the success of diet management. Parents have their own views regarding their child's progress and may differ in their conceptions of an acceptable level of dietary control. One family may consider their child to be doing quite well, while another family with the identical situation may express concern about their youngster's behavior and language skills. When one parent may consider blood levels of 10–12 mg/100 ml acceptable, another parent may be quite concerned and consider that level of dietary control cause for alarm. Individual differences such as these have an important impact on a child's progress and on diet implementation and should be carefully considered.

Evaluation plays a central role in determining the most desirable level of dietary control and in assessing the effects of changes in PA blood level on the child's functioning. Although general guidelines of dietary control are useful, regular interdisciplinary evaluation of the child's physical, nutritional, cognitive, academic, behavioral, and emotional functioning is needed because of the potentially broad implications of poor dietary management. Since the effects of PA elevation vary, individualized evaluation is needed in making specific recommendations to each family. While full evaluation is not always needed, regular monitoring of the child's progress is suggested. Changes in dietary control or parental concerns may necessitate additional evaluation. At the University of Oregon Health Sciences Center, PKU Clinic families are evaluated by interdisciplinary teams every six months for the first two years and then once yearly for the next four or five years. Frequent contact with families between evaluations is also common. While regular follow-up is most important in the early years, periodic evaluation must continue after the diet has been terminated or relaxed, since changes in functioning level have been identified two or more years after diet discontinuation or relaxation.

Clinicians vary in their use of assessment instruments. A typical protocol might include physical/neurological and nutritional evaluation, developmental exam (during the first two years), intellectual assessment (every other year after age two), a measure of adaptive skills and behavioral functioning, observation of parent–child interaction, and evaluation of motor/perceptual–motor abilities. Evaluation of academic achievement, self-esteem, and other related aspects are often included as the child reaches school age. Specific concerns may suggest additional testing procedures.

The interpretation of test results can be difficult and should be made in conjunction with a clinic team. Where the effects of poor diet management are clear, or when diet control is good and no problems are evident, the clinician's report to the team may be straightforward. Often the results of evaluation are less clear, and the clinician is asked to provide information needed to evaluate the effects of intermediate levels of dietary control. The evaluator, for example, may be asked whether this level of functioning reflects true potential, environment/family factors, other medical/neurological problems, or an inadequate level of diet control. While there is a temptation to use the ability of parents or unaffected siblings as a guide to the child's potential, one must be wary because there is often a great deal of intrafamilial variation in intelligence due to factors not associated with the disease. In such instances, the appraisals of the entire team should be considered before recommendations regarding possible changes in diet are made to the family.

The clinician is also often asked to provide information regarding the possible effects of elevations in PA blood level due to changes in dietary control. Although temporary elevations may or may not affect the child's behavior, it is often difficult to determine whether other areas of functioning have been affected. With the varied effects of PA elevation, the clinician must consider a broad range of functioning and all problems which may have occurred in the school, as well as home, environment. As the effects of poor diet control may be cumulative, it is difficult to determine whether the apparent absence of problems is an indication of adequate diet management or whether the effects of the PA elevation are accumulating and will be seen in the future. Changes may be gradual and only identified with regular and careful evaluation. Again, cautious interpretation of results, by the entire clinic team, is called for in making recommendations and providing the family with guidance.

Intervention Methods

Although diet intervention is the primary form of treatment, a psychologist can play an important role in helping families resolve problems and avoid potential problems. Providing families with the opportunity to air their feelings and discuss their problems can alleviate stresses, improve family and marital relationships, and result in improved diet control. Support from other parents with PKU children can be quite helpful, although individualized family counseling may be needed in some instances (Schild, 1979). Reeducation, practical suggestions regarding diet implementation, and assistance with behavior management problems can be useful, and it is often beneficial for professionals to work together (e.g., nutritionist and psychologist) in helping a family. School consultation may also be helpful. Intervention is most effective when it is interdisciplinary, when the team works together with the family in resolving difficulties as they arise in home and school.

TURNER'S SYNDROME

The Physical Disability

Definition and Incidence. Turner (1938) first described the syndrome which later came to bear his name, as one of "infantilism, congenital webbed neck, and cubitus valgus" (that is, where the arm turns out more than usual at the elbow). Persons affected are clinically female. Its incidence is about one in 2,500 live female births.

Today the most common medical term for Turner's Syndrome is chromosomal ovarian dysgenesis (Plumridge, 1976), meaning a defect in the ovaries or a lack of ovaries due to a missing or malformed X chromosome. As a consequence, there is no menstruation and a failure to develop secondary female sexual characteristics, with infertility the general rule.

Genetic Factors. The genetic defect in 80% of the cases with Turner's Syndrome is one in which the individual is missing one of the sex chromosomes, as discovered by Ford (1959). In genetic terminology, this is written as 45,X0, with the 0 designating the missing chromosome. The remaining percentage of cases have two populations of cells developing simultaneously (mosaicism), one having the normal complement of 46 chromosomes and the other an abnormal count; for example, 45,X0/46,XX or 45,X0/47,XXX. There may also be partial deletions of the X chromosome, where one X divides horizontally rather than vertically, and part of the chromosome duplicates itself, while the other part disappears (isochromosome). The X and Y chromosomes have few, if any, homologous loci and thus form a very unstable synapsis which may account for the many types of chromosomal variations. In general, the more X chromosomes (past three) the more severe the retardation in either sex.

Clinical Characteristics. An individual may be diagnosed as having Turner's Syndrome at any time from birth to adulthood. The diagnosis is suggested by the clinical features (Lemli & Smith, 1963; Beals, 1973) described in Table I. There is considerable variation from individual to individual in the extent to which each of the clinical findings is present; not all anomalies are present in each female. The majority of the defects are minor in character and of little consequence to the patient. Life expectancy is not reduced and there is usually normal or near normal intelligence. It is generally assumed that the earlier the diagnosis is made, the easier it is for the family and client to grow up accepting any modifications that may be necessary in their lives.

According to LaFranchi (1980), approximately 25% are diagnosed in the newborn period, 50% in the 3–10 year period, with the peak coming at ages 5 and 6 with the beginning of school and various screening programs; the remaining 25% occurring in early adolescence between 12 and 16.

At birth, length may be a significant indicator. Although the average length of an infant is 20 in., in Turner's Syndrome the birth length is usually under 18½ in. (Lemli & Smith, 1963). There may be extra folds

TABLE I
Clinical Features That May Be Associated with Turner's Syndrome

Shortness of stature	Extra folds of skin at the back of the neck (webbed neck)
Lack of secondary sexual characteristics	Short neck
A broad, shield-like chest with widely spaced nipples	Small brown moles (pigmented nevi)
Inverted nipples	A permanent lateral or medial deviation of one or more fingers (clinodactyly)
Puffiness of the fingers and soft finger nails which may turn up at the end	Short fifth finger
Low hairline on the back of the neck	Drooping eyelids (ptosis)
A narrow high-arched palate	Inner epicanthal folds
A small jaw line (micrognathia) resulting in unusual facies	Heart disease (20–50% of the cases)
The arm turning out at the elbow more than 15° deviation (cubitus valgus)	Renal disease (about 50% of the cases)
Prominent ears	Orthopedic problems

of skin at the back of the neck (webbing), and the top of the hands and feet may be puffy (lymphedema).

As the child gets older, the diagnosis may derive from short stature. In adults, the dividing point between abnormal smallness and normality is generally 4 ft., 11 in. The average height for a female with Turner's Syndrome is 4 ft., 7 in. (Plumridge, 1976). If not previously diagnosed, the syndrome becomes clearly evident when the young woman enters adolescence without menstruation, without the development of secondary sexual characteristics, and with no further growth.

Almost all girls with Turner's Syndrome are overweight for their height. Excess weight may be a lifelong problem and should be attended to early with careful dieting.

Medical Management. The primary physician responsible for the female with Turner's Syndrome is usually an endocrinologist, often part of an interdisciplinary team in a genetics or endocrinology clinic. The description below relies heavily on the procedure used in the Genetics Clinic of the University of Oregon Health Sciences Center (LaFranchi, 1980). The diagnostic process usually takes three visits in order to get the necessary blood samples, complete the laboratory tests, and then provide a report for the family. The time of diagnosis will in large part determine how involved the follow-up will be. If the diagnosis is during infancy, follow-up may require having the family return periodically. If the diagnosis is later in adolescence, the client herself needs to be carefully involved in the follow-up process, particularly if the hormone treatment described below is started immediately. In interdisciplinary clinics there are social workers and psychologists available to help the family through the shock, denial, and adaptation process described in Chapter 1, to provide information, to help the family make decisions, and to consult with the schools should difficulties arise.

Growth Hormones. Somewhere between 10 and 13 years of age, the female with Turner's Syndrome is started on hormone therapy to increase the growth rate. The male sex hormones (androgens) are used, because it is felt there is potential for promoting greater growth. The pros and cons of the medication are discussed with the family, since the evidence is not conclusive regarding how much the height may ultimately be increased. When hormone therapy has begun, there are checkups at three-month intervals to evaluate the medication and to look for side effects, the most important of which is too rapid an increase in bone age. X-rays of the hand and wrist are taken periodically to monitor rate of bone maturation. Other less common side effects include enlargement of the clitoris, deepening of the voice, and an increase in body hair growth. Occurrence of any of these is reason for modifying the hormone therapy. Growth hormones are given until the bone age reaches about 13 years, indicating maximum stature has probably been reached.

Sexual Development. Since she may not have any functioning ovaries, a woman with Turner's Syndrome is unable to create her own supply of sex hormones, estrogen and progesterone. Therefore, secondary sex characteristics and menstrual periods do not spontaneously develop. When the bone age reaches approximately 13 years, the physician may begin administering low doses of estrogen. The mean age of onset of the female menstrual cycle is 12.8 years. The young woman with Turner's Syndrome's menstrual cycle begins 6–12 months after starting estrogen therapy. Many girls are willing to delay their periods on the chance of obtaining some increased height.

When the decision is made to begin the more natural menstrual cycle, progesterone is used in combination with the estrogen to create a process similar to that occurring with the use of the standard birth control pills in normal women. However, since the dosage is equal only to what the body should produce, this reduces the possibility of the side effects associated with birth control pills, which supply excess amounts of estrogen to the fertile woman.

A woman with Turner's Syndrome must stay on the medication of estrogen and progesterone until menopausal time, when a low amount of estrogen may or may not be given on a daily basis. Some women, particularly those in their early 20s, would rather not have a period because they are sterile and ask if they must continue the medication. Doctors generally advise the patient to continue the medication, since there is some evidence that without the sex hormones early aging or other problems such as osteoporosis and arteriosclerosis are more likely to develop.

There are some cases reported in which women with Turner's Syndrome may have spontaneous menses and be fertile (cf. King, Magenis, & Bennett, 1978). Reyes, Koh, and Faiman (1976) warn however, that young women with gonadal dysgenesis who exhibit spontaneous menses may have reduced fertility and an increased chance of abortion or abnormal offspring.

Common Psychological Characteristics and Problems

Individuals with Turner's Syndrome are usually seen as being free of major psychopathology. They are described as being stable, free of behavior disorders, and easy to get along with, usually having good relations with siblings, schoolmates, and teachers (Nielsen, 1970). Gender identity and role are strongly feminine, as described by Money and

Mittenthal (1970), often more so than the patients' sisters. They also enjoy working with small children. Low sexual libido is common, and women who have sexual relations may experience difficult or painful coitus (Nielsen, 1970).

Personality Development. The cosmetic disfigurements of Turner's Syndrome have been found to be of less concern than the lack of growth and breast development. The short stature and immature appearance, particularly between 14 and 18 years of age, almost universally lead to girls' being seen and treated as immature for their age. With hormone treatment this is reduced. However, teasing by peers may create difficulties. Although the girl may have grown up with and adapted to disfigurement and small stature, lack of pubertal development may represent a dramatic failure which makes her feel different at a time when similarity to peers is a high priority. Beyond the age of 19, individuals with Turner's Syndrome may be able to achieve full acceptance on a basis appropriate to age.

How well the female child is adjusted socially may be related to the child's acceptance in the family structure. The more appropriately family and parents treat the young woman at any given age, the more likely she will be to make a satisfactory adjustment outside the family sphere. On the other hand, Money and Mittenthal (1970) found that parental pathology, or the parents' inability to cope with the implications of the diagnosis, constituted a greater psychological hazard to the girl than did physical deficits.

Girls with the shortest height were found to be more bland and overcompliant and to show a general lack of concern which was interpreted as a denial of problems by Sabbath, Morris, Menzer-Beneron, and Sturgis (1961). Overall, girls with Turner's Syndrome may show a personality that is immature and passive, to the degree that Watson and Money (1975) coined the term *inertia of emotional arousal* to describe these women's complacency and slowness in asserting initiative. Watson and Money also suggest that the same behavior may serve as a strength, for evidence suggests that women with Turner's Syndrome have an unusual capacity to deal with stress and adversity.

Intelligence and Schooling. Although we are aware that individuals with Turner's Syndrome are usually normal or near normal in intelligence, one young woman known to the author reported finding Down's Syndrome and Turner's Syndrome listed together in her health textbook as examples of genetic disorders resulting in retardation. Research using the Wechsler Intelligence Scale for Children—Revised (WISC–R) and Wechsler Adult Intelligence Scale (WAIS) indicate that verbal IQs approximate average, whereas performance IQs may be lower by 10 to 20 points (Money, Klein, & Beck, 1979). Women with Turner's Syndrome do best on the Information, Similarities, Vocabulary, and Comprehension subscales (Garron, 1977) and may have difficulty with Arithmetic, Digit Span, and Block Design (Shafer, 1962). More specific testing, matching a Turner's Syndrome group with normal controls on the verbal subscales described above, found deficits in recall of digits backward, general visual memory, word fluency, and right/left discrimination (Waber, 1979). Some academic tasks, such as map-reading, figure-drawing, geometry, and arithmetic may be difficult (Money, Klein, & Beck, 1979). In the Oregon sample, it has been estimated that one third of the Turner's Syndrome patients were having some difficulty in arithmetic (LaFranchi, 1980). However, many of the young women reported receiving no special help in school. This may be in part because a number of them had not informed the school of their illness. The reason was described by one young woman: "Everyone used to know I had Turner's Syndrome, but then we moved. I haven't told anyone at the new school, and I like it that way."

The motor clumsiness and problems with directionality may present a specific challenge in driving a car. Most of the girls with Turner's Syndrome are able to obtain a driver's license, but much frustration and many attempts at taking the driving test may be required. The problem is compounded if the family views the girl as overly immature and postpones the opportunity for her to drive. The importance of driving as a developmental milestone is described in Chapter 1.

In summary, one must remember that the intellectual, academic, and motor problems related to Turner's Syndrome are generally mild and that they may not always occur, any more than all the physical stigmata described in Table I will occur in every case.

Evaluating Persons with Turner's Syndrome

Typically, establishing a relationship and undertaking psychological testing does not pose any special problem for an individual with Turner's Syndrome. It is helpful for the interviewer to have some background knowledge and experience with the syndrome. There is often a close mother–daughter relationship, and at times the mother and daughter may prefer to be interviewed together. Observation of the interaction between them during the interview may contribute information about how age-appropriate the mother's expectations are for the child. The whole family should be seen, if possible, so that everyone's expectations for the patient may be explored.

Preparations for the interview should include speaking with the endocrinologist (with the family's permission), as he/she may have been working with the family over an extended period of time and can help put some problems, such as the adjustment to the diagnosis, into perspective.

If the child is of school age, contact with the school would be extremely helpful to obtain information regarding specific academic performance and special help that is being given. Behavior in physical education might be discussed because of the potential motor clumsiness and small stature. One patient felt that she had been dropped from the volleyball team because she was so short and not because of her ability.

If the patient is an adolescent, time should be taken to determine to what point the medical treatment program has progressed and the attitude of the patient toward the development of puberty and the taking of the medication. In an adult, the issues of marriage, sterility, and career planning may be important.

Questions the author always asks are, "Whom have you told about the diagnosis?" and "What do you tell others about your problem when they ask?" The literature suggests that the information given by the client may vary, depending upon who is asking the question. For example, a friend may be told, "I have a growth problem for which I am taking medication"; the school nurse may be told the diagnosis; and close family or a fiancé may be told specifically some of the implications, such as sterility. How such situations are handled by the client helps to reveal the overall adjustment pattern.

If the patient is of preschool age, there should be a developmental baseline evaluation using standard developmental assessment instruments. Strengths as well as potential weaknesses should be explored.

It is imperative that a very careful intellectual and academic evaluation be undertaken with the school-age child. Careful attention should be given to scatter among intelligence test subscale scores and to the individual's school performance.

Attention should be paid to adaptive behavior both within the family and in the larger environment. For example, there are various problems stemming from being short: reaching high places, finding clothes that are stylish and will still fit, and adapting to driving.

An older client may need some help planning career choices. If the client is immature and tends toward a denial of problems, an ongoing therapeutic relationship may be required for adequate adjustment. Although major psychopathology is rare, it may be present, and standard psychological assessment instruments should be used in making the diagnosis.

Intervention Methods

Since the diagnosis of Turner's Syndrome may be made prior to birth (amniocentesis) and up through late adolescence, the choice of intervention is in large measure determined by the time and circumstances of the diagnosis. The first priority for treating new parents is to provide them with information which will help them understand and accept the diagnosis. Presenting information to the family should be done in terms of probability statements and in a positive context rather than a negative one. *Good Things Come in Small Packages* is a booklet written specifically for families where Turner's Syndrome is present. The patient is described as: "A girl who is short and who will need medication to help her mature sexually. There is a strong possibility that she may not be able to become pregnant and if she marries she and her husband may consider adoption if they wish to become parents" (Plumridge, 1976, p. 1).

In the author's experience, an adult female with Turner's Syndrome may be asked to visit with the parents of a newly diagnosed child. This has been extremely helpful to the family. Often parent groups can be very supportive and informative, particularly when there are children of varying ages within the families. Positive results come from a group approach for adolescent girls with Turner's Syndrome. They tend to be supportive of one another, and find strength in sharing their feelings. However, some girls, usually those with mild clinical symptoms, may resist coming because it becomes a reminder there is a problem which they try and avoid thinking about. Furthermore, wide geographic distribution of families may make it difficult for such a group to meet regularly.

When the diagnosis is made early, it is important that an appropriate relationship be established with the family, since there will be regular visits to the clinic, particularly during the years when the youth is on medication. Then, when sensitive issues such as sterility come up, they can be dealt with in an open and straightforward manner. Within the positive context of an understanding interdisciplinary staff, the parents can be given counsel about treating their daughter in the most age-appropriate manner possible. If the positive parent-child interaction is maintained, there can be optimal adaptive behavior on the part of the child.

As part of the routine follow-up, school progress should be monitored. If achievement problems surface, a complete evaluation and consultation with the school personnel is in order to help them understand the general immaturity and nonverbal deficits and their implications for social adaptation and academic achievement.

One goal is to help the individual with Turner's Syndrome know how to inform others of the kinds of problems that are being experienced. If this is done appropriately, the circle of support can widen and bring additional growth.

Because teasing from peers may be part of a response to short stature and the lack of secondary sex characteristics, counseling in this area may be required. Both accepting the teasing as well as learning more direct ways of responding to it can help, for example, ignoring remarks, responding with humor, or, perhaps, directly telling the other person how a remark has hurt (Plumridge, 1976). There may be other times when the individual with Turner's Syndrome may want to be treated as an adult while still engaging in practices which lead to ambivalence, such as using small size to get into the movies at the cheaper price.

As our knowledge in the area of genetics continues to mushroom, prevention may be the ultimate intervention.

KLINEFELTER'S SYNDROME

The Physical Disability

Definition and Incidence. Klinefelter's Syndrome is a clinical condition affecting only males. It occurs approximately 1–2 times in 1,000 live male births (Court-Brown & Smith, 1969; Money, Klein, & Beck, 1979).

Klinefelter's is marked by only two features which may have serious consequences for the individual: extremely small testes in which spermatogenesis is absent or slight (seminiferous tubule dysgenesis) and mild mental retardation. There is usually increased height. Court-Brown and Smith (1969), in a study of 13,000 males who were retarded, found an incidence of 9.4 per 1,000.

Genetic Factors. In contrast to Turner's Syndrome, which affects only females and is characterized by a missing X chromosome, Klinefelter's Syndrome involves only males who have one or more extra X chromosomes (47,XXY). The parents do not have the condition. The 47,XXY configuration derives from errors occurring when the chromosomes separate in meiosis and mitosis. Ferguson-Smith (1966) suggests that about two thirds of Klinefelter's patients have the classic karyotype 47,XXY, while others may have two populations of cells, such as

46,XY/47,XXY. Some Klinefelter's cases with the two populations of cells can show normal fertility in combination with many of the clinical features of the XXY Syndrome. There is evidence that physical and mental disability increase with the number of additional X chromosomes.

Clinical Characteristics. Diagnosis can occur at various times, but unless a karyotype analysis is performed, one is unlikely to make the diagnosis of Klinefelter's in the prepubertal male. Thus, the syndrome remains covert until after the onset of puberty. In adulthood, the diagnosis is most frequently made as part of an infertility or mental retardation evaluation. Some individuals may be diagnosed in endocrinology clinics because of obesity or complaints of breast enlargement (gynecomastia).

The clinical effects which are commonly seen seem to result from the intermediacy of sex conferred by the chromosomes. Thus, these males tend to have enlarged breasts, female distribution of abdominal and facial hair, small phallus, and a tendency to tallness and obesity (Ford, 1973). Since most of these characteristics are prominent only after puberty, it is not surprising that little is known about the physical characteristics before puberty.

Robinson, Lubs, Nielsen, and Sorenson (1979), on the basis of their follow-up of Klinefelter's Syndrome infants, developed the profile presented in Table II.

This profile represents the average and thus may not fit a specific individual child; it does mark the prepubertal stigmata of the syndrome.

Medical Management. The usual treatment is male hormone (testosterone) replacement. About one half of those coming into the genetics clinic at the University of Oregon Health Sciences Center receive the male hormone; for the rest, no treatment is required (LaFranchi, 1980). When there are specific symptoms such as enlarged breasts or obesity,

TABLE II
Profile of Children Who Were Found to Have Klinefelter's Syndrome

Low birth weight, but within the normal range
Increased incidence of major and minor congenital anomalies; for example, cleft palate and inguinal hernia
Height percentiles increased with age
An increased incidence of late speech development
Verbal IQ below normal
Delayed emotional development
Frequent school problems: 44% as compared with 24% in siblings and controls
Poor gross motor coordination

these are dealt with according to current medical practice. Considerable effort is made to help the individual become informed about his condition and to help him plan for the consequences of the disorder (see the section on "Genetic Counseling" in this chapter).

Common Psychological Characteristics and Problems

Money, Klein, and Beck (1979) suggest there are three basic characteristics of the syndrome: sexual apathy, easy fatigability, and low dominance assertion, all of which may stem from an insensitivity or hyporesponsiveness of the XXY cells to androgen. These characteristics create the impression of an inadequate personality. Overall, individuals with Klinefelter's Syndrome are seen as more immature than their normal peers just as are the individuals with Turner's Syndrome.

Males with Klinefelter's Syndrome have an immature and somewhat insecure male gender role compared to females with Turner's Syndrome, who tend to have a clear well defined female gender role identity (Nielsen, 1972). Interestingly, few problems have been found to be directly connected with the enlarged breasts, hypogonadal signs in general, hormone levels, or treatment with hormones. Because of the intermediacy of the biological sex gender, the development of role gender problems is more likely when there are problems in the environment or in the parent–child interaction. In adults with Klinefelter's, marriages have been found to be more stable when children were adopted, and divorce more frequent when there were no children. In many of the marriages, it was the wife who had been active in the courting and proposing. Finally, a close relationship has been noted between men with Klinefelter's Syndrome and their mothers, often continuing to adulthood.

In spite of the insecure male identity, the frequency of homosexuality does not appear to be higher than expected, considering that most of the studies have been conducted among institutionalized men. Males with Klinefelter's have been accused of sexual misconduct toward children. The low sexual potency and shyness toward more mature women may shift their focus to younger children.

In Denmark, where excellent records are kept, Nielsen (1969) found that Klinefelter's Syndrome patients have a high incidence of legal offenses (32% versus the national norm of 19%), a greater number of psychiatric admissions as children, fewer years of secondary and higher education, more frequent rejection from the military service, more sexual offenses against juveniles, and a lesser probability of marrying. In a controlled study using hypogonadal men as matched controls, Nielsen (1969) also found males with Klinefelter's Syndrome had a mean of 12.9 psychiatric symptoms versus only 5.1 for the controls.

There is a higher incidence of retardation with Klinefelter's Syndrome than with Turner's Syndrome. Robinson *et al.* (1979) found the distribution of WAIS full scale IQs was skewed, with 29% of the males having IQs below 90. They found lower scores in the verbal subtests than in the performance subtests. On the other hand, Funderburk and Ferjo (1978) found no significant difference in WAIS verbal and performance scores. Results of the study by Funderburk and Ferjo did find concreteness, poor abstraction, a limited range of expressivity, and problems in speech production. It is felt that the speech and language problems are not always reflected in the IQ scores. The behaviors described above seem to contribute to later underachievement and social maladaptation.

Whereas females with Turner's Syndrome are feminine, have good abilities for social interaction, and are often well liked and supported by family and friends, individuals with Klinefelter's Syndrome may have considerable difficulty in social interactions, including behavioral difficulties in childhood.

Evaluating Persons with Klinefelter's Syndrome

Although Klinefelter's Syndrome is four to five times more common than Turner's Syndrome, the number of individuals seen within the typical endocrinology clinic for Klinefelter's may be smaller. Whenever the diagnosis is made of a child or adolescent, there is often a feeling of relief in the family, because there is now a way of accounting for concerns which may have been present. The psychological evaluation is, in large part, determined by the referral question rather than by the specific characteristics of the syndrome.

Since the literature suggests that there is likely to be a history of some minor problems within the individual's environment, for example, home, school, or community, a thorough interview should be undertaken with the family. The interview will be most productive if it focuses on the developmental history and the interaction between the parents and the child. It is important that the parents' attitude toward the child be carefully reviewed. A direct observation of an interaction between the child and parents may document specific problems.

A thorough intellectual evaluation, preferably using the WISC–R (Wechsler, 1974) should be undertaken because there can be a wide range of IQ and there is a fairly high probability that the verbal subscales scores will be low–average or below average. Current academic achievement should be assessed using the instruments the examiner is competent to administer.

If the diagnosis occurs during adolescence, the focus may shift to the individual's concerns about self-concept and sexual identity. The concerns about behavior and academic performance may still be present. An interview with the client should be very supportive, while exploring his feelings about his physical appearance (e.g., enlarged breasts and poor male sexual development). The reader may refer to Chapter 1 for some ideas about interview strategies. In addition, the client's relationships with his peers should be explored in relation to teasing or covert pressures from the peer group. Since achievement drive may be low, the client's general level of motivation should be assessed. Vocational guidance can be very helpful.

In an adult with Klinefelter's Syndrome, it is helpful to review the client's understanding of the disorder to determine where he is in the genetic counseling process.

In the adult it is not unusual to find a lower energy level, and some effort at helping him to be as realistic as possible about his drive level may be important. Specific attention should be paid to the demands of his employment and family and to other factors which may be providing stress. Particular attention should be focused on determining whether a significant depression is present. Adequacy of sexual relationships should be explored to determine the extent of any difficulties in this area and sexual counseling recommended if appropriate.

Intervention Methods

The literature of child development documents how infants have differing levels of activity and temperaments at birth (Thomas & Chess, 1977). Researchers present a rationale for developing an appropriate synchrony between parents and their child (cf. Goldberg, 1977). Early identification of Klinefelter's Syndrome and periodic appraisal of parent–child interaction may make it possible to help parents develop the desired synchrony of interaction to prevent some of the minor behavioral difficulties which are usually present.

Early educational consultation and speech therapy help alleviate school concerns (Puck, Tennes, Frankenberg, Bryant, & Robinson, 1975). Screening and early diagnosis are not without problems, however, especially when there is no specific treatment. This issue will be discussed in more detail in the next section on Huntington's Disease.

In the years of puberty there are risks for these young men, whose lack of virility and sexual apathy may make them feel like social outcasts in their peer group. This may be compounded by other people's negative reactions. The issues of sexual adequacy, teasing, and independence are three fundamental sources of conflict with which the counselor must be prepared to help the individual.

In adulthood, the individual with Klinefelter's Syndrome usually comes to light because of sterility. It has been noted by Nielsen (1972) that informing a male that he has small testes and sterility can be a very traumatic event. Nielsen recommends that the patient not be told that he has small testes and that the information about sterility be given in the form of the more positive statements about the possibilities of having children (as we discussed previously for Turner's Syndrome).

Some studies have found a correlation between the amount of sexual apathy and the testosterone production in the body. There appears to be increased sexual interest in those who are married and receiving testosterone. In addition, the amount of ejaculate appears to be greater (Money, 1971).

In some individuals, the plasma testosterone levels may be within normal range, but the patient may still get a positive response by regular injections of long-acting testosterone. Money, Kline, and Beck (1979) describe a mild positive response manifested by increased frequency of erotic imagery and increased strength and energy, as well as decreased fatigue and sleepiness.

There may also be specific instances, such as the presence of depressive symptoms, when the administration of testosterone may also have specific positive results (cf. Rinieris, Malliaras, Batrinos, & Stefanis, 1979). The therapist may also need to be supportive when the patient is confronted with his inability to achieve on par with his peers.

If diagnosis is made of Klinefelter's Syndrome as part of a mental retardation evaluation and the retardation is the significant issue, the intervention should be planned as appropriate for the level of retardation (see Chapter 7).

Finally, there may be some specific instances in which psychological intervention is required. For example, prior to as well as following a mastectomy, there may be a need to help the individual work through his sensitivity to the loss of part of his body, just as must be done with women who have breast cancer.

HUNTINGTON'S DISEASE

The Physical Disability

Definition and Incidence. The incidence of Huntington's Disease has been estimated to be somewhere between 4 and 7 per 100,000 population (Myrianthopoulous, 1973) and has been found in all races and countries of the world. Its prevalence in the United States and Canada is estimated to be 100,000 (Committee to Combat Huntington's Disease, 1980).

Huntington's Disease is an autosomal dominant disorder, which progressively affects the central nervous system. It progresses without remission until death results, some ten to twenty years after the initial onset of the symptoms. The disorder is characterized by abnormal involuntary movements (chorea), progressive intellectual impairment (dementia), and a variety of emotional and psychiatric disturbances.

The risk of the disorder's being passed to the offspring by an affected parent is 50% regardless of sex. If children do not inherit the gene, they will not have the disease. The gene is fully penetrant, and if it is inherited and the patient lives long enough, the disease will develop. Clinical records show that children born to parents, both of whom have had Huntington's Disease, do not have earlier onset or a more severe course (Eldridge, O'Meara, Chase, & Donnelly, 1973). The age of onset of symptoms, the nature of the presenting symptoms, the clinical course, and the response to treatment are all variable. The age of onset may vary from 2 to 80 (Wexler, 1979). Approximately 1–2% develop the symptoms prior to 10 years of age, about 3% between 10 and 20 years of age, and approximately 5% develop the symptoms after 60 years of age. The mean duration of the illness until death is 8 years in children under 10 and approximately 15 years for adults. The onset of symptoms sufficient for diagnosis usually occurs between 35 and 45 years of age (Menkes, 1971).

Diagnosis. There is no known test to detect Huntington's Disease prior to the onset of symptoms. Thus, it cannot be determined whether a specific individual is a carrier of the lethal gene. Early detection attempts of at-risk individuals have occurred on three different levels: (1) clinical studies of abnormal muscle movements and various areas of cognitive functioning, (2) biochemical tests, and (3) genetic linkage and chromosome studies.

There was a brief flash of hope when a treatment breakthrough was made in Parkinson's Disease with the use of L-dopa. However, the Committee to Combat Huntington's Disease (1977) does not recommend this test because: (1) a negative result does not rule out the presence of Huntington's Disease; (2) it is not known whether its administration may precipitate the onset of the disease; and (3) if the actual symptoms of Huntington's Disease are induced, serious psychological problems may result. Many ethical issues will be raised if a test is discovered to determine whether an individual has the disease, but there is still no means of preventing its occurrence. On the other hand, such a test may mean relief for those who do not have the disease.

In reality, Huntington's Disease might be defined as any of the following: an illness, a long-term physical disability, a chronic illness, or a genetic disorder. As part of the variability of Huntington's Disease, the first symptoms may be in any of three areas: motor, cognitive or emotional. For an unequivocal diagnosis to be made (Chiu & Teltscher, 1978), it is necessary to have (1) a positive family history, (2) unequivocal, abnormal involuntary movements, and (3) progressive dementia.

Even in the presence of abnormal movements and progressive dementia, the diagnosis is listed as pending if the family history is unavailable. Its symptoms are often diagnosed as Parkinson's Disease, multiple sclerosis, epilepsy, schizophrenia, depression, manic–depressive psychosis, or a variety of other disorders. Seven percent of the postmortems of individuals presupposed to have had Huntington's Disease have shown the diagnosis to have been incorrect (Committee to Combat Huntington's Disease, 1980).

History. Careful observation of families over a long period of time led Dr. George Huntington (1872), a physician who was practicing in Long Island, New York, to describe for the first time the disease which bears his name. He pointed out that the disease was hereditary in nature, that there was a tendency to insanity and suicide, and that it usually manifested itself as a grave disorder only in adult life. The observations upon which his diagnosis was made covered a period of 78 years. The notes of his father and grandfather, who were also physicians in the same locale, were also used.

From 1872 to 1966, progress in understanding and treating Huntington's Disease was painfully slow. Myrianthopoulous (1973, p. 158) made the following statement seven years ago: "More progress has been made in the last five years than in the last fifty, and I venture to predict that the genetic problem in Huntington's Chorea will be resolved before the decade is out."

The decade has ended, and the mystery of Huntington's Disease has not yet been solved. However, there has been an explosion of research and information regarding Huntington's Disease because of the progress in scientific technology and the efforts of Marjorie Guthrie, who spent fifteen years watching her husband deteriorate in hospitals from Huntington's Disease. She made a request of her doctor following her husband's death in 1967: "Please educate me; I want to do something about this devastating hereditary illness" (Committee to Combat Huntington's Disease, 1977, p. 1).

Armed with the basic information about the disease, Mrs. Guthrie began working with the National Institutes of Health (NIH) and was instrumental in getting support for the organization of the first workshop on Huntington's Disease within a year. When she asked professionals at that workshop how she could help, their response was, "Find families with Huntington's Disease" (Committee to Combat Huntington's Disease, 1977, p. 3). With the establishment of the Committee to Combat Huntington's Disease (a nonprofit organization) by Mrs. Guthrie, new Huntington's Disease cases were found and a roster developed.

Progress reached a high point when the 94th Congress, through Public Law 94–63, established the Commission for the Control of Huntington's Disease and Its Consequences. The plan this commission produced in 1977 now serves as a model because of its generic approach and problem orientation. Huntington's Disease is seen as a prototype for many physiological and psychiatric illnesses, and any major breakthrough in Huntington's Disease cause and cure will be felt throughout all science. The commission suggested the change of name from Huntington's Chorea to Huntington's Disease, because the involuntary movements were only one symptom of the disorder (Committee to Combat Huntington's Disease, 1977).

Motor Symptoms. The patient with Huntington's Disease demonstrates an extrapyramidal movement disorder. The motor problems may begin with restlessness and nervousness: the individual cannot sit still for a long period of time. Clumsiness, falling, dropping objects, problems with balance, impairments in driving, slurred or grunting speech, altered handwriting, and difficulty in swallowing are common symptoms (Shoulson, 1978). The patient may then develop visible twitches or grimaces of the face and mouth, tremors and jerkings of the head and neck. Finally, uncontrolled movements of the trunk, arms, hands, and legs develop. The movements generally increase during voluntary effort or stress and diminish during sleep. Binswanger (1973, p. 7) described locomotion in the middle stages as "a reeling gait with wide stance . . . with feet inverted, and weight maintained at the heels. Difficulty in turning and walking backwards and sidewards was exhibited." As the disease progresses, there is difficulty focusing the eyes and swallowing and trouble controlling elimination. In the end, the patient is strapped in bed and is unable to handle any self-care activities.

Treatment. There is presently no cure for Huntington's Disease. The complexity and long-term management of Huntington's Disease requires the effort of a physician, generally a neurologist, who can meet the extensive needs of the family as well as those of the patient. Additional health care team members will be involved as the patient develops a broad range of symptoms and requires more care. Psychologists may recommend treatment for emotional and intellectual disturbances. Further consultation may be required from social workers, nurses, speech clinicians, dietitians, and recreational, occupational, and physical therapists in the day-to-day care of the patient. Genetic counseling is probably one of the most potent tools available, and information and support must be given the family as various decision-making points occur.

Treatment is primarily through a wide variety of medications in addition to basic nursing care. Medication is used to help control the chorea and emotional symptoms in order to prolong the patient's ability to care for himself and function independently. Researchers are now looking for a drug that will provide symptomatic relief.

A smaller number of patients who have an early onset of symptoms may exhibit hypokinetic motor impairment resembling Parkinsonism. These individuals respond positively to a group of medications different from those effective with the later onset of symptoms.

A large percentage of Huntington's Disease patients exhibit an affective disorder. Since depression is the most frequent, these patients seem to respond to the antidepressant medications. Tranquilizers may be useful in reducing anxiety.

In general, the psychotic symptoms respond to antipsychotic drugs but may require dosages that are higher than those needed for the antichorea effect.

As the disease progresses, the patient moves from the family to an institution until the time of death, which usually results from secondary infections, heart failure, or aspiration.

The medication therapy requires regular reevaluation and dose adjustment. The long-term efficacy of these agents is not known, but some clinicians feel they may lose their therapeutic effect with passage of time. It may be advisable to reduce dosage or discontinue these drugs periodically to reassess the patient's motor status and determine side effects.

Common Psychological Characteristics and Problems

Being "At Risk." The person at risk for Huntington's Disease is an individual whose parent had the disease and who has a 50:50 chance of developing it himself. At the absolute level of chance, either investing in the future or failing to do so may result in a personal loss of an intense nature. There is a "damned if I do, damned if I don't" attitude about marriage, children, and vocation.

The fear of losing one's mind and the fear of losing control of one's body are among the most profound fears known to mankind, and both losses occur in Huntington's Disease. The strain of living with this possibility is so great that family members may show irrational behavior even if they have not become affected.

Oliver studied individuals at risk in England and reported that there was a high incidence of psychosis, neurosis, divorce, alcoholism, and child neglect among the members of these families who proved to be unaffected by the disease (1970a, 1970b). The conclusion is that growing up with an affected parent has serious, unfavorable effects upon the offspring. For example, one woman at risk described growing up with a mother who held her out of school beginning in the fourth grade. As she looked back, she could now understand that this devastating step was the result of her mother's experiencing personality changes from Huntington's Disease and becoming paranoid. The person at risk frequently becomes the confidant of the well parent, who pours out his or her grievances toward the ill parent.

In addition, the at-risk individual has a constant dread of developing Huntington's Disease and may have a complicated procedure for monitoring mood and movement. Thus, if moodiness, suspicion, jealousy, or disagreeableness develop, it is considered a sign that the disease is impending. As one spouse of an at-risk husband who had no clinical sign of Huntington's Disease said, "He had better have Huntington's Disease, or our marriage is really in sad shape." It was easier to attribute the problems to the disease than to the deterioration of the relationship.

The nature of each at-risk individual's exposure to Huntington's Disease appears to be critical in determining adjustment in adulthood. The longer the parent had been maintained in the home and included as part of the family, the better was the adjustment of the at-risk person.

Wexler (1979) found that approximately one half of her at-risk sample would seriously consider suicide as an option if and when they contracted the disease. Most of these individuals came from families in which the ill parent had made at least one suicide attempt. The threat of suicide is ever present.

However, in the same study by Wexler (1979), few of the at-risk individuals expressed conscious anger toward the parent who had passed the disease on to them. The more common feelings were compassion and grief.

Wexler (1979) found that one fourth of the at-risk individuals interviewed in her study had children *after* learning the hereditary nature of the disease. Thus, it is apparent that those at risk may still continue to have children, in spite of the fact that there is no other disorder with such a strong argument against having children. Huntington's Disease is the example in most textbooks of a genetic disorder which should rule out reproduction. Strong ambivalent feelings are present. An individual may feel devastated to deny the future spouse natural children. On the other hand, some individuals have indicated that to choose sterility and not have children is to maintain the belief that one would get the disease. The decision not to have children is complicated by the fact that many adoption agencies consider a person at risk for Huntington's Disease an unsuitable parent.

The Identified Patient. Informing the affected individual of the diagnosis of Huntington's Disease is a critical part of a comprehensive care program. How to inform and whom to inform can be difficult decisions. For example, I encountered this situation in my clinic: A new patient informed the staff that he would commit suicide if a diagnosis of Huntington's Disease were made. When the evidence pointed to his having the disease, there was considerable discussion about how and when to tell him. The neurologist decided to tell him immediately and straightforwardly. A week later, the patient carried out his threat and took his life.

Not all patients react so strongly or with the frequently seen denial and shock. Whittier, Heimler, and Korenyi (1972) found that a majority of Huntington's Disease patients expressed relief when finally given a verified diagnosis. This was particularly the case when there had been many previous misdiagnoses or uncertainties as to what the problem might be. These authors conclude that the certainty of something even as horrendous as Huntington's Disease is more bearable, for most people, than the uncertainty of not knowing.

Some individuals may accept the information calmly. A young man who had been a helicopter pilot in Vietnam, when he was informed that his father had Huntington's Disease, responded, "I've been living with a 99% chance of death for thirteen months, so a 50:50 chance sometime in the future looks pretty good to me" (Harmetz, 1971, p. 46).

Since Huntington's Disease is a genetic disorder, its diagnostic confirmation affects not only an individual but an entire family. The Huntington's Disease patient must decide whether or not to tell the rest of the family. The decision includes whether to seek out and inform members of the extended family if they live in different cities. How other family members have handled the same situation may dictate a present course of action. If at all possible, other family members should be present for the diagnostic conference. Physicians have their own dilemmas about informing affected individuals in their care. The physician may be in the best position to provide the diagnosis to the spouse or a responsible relative. Information to others is privileged and confidential. The informing professional cannot merely provide information to a patient, who may already know or suspect much of what he is told, but must be available to help the patient work through feelings and to make decisions about the future. Some patients gain an enriched perspective on life, living more in the present and focusing on meaningful activities and relationships.

One of the realities a patient faces as the motor problems become more apparent is his unsteady gait and impaired coordination, which may precipitate ridicule and accusations of excessive drinking. Further frustration results from the patient's not being able to keep as clean and neat as before.

Emotional Symptoms. Once the diagnosis of Huntington's Disease has been made, one can usually look back and see the personality changes that may have predated the diagnosis of the disease by some 10 years. At the time of diagnosis, emotional symptoms, although variable in character and severity, are usually becoming apparent. The initial emotional disturbances are frequently vague; but as the disease progresses, the increasing manifestation and severity of the symptoms significantly influence the clinical approach to the patient and family (Shoulson, 1978). Depression may be part of the early clinical picture and significant depression is the most frequent affective disorder attending Huntington's Disease. As time progresses, there may be irritability, emotional lability, impulsivity, and agitation. On the other hand, some patients may be described as apathetic, seclusive, and withdrawn. The symptoms are sufficiently variable that there may be alcoholism, inappropriate sexual behavior, delusional or persecutory beliefs, or hallucinations. Palm (1973) found that MMPI profiles for individuals with Huntington's Disease were not representative of the normal population. Huntington's Disease patients tended to be rebellious of social and ethical codes and have difficulty dealing with people. Activity drive was extremely high or low, and there was a tendency noted to avoid immediate problems. Lyle and Gottesman (1977) found similar results for their sample of Huntington's Disease individuals on the MMPI. However, only 56% of the affected persons in the sample took the tests; those with the most acute anxiety may have screened themselves out. In summary, there are no clear symptoms specific to Huntington's Disease, and diagnosis is not possible on the basis of emotional symptoms alone.

Cognitive Deficits. All Huntington's Disease patients appear to have some degree of intellectual impairment, although dementia may not be a prominent feature early in the disease. Attempts have been made with relatively little success to diagnose Huntington's Disease through use of standard psychological assessment tools: WAIS, Wechsler Memory Scale, Bender–Gestalt Test, Halstead's Neuropsychological Test Battery, the Trail Making Test, and the MMPI. It has been concluded that an instrument like the WAIS is too gross a measure and its results too easily confounded with anxiety to be an accurate predictor of whether an individual at risk actually has Huntington's Disease (Wexler, 1976).

When interpreting the studies in the literature, one must pay careful attention to the point in the 20- to 30-year span of the disease at which the assessment is undertaken. Four general categories may be used: (1) early, when the individual is at risk, (2) in adulthood, but prior to a diagnosis, (3) soon after the diagnosis, and (4) more than five years after the diagnosis.

Although an individual may score within the average range on the WAIS until more than five years after the diagnosis, retrospective studies of at-risk individuals demonstrate that those who later develop the disease score lower as a group than those who do not get the disease.

The earliest signs of the disease are loss of ability to use environmental cues, difficulty in planning, and deterioration of recent memory (Shoulson, 1978). However, some researchers (Caine, Hunt, Weingartner, & Ebert, 1978) feel that concepts such as *immediate memory* are ambiguous and affected by so many other variables, such as rate of presentation, type of memory tested, time between tests, and anxiety, that they are not useful. It is felt that very specific tests of planning, thinking, and memory must be developed before the cognitive deficits can be clearly documented. At present, complex memory tasks may serve as the most sensitive predictor of Huntington's Disease (Butters, Sax, Montgomery, & Tarlow, 1978).

With the progression of the disease, intellectual impairment becomes more global in nature. Lyle and Gottesman (1977) did a follow-up study of potential Huntington's Disease victims who had been tested 15 to 20 years earlier. Test scores were progressively lower with increased closeness to symptomatic Huntington's Disease. The authors felt this decline was diffuse. Other researchers maintain that there are very specific deficits present. Caine, Hunt, Weingartner, and Ebert (1978) found the following factors present: an inability to plan and organize factual material requiring advanced preparation; difficulty recalling information upon command, but an ability to recall it later; loss of finely detailed memories; and failure to initiate activities spontaneously. A final factor was that some functional impairments were reduced by great emotional investment in a task.

Another group of investigators (Butters, Sax, Montgomery, & Tarlow, 1978) found that persons with recently diagnosed Huntington's Disease did more poorly on the Digit Symbol and Picture Arrangement subtests of the WAIS than did a control group. Lower scores on the Logical Memory and Associative Learning tasks of the Wechsler Memory Scale were also documented.

The sharp decline in IQ during the five years after diagnosis may indicate a relatively late involvement of the neocortex. The most severe deterioration during the five years after diagnosis involves the Verbal, Spatial, Arithmetic and Perceptual Functions measured by the WAIS (Butters, Sax, Montgomery, & Tarlow, 1978).

In the later stages of the disease, the patient not only has gross intellectual deficits, but has now lost the ability to communicate effectively and handle any activities of daily living. At this point the patient's limited responses make formal testing difficult or impossible.

Spouse and Family. The spouse, although not at risk or affected with the disease, may be as overwhelmed by the prospect of the partner's getting the disease as the person at risk. If, for whatever reason, the spouse has not been told before, the diagnosis comes as a major shock. The past avoidance foretells further difficulties in the family unless counseling follows. The spouse needs considerable support and help in working through any unrealistic concerns, with the goal of making him or her an ally with the professional in the treatment. A successful care arrangement will almost always include the marriage partner.

Huntington's Disease pushes a family toward a lower economic status. Its occurrence in the prime of life may prevent financial and personal achievement. There is an exorbitant financial cost for long-term care. The estimated annual cost of a nursing home in 1977 was $12,700, which would amount to almost $200,000 over the 15-year period of expected life span (Commission for the Control of Huntington's Disease, 1977). In addition, many patients have been affected by the previous generation's affliction with the disease. Individuals may have been compelled to leave school early because of parental illness or may have been required to support the family or care for the sick parent.

Family members are less active socially because of preoccupation with survival, shame over the disease, discouragement, physical limitations, economic difficulties, and inability to gain satisfaction from giving their offspring that which they didn't have (Hans & Gilmore, 1968). Wexler (1973) reviews some of the complex family dynamics which may occur. For example, a sibling may deny the presence of Huntington's Disease symptoms in another sibling out of guilt for the inevitable wish held by each that the other will get the disease. Parents may deny symptoms in the children because of guilt at having passed on the defective gene or because they dread going through the deterioration and death of a loved one again. Anger may be displayed to anyone by the patient; and family members and friends often take this personally and react with equal anger and guilt. The spouse may feel guilt over good health and make a sacrifice by taking more assiduous care of the afflicted individual. Overall, the disease bears the seeds of desocialization and cultural alienation.

As the disease progresses, the daily demands of patient care can become wearing for the spouse. The patient's anxiety, depression, emotional lability, and mental deterioration cause family members to become emotionally drained. They seek individual activities outside the home as an important respite. At the point at which the patient is excluded from the family interaction, the patient's ability to cope will become more problematical. Only by maintaining an active rapport with each other through changes in family roles, the many anxieties, and increasing demands of daily care can a family survive the stress (Power & Sax, 1978).

Evaluating Persons with Huntington's Disease

Since the most frequent initial symptoms of Huntington's Disease are emotional in nature and usually occur some years before the diagnosis is made, there is some probability that a clinician may encounter the undiagnosed Huntington's Disease individual. The clinician must have an understanding of the disease, do a thorough assessment, and obtain a family history even to suspect Huntington's Disease. It is wise to include a minimal number of questions about family background in the initial interview with any adult, for example: "Are your parents still living and in good health?" "How old are they?" "Have there been any psychiatric or unusual illnesses in your family?" and "Are there any diseases which have been passed from one generation to another in your family?"

A typical assessment battery for the at-risk individual might include the WAIS, the Wechsler Memory Test, a perceptual motor test (e.g., Finger Tapping, Bender–Gestalt, or Trail Making Test), the MMPI, and a general mental status examination. Often anxiety is so pronounced that the individual will not be able to undertake the assessment. If the patient does complete the assessment battery, the results should be interpreted with caution. A thorough interview with family members as well as the patient is desirable.

When the diagnosis is made, an interdisciplinary approach is critical to deal with all of the patient's needs. If the patient has been referred, contact with the patient's physician, usually a neurologist, will help to confirm the diagnosis and provide information about how the patient and the family have responded to the diagnosis and to any genetic counseling which followed. While the physician will make, and ordinarily convey, the diagnosis, other members of the team may provide much of the extended counseling and support services. Often the family members can provide considerable information and insight. For example, family members are frequently the first to suspect the diagnosis, which is then later confirmed by the physician when the patient and family are more ready to face the reality.

Any evaluation should include a careful review of the community resources, including vocational retraining and nursing homes. Direct help from the community in the form of homemaker service, public health nursing, financial assistance, or respite care may be required. Often there is need for an advocate, since some rehabilitation programs are intended only for those with permanent disabilities and not for those whose condition will deteriorate over time (see Chapter 8).

One of the goals of an evaluation is to begin sorting out the Huntington's Disease problems from all of the other anxieties and problems which may exist. It is easy for the patient and family to attribute more or less to the disease than is warranted. One must also lay the groundwork for open communication regarding changing roles.

If the diagnosis has already been made, the clinician must be aware that the suicide rate is extremely high and should be considered as a serious possibility in every Huntington's Disease patient. Background information about the family and how those with the disease have coped is essential. Suicide attempts of parents and other family members should be explored as well. An interview procedure similar to that described in Chapter 1 may be used to elicit the patient's current feelings and explore the probability of a suicide attempt. Even if there is no evidence of suicidal ideation, there is a high probability of depression being present which should also be explored.

There are major difficulties regarding self-esteem as the disease progresses. As the motor symptoms begin to affect gait and cause the dropping and spilling of things, severe frustration occurs. Changes may be necessary in employment, in driving a car, and in maintaining self-help skills. (See Chapter 10 for some of the specific implications of losing motor control over time and becoming dependent on others.) As the cognitive deterioration progresses, there is severe stress when even such basic tasks as following a cake recipe become difficult. How the patient is being included or excluded from family activities needs to be explored in detail. There are stresses at the individual, family and community levels. The clinician must not be overwhelmed by all of the needs that may present themselves once a commitment has been made to work with the family.

Intervention Methods

The specific strategy for intervention will depend upon the presenting problem. Besides the individual at risk, there may be a young couple coming in for genetic counseling about having children, a spouse wanting to know how to deal with the patient's behavior, a suicide attempt, an extended-family member who must be persuaded to seek help, or a family needing help in arranging residential care.

Conveying the Diagnosis to the Family. When the patient is told of the diagnosis, the spouse and selected family members should be involved in the discussion. The professional should describe the disease in simple, honest terms, for, although the patient may be well informed about the disorder, the spouse may have little or no information. A primary goal should be to create an atmosphere in which the patient and family can express *feelings* about the diagnosis. Power and Sax (1978) suggest three guidelines for presenting the information to the patient: (1) use clinical judgment about the patient's readiness to receive the information, (2) use the patient's and family's own questions about the disease as a focus of discussion, and (3) take into account any communication barriers which may exist, such as impairment of the patient's mental status. The strengths of the patient and the usefulness of treatment programs are emphasized. A discussion of the family's adjustment to previous illnesses, their style of communication, and the community resources available will lead naturally to consideration of further implications.

Marjorie Guthrie, chairperson of the Committee to Combat Huntington's Disease, attempts to show newly diagnosed Huntington's Disease patients "that it's not the end of the world. That it's the quality, not the quantity, of life that's important. What's wrong with 40 to 50 fine productive years." (Cole, 1973, p. 66).

Informing Children of Huntington's Disease in a Parent. After the patient's illness has been diagnosed, many families ask what to tell the children. It is generally suggested that the questions of younger children be answered as they come up, an approach followed in other sensitive subjects such as sex education. When a parent asks, "When is my child ready to learn that there is Huntington's Disease in the family?" he may be asking, "When will I be ready to tell him that there is Huntington's Disease in the family?" (Whittier, Heinler, & Korenyi, 1972). These same authors suggest that if the parent is to bring up the issue directly, the following question be used: "Mother/Father hasn't been feeling well lately. What do you think could be wrong?" The parent can then make the explanation according to the child's understanding. Children should not be told too much, particularly the name or the hereditary nature of the disease, until they can grasp the implications and make a responsible decision about whether there is reason to keep the information private. The child can be informed that the illness is responsible for the parent's unusual behavior.

Counseling Parents Who Are At Risk about Having Children. Even with the 50:50 chance of each child's having Huntington's Disease, individuals at risk may decide to have children after the diagnosis has been made. The Committee to Combat Huntington's Disease takes the stand that reliable information should be imparted to the family but that it then becomes their decision whether or not to have children. Although few professionals advocate directly counseling parents not to have children, some are raising questions about what should be done (Pearson, 1973). Others are prepared to assert an influence: when asked, "What would you do if you were in my shoes?," they would respond, "I would avoid having children." With the rapid progress in research, a realistic approach may be to encourage a young couple to wait five years before deciding about children to see what the future will bring. Otherwise, the parents may decide to begin having children immediately for the complex reasons previously discussed.

Counseling Individuals At Risk for Huntington's Disease. Although for most at-risk individuals the only contact with professionals about Huntington's Disease has been their parent's physician, almost all could benefit from counseling focused on coping with Huntington's Disease in the family (Wexler, 1979). Wexler (1979, pp. 217–220) gives some specific suggestions for working with this group: (1) listen; (2) do not minimize the gravity of the concern but offer realistic hope; (3) avoid pointing out that anyone might die suddenly in an accident, because this is not an effective consolation; (4) let the individual know that it is not unusual for the 50:50 risk to become a 100% certainty that one will or will not develop the disease; (5) stress that it is normal for those who are at risk to become anxious when they see any behavior patterns which might be attributable to the disease; (6) differentiate Huntington's Disease from the rest of the environment; (7) try to relieve guilt; (8) if the patient is not manifesting any signs of the illness at that moment, tell him so.

Intervention at the Community Level. One of the most pressing needs within the community is an alternative care facility which would provide the transitional step from the home to a nursing care facility. There is also a need for chronic care facilities providing care with dignity by highly motivated personnel who understand both the immediate nursing problems and the long-term prognosis. Competent nursing care means acting upon sympathetic observation, for example, changing a styrofoam cup to a sturdy tumbler when the motor problems become severe or taking time to communicate with the patient so there can still be some individual control over the daily schedule, such as whether to take a bath or not. There is a great need for an interdisciplinary team approach involving the nutritionist, recreational therapist, and occupational therapist. Such team members bring suggestions and new perspectives. Simple strategies such as making a patient responsible for a bedside plant can make a positive difference (Swiatek, 1973). Continuing, realistic, and positive communication with the family is important, because there is a tendency to stop visiting once the patient has entered a chronic care facility.

Overall, there is an ongoing need to provide health service professionals, every Huntington's Disease family, and the general public with current reliable information so that Huntington's Disease can continue to come out of the closet where it has been for so long.

TRENDS AND NEEDS

Although the specific mechanisms of gene interactions and biochemistry of inheritance still elude us, we have come to have a much clearer understanding of the disorders discussed in this chapter. Where uncertainties do exist, we must be straightforward with families and keep them informed of the basis on which decisions are made that effect them: for example, diet changes in PKU, medications used in Turner's and Huntington's Diseases.

The rapid rate of advances in applied human genetics has outdistanced the integration of the new knowledge and technology into the norms and values of our society. "Couples facing reproductive decisions have an array of new options open to them, some inimical to previously held moral and religious beliefs, some offering hope where there was none before, and all raising questions for which satisfactory answers are still difficult to obtain" (Kenen & Schmidt, 1978, p. 1116). A combination of effective screening and selective abortion will enable more couples with a wider and wider range of disorders to achieve desired normal biological parenthood without the risk of giving birth to a defective child. In the case of recessive disorders, carriers are still in danger of self-imposed and social stigma and therefore require further educational programs.

In the meantime, it is clear that the need goes beyond identifying the disorder in a family and informing them of the facts of the disease.

Thus, a single professional is no longer able to bear the whole burden of treatment. Interdisciplinary teams provide for the broader base of intervention. With each disorder, there are psychological and behavioral implications for the whole family which must be addressed in the family context for optimal adaptation and for prevention of secondary problems. Finally, positive community attitudes and adequate resources become critical to a successful outcome.

APPENDIX: SOURCES OF INFORMATION

Genetic Counseling:
>The National Foundation/March of Dimes
>Box 2000
>White Plains, NY 10602

Kessler, S. (Ed.). *Genetic counseling: Psychological dimensions.* New York: Academic Press, 1979.

Milunsky, A. *Know Your Genes.* Boston: Houghton Mifflin, 1977.

Barbeau, A., Chase, T. N., & Paulson, G. W. (Eds.). *Advances in neurology. Vol. 1.* New York: Raven Press, 1973.

Plumridge, D. *Good things come in small packages: The whys and hows of Turner's Syndrome.* Portland: University of Oregon Health Sciences Center, 1976.

>Committee to Combat Huntington's Disease
>250 West 57th Street, Suite 2016
>New York, NY 10019

Living with PKU. Evanston, Ill.: Mean–Johnson, 1972.

Acosta, P. B., Wenz, E., Schaeffler, G., and Koch, R. *PKU: A diet guide for parents of children with phenylketonuria.* Los Angeles: Bureau of Public Health Nutrition of California State Department of Public Health, 1969.

REFERENCES

Acosta, P. B., & Elsas, L. J. *Dietary management of inherited metabolic disease.* Atlanta, Georgia: ACELM Publishers, 1975.

Acosta, P. B., Fiedler, J. L., & Koch, R. Mothers' dietary management of PKU children. *Journal of the American Dietetic Association,* 1968, 53, 460–464.

Acosta, P. B., Wenz, E., & Williamson, M. Nutrient intake of treated infants with Phenylketonuria. *American Journal of Clinical Nutrition*, 1977, *30*, 198–208.

Ad hoc committee on genetic counseling. Genetic counseling. *American Journal of Human Genetics*, 1975, *26*, 240–242.

Allen, R. J., & Gibson, R. M. Phenylketonuria with normal intelligence. *American Journal of Diseases in Childhood*, 1961, *102*, 115–122.

Anderson, V., Siegel, E., & Bruhl, H. Behavioral and biochemical correlates of diet change in phenylketonuria. *Pediatric Research*, 1976, *10*, 10–17.

Armstrong, M. D., & Tyler, F. H. Studies on phenylketonuria. 1. Restricted phenylalanine intake in phenylketonuria. *Journal of Clinical Investigation*, 1955, *34*, 565–580.

Bartholome, K., Byrd, D. J., Kaufman, S., & Milstein, S. Atypical phenylketonuria with normal phenylalanine hydroxylase and dihydropteridine reductase activity in vitro. *Pediatrics*, 1977, *59*, 757–761.

Baumeister, A. A. The effects of dietary control on intelligence in phenylketonuria. *American Journal of Mental Deficiency*, 1967, *71*, 840–847.

Beals, R. K. Orthopedic aspects of the X0 (Turner's Syndrome). *Clinical Orthopedics and Related Research*, 1973, *97*, 19–30.

Beckner, A. S., Centerwall, W. R., & Holt, L. Effects of rapid increase of phenylalanine intake in older phenylketonuria children. *Journal of the American Dietetic Association*, 1976, *69*, 148–151.

Berman, J. L., & Ford, R. Intelligence quotient and intelligence loss in patients with phenylketonuria and some variant states. *Journal of Pediatrics*, 1970, *77*, 764–770.

Berman, P. W., Waisman, H. A., & Graham, F. K. Intelligence in treated phenylketonuria children: A developmental study. *Child Development*, 1966, *37*, 731–747.

Berry, H. K., O'Grady, D. J., Perlmutter, L. J., & Bofinger, M. K. Intellectual development and academic achievement of children treated early for phenylketonuria. *Developmental Medicine and Child Neurology*, 1979, *21*, 311–320.

Bickel, H., Gerrard, J., & Hickmans, E. M. The influence of phenylalanine intake on phenylketonuria. *Lancet*, 1953, *2*, 812–813.

Binder, J., Johnson, C. F., Saboe, B., & Krug-Wispe, S. Delayed elevation of serum phenylalanine level in breast-fed children. *Pediatrics*, 1979, *63*, 334–336.

Binswanger, C. Physical therapy as possible modality used to extend the creative functional lives of patients with Huntington's Disease: A pilot study. In *HD Handbook for health professionals*. New York: Committee to Combat Huntington's Disease, 1973.

Buist, N. R., Lis, E. W., Tuerck, J. M., & Murphy, W. H. Maternal phenylketonuria. *Lancet*, 1979, *2*, 589.

Butters, N., Sax, D., Montgomery, K., & Tarlow, S. Comparison of the neuropsychological deficits associated with early and advanced Huntington's Disease. *Archives of Neurology*, 1978, *35*, 585–589.

Caine, E. D., Hunt, R. D., Weingartner, H., & Ebert, M. H. Huntington's dementia: Clinical and neuropsychological features. *Archives of General Psychiatry*, 1978, *35*, 377–384.

Chiu, E., & Teltscher, B. Huntington's Disease: The establishment of a national register. *The Medical Journal of Australia*, 1978, *2*, 394–396.

Cole, W. Marjorie Guthrie's fight against her husband's killer. *Good Housekeeping*, 1973, *176*, 64–67.

Commission for the Control of Huntington's Disease and its Consequences. Report: Vol. I—Overview, DHEW Pub. No. (NIH) 78–1501. Bethesda, Md.: National Institutes of Health, 1977.

Committee to Combat Huntington's Disease. *A decade of progress and hope, 1967–1977*. New York: Committee to Combat Huntington's Disease, 1977.

Committee to Combat Huntington's Disease. Newsletter No. 27, Spring, 1980.
Court-Brown, W. M., & Smith, P. G. Human population cytogenetics. *British Medical Bulletin,* 1969, *25,* 74–80.
Cunningham, G. C., & Day, R. Phenylalanine tolerance tests in families with phenylketonuria and hyperphenylalaninemia. *American Journal of Diseases in Childhood,* 1969, *117,* 626–635.
Dobson, J. D., Kushida, E., Williamson, M., & Friedman, E. G. Intellectual performance of 36 phenylketonuria patients and their non-affected siblings. *Pediatrics,* 1976, *50,* 53–56.
Eldridge, R., O'Meara, K., Chase, T. N., & Donnelly, E. F. Offspring of consanguineous parents with Huntington's Chorea. In A. Barbeau, T. N. Chase, & G. W. Paulson (Eds.), *Advances in Neurology* (Vol. 1). New York: Raven Press, 1973.
Ferguson-Smith, M. A. Sex chromatin, Klinefelter's syndrome, and mental deficiency. In K. L. Moore (Ed.), *The sex chromatin.* Philadelphia: W. B. Saunders, 1966.
Fisch, R. O., Conley, J. A., Eysenbach, S., & Chang, P. Contact with phenylketonurics and their families beyond pediatric age: Conclusion from a survey and conference. *Mental Retardation,* 1977, *15,* 10–12.
Fisch, R. O., Solberg, J. A., & Borud, L. Responses of children with phenylketonuria to dietary treatment. *Journal of the American Dietetic Association,* 1971, *58,* 32–37.
Folling, A. Phenylpyruvic acid as a metabolic anomaly in connection with imbecility. *Zeitschrift für physiologische Chemie,* 1934, *227,* 169–176.
Ford, C. E., Jones, K. W., Polani, P. E., de Almeida, F. C., & Briggs, F. H. A sex-chromosome anomaly in a case of gonadal dysgenesis (Turner's Syndrome). *Lancet,* 1959, *1,* 711–713.
Ford, E. H. R. Abnormalities of the sex chromosomes (Chapter 10). *Human chromosomes.* New York: Academic Press, 1973.
Frankenburg, W. K., Goldstein, A. D., & Olson, C. O. Behavioral consequences of increased phenylalanine intake by phenylketonuria children: A pilot study describing methodology. *American Journal of Mental Deficiency,* 1973, *77,* 524–532.
Fuller, R., & Shuman, J. Treated phenylketonuria. Intelligence and blood phenylalanine levels. *American Journal of Mental Deficiency,* 1971, *75,* 539–545.
Funderburk, S. J., & Ferjo, N. Clinican observations in Klinefelter's (47,XXY) syndrome. *Journal of Mental Deficiency Research,* 1978, *22,* 207–212.
Garron, D. Intelligence among persons with Turner's Syndrome. *Behavior Genetics,* 1977, *7,* 105–127.
Goldberg, S. Social competence in infancy: A model of parent–infant interaction. *Merrill-Palmer Quarterly,* 1977, *23,* 163–175.
Guthrie, R. Blood screening for phenylalanine. *Journal of the American Medical Association,* 1961, *178,* 863–868.
Hackney, J. M., Hanley, W. B., Davidson, W., & Lindsao, L. Phenylketonuria: Mental development, behavior and termination of low phenylalanine diet. *Journal of Pediatrics,* 1968, *72,* 646–655.
Hans, M. B., & Gilmore, T. H. Social aspects of Huntington's Chorea. *British Journal of Psychiatry,* 1968, *114,* 93–98.
Harmetz, A. Must they sacrifice today because of threatened tomorrows? *Today's Health,* 1971, *49,* 44–47.
Hecht, F., Wyandt, H. E., & Magenis, R. E. H. The human cell nucleus: Quinacrine and other differential stains in the study of chromatin and chromosomes. In *The cell nucleus* (Vol. 2). New York: Academic Press, 1974.

Holtzman, N. A., Mellits, E. D., & Kallman, C. H. Neonatal screening for PKU II: Age dependence of initial phenylalanine in infants with PKU. *Pediatrics*, 1974, *53*, 353–357.

Holtzman, N. A., Welcher, D. W., & Mellits, E. D. Termination of restricted diet in children with PKU: A randomized controlled study. *New England Journal of Medicine*, 1975, *293*, 1121–1124.

Hsia, D. Y. Y. Phenylketonuria. *Developmental Medicine and Child Neurology*, 1967, *9*, 531–540.

Hsia, D., Knox, W. G., Quinn, K. V., & Paine, R. S. A one–year controlled study of the effect of low phenylalanine diet on phenylketonuria. *Pediatrics*, 1958, *21*, 178–202.

Huntington, G. On chorea. *The Medical and Surgical Reporter*, 1872, *26*, 320–321.

Johnson, C. F. Phenylketonuria: A diagnosis that affects the entire family. *Medical Times*, 1979, *107*, 37–40.

Kang, E. S., Kennedy, J. L., Gates, L., Burwash, I., & McKinnon, A. Clinical observations in PKU. *Pediatrics*, 1965, *35*, 932–943.

Kang, E. S., Sollee, N. D., & Gerald, P. S. Results of treatment and termination of diet in phenylketonuria. *Pediatrics*, 1970, *46*, 881–889.

Keleske, L., Solomons, G., & Opitz, E. Parental reactions to PKU in the family. *Journal of Pediatrics*, 1967, *70*, 793–798.

Kenen, R. H., & Schmidt, R. M. Stigmatization of carrier status: Social implications of heterozygote genetic screening programs. *American Journal of Public Health*, 1978, *68*, 1116–1120.

Kennedy, J. L., Wertleki, W., Gales, L., Sperry, B. P., & Cass, V. M. The early treatment of PKU. *American Journal of Diseases in Childhood*, 1967, *113*, 16–21.

Kessler, S. The psychological foundations of genetic counseling. In S. Kessler (Ed.), *Genetic counseling: psychological dimensions*. New York: Academic Press, 1979.

King, C. R., Magenis, E., & Bennett, S. Pregnancy and the Turner Syndrome. *Obstetrics and Gynecology*, 1978, *52*, 617–624.

Kirkman, H. N. Single-gene disorders. *Pediatric Annals*, 1978, *7*, 69.

Kleinman, D. S. Phenylketonuria: A review of some deficits in our information. *Pediatrics*, 1964, *33*, 123–133.

Knox, W. E. An evaluation of treatment of phenylketonuria with diets low in phenylalanine. *Pediatrics*, 1960, *26*, 1–11.

Koch, R., Fishler, K., Schild, S., & Ragsdale, N. Clinical aspects of PKU. *Mental Retardation*, 1964, *2*, 47–54.

Koch, R., Shaw, K. N. F., Acosta, P. B., Fischler, K., Schaffly, G., Wenz, E., & Wohlers, A. An approach to the management of PKU. *Journal of Pediatrics*, 1970, *76*, 815–828.

Koff, E., Boyle, P., & Pueschel, S. Perceptual–motor functioning in children with PKU. *American Journal of Diseases in Childhood*, 1977, *13*, 1084–1087.

Komrower, M., Saroharwalla, I. B., Coutts, J. M. J., & Ingham, D. Management of maternal phenylketonuria: An emerging clinical problem. *British Medical Journal*, 1979, *1*, 1383–1387.

La Franchi, S. Personal Communication. September, 1980.

Langdell, J. I. PKU: Eight year evaluation of treatment. *Archives of General Psychiatry*, 1965, *12*, 363–367.

Lemli, L., & Smith, D. W. The X0 syndrome: A study of the differentiated phenotype in 25 patients. *Journal of Pediatrics*, 1963, *63*, 577–588.

Leonard, C. O., Chase, G. A., & Childs, B. Genetic counseling: A consumer's view. *New England Journal of Medicine*, 1972, *287*, 433–439.

Lowe, T. L., Tanaka, K., Seashore, M. R., Young, G. J., & Cohen, D. Detection of phenylketonuria in autistic and psychotic children. *Journal of the American Medical Association*, 1980, *243*, 126–128.

Lyle, O. E., & Gottesman, I. I. Premorbid psychometric indicators of the gene for Huntington's Disease. *Journal of Consulting and Clinical Psychology*, 1977, *45*, 1011–1022.

Mabry, C. C., Denniston, J. C., & Caldwell, J. G. Mental retardation in children of PKU mothers. *New England Journal of Medicine*, 1966, *275*, 1331.

McKusick, V. A. *Mendelian inheritance in man: Catalogs of autosomal dominant, autosomal recessive, and X-linked phenotypes* (5th ed.). Baltimore: Johns Hopkins Press, 1978.

Menkes, J. H. The pathogenesis of mental retardation in phenylketonuria and other inborn errors of amino acid metabolism. *Pediatrics*, 1967, *39*, 297–308.

Menkes, J. H. Summary of a workshop on Huntington's Disease sponsored by the Committee to Combat Huntington's Disease. Pacific Palisades, Calif., March 12–13, 1971.

Moen, J. L., Wilcox, R. D., & Burns, J. K. PKU as a factor in the development of self-esteem. *Behavioral Pediatrics*, 1977, *90*, 1027–1029.

Money, J. Psychologic findings associated with the X0, XXY, and XYY anomalies. *Southern Medical Journal*, 1971, *64* (Supplement No. 1), 59–64.

Money, J., Klein, A., & Beck, J. Applied behavioral genetics: Counseling and psychotherapy in sex-chromosomal disorders. In S. Kessler (Ed.), *Genetic counseling, psychological dimensions*. New York: Academic Press, 1979.

Money, J., & Mittenthal, S. Lack of personality pathology in Turner's syndrome: Relation to cytogenetics, hormones and physique. *Behavior Genetics*, 1970, *1*, 43–56.

Myrianthopoulos, N. C. Huntington's chorea: The genetic problem five years later, In A. Barbeau, T. N. Chase, & G. W. Paulson (Eds.), *Advances in neurology* (Vol. 1). New York: Raven Press, 1973.

Nielsen, J. Turner's Syndrome in medical, neurological, and psychiatric wards. *Acta Psychiatrica Scandinavica*, 1970, *46*, 286–310.

Nielsen, J. Gender role-identity and sexual behaviour in persons with sex chromosome aberrations. *Danish Medical Bulletin*, 1972, *19*, 269–275.

Oliver, J. E. Huntington's Chorea in Northamptonshire. *British Journal of Psychiatry*, 1970a, *116*, 241–253.

Oliver, J. E. Socio-psychiatric consequences of Huntington's Disease. *British Journal of Psychiatry*, 1970b, *116*, 255–258.

Palm, D. J. Longitudinal study of a preclinical test program for Huntington's Chorea. In A. Barbeau, T. N. Chase, & G. W. Paulson (Eds.), *Advances in neurology* (Vol. 1). New York: Raven Press, 1973.

Pearson, J. E. Behavioral aspects of Huntington's Chorea. In A. Barbeau, T. N. Chase, & G. W. Paulson (Eds.), *Advances in neurology* **(Vol. 1). New York: Raven Press, 1973.**

Plumridge, D. *Good things come in small packages: The whys and hows of Turner's Syndrome.* Portland: University of Oregon Health Sciences Center, 1976.

Power, P. W., & Sax, D. S. The communication of information to the neurological patient: Some implications for family coping. *Journal of Chronic Diseases*, 1978, *31*, 57–65.

Puck, M., Tennes, K., Frankenburg, W., Bryant, K., & Robinson, A. Early childhood development of four boys with 47,XXY karyotype. *Clinical Pediatrics*, 1975, 7, 8.

Reyes, F. I., Koh, K. S., & Faiman, C. Fertility in women with gonadal dysgenesis. *American Journal of Obstetrics and Gynecology*, 1976, *126*, 668–670.

Rinieris, P. M., Malliaras, D. E., Batrinos, M. L., & Stefanis, C. N. Testosterone treatment of depression in two patients with Klinefelter's Syndrome. *American Journal of Psychiatry*, 1979, *136*, 986–988.

Robinson, A., Lubs, H. A., Nielsen, J., & Sorensen, K. Summary of clinical finding: Profiles of children with 47,XXY, 47,XXX and 47,XYY karyotypes. *Birth Defects: Original Article Series*, 1979, *15*, 261–266.

Rouse, B. M. Phenylalanine deficiency syndrome. *Journal of Pediatrics*, 1966, *69*, 246–249.

Sabbath, J. C., Morris, T. A., Menzer-Benaron, D., & Sturgis, S. H. Psychiatric observations in adolescent girls lacking ovarian function. *Psychosomatic Medicine*, 1961, *23*, 224–231.

Sanchez, O., & Yunis, J. J. New chromosome techniques and their medical applications. In J. J. Yunis (Ed.), *New Chromosomal Syndromes*. New York: Academic Press, 1977.

Sankaranarayanan, K. The role of non-disjunction in aneuploidy in man: An overview. *Mutation Research*, 1979, *61*, 1–28.

Schild, S. Psychological issues in genetic counseling of PKU. In S. Kessler (Ed.), *Genetic counseling: Psychological dimensions*. New York: Academic Press, 1979.

Shaffer, J. W. A specific cognitive defect observed in gonadal aplasia (Turner's Syndrome). *Journal of Clinical Psychology*, 1962, *18*, 403–406.

Shoulson, I. *Clinical care of the patient and family with Huntington's Disease*. New York: Committee to Combat Huntington's Disease, 1978.

Sibinga, M. S., & Friedman, C. J. Complexities of parental understanding of phenylketonuria. *Pediatrics*, 1971, *48*, 216–224.

Smith, I., Clayton, B. E., & Wolff, O. H., New variant of PKU with progressive neurological illness unresponsive to phenylalanine restriction. *Lancet*, 1975, *1*, 1108.

Smith, I., Lobascher, M. E., Stevenson, J. E., Wolff, O. H., Schmidt, H., Gruber-Kaiser, S., & Bickel, H. Effect of stopping low-phenylalanine diet on intellectual progress of children with phenylketonuria. *British Medical Journal*, 1978, *2*, 723–726.

Smith, I., & Wolff, O. H., Natural history of PKU and influence on early treatment. *Lancet*, 1974, *2*, 540–544.

Solomons, G., Keleske, L., & Opitz, E. Evaluation of the effects of terminating the diet in phenylketonuria. *Journal of Pediatrics*, 1966, *69*, 596–602.

Steisel, I. M., Friedman, C. J., & Wood, A. C., Jr. Interaction patterns in children with phenylketonuria. *Journal of Consulting Psychology*, 1967, *31*, 162–168.

Stevenson, J. E., Hawcroft, J., Lobascher, M., Smith, I., Wolff, O. H., & Graham, P. Behavioral deviance of children with early treated phenylketonuria. *Archives of Disease in Childhood*, 1979, *54*, 14–18.

Sutherland, B. S., Umbarger, B., & Berry, H. K. Treatment of PKU: A decade of results. *American Journal of Diseases in Childhood*, 1966, *111*, 505–523.

Swiatek, M. Nursing and boarding homes try a new medicine, recreation therapy. In *HD Handbook for health professions*. New York: Committee to Combat Huntington's Disease, 1973.

Thomas, A., & Chess, S. *Temperament and development*. New York: Brunner/Mazel, 1977.

Turner, H. H. A syndrome of infantilism, congenital webbed neck and cubitus valgus. *Endocrinology*, 1938, *23*, 566–574.

Vandeman, P. R. Termination of treatment for PKU. *American Journal of Diseases in Childhood*, 1963, *106*, 492–495.

Waber, D. P. Neuropsychological aspects of Turner's Syndrome. *Developmental Medicine and Child Neurology*, 1979, *21*, 58–70.

Watson, M. A., & Money, J. Behavior cytogenetics and Turner's Syndrome: A new principle in counseling and psychotherapy. *American Journal of Psychotherapy*, 1975, *29*, 166–178.

Wechsler, D. *Wechsler intelligence scale for children—Revised*. New York: The Psychological Corporation, 1974.

Wexler, N. S. Living out the dying: HD, grief, and death. In *HD Handbook for health professionals*. New York: Committee to Combat Huntington's Disease, 1973.

Wexler, N. S. Personal communication. November 2, 1976.

Wexler, N. S. Genetic "Russian Roulette": The experience of being "at risk" for Huntington's Disease. In S. Kessler (Ed.), *Genetic counseling: Psychological dimensions*. New York: Academic Press, 1979.

Whittier, J. R., Heimler, A., & Korenyi, C. The psychiatrist and Huntington's Disease (Chorea). *American Journal of Psychiatry*, 1972, *128*, 1546–1550.

Williamson, M., Koch, R., & Berlow, S. Diet discontinuation in phenylketonuria. *Pediatrics*, 1979, *63*, 823–824.

Wood, A. C., Jr., Friedman, C. J., & Steisel, I. M. Psychosocial factors in phenylketonuria. *American Journal of Orthopsychiatry*, 1967, *37*, 671–679.

Wood, B. Neurological disturbance in a phenylketonic child after discontinuance of dietary treatment. *Developmental Medicine and Child Neurology*, 1976, *18*, 657–665.

5

Cerebral Palsy

When William J. Little (1862) attributed certain deformities to "abnormal parturition, difficult labors, premature birth and asphyxia neonatorum," he produced a brilliant contribution to clinical medicine and a colossal headache for taxonomists. The disorders once known as Little's disease and now known as cerebral palsy have been described by Nelson and Ellenberg (1978) as "not a single disease, but rather a group of conditions differing in topographic distribution, specific manifestations, and associated handicaps, and probably (but to a degree as yet unknown) varying in etiology." Cohen and Kohn (1979) call cerebral palsy a syndrome, not a definitive diagnosis, and Minear (1956) points out that its treatment is a treatment of symptoms, not of etiology.

THE PHYSICAL DISABILITY

Definition

There is common agreement that cerebral palsy involves a lesion of the central nervous system which causes motor dysfunction and, frequently, concomitant sensory, cognitive, or emotional disturbances. The lesion is nonprogressive and, while it may occur during the neonatal, perinatal, or postnatal period, is one that is incurred early in life. Contemporary attention to developmental disorders, among them cerebral palsy, should serve to strengthen the latter criterion, that is, that the disability is one that is incurred early enough in the maturational process to interfere with the normal progression through the developmental milestones. In earlier times, the diagnosis of cerebral palsy was sometimes applied to disabilities sustained later in life if they resulted in a similar motor dysfunction.

Types of cerebral palsy are defined according to motor symptom complexes and topography, that is, parts of the body involved. To appreciate motor function, the reader is invited to hold his arm out straight with the palm up, and bend it. The muscles inside the arm (flexors) contract as those outside (extensors) relax. These opposing muscles move in smooth coordination by signals from the brain through the spinal cord. The movement is simultaneously monitored and modified on the basis of sensory feedback from the muscles. The body also uses certain primitive and automatic reflexes to maintain functions such as balance and body coordination in an upright position. The disturbance of the system that signals this finely tuned motor functioning is seen as cerebral palsy. Johnston (1976) summarizes this as an improper balance between voluntary and involuntary controls, stimulating and suppressing influences, and flexion and extensor postures.

If the disturbance is characterized by a hyperactive muscle stretch reflex, it is called *spasticity*. Muscles will be tight (hypertonic) and movement will be jerky, caused by sudden relaxation of the hypertonic muscles and by spasms of contraction and relaxation. If the disturbance is characterized by an abnormal amount of involuntary motion resulting in bizarre, purposeless, writhing movements, it is called *athetosis*. If the disturbance is characterized primarily by incoordination and poor balance, it is called *ataxia*. Other less frequently used classifications on motor function are *rigidity, tremor,* and *atonia*.

Common classifications of cerebral palsy based on topography usually relate to the spastic type, and include: (1) *Hemiplegia:* involvement of the arm and leg on one side of the body; (2) *Diplegia:* involvement of all four limbs, legs more than arms; (3) *Quadriplegia (tetraplegia):* involvement of all four limbs; (4) *Paraplegia:* involvement of legs only.

Incidence

Nelson and Ellenberg (1978) reviewed a number of clinical surveys and report the ranges of occurrence of the common types of cerebral palsy shown in Table I.

Differences in findings vary with the time of the study and nature of the sample, as well as with the diagnostic system utilized. In addition to variations of the diagnostic categories already described, there may be differences in the degree of severity required to warrant the diagnosis of cerebral palsy. Levels of severity are commonly defined as mild (little or no interference with independent motor functioning), moderate (sub-

TABLE I
Common Forms of Cerebral Palsy[a]

Spastic hemiplegia	25 to 40%
Spastic diplegia	10 to 33%
Spastic quadriplegia	9 to 43%
Extrapyramidal (including athetoid ataxic and dystonic forms)	9 to 22%
Mixed	9 to 22%

[a] Adapted from Nelson and Ellenberg (1978).

stantial handicap with need for wheelchair, bracing, or other assistance), and severe (inability to function independently). The reader should be aware that in some instances people who should be called awkward or incoordinated may be labeled *cerebral palsied.*

Nelson and Ellenberg (1978) point to the need for a current and perhaps continuing national statistical survey of the incidence and prevalence of cerebral palsy. In the absence of uniform data, figures are based on studies which apply slightly differing criteria to a variety of populations. The medical director of the United Cerebral Palsy Research and Educational Foundation (Sternfeld, 1979) reports that his organization estimated the incidence of congenital cerebral palsy at six per 1,000 live births in 1965 and further estimated that it had decreased to three per 1,000 live births by 1978. He observes, "Much of this decrease has occurred as a result of the decrease in spastic diplegia and athetoid forms of palsy. The former is attributable to the increased use and effectiveness of neonatal intensive care, and the latter to the control of neonatal jaundice through the prevention of blood incompatibility and the use of phototherapy."

A cerebral palsy prevalence rate of 4.6 per 1,000 at seven years of age was found by the National Collaborative Perinatal Project as reported by Nelson and Ellenberg (1978). This was a prospective study based on a population of 54,000 children born between 1959 and 1966. This prevalence figure compares closely to that of 4.3 per 1,000 utilized by the National Significance Project conducted by the United Cerebral Palsy Association of California (Orr-Kissner, 1978). Interpretation of prevalence in adults, however, should be tempered by the findings of Keiter (1979), who surveyed known adult cerebral-palsied individuals in Oregon. He found a rapid decrease in those receiving services for cerebral palsy at increasing age levels, with the 21- to 40-year age group three times larger than the 41- to 60-year age group, and seven to eight times larger than the 61+ age group. His study did not include those who had mainstreamed themselves and no longer received services. He found 60% of those studied to be living in institutions and almost all of these had secondary diagnoses of severe mental retardation, epilepsy, or an uncontrolled medical problem, while those in the community had a very small incidence of serious secondary diagnoses.

Motor

Johnston and Magrab (1976) stress the need for early diagnosis in developmental disorder, including cerebral palsy, but caution against the "Rumplestiltskin complex," which holds that coming up with a name for something will solve every problem. Early intervention should follow on the heels of early identification. Surgery, bracing, and physical therapy are commonly used with cerebral-palsied children. Surgical procedures are more often palliative than curative and more frequently involve the lower extremities than the upper extremities. They may include procedures to lengthen or release muscles or tendons or interrupt nerve pathways in order to better balance opposing muscles or stabilize bones. As stated by Keats (1965), the goals are to correct deformity, improve muscle function and skill, restore muscle balance, assure proper alignment of the joints concerned with weight bearing, and establish correct posture. Bracing may also be used to correct deformities, control unwanted motions, and assist in training desired motions.

Surgical or bracing approaches to motor problems of cerebral palsy are almost always in the context of a program of physical therapy and are usually influenced by the theory underlying the program. Wolf (1969) outlines no fewer than 10 systems of treatment, and this is not an exhaustive list. They may be divided into three major groups: (1) those which are peripheral and stress the relaxation and training of muscles, (2) those which are central or neurophysiological and use reflexes to develop more orderly neuromuscular patterns, and (3) those which are eclectic. Although there are basic principles and techniques common to all of these systems, there exists considerable controversy among schools of thought, fueled by the absence of good prospective studies to document the long-term effectiveness of *any* treatment, let alone a particular system. This is a regrettable lack in view of the considered value of physical therapy treatment which, in the words of Phelps (1958, p. 251), "is physical education of the motor apparatus of control of the body to carry out activities which are learned automatically by the normal child."

The role of the physical therapist in teaching mobility and muscle coordination is frequently supplemented by the occupational therapist in teaching activities of daily living, with particular emphasis on the upper extremities and on the use of special techniques or devices as required by the handicapping condition. Cruickshank (1976), in speaking of young cerebral palsy patients, has said, "No other single group of children demands the services of so many different professionals in the habilitation process." There is uniform agreement on the desirability, if not the absolute necessity, of the interdisciplinary team in the treatment of cerebral palsy. In addition to the motor dysfunction already described, the team directs its attention to the problems of speech, hearing, vision, intellectual deficits, emotional adjustment, and seizure activity which are commonly associated with cerebral palsy.

Speech

Ingram and Barn (1961) review reports of four series of cerebral-palsied children in which 30% to 70% were considered to have significant speech disorders. Many of these are motor problems due to lack of control of the speech structures. Slow, labored, and imprecise tongue and lip movements may result in problems of articulation (dysarthria). Difficulty with the swallow reflex or breath control may cause problems of phonation, such as broken or high-pitched speech. Speech problems may also be due simply to delay in motor development. Less common in cerebral palsy are language problems, such as aphasia, which are due to brain damage and result in difficulty in word-finding or in inability to comprehend the meaning of words. Language problems may also be caused by delayed intellectual development. Finally, speech and language problems in cerebral palsy may be related to the inability to hear.

Hearing

Nober (1976) reports that estimates of hearing loss in cerebral palsy range from 6% to 41%. He attributes the range to varying criteria for determining loss and to the fact that athetoid persons have the highest incidence of loss, so that estimates will vary with the percentage of athetoids in the cerebral palsy group being studied. Common problems include high-frequency hearing loss and auditory agnosia. The latter may also be called receptive aphasia and is a condition in which word sounds are heard but have no associated meaning. Holt and Reynell (1967) point out that children with cerebral palsy develop otitis media as easily as other children and through this disease may develop acquired deafness. Cerebral-palsied persons who have otherwise normal auditory acuity may have difficulty in localizing sounds due to inability to stabilize the head or to hold it in an upright position.

Vision

It has been estimated (Holt & Reynell, 1967; Keats, 1965) that 50% of the cerebral-palsied persons have defects of vision. Of these defects, strabismus is by far the most common. This is usually internal strabismus (one or both eyes turned inward) and is most frequently seen in persons with spastic diplegia or spastic quadriplegia. Problems of impaired visual acuity are the next most common. These are generally assumed to be in the central nervous system (cortical) rather than in the eye (ocular) and may include defects of visual imagery or inability to perceive a three-dimensional field. Nystagmus (rhythmic involuntary eye movements) is also fairly common. Difficulties in head stabilization and orientation which cause hearing problems pose similar vision difficulties, in that the eyes do not have a stable position from which to perceive the surroundings.

Intelligence

Estimates of intelligence and mental retardation in the cerebral palsied have varied widely with the populations studied and the measures of intelligence used. This is a matter that is controversial and sensitive in this population, which is so easily labeled "stupid" on the basis of superficial characteristics of appearance, speech, and gait. It is clear that the range of intelligence for the cerebral palsied is the same as that for the population at large, and there are numerous cerebral-palsied persons with very superior intelligence. The author is reminded of friends whose labored and difficult speech rewards those with the wit to listen with prize insights and droll humor. He has described this elsewhere (Lindemann, 1972).

After reviewing many studies, Cruickshank (1976) concluded that 50% of cerebral-palsied persons fall below IQ 70 (mental retardation) and 50% fall in normal and superior classifications. He also observed that there is no essential difference in the measurable intelligence of the spastic and athetoid, contrary to earlier belief. See the latter sections of this chapter for further discussion of intelligence and emotional adjustment.

Seizures

Denhoff (1976) reports that between 35% and 60% of the cerebral palsied have seizures at some period during their life and that the incidence is 3 times higher among the spastic than among the athetoid.

Seizures may be major (grand mal or Jacksonian) or minor (petit mal). Onset may be at any time during the developmental process, and it is not uncommon for seizures to continue for a number of years and then disappear spontaneously. For further discussion of characteristics, problems, and procedures associated with seizures, see Chapter 6.

COMMON PSYCHOLOGICAL CHARACTERISTICS AND PROBLEMS

The concepts of the *whole person,* of the inseparability of the physical and the psychological, or body and mind, are truisms which nowhere are better illustrated than in cerebral palsy; nowhere is it more necessary to have an appreciation of the developmental process as experienced by the individual. The motor, sensory, or perceptual problems of the newborn infant may not be immediately manifest and may await notice of delayed motor development such as difficulty in raising the head, rolling over, or reaching for objects. Nevertheless, the very early losses in quality of perception, with limitation in exploring and manipulating the environment, already begin to delay and distort the experiences which are necessary for cognitive development and cumulatively result in limitations in experience and perspective which pose great burdens to the development of a sense of competence, personal worth, and social acceptance.

Family

Unlike the families of those with traumatic injury (see Chapter 8), the parents of the cerebral-palsied child are likely to have a somewhat more gradual introduction to the fact of disability and its permanence. Nevertheless, they are likely to experience analogous shock and depression during what Kessler (1977) has described as the diagnostic period. Parks (1977) has described the same period of adaptation in terms of changes in the way in which the parents originally thought of their expected child. They cannot make an honest attachment to their real child until they have withdrawn their affection from the normal, wished-for child. Parks sees the process as relating to the wished-for child, relating to the handicap of the real child and, finally, relating to the person, the actuality of the real child.

The dynamics of the interaction between parent and child have seemingly contradictory characteristics that appear to reflect affection, withdrawal, sense of duty, and ambivalence on the part of the parents.

On the one hand, Keith and Markie (1969) report that parents as a group overestimate the abilities of their children as compared with the estimates of professionals. On the other hand, Kogan, Tyler, and Turner (1974), in a study of the mothers of young cerebral-palsied children observed a gradual reduction in expressions of affection and acceptance, particularly in mothers whose children were not walking by the end of the three-year study. Their suggestions were surprisingly convergent: Kogan *et al.*, that health workers put more emphasis on the child's gain than on the disability in working with families; and Keith and Markie, that it might be judicious not to make great efforts to influence parents to concur with the professionals, but to permit some divergence and a degree of optimism.

The overprotectiveness of many families of the cerebral palsied is legendary (Cruickshank, 1976). Although more frequently mentioned in reports from clinical observation than in those from a more structured data base, these reports appear with a regularity that is convincing. Kessler (1977) points out that conservative overprotection is often the easiest and safest approach to care. She observes that children will regard their disability much as their parents do. If they are seen as helpless, they are apt to respond with passivity. In a study of adult cerebral-palsied persons, Minde (1978) observes life outcomes which appear to be an extension of this; those with psychiatric problems came from disturbed families at one of the extremes, insisting that their child was either completely normal or forever crippled.

Differences of perception between family and professionals regarding ability level may have some basis in reality, since families have extended opportunities to see the patient in action and can observe the unique insights or circumscribed but impressive abilities of which the patient may be capable. "If he can memorize the batting average of every player in the American League, he ought to be able to do some kind of job." "What do you mean, limited social insight and skill? She knows every one of her relatives like a book and is a past master at getting her way." When these admittedly valid family observations are combined with deep compassion, denial, or guilt about rejection, the result may be a formidable barrier to observations or suggestions that lead to conclusions or goals at variance with those of the family.

It is characteristic of developmental delay or deficit that it causes differences that become more apparent with age. To oversimplify: If the characteristic (e.g., motor ability, intellectual capacity) is developing at a rate 50% of normal, then the child will differ from his peers by one year at age two, two years at age four, and so on. Although children cannot be expected to develop at a precisely fixed proportionate rate, nevertheless it is likely that differences will become more noticeable (and functionally more significant) as they grow older. When the six-month-old does not roll over, it is a matter of concern. When the five-year-old does not climb stairs, it starts to become a significant life problem.

The multiple handicaps of the cerebral palsied tend to contribute to each other. There may be intellectual delay, which is compounded by a hearing problem, which interferes with development of language skills. Lack of mobility may interfere with early opportunities for socialization, and delayed social maturation may later be compounded by a speech (communication) problem. Needless to say, the impact of each deficit will be related to its severity but may also be influenced by its interaction with other deficit areas.

Intellectual and Emotional Functioning

As the child approaches school age, his general intellectual development, as well as the possibility of specific cognitive deficits, will become a matter of concern. These difficulties, plus the severity of any sensory or motor problems, will be considered in a choice of school settings: Regular school? Special school for those with motor handicaps? Special school for those with sensory handicaps? For the multiply handicapped? For those with normal intelligence? Educable level of retardation? Trainable level of retardation? If the child is fortunate, at least this range of choices will be available. The absence of choices in the past has meant that many normal or intellectually superior cerebral-palsied persons with severe motor and/or speech involvements have spent years learning (too often without success) to make a social adaptation to a setting for the mentally retarded, or to a restricted, homebound existence. These circumstances undoubtedly contributed to the conditions that caused Allen and Jefferson (1962) to observe, "From a behavioral point of view 70 per cent conduct themselves as if they were intellectually retarded."

As reported previously, approximately 50% of cerebral-palsied persons fall within the range of intellectual retardation. A discussion of some of the psychological, social, and educational problems associated with general mental retardation will be found in Chapter 8. There are some specific cognitive deficits associated with cerebral palsy which should be discussed here. On tests of intelligence, most cerebral-palsied persons will score better on measures of verbal ability than on measures of performance ability. This may reflect a purely motor deficit with resultant difficulty in physically manipulating the materials. It may also reflect a deficit in visual-motor coordination. Cruickshank, Bice, Wallen, and Lynch (1965) quote the child who says "Why can't I make my hand do what my eyes see?" The problems in developing adequate handwriting are evident. Lowered scores on intelligence scales may also reflect a deficit in perception, in the ability to perceive three dimensions, or to organize percepts. These may translate into a specific learning disability, with resultant problems in learning to read and spell. Difficulty in integration may be found in relation to the organization of abstract concepts as well as in the organization of sensory percepts.

Allen and Jefferson (1962) observe a shortened concentration span in many cerebral-palsied persons. The quality of slowness is also characteristic. This may, again, be simply slower motor function, but also frequently reflects a general slowness in tempo and may include increased time needed for conceptual processing. A related characteristic of cerebral-palsied persons is difficulty in carrying out two functions (e.g., walking and talking) at the same time. This may reflect a problem in coordination or the intensity of concentration needed to make the limbs carry out a single function, such as walking, in an acceptable fashion. Keats (1965) describes this in another way, saying that attention must shift from what the person wants to say to how to control the muscles to say it. In any event, if the clinician is walking down the hall with a cerebral-palsied patient and asks him a question, he must not be surprised if the patient stops walking to deliver the answer.

Minear (1956) describes "emotional release," usually seen in athetosis but also seen in other cerebral-palsied persons. In this, a very slight stimulus to laugh or cry will result in that emotional expression with an inappropriate intensity and duration. The person will usually be intellectually aware of the inappropriateness of the display, dislike it, and be unable to control it. A related characteristic is the exaggerated startle reflex to be found in many cerebral-palsied persons. A sudden, unexpected noise or movement will result in an exaggerated motor response, crying out, or the emotional release previously described. Flechsig (1978) refers to the discomfiture of this in her brief but illuminating autobiographical account of living with cerebral palsy.

Speech

We have noted that as many as 50% of the cerebral-palsied population have speech problems. These warrant special mention as psychological characteristics or problems because of the profound effect they may have on communication and social adjustment. The labored, broken speech, with grimacing and problems of intonation, contributes probably more than any other secondary factor to the misperception and erroneous labeling of cerebral-palsied persons as "dumb" or "strange." This stereotyping feeds back into the person's self-image and may cause him to devalue himself or to become socially withdrawn and uncomfortable. Impaired speech may also have extra vocational significance. The person whose verbal intellectual skills clearly exceed his motor skills may find his aspiration to be a radio announcer or even a store clerk to be seriously impeded, if not negated, by his reduced effectiveness in communication, or (even harder to take) by the image which it projects.

Self-Concept

Minde (1978) observed in the adolescents he studied that between the ages of 10 and 14 they developed an increased realization that their handicap was permanent and that there was little hope for improvement. This resulted in lowered self-esteem and passivity. Minde's observation carried in it the interesting implication that, until adolescence, his subjects nurtured the expectation, or at least the hope, that somehow their disability would diminish. It is in the delicately balanced area of the relationships among actual ability, appraisal of performance, and hope for the future that most of the grave psychological and social problems of cerebral palsy lie. Parents and teachers have the wisdom to know that some hope is necessary for survival and that the disabled person must see some positive reflection of the abilities he does have. In too many cases, however, parents and teachers lack the skills and ability to give feedback, as well as the resources to organize the environment so that the person is led to a gradual accommodation between the way he perceives himself and what is possible. Let us hasten to acknowledge the enormous difficulty of that task under any circumstances. It is sometimes made impossible by the fact that our society has failed to accommodate these extreme individual differences by organizing job and educational experiences that utilize partial or single abilities in the absence of all-around competence.

In giving feedback, the performance of the cerebral-palsied person may be dismissed or criticized. More commonly, it is overvalued through extravagant praise or by inaccurately comparing it favorably with other standards and allowing the person to believe that he is competitive when he is not. The tragedy of this tactic is that it may reduce the person's aspiration to the highest level of excellence of which he is capable.

The attempt to associate a particular personality type with cerebral palsy has been as fruitless as that attempt in relation to other physical disabilities (Allen & Jefferson, 1962; Linde & Patterson, 1958). There is agreement about the presence of increased maladjustment, including anxiety, withdrawal, and poor self-concept. In contrasting groups with different observable disabilities, Richman and Harper (1978) conclude that the presence of disability is more important than the type of disability, with regard to its effect on adjustment.

The National Significance Project (Orr-Kissner, 1978) reports that one of the most frequently mentioned areas of concern to disabled young adults is identity and that sorting out "who I am" from "who I am expected to be" is especially difficult. The powerful social stereotypes associated with disability are seen as a great (and, by implication, negative) influence on this process. Nigro (1976) observed in cerebral-palsied adolescents and young adults a lack of skills for relating with peers because of a tendency to relate to and rely on authorities. She linked the problem to what she called the maturation stage of the parents, in which the parents of the handicapped remain at the parent–infant stage and are unable to let go of their children. She concluded that most of the subjects of her study could not have sexual relationships because they did not know how to form social relationships. Minde (1978) observed that fewer than 10% of those who had a nonhandicapped friend were labeled psychiatrically deviant, while almost 50% of those who did not have a nonhandicapped friend were so labeled.

Social and Work Adjustment

Underachievement, especially in employment, is also characteristic of cerebral-palsied persons. While the contribution of emotional maladjustment to vocational maladjustment is well documented, there are a number of findings which suggest caution in applying this interpretation too freely to the cerebral-palsied population. In a study of 50 intellectually normal cerebral-palsied adults in New South Wales, Australia, Andrews *et al.* (1977) found that social adjustment and work adjustment scores were independent of mental health scores. In contrast, they found that social and work adjustment were directly related to degree of disability. In a similar vein, Cohen and Kohn (1979), studying 209 cerebral-palsied adults, concluded that high level of intelligence and low severity of disability were directly related to degree of independent functioning. It appears that, for now, the effects of intellectual and motor impairment overpower the influence of emotional maladjustment. It is probable that the effects of emotional maladjustment will become more apparent as there are developed more work settings and social opportunities which accommodate the other impairments.

In a follow-up of 48 young adult cerebral-palsied students from a state residential school for the handicapped, Magyar et al. (1977) found that 26 remained students and 13 were employed. Of those employed, nine earned $1,000/year or less, and none earned more than $4,000/year. In their follow-up of intellectually normal cerebral-palsied persons, the National Significance Project (Orr-Kissner, 1978) found that 14% were in competitive employment. Of these, 27% were dissatisfied, half of them saying the work was not challenging. The National Significance Project found an additional 12% employed in workshops and 5% in training or other settings. Of the group they studied, 91% did not have a driver's license and/or liability insurance. Fifty-eight percent were not able to use public transportation systems. Studying Oregon cerebral-palsied persons in the community, Keiter (1979) found 9% competitively employed, 47% in workshops, and 11% in work activity centers. He also found that employment decreased with age. The rather grim prospect for employment among the cerebral palsied as a group should not be allowed to obscure the achievements of numerous cerebral-palsied individuals, who have held positions such as judge, business executive, college professor, and Emperor of the Holy Roman Empire. In few disabilities is the range of differences so great.

EVALUATING PERSONS WITH CEREBRAL PALSY

Interview

The rewards of interviewing a person with cerebral palsy are closely associated with the problems in doing so. One is frequently dealing with a relatively isolated person who communicates (and is understood) with difficulty and who does not often have the experience of talking at length with a patient listener. When a relationship is established, the pleasure evidenced at this opportunity to share confidence may be as gratifying to the interviewer as the imparted information is useful.

Patience is required. The pace is often slow, both in verbal and motor expression. Scheduling for interview and testing should take this into account, and sometimes more than one session should be planned, in order to avoid wearing out the examiner as well as the patient.

A 30% to 70% incidence (Ingram & Barn, 1961) of speech disturbance has already been mentioned. While there are many variations in phonation and articulation, the suh-air-uh-buh-rul puh-al-sie-ed patient often speaks like thee-is, with syllables broken, unevenly spaced, and dragged out. Listening takes time and resistance to the temptation to interrupt and can be improved with practice. I find it useful to say fairly early on that I cannot always understand the patient the first time and that, from a desire to understand him, I will not do the socially acceptable thing and fake comprehension, but rather will ask the patient to repeat and will work with him until communication is clear. This is usually appreciated.

More often than not, the cerebral-palsied person will be accompanied when he comes for his appointment (a reflection of problems of mobility and/or protectiveness). It is helpful, at the beginning, to establish the contract with both the patient and companion with a brief statement of the reason for the appointment, procedures to be carried out and time duration anticipated. If appropriate, it may be useful to explain deliberately in the presence of the patient and significant others the concerns or problems which may have prompted the evaluation. This may be a matter of some delicacy, especially for families in which handicaps and their attendant concerns are not discussed openly. Minde (1978) found that 60% of the families he studied did not discuss the handicap in front of the child. A sensitively conducted public airing may be of great value in promoting communication in such families.

If the patient is a child or otherwise dependent person, it may be necessary to obtain information from parents or others, taking care, as Keats (1965) points out, not to talk "around, about or above the head of the child." Information may be obtained through interview or through more formal assessment methods, as described under "Psychological Testing."

The content of the interview will vary, of course, with its purpose, be it mental health, educational–vocational or some other evaluative end. Note should be made of the tendency of cerebral-palsied persons to reflect the standards to which they have been exposed. Thus, if the family interpretation is that their "special" class is "regular," they will report it as such. If their skill and interest in radio repair have been deprecated, they will also reflect that. Care must be taken to get detail, for example, name and content of courses and behavioral description of activities, and not to accept without scrutiny generalizations and global evaluations. As with most interviews, the progression should generally be from more objective and factual material to the more sensitive aspects such as perception of self and others, hurts, fears, and aspirations. Some degree of anxiety and mild depression is common, often in relation to social isolation. Where significant depression becomes apparent, it should be probed, with attention to possible suicidal thinking as described in Chapter 1. Personality characteristics and psychopathology may also be explored through psychological testing, as described in the following section.

Psychological Testing

Standardized Administration and Norms. Psychological testing with the cerebral-palsied brings into bold relief the question of using tests and norms with a population which may systematically differ from that which was the original focus of the test development. Allen and Jefferson (1962, p. 9) meet this head-on when they say, "The sentimental view that the handicapped should be assessed with tests standardized with this segment of the population is untenable and unrealistic." Keats (1965, p. 189), more diplomatically but no less clearly, says "It is important to use with any child a test that was prepared for the general run of children. The goal of the parent is to promote the child's development so that he will be as much like the nonhandicapped as he can become." Despite their position, Allen and Jefferson continue with an extended discussion of ways to modify test administration, select feasible items, and interpret appropriately. They go on to suggest (Allen & Jefferson, 1962, p. 69–70) the use of an extended battery of tests because the purpose "is not to arrive at a series of IQs but to reveal the spread of intellectual capability as it expresses itself in the client's handling of different types of test materials." Though Cruickshank, Hallahan, and Bice (1976, p. 122) object to the "total use" of any single intelligence test, they go on to say, "Quantitative results of intelligence evaluations are helpful if done accurately, but are at best limited in their usefulness with cerebral-palsied children and youth; qualitative assessments which bridge psychology and education are significant and can lead to realistic educational planning for these handicapped persons." Magrab (1976) stresses planning as the primary objective of psychological evaluation, rather than prediction. Recognizing the value of early intervention and that motor development is the most readily observed and easily recorded of all spheres, Johnston and Magrab (1976, p. 49) warn that "motor delay in and of itself is a poor predictor of future intelligence and should bear little weight in overall judgments in this regard." Holt and Reynell (1967) recommend repeated assessments as the child develops and suggest that the examiner modify most tests and then not use numerical scoring.

Through the rhetoric comes general agreement that the cerebral-palsied individual should be exposed to standardized test materials, that items should be chosen and/or modified for their appropriateness when motor, sensory, or speech deficits are present, and that the results should be evaluated against a backdrop of standard norms. Everyone advocates the sensible precautions, which should be applied in using tests with anyone, of not overgeneralizing the interpretation of a single score nor of assuming that its applicability will remain constant over long periods of time in the life of the patient. No author has been found to advocate precisely standardized administration and literal application of norms. The principal reason for using standardized materials as a reference point appears to lie in the inadequacy of alternate approaches. A statement by Holt and Reynell (1967, p. 140–141) may be related to this:

> It is unwise to draw conclusions about "brain damage" on the basis of psychological testing alone; it can be equally unwise to draw conclusions about "intelligence" on the basis of conversation and unstandardized "tests" carried out during the course of a clinical examination.

The same objection could be made to drawing conclusions about intelligence from subjective observations in home or classroom.

Reports. Examiners should be aware that the precaution against overgeneralizing their findings can be too zealously applied. Test reports can be too atomistic. The author is familiar with reports that appear to be an endless listing of items on which the subject has been successful or unsuccessful, with no attempt at generalization. "He is able to add 15 and 6, but not 11 and 13"; "She knew 26 out of a list of 37 words." Such reports, besides being tedious, are of little utility. The clinician is usually in a better position than the report reader to venture some judgment about comparative strengths and the kinds of activities to which findings might be related in making plans for the near future of the patient.

Examiners should also be cautioned to take seriously the need to measure a number of kinds of skills. The common practice of using only verbal tests with the cerebral palsied fails: (1) to take into account the fact that all cerebral-palsied patients, even with serious motor involvement, do not necessarily have perceptual deficits, (2) to provide a qualitative analysis of such perceptual deficits as may exist, particularly as they may relate to learning (e.g., reading, writing) problems, and (3) to assess skills in organizing percepts, which may not be measured by verbal subtests.

The general goal of a psychological test evaluation is to sample a number of intellectual skills (e.g., verbal, numerical, spatial, motor, memory, organization) and, through interview, behavioral observation, adaptive behavior ratings, or other means, to obtain measures of the patient's current functioning in social, educational, and vocational spheres, as well as activities of daily living. The latter are examined to see if the basic skills, which the patient has now, are being used effectively. Where the patient is not functioning up to the level of his potential as suggested by his basic skills, presumably there will be suggestions as to how this may be accomplished. In any event, a report should contain suggestions about the application and development of these skills in the near future of the patient.

A number of points should be added to the qualitative analysis and interpretation which is part of every competent test evaluation. Lapses in responsivity may reflect problems of vision, hearing, or speech fluency. They may also reflect petit mal seizures which are not infrequent among the cerebral-palsied. The examiner should be particularly alert for those interruptions which seem to appear arbitrarily, particularly if they leave the subject in a state of mild disorientation. The examiner should also be alert to differentiate speech problems which reflect motor difficulty or general delay in speech development from those which reflect an aphasic inability to associate word and meaning. Similarly, the examiner should attempt to differentiate the peripheral motor problem of focusing vision on something while trying to manipulate it from the central problem of coordinating visual perception with motor response. The latter may be reflected in more serious problems of reading and writing.

Tests of Ability and Development. In the very young child one ordinarily wishes to assess the ability to move and coordinate, to communicate, to understand, and to make himself understood. For the child under two years of age the Denver Developmental Screening Test (Frankenburg, Dodds, & Fandal, 1970) or the Bayley Scales of Mental and Motor Development (Bayley, 1969) may be used, in conjunction with interview and observation.

From age two to four the Boyd Developmental Progress Scale (Boyd, 1974) will be suitable. *Prediction* of intellectual functioning at this age is precarious, if not impossible. One may use items from the Revised Stanford–Binet (Terman & Merrill, 1960), but calculation of an intelligence quotient is discouraged. It is useful, however, to compare performance on items which are specifically affected by deficits due to cerebral palsy, in contrast to performance on items not so affected. Although many of these items require vision, hearing, speech, or hand use, many do not and can be adapted.

The Wechsler Intelligence Scale for Children–Revised (Wechsler, 1974) may be used beginning at age eight (if the patient is near average in general intellectual development) and the Wechsler Adult Intelligence Scale (Wechsler, 1955) at 16. These scales require various combinations of the abilities to see, hear, speak, and manipulate materials, but some lend themselves to modification and, as Cruickshank, Hallahan, and Bice (1976) point out, a large percentage of cerebral-palsied persons can see, hear, or speak well enough, and have at least one good hand, so that little modification is necessary. On occasion, one may wish to supplement these measures with tests such as the Illinois Test of Psycholinguistic Abilities (Kirk & McCarthy, 1961), Columbia Mental Maturity (Burgemeister, Blum, & Lorge, 1972), Raven's Progressive Matrices (Raven, 1960), or Peabody Picture Vocabulary Test (Dunn, 1959). Parts of the Vineland Social Maturity Scale (Doll, 1965) may be used in obtaining information about areas of personal function, although some of the items appear to be outdated, and calculation of an actual social age or quotient is discouraged. The AAMD Adaptive Behavior Scale for Children and Adults (American Association on Mental Deficiency, 1974) is useful for assessing a wide range of living skills, especially if there are limitations due to physical or intellectual deficits. It requires the participation of a person who is familiar with the daily activities of the patient.

Logistics. As suggested previously, the examiner will find that his cerebral-palsied patient speaks with difficulty and is slow in his motor activity. This should be anticipated in scheduling, so that ample time is allowed (perhaps more than one session). If the patient is in a wheelchair, it will be useful to have a table the lower edge of which is three to four inches higher than standard. In general, it is good to have a variety of furnishings available: tables and chairs of different sizes and heights. Testing on the floor can be fun when you get into the spirit of it.

As a general principle, it is useful to allow the subject a bit of time to adjust to test surroundings and the examiner. When the subject is hyperactive or distractible, however, it is best to proceed as soon as possible, to minimize the emergence of distracting stimuli from the environment, and make the best use of available concentration time.

Adaptation to test tasks is limited only by the ingenuity of the examiner and the cooperation of the subject. Communication may be effected through careful enunciation by the patient and careful listening by the examiner. Many tests will allow the patient to point to the answer (noses as well as limbs can be used for pointing). The academically and motorically skilled subject may write his answers. Where speech and motor ability are severely limited, a code system may be set up. "Blink once for 'yes,' twice for 'no.' " Language boards may be used.

If hearing is impaired, but the person can see and read with comprehension, material may be presented in written form. Conversely, most verbal tests can be presented entirely through oral presentation, without the requirement of vision. Hearing alone is sufficient for all of the verbal subtests of the Wechsler scales, and all but Arithmetic and Digit Span can be administered through vision (with reading comprehension) alone. For further discussion of methods for evaluating persons with hearing and vision disorders, see Chapters 13 and 14. Vision is required for all of the performance subtests of the Wechsler scales, and arm–hand use for most of them. Some adaptation is possible on the performance scales: Picture arrangement cards may be aligned at the verbal direction of the subject; the subject may point to the area of the missing part in Picture Completion; and specified sides of blocks may be turned up at the direction of the subject (who has hand but not finger use). Allen and Jefferson (1962) have classified the 142 items of Form L of the Revised Stanford–Binet (Terman & Merrill, 1960). They find that 22 of them must have arm–hand use and that 16 others ordinarily require it, but are adaptable.

Flexibility and adaptiveness in test administration and interpretation should not be mistaken for laxness and certainly not for lessened rigor in the preparation of the examiner. On the contrary, this kind of evaluation calls for the skills of the fully trained psychologist. A solid knowledge of the meaning of standardized test administration, application of norms, and limits of interpretation is necessary so that the examiner knows what he is doing when he adapts and compares and can demonstrate this appropriately in his interpretation.

Tests of Personality and Interest. Emphasis has been placed upon ability testing because it is the area of greatest difficulty with the cerebral-palsied. Many of the adaptations, for example, vision to hearing and the reverse, may be applied in personality or interest testing. When the patient is unable to mark the answer sheet of a paper and pencil test, it may be possible to utilize a tape recorder or to have a second person mark the sheet. This is best done by a neutral person, not a family member, who, in the presence of the patient, has been instructed to avoid influencing responses by verbal or nonverbal comment.

Most of the personality and interest tests are applicable, with the same limitations which apply to their use with any population. The examiner may wish to suggest to the patient that he do take into account his physical disability in responding to the interest test, contrary to the usual instruction. Because of the close ties which frequently exist between cerebral-palsied persons and family, as described earlier in this chapter, it is usually desirable to obtain information which reflects that interaction, as well as that which pertains to the patient alone. Taylor (1970) studied the moderator-variable effects on the MMPI profiles of physically disabled patients, finding that physical description items did cause spurious profile elevations. He has listed those items which were affected in the spinal-cord injured population which he studied. The examiner may wish to inspect items on MMPI scales which may have been influenced by the specific physical dysfunctions of his cerebral-palsied patient.

INTERVENTION METHODS

The Family

Psychological intervention with the family of a cerebral-palsied child should begin when there is suspicion that, indeed, this diagnosis will be the appropriate one to describe the observed malfunction or delayed development. Kessler (1977) has suggested that the pediatrician should: (1) indicate a positive interest in the child's development; (2) identify needs for treatment; and (3) reinforce the parents' attitude regarding their capability in providing care. This advice to physicians is especially appropriate because they are apt to be the first health professionals involved. In clarifying the diagnosis and carrying treatment forward, the child (and adult) will more likely and more appropriately receive the services of a treatment team which may include physicians of a number of specialties, physical and occupational therapists, speech and hearing specialists, psychologist, educator, social worker, vocational rehabilitation counselor, and others. As each provides a specialized service, each will have the opportunity to provide psychological and social support to patient and family. Individual members of the team from any discipline may be chosen, during a given period of time, to be a special source of advice, supportive counseling, or merely empathic listening, for the patient or family. At times this role may be supplemented with the diagnostic or therapeutic expertise of the psychologist or other mental health specialist. Kogan, Tyler, and Turner (1974) have stated the importance of emphasizing the child's gains rather than the disabilities, and Keith and Markie (1969) point to the necessity for parents to maintain a degree of optimism. Contact with other parents who have experienced success in helping their cerebral-palsied child may be useful. This is also a time when a great deal of information, chosen judiciously, presented clearly, and repeated as often as required is of maximum efficacy. Cerebral palsy involves difficult concepts (e.g., neuromuscular coordination) and complex interaction (e.g., interplay between speech, social, and intellectual development).

Realistic Expectations, Self-Appraisal, Self-Concept

The difficulty in maintaining a balance in appraisal of ability, response to the patient, and expectations and hope for the future has been mentioned. Parents and teachers frequently need help in setting realistic expectations for child or adult. This may be the case even when the capacity to perform a task may be obvious to the professional. There is the nonprofessional's fear of being unfair because of lack of awareness of some subtle deficit, or sometimes simple inability to be so "tough" as to demand that the cerebral-palsied child dress himself, make his own bed, read as many chapters as the rest of the class, or study algebra. Frequently, the reassurance of the professional is a necessary impetus so that demands are set which will stimulate, rather than delay, growth. Parents and teachers need to know that disciplinary methods are as necessary for the cerebral palsied as for any other child. These children are not born with a capacity to learn limits any more readily than others. On the contrary, they suffer the blunting effects of patronizing sympathy in learning what is expected of them in the world and how they measure up to ordinary standards.

In the author's experience, results have been best with families who were good-humoredly realistic in talking to and about their cerebral-palsied member and were slightly demanding in their expectation of what he should do for himself in everyday activities. An error in expecting slightly too much has seemed to work better than an error in the direction of too much protection. Reflecting a similar sentiment, the adults followed up by Minde (1978) reported (approvingly) that regular schools had "babied" them less than special schools. It seems apparent that unsophisticated benevolence is no favor to the cerebral palsied.

Parents of the cerebral palsied often need encouragement and support in broadening the experiences to which their child is exposed. One of the earliest examples is encouragement to leave the child with a competent baby sitter, thus to learn to relate to others besides mother and father. A bit later, staying with relatives is a further expansion, to be followed still later by staying at the house of a friend. Enrollment in nursery school and kindergarten should be encouraged if at all feasible. School attendance is vastly superior to home teaching, academically as well as socially. When there is a choice between regular facilities and special facilities for the handicapped, regular facilities should be chosen if there is a reasonable possibility that the person will be able to function competently in that setting. Sometimes that can be done with only minor modifications (e.g., of architectural barriers or schedule) or a small amount of additional support (e.g., special physical education or occasional supportive counseling). The goal is to challenge the cerebral-palsied person to stretch his capacities a bit, not to do the impossible. Mainstreaming should not be "sink or swim," and Public Law 94–142 does provide for the least restrictive environment in which the individual can achieve *optimal* functioning.

Similar considerations for degree of challenge should be given to the choice of a summer camp—regular camp if possible, but definitely a special camp for the handicapped in preference to none. Meacham and Lindemann (1975) have described a summer program for underachieving handicapped adolescents at the Oregon Crippled Children's Division. The emphasis was on group cohesiveness and functioning directed toward a productive goal in order to develop skills in relating to peers and a sense of personal competence. An interaction (therapy) group was used to help in consolidating these gains through verbalizing feelings and conflicts regarding participation in the program.

Identity and Competence

Many cerebral-palsied adolescents and adults can profit from help in working through their feelings about identifying with the handicapped. Those persons seem to do best who can move back and forth between social interaction with the handicapped and with the general population. Individual or group counseling may help in resolving feelings and developing skills which facilitate this adaptability. The cerebral-palsied person who avoids identification and contact with handicapped persons may do so realistically but is more likely to be repressing feelings the resolution of which would leave him with greater inner comfort and assurance. The National Significance Project (Orr-Kissner, 1978) also suggests that assertiveness training be provided.

In attempting to help adolescent and young adult cerebral-palsied people to establish sexual relationships, Nigro (1976) suggested, first, the need for improved ability to establish meaningful personal relationships which might then become sexual. Her further suggestions were: (1) improve the attitudes of professionals and the public (e.g., that sexual expression is a birthright), (2) provide knowledge about sexuality, and (3) promote opportunities for sexual experiences. With regard to the latter, it should be obvious that one's opportunities are quite restricted if one never goes anywhere without Aunt Emma. In a similar vein, Kessler (1977) points out that boredom may provoke misbehavior among cerebral-palsied youth and that life should have some novelty.

In addition to expanding experiences such as at school or camp, the families of the cerebral palsied frequently need encouragement to foster skills such as dressing oneself, doing household and garden chores, simple cooking, eating in a restaurant, and going about town alone. While the rather direct relationship between these skills and later employability may seem obvious, this is not always so to the cerebral-palsied person or his family. I have encountered parents who brought their mildly cerebral-palsied, moderately mentally retarded 18-year-old son for consultation and said, "We brought him to see about getting a job." Within a few minutes, one of these parents said (in giving some background information), "Of course, he never goes out of the house without one of us." These sincere and conscientious people had literally not seen a connection between their overprotectiveness and their son's vocational potential.

The development of skills within the capability of the handicapped person is extremely important to the achievement of relationships with parents, teachers, and others; it is in these relationships that he develops standards of self-appraisal that are compatible with those which he will meet in the community. If the person develops a sense of competence in some areas and if there are achievements with which others can be genuinely impressed, then it becomes possible to be honestly critical in other areas where the person has limitations of which he should be aware. Positive feedback should praise accomplishments for themselves without overrating them in relation to external criteria. The matter of feedback is discussed further in Chapter 1.

Employment and Vocational Counseling

The underemployment of cerebral-palsied persons has been documented under "Common Psychological Characteristics and Problems," with Keiter's (1979) finding of 9% competitively employed and the National Significance Project's finding of 14% (Orr-Kissner, 1978). It should be pointed out that the 14% figure refers to non-mentally-retarded cerebral-palsied persons. That report goes on to observe that a lack of support services deprives many of this group of their chance to attain their full potential "even though drastic improvements could be effected by small investments in transportation, educational aids, and attendant care." The authors note that procedures necessarily designed for the large proportion of the developmentally disabled population have led to restraints on the options of the nonretarded segment of that group. This could be amplified with the suggestion that workshops should provide not only work which is sheltered in terms of simplicity and flexible production demand, but complex and difficult work which is divided and organized so that it requires only limited kinds of intellectual, motor, or sensory ability, albeit at a high skill level. Given the large numbers of unemployed and seriously involved cerebral-palsied persons, it would appear desirable, also, that there be a greater number of modified employment settings that can provide semipermanent employment to skilled handicapped workers, instead of merely transitory jobs.

In helping to set employment goals for cerebral-palsied persons, I found it useful to consider some minimum criteria for competitive employment. These are presented in Chapter 1, Table III.

In providing vocational evaluation and career counseling to handicapped persons, I found it useful to allow evaluative data and occupational information to speak for themselves. This procedure, advisable for most people, is especially suited to the cerebral-palsied person and his family, who are reluctantly and painfully adjusting goals to realities. When ability testing is available, a chart or graph is presented on which the results of the various tests are displayed in the context of the general population; noting the fallibility of tests. Academic achievement scores are often available in terms of grade level and, again, should be presented with a word about fallibility. Client and family are encouraged to read the requirements for various occupations as presented in sources such as the United States Department of Labor's Occupational Outlook Handbook (1978). Plans are discussed in terms of probability of achievement, and rarely is anything labeled impossible. I have scars of experience from too frontal an attack on the goals of cerebral-palsied persons and their families, no matter how unrealistic the goal or how objectively reasonable my presentation. Needless to say, it is virtually impossible to modify such significant self-concepts without first having established a relationship which demonstrates sensitivity to the feelings and aspirations of the person.

Behavior Modification

It is not the purpose here to describe the intervention methods of the physical therapist, occupational therapist, or speech pathologist, although they regularly make significant contributions to the psychological and social well-being of the patient. It is appropriate, however, to give examples of some of the contributions which can be made to their procedures by the psychologist or other persons who may be trained in the application of behavior modification principles.

Ball, Combs, Rugh, and Neptune (1977) describe a simple joint switch which can be adjusted for extension or flexion and which will reinforce a desired action by activating a radio to play music for a certain period of time. They note its usefulness for range of motion exercises which may be dull and repetitious but are often needed by young patients and will not be effective if postponed.

Sacks, Martin, and Fitch (1972) describe the use of visual feedback in improving the fine finger movement of an 11-year-old deaf athetoid child. This was done by reducing the latency of the finger response.

They raise the interesting hypothesis that there may have been afferent (sensory input) dysfunction as well as efferent (motor output) dysfunction and consider that perhaps their greatest contribution was to provide the patient with better sensory feedback about what the fingers were doing, rather than reinforcing the motor function *per se*.

Harrison (1977) suggests augmented feedback to highlight natural (intrinsic) movement signals so that they can be distinguished from the abundance of other sensory impulses. She goes on to caution, however, that teaching a cerebral-palsied person to produce more normal movement sequences may be antithetical to making him more skillful, as the fastest, most economical and skillful way for him to perform a task may involve highly idiosyncratic patterns of movement.

Block (1978) tells the interesting story of a young man who wished to be able to read for more than 15 minutes at a time without tiring and either to write with a pencil or listen and typewrite simultaneously. The object of these skills was to complete the college training necessary to become a counselor. He achieved these skills through the application of biofeedback methods to fixation and tracking in reading and elemental finger, hand, and arm movements in writing. In this instance, the approach also included more traditional teaching and counseling.

Martin (1976) has compiled an extensive review of the use of behavior modification in lower extremity functioning, upper extremity functioning, head control, drooling, and control of irrelevant movements. These methods are useful and promising. They should not be approached lightly, however, for they require theoretical and procedural expertise in a number of areas, as well as the innovative use of relatively sophisticated equipment.

From earlier studies, Cruickshank, Bice, Wallen, and Lynch (1965) made a number of practical recommendations for teaching cerebral-palsied children. Their framework was studies in perception and they suggested: (1) more time exposure for better perception; (2) large materials; (3) color presentations to increase the stimulus value of the thing to which attention is desired; and (4) three-dimensional objects as a transition to seeing things (e.g., pictures) in two dimensions.

Using yet another theoretical approach, Lazar (1977) notes that purposeless athetoid movements tend to increase when voluntary movements are attempted and to disappear during relaxation. He believes that even a light hypnotic trance is sufficient to reduce athetosis and increase function, and he reports a case in which this end was achieved with a 12-year-old boy. He also describes the use of imagery (e.g., to imagine watching television) in subjects who are resistant to relaxation and hypnosis.

TRENDS AND NEEDS

As with every major disease, the ultimate goal is prevention of cerebral palsy rather than cure. To that end, there is continuing research (United Cerebral Palsy Research and Education Foundation, 1978) to prevent premature delivery of babies (e.g., study of the control of gestation by the chemical agent relaxin) and in the treatment of the prematurely born (e.g., minicomputers to monitor and control oxygen and carbon dioxide levels).

Under current evaluation is the neurosurgical implantation of a chronic cerebellar stimulation device. Cooper, Amin, Upton, Riklan, Watkins, and McLellan (1977–78) report that 68% of their patients so treated show improvement through reduction of spasticity or cumulative long-term improvement in athetosis. They report greatest success with younger (e.g., 18-years-old), more intelligent patients and go on to describe psychological gains in alertness, concentration, and reduced depression, anger, and aggression.

Behavior modification applications to date have been concentrated on improving motor function. Little attention has been given to their use in teaching activities of daily living, such as eating, dressing, and the performance of simple chores, or in teaching recreational skills. Such applications would be especially appropriate in conjunction with the development of additional resources for independent living and for employment. Much could be accomplished in the normalization of the lives of the cerebral palsied by the provision of settings in which the demands (e.g., job skills) and the support services (e.g., occasional attendant service) could be precisely tailored to the requirements of the individual and in which specialized training programs could be made available to develop those skills which might be attainable by the individual. Particularly needed are long-term work settings for cerebral-palsied persons capable of higher-level vocational functioning.

APPENDIX: SOURCES OF INFORMATION

General:
United Cerebral Palsy
Research and Educational Foundation, Inc.
66 E. 34th Street
New York, NY 10016
(212) 481–6347

The National Easter Seal Society
for Crippled Children and Adults
2023 W. Ogden Ave.
Chicago, IL 60612

Information for the patient and his family: *The Sourcebook for the Disabled*, G. Hale (Ed.). New York: Paddington Press, 1979.

Information for the professional: *Cerebral Palsy: A Developmental Disability*, W. M. Cruickshank (Ed.). Syracuse University Press, 1976.

Assessment of Cerebral Palsy (2 vols.), K. S. Holt and J. K. Reynell. London: Lloyd-Luke, 1965–1967.

REFERENCES

Allen, R. M., & Jefferson, T. W. *Psychological evaluation of the cerebral palsied person.* Springfield, Ill.: Charles C Thomas, 1962.

American Association on Mental Deficiency. *AAMD adaptive behavior scale for children and adults.* Washington, D.C.: American Association on Mental Deficiency, 1974.

Andrews, G., Platt, L. J., Quinn, P. T., & Nelson, P. D. An assessment of the status of adults with cerebral palsy. *Developmental Medicine and Child Neurology*, 1977, *19* (6), 803–810.

Ball, T. S., Combs, T., Rugh, J., & Neptune, R. Automated range of motion training with two cerebral palsied retarded young men. *Mental Retardation*, 1977, *15* (4), 47–50.

Bayley, N. *Bayley scales of infant development.* New York: The Psychological Corporation, 1969.

Block, J. D. Teaching reading and writing skills to a teen-aged spastic cerebral palsied person: A long-term case study. *Perceptual and Motor Skills*, 1978, *46*, 31–41.

Boyd, R. D. *Boyd developmental progress scale.* San Bernardino, Calif.: Inland Counties Regional Center, 1974.

Burgemeister, B. B., Blum, L. H., & Lorge, I. *Columbia mental maturity scale.* New York: Harcourt Brace Jovanovich, 1972.

Cohen, P., & Kohn, J. G. Follow-up study of patients with cerebral palsy. *Western Journal of Medicine*, 1979, *130*, 6–11.

Cooper, I. S., Amin, I., Upton, A., Riklan, M., Watkins, S., & McLellan, L. Safety and efficacy of chronic cerebellar stimulation. *Applied Neurophysiology*, 1977–78, *40*, 124–134.

Cruickshank, W. M. (Ed.), *Cerebral palsy: A developmental disability.* Syracuse, N.Y.: Syracuse University Press, 1976.

Cruickshank, W. M., Bice, H. V., Wallen, N. E., & Lynch, K. S. *Perception and cerebral palsy.* Syracuse, N.Y.: Syracuse University Press, 1965.

Cruickshank, W. M., Hallahan, D. P., & Bice, H. V. The evaluation of intelligence. In W. M. Cruickshank (Ed.), *Cerebral palsy: A developmental disability.* Syracuse, N.Y.: Syracuse University Press, 1976.

Denhoff, E. Medical aspects. In W. M. Cruickshank (Ed.), *Cerebral palsy: A developmental disability.* Syracuse, N.Y.: Syracuse University Press, 1976.

Doll, E. A. *Vineland social maturity scale.* Circle Pines, Minn.: American Guidance Service, 1965.
Dunn, L. M. *Peabody picture vocabulary test.* Circle Pines, Minn.: American Guidance Service, 1959.
Flechsig, L. Living with cerebral palsy. *American Journal of Nursing,* 1978, *78*(7), 1212–1213.
Frankenburg, W. K., Dodds, J. B., & Fandal, A. W. *Denver developmental screening test.* Denver: University of Colorado Medical Center, 1970.
Harrison. A. Augmented feedback training of motor control in cerebral palsy. *Developmental Medicine and Child Neurology,* 1978, *19*(1), 75–78.
Holt, K. S., & Reynell, J. K. *Assessment of cerebral palsy. II. Vision, hearing, speech, language, communication and psychological function.* London: Lloyd-Luke, 1967.
Ingram, T. T. S., & Barn, J. A description and classification of common speech disorders associated with cerebral palsy. *Cerebral Palsy Bulletin,* 1961, *3*, (1), 57–69.
Johnston, R. B. Motor function: Normal development and cerebral palsy. In R. B. Johnston and P. R. Magrab, *Developmental disorders: Assessment, treatment, education.* Baltimore: University Park Press, 1976.
Keats, S. *Cerebral palsy.* Springfield, Ill.: Charles C Thomas, 1965.
Keiter, J. B. *Characteristics of the AADD population.* Presented at the annual meeting of the American Academy on Mental Retardation. Miami, 1979.
Keith, R. A., & Markie, G. S. Parental and professional assessment of functioning in cerebral palsy. *Developmental Medicine and Child Neurology,* 1969, *11*, 735–742.
Kessler, J. W. Parenting the handicapped child. *Pediatric Annals,* 1977, *6*, 654–661.
Kirk, S. A., & McCarthy, J. J. *Illinois test of psycholinguistic abilities.* Urbana: Institute for Research on Exceptional Children, 1961.
Kogan, K., Tyler, N., & Turner, P. The process of interpersonal adaptation between mothers and their cerebral palsied children. *Developmental Medicine and Child Neurology,* 1974, *16*, 518–527.
Lazar, B. S. Hypnotic imagery as a tool in working with a cerebral palsied child. *International Journal of Clinical and Experimental Hypnosis,* 1977, *XXV*(2), 78–87.
Linde, T., & Patterson, C. H. The MMPI in cerebral palsy. *Journal of Consulting Psychology,* 1958, *22*(3), 210–212.
Lindemann, J. E. The beauty inside. *Portlander,* 1972, *4* (4). (Publication of Junior League of Portland, Oregon.)
Little, W. T. On the influence of abnormal parturition, difficult labors, premature birth and *asphyxia neonatorum. Transactions Obstetrical Society,* (London) 1862, *3*, 293–344.
Magrab, P. R. Psychology. In R. B. Johnston & P. R. Magrab, *Developmental disorders: Assessment, treatment, education.* Baltimore: University Park Press, 1976.
Magyar, C. W., Nystrom, J. B., & Johansen, N. A follow-up of former cerebral palsied students at a school for neuro-orthopedically disabled children. *Rehabilitation Literature,* 1977, *38*, (2), 40–42.
Martin, J. A. Behavior modification and cerebral palsy. *Journal of Pediatric Psychology,* 1976, *1* (3), 48–50.
Meacham, R., & Lindemann, J. E. A summer program for underachieving adolescents. *American Journal of Occupational Therapy,* (AJOT) 1975, *29*(5), 280–283.
Minde, K. K. Coping styles of 34 adolescents with cerebral palsy. *American Journal of Psychiatry,* 1978, *135* (11), 1344–49.
Minear, W. L. A classification of cerebral palsy. *Pediatrics,* 1956, *18*, 841–852.
Nelson, K. B., & Ellenberg, J. H. Epidemiology of cerebral palsy. In B. S. Schoenberg, *Advances in Neurology.* New York: Raven Press, 1978.

Nigro, Giovanna. Some observations on personal relationships and sexual relationships among lifelong disabled Americans. *Rehabilitation Literature,* 1976, *37,* 328–330, 334.

Nober, E. H. Auditory processing. In W. M. Cruickshank (Ed.), *Cerebral palsy: A developmental disability.* Syracuse, N.Y.: Syracuse University Press, 1976.

Orr-Kissner, C. (Project Director). *National Significance Project: Developmentally Disabled Individuals of Normal Intelligence.* United Cerebral Palsy Association of California, 1978.

Parks, R. M. Parental reactions to the birth of a handicapped child. *Health and Social Work,* 1977, *2* (3) 51–66.

Phelps, W. M. The role of physical therapy in cerebral palsy. In R. S. Illingworth (Ed.), *Recent Advances in Cerebral Palsy.* Boston: Little Brown, 1958.

Raven, J. C. *Standard progressive matrices.* London: H. K. Lewis, 1960.

Richman, L., & Harper, D. School adjustment of children with observable disabilities. *Journal of Abnormal Child Psychology,* 1978, *6*(1), 11–18.

Sachs, D. A., Martin, J. E., & Fitch, J. L. The effect of visual feedback on a digital exercise in a functionally deaf cerebral palsied child. *Journal of Behavior Therapy and Experimental Psychiatry,* 1972, *3,* 217–222.

Sternfeld, L. Medical Director, United Cerebral Palsy Research and Educational Foundation, New York. Personal communication, August 29, 1979.

Taylor, G. P. Moderator-variable effects on personality-test item endorsements of physically disabled patients. *Journal of Consulting and Clinical Psychology,* 1970, *35,* 183–188.

Terman, L. M., & Merrill, M. A. *Stanford-Binet intelligence scale—Form LM.* Boston: Houghton Mifflin, 1960.

United States Department of Labor. *Occupational outlook handbook.* Washington: U.S. Government Printing Office, 1978.

United Cerebral Palsy Research and Educational Foundation, Inc. "The time has come . . ." Annual Report, 1978.

Wechsler, D. *Wechsler adult intelligence scale.* New York: The Psychological Corp., 1955.

Wechsler, D. *Wechsler intelligence scale for children—Revised.* New York: The Psychological Corp., 1974.

Wolf, J. M. *The results of treatment in cerebral palsy.* Springfield, Ill.: Thomas, 1969.

6

Epilepsy

LEIF G. TERDAL

John Smith, a successful 24-year-old sales representative for an electrical firm, was invited by his boss for a day of salmon fishing off the Oregon coast. He stayed at a motel adjacent to the marina, and awoke at 4:00 A.M. They planned to leave the dock at 5:00 A.M.. Mr. Smith realized that he had forgotten to bring along his medication. He had been taking Dilantin regularly to control his grand mal epilepsy. He was sleepy from the early morning hour, but rising early was especially difficult because the Dilantin made him a little drowsy. He had set the alarm early to give himself a little extra time to be alert and ready. But no medication! A fishing trip with his boss! He couldn't believe the predicament. What should he do? Should he risk a day—with less sleep than normal—without Dilantin? Should he somehow get lost and miss the boat? Should he feign illness and as politely as possible excuse himself from the trip? Should he make some effort to obtain Dilantin? In all, the grand mal seizures experienced by Mr. Smith, if added together, would equal less than 20 minutes. But the predicaments brought on by seizures or anticipation of them would have added considerable stress.

John Smith chose not to go fishing without taking Dilantin. There was a small hospital with a 24-hour emergency facility only a quarter mile from the harbor. He went to it at 4:00 that morning, explained his situation, and was promptly given a day's supply. He was profoundly thankful when the nurse said, "I'd rather give you Dilantin now than have you risk an unnecessary seizure." He returned to the marina in time to go on his fishing trip. John had learned to manage his epilepsy.

The preparation of this chapter was supported in part by the Bureau of Community Health Services, Maternal and Child Health Services Project 920.

The purpose of this chapter is to provide an overview of epilepsy with an emphasis on its impact on the individual and family and with some recommendations for assessment and intervention.

THE PHYSICAL DISABILITY

The term *epilepsy* comes from a Greek word for seizure. Seizures are the result of an abnormal cortical discharge which may be caused by a variety of stimuli. The seizure is characterized by some abrupt altered control over motor, sensory, or autonomic functions of the body, and it may involve loss of consciousness or altered state of consciousness. A seizure is not synonymous with epilepsy. Epilepsy describes disorders in which the source of the seizure is within the brain itself; if the source of the seizure is external to the brain, as, for example, a convulsion related to low blood sugar or to the taking of a drug, the disorder is not identified as epilepsy.

The nature of the symptoms depends upon (1) the area of the brain in which the abnormal electrical discharges occur, (2) the relative number of brain cells involved, (3) the duration of the abnormal discharges, and (4) the age of the individual (the pattern of seizures and susceptibility to seizures change during developmental stages).

Classification of Epileptic Seizures

Most authorities recommend the International Classification of Epileptic Seizures, which groups seizures according to the area of the brain involved. The system does not incorporate etiology into the diagnosis but focuses on characteristics of the seizure disorder and manifestations of EEG recordings, that is, generalized or partial. The main classifications are partial (part of the brain involved) and generalized (involving the entire brain). Table I outlines the International Classification System.

The most common forms of generalized seizures are petit mal and tonic–clonic. Also included among generalized seizures are myoclonic, akinetic, and infantile spasms.

Absences (Petit Mal). Petit mal is one of the generalized seizures. It is a generalized seizure in that the EEG recordings show a three-per-second spike–wave pattern over all the brain recordings. To an observer, petit mal may appear as a little seizure. Behavior that may indicate petit mal includes staring spells, lack of response, dropping things without apparent reason, a cessation of motor activity, or a sudden loss of muscle

TABLE I
International Classification of Epileptic Seizures[a]

I. Partial Seizures (seizures beginning locally):
   A. Partial seizures with elementary symptomatology (generally with impairment of consciousness):
       1. With motor symptoms (includes Jacksonian seizures)
       2. With special sensory or somatosensory symptoms
       3. With autonomic symptoms
       4. Compound forms
   B. Partial seizures with complex symptomatology (generally with impairment of consciousness) (temporal lobe or psychomotor seizures):
       1. With impairment of consciousness only
       2. With cognitive symptomatology
       3. With affective symptomatology
       4. With "psychosensory" symptomatology
       5. With "psychomotor" symptomatology (automatisms)
       6. Compound forms
   C. Partial seizures secondarily generalized

II. Generalized seizures (bilaterally symmetric and without local onset):
       1. Absences (petit mal)
       2. Bilateral massive epileptic myoclonus
       3. Infantile spasms
       4. Clonic seizures
       5. Tonic seizures
       6. Tonic-clonic seizures (grand mal)
       7. Atonic seizures
       8. Akinetic seizures

III. Unilateral seizures (or predominantly)

IV. Unclassified epileptic seizures (due to incomplete data)

[a] Abstracted from Gastaut, 1970.

tone. Petit mal is thus characterized by brief absences (blank spells) without falling. Consciousness and mental and physical functions may return immediately. Petit mal is more common in children than adults; seizures may occur as often as 100 times a day. Petit mal seizures are often first suspected by school teachers or school nurses.

Tonic-Clonic Seizures (Grand Mal). Like petit mal, grand mal is one of the generalized seizures and involves the entire brain. An aura may precede a grand mal seizure. Sudden loss of consciousness, falling to the ground, momentary interruption of breathing, and jerking movements of the whole body all characterize a grand mal seizure. The person may bite his tongue and may lose bladder and bowel control. The person may be drowsy, weak, and confused for some time after a seizure. A grand mal seizure may last two or three minutes.

Myoclonic Seizures. Myoclonic seizures generally are very brief and involve a sudden massive jerk of the entire body which may throw the subject to the ground.

Akinetic Seizures. Akinetic seizures occur more commonly in children than in adults. They are characterized by falling to the ground with loss of mobility but retention of muscle tone. There is either loss or clouding of consciousness.

Infantile Spasms. Infantile spasms occur usually in the first year of life and are characterized by frequent tonic contractions of brief duration. Infantile spasms signal very serious problems. Approximately 20% of infants die within a few months of the first seizure, and of those who survive only 10% achieve normal intellectual functioning.

Dancing Eyes Syndrome. A rare form of generalized seizure is the "dancing eyes syndrome," described by Ford (1966). The dancing eyes syndrome is characterized by irregular flickering and jerking of the eyelids, ataxia, and extreme irritability. The onset is generally acute and the course, though nonprogressive, is protracted.

Jacksonian Epilepsy. Jacksonian seizures (one of the partial seizures) usually start in one part of the body and spread gradually to other parts of the body. The seizures may start in part of a limb, for example, a thumb or toe, or they may start in the mouth or tongue. The individual may lose consciousness if, as the seizure activity spreads, it crosses the midline. A Jacksonian seizure may proceed to a grand mal seizure.

Complex Partial Seizures (Formerly Called Psychomotor Seizures). A psychomotor seizure is one of the partial seizures and is generally caused by disturbances in the temporal lobe of the brain. The individual may show patterned movements (automatisms), such as turning of the head or eyes, smacking lips, walking aimlessly, rubbing hands, unbuttoning clothes, or other such patterns. Psychomotor seizures may be brief but could last for many minutes. They can lead to a generalized seizure. The person may not lose consciousness, but awareness may be affected in a number of ways. For example, the individual may feel that he/she is in unfamiliar surroundings when the surroundings are familiar, or the individual may have a feeling that he/she is in a familiar setting when that is not the case. The individual may experience and describe vivid illusions or hallucinations or may be confused. Generally, after a partial seizure the individual will not recall events that occurred during the seizure.

Status Epilepticus. Status epilepticus describes recurrent severe seizures which occur with little or no interval between them. This represents a severe medical emergency because the individual may become exhausted and hyperthermic and die.

Differential Diagnosis. A number of behavioral patterns may be mistaken for seizures. Among children, day-dreaming may be confused with an episode of petit mal seizures; breath-holding attacks and tantrums are sometimes confused with epilepsy. Among adults, hysteria may be confused with epilepsy.

Febrile Convulsions. Febrile convulsions or convulsions associated with fever occur among approximately 2% of children. Reports vary as to how many of those children eventually develop epilepsy, with Millichap (1968) reporting that as many as 20% later develop epilepsy, while the Commission for the Control of Epilepsy and its Consequences (1978) reports that approximately 4% of the children who have febrile convulsions later develop epilepsy.

Prevalence

An estimated 1% of the population of the United States, or just over two million individuals, have epilepsy (Millon, 1969). Most keep seizures under control through the use of medications. Approximately 200,000 Americans have uncontrolled seizures. The Commission for the Control of Epilepsy and its Consequences (1978) reports that approximately 80,000 Americans with epilepsy live in institutions.

Goodglass, Folson, Morgan, and Quadfasel (1963) studied the distribution of kinds of epilepsy among adults. Almost three quarters of those with epilepsy (69%) had grand mal seizures only, 12% had grand mal and partial seizures, 5% had grand mal and petit mal, 7% had psychomotor seizures, and 7% had minor and focal seizures. Other studies differ somewhat, but there is general agreement that grand mal is the most common and makes up about half or more of cases of epilepsy.

In a major study, Rutter, Graham, and Yule (1970) investigated the distribution of seizures among children. Of children with seizures, 51% had grand mal seizures only; 17% had grand mal and other combinations including partial; 9% had grand mal and petit mal; 3% had petit mal only, and 20% had minor motor attacks.

Approximately 75% of those with epilepsy have the first seizure before age 20. Developmental periods in which onset is most likely to occur are between the ages of 4 to 7 and during puberty (Debakan, 1959). The distribution of epilepsy is approximately the same for males as for females (Millon, 1969). The age of onset relates to the presence and severity of other handicapping conditions.

Etiology

Epilepsy is not a specific disease but a symptom complex. The causes are varied and include the broad range of diseases or accidents that can cause damage to the brain. Brain injury may occur during pregnancy. Mothers at risk to produce a child with epilepsy include pregnant teenagers, mothers addicted to drugs (including alcohol), and mothers who have complicating conditions such as diabetes, hypertension, or epilepsy.

Diseases such as meningitis and viral encephalitis sometimes result in epilepsy. Common illnesses such as mumps and measles less frequently but occasionally have been implicated in the precipitation of epilepsy. Toxic agents, including lead, can cause epilepsy.

Severe alcoholism can cause epilepsy. In cases of chronic alcoholism, brain damage may occur which may result in epilepsy. In individuals who use alcohol continuously, a sudden increase in or withdrawal from alcohol may precipitate seizures. The use of alcohol is common in our society and its use among those with epilepsy presents some specific problems. It is known that alcohol and anticonvulsant medication do interact in such a way that the effects of alcohol are potentiated, and also that alcohol tends to lower the threshold for seizures. Because of this, it is advised that individuals with seizure disorders abstain from alcohol or drink only in moderation and that they be fully apprised of the effects of alcohol.

Head trauma is a major cause of epilepsy. However, of individuals who suffer head injuries, only a small proportion later develop epilepsy. These statements are in apparent contradiction. The relationship between head trauma and epilepsy is appreciated only when viewed from the perspective of the absolute number of head injuries that occur. The number of head injuries is very high. In the United States, some 46,000 people are killed in highway accidents each year. Of the nearly 2,000,000 who are seriously injured, 540,000 suffer head injuries. It is not known how many of those later develop epilepsy. However, population studies that specifically seek to identify the incidence of seizures after head injury, and the factors that predict risk, provide a framework.

Annegers *et al.* (1980) studied 2,747 cases of individuals who received medical services between the years of 1935 and 1974 because of head injuries. The cases were divided according to severity of injury into categories of mild, moderate, and severe head injury. The categories included the following definitions:

1. *Mild* (1,640 cases): no skull fracture, but either unconsciousness or post-traumatic amnesia for not more than 30 minutes
2. *Moderate* (912 cases): skull fracture or head injuries with more than one–half but less than 24 hours of either unconsciousness or post-traumatic amnesia
3. *Severe* (195 cases): head injury with one or more of the following: brain contusion, intracranial hematoma, or 24 hours or more of either unconsciousness or post-traumatic amnesia.

Of the 195 cases of severe head injury, 23, or 11.6%, later developed epilepsy. Of the 912 cases suffering moderate head injury, 16, or 1.6%, later developed epilepsy. Of the 1,640 cases suffering mild head injury (but still requiring medical care for the head injury), 12, or 0.6%, later developed epilepsy. The incidence of epilepsy among the group who suffered mild head injury was not more than the expected rate of new epilepsy cases in the general population.

The study by Annegers *et al.* shows that risk for developing epilepsy is directly related to the severity of the head injury. The problem is compounded in cases with severe head injuries by the possibility of impairment in cognitive functioning, behavioral disturbances, and other neurological dysfunctions.

Studies of soldiers who suffered head injuries also show a relationship between severity of head injury and the later development of seizures. Cases of gunshot wounds with penetration of the skull resulted in incidence of epilepsy as high as 43% among British soldiers wounded in World War II (Russell & Whitty, 1952). Closed head injuries less often resulted in the onset of seizure disorders.

Considering the absolute number of head injuries that occur, this represents an area where prevention can be undertaken, for instance, much more stringent control of alcohol abuse (and driving while intoxicated), further safety design improvements in automobiles, increased use of safety belts, enforcement of speed limits, and mandatory helmet use for motorcyclists.

Current Treatment Procedures

The first seizure in a previously healthy individual brings on a crisis. A physician is called, or the individual may be brought to an emergency room. The seizure itself may be brief and self-limiting in duration. It may mark, however, the beginning of a chronic condition that may require lifelong management and ongoing monitoring and which may have implications for personal and social adjustment. If the condition is diagnosed as epilepsy, a very detailed and comprehensive medical assessment is required. Effective management and treatment require that any underlying neurological disease be identified and treated. Epilepsy may be associated with clearly identified organic causes, such as preexisting brain injury, presence of a systemic or brain disease such as meningitis, the presence of a metabolic disorder or brain tumor. Epilepsy may occur without an identifiable organic reason. In these cases the epilepsy is considered idiopathic. An accurate description of the seizure facilitates diagnosis by the International Classification of Epilepsy and may assist in determining the presence of an organic as opposed to an idiopathic basis to the epilepsy. The following characteristics suggest a neurological disease or impairment: seizures preceded by an aura; seizures starting in one area of the body and carrying or shifting to other parts of the body; seizures that do not begin with loss of consciousness; and a pattern of progressive worsening of seizures. But a description of the seizure and a diagnosis by the International Classification of Epilepsy is just the beginning of the diagnostic process.

The Commission for the Control of Epilepsy and its Consequences in 1978 recommended standards of medical care to be followed for services provided to individuals with epilepsy. Table II provides a summary of their recommendations in outline form. A more complete report is available from the U.S. Department of Health, Education and Welfare.

The exhaustive and detailed diagnostic service recommended as a minimal standard of care for individuals with epilepsy is suggested for a number of reasons.

First, early control of some seizures (caused by trauma) provides the best chance that the individual will eventually obtain seizure control.

Second, while a few uncomplicated seizures may not cause permanent harm, an individual with uncontrolled epilepsy runs a risk of status epilepticus, which, as we stated above, constitutes a major medical emergency. Studies indicate that as many as 10% of the deaths of individuals with epilepsy occur because of an attack of status epilepticus. About 8,000 persons are hospitalized with status epilepticus each year in the United States. An episode of status epilepticus is more likely to occur in individuals not receiving treatment for epilepsy or in individuals who are not taking the medication as prescribed.

Third, comprehensive evaluation and early treatment of epilepsy may minimize the compounding of psychological problems with the medical problems associated with epilepsy and also make the treatment of the psychological problems easier.

Fourth, early and comprehensive neurological evaluation offers the opportunity to detect potentially treatable medical conditions associated with epilepsy.

Patient Management Through Anticonvulsant Medication. Developments in the area of anticonvulsant medication have brought about substantial control of seizures for the majority of individuals with epilepsy. In instances in which the patient follows the prescribed medication plan, seizures are completely controlled in about 50% of cases. Sufficient control occurs in another 30% of cases to permit the individual to live virtually a normal life. Approximately 12%–15% of individuals with epilepsy do not respond to anticonvulsant medication.

Rapport and effective communication are required between the physician and client to insure good treatment results. Intelligent cooperation is likely to follow if the physician takes time over a number of sessions to explain the client's individual condition and the need for prolonged care and continued monitoring.

The administration of a proven anticonvulsant drug to a patient new to the drug requires individual experimentation and careful evaluation. Aird and Woodbury (1974) recommend that in each case the administration of an anticonvulsant medication be started in small doses (below the level at which it is assumed to be effective) and that the physician monitor the patient to assess possible sensitivity to the drug. As the patient shows tolerance for the drug, the physician may increase the dosage level to the point of the usual therapeutic dose level. Monitoring again is required for assessing the effectiveness of the drug and detecting severity and type of side effects.

The selection (and dosage level) of the anticonvulsant drug is generally made on the basis of the type of epilepsy, as well as patient characteristics, such as age and size. Sudden discontinuance of an anticonvulsant medication should always be avoided. Monitoring of plasma levels can assist the physician in ascertaining whether the patient is taking the drug in the amount prescribed.

Special Problems. Aird and Woodbury stress that special care and monitoring must be employed in the management of anticonvulsant medication in children. Dosage levels might need adjustment to match changes in the physical growth and maturation of the child. In addition, as a child matures there may be changes in susceptibility to seizures and changes in the form of the seizures. These two factors sometimes require a change in dose levels or a change in medication. A review of anti–epileptic therapy in childhood is provided by Davison (1970) and Livingston (1972).

A continuing problem in the management of epileptic patients is

TABLE II
Medical Services—Minimum Standards of Care[a]

Minimum standards of medical care must be adhered to for services available to any person—whether residing in an institution or in other parts of the community. These standards are outlined as follows:

I. Initial medical evaluation
   A. To determine the cause and nature of the epileptic process
       1. Medical history
       2. Accurate subjective and objective description of seizures
       3. Developmental history
       4. Family history
       5. Physical and neurological examination
       6. Diagnostic tests
          a. Biochemical, hematological, and serological studies
             (1) Complete blood count
             (2) Urinalysis
             (3) Serum calcium and phosphorus
             (4) Studies to exclude tuberculosis and syphilis
             (5) Fasting blood sugar
          b. Electrophysiological studies
             (1) Electroencephalogram (EEG)
          c. Radiological studies
             (1) Computed tomogram of brain
             (2) Angiogram or pneumoencephalogram (if indicated)
   B. The following additional studies may be required in selected cases:
       1. Five-hour glucose tolerance test for atypical seizures
       2. Chromosome studies for congenital malformations
       3. Amino acid screen for metabolic disorders
       4. Spinal fluid examination for infection of nervous system
       5. Special EEF activation procedures
          a. Sleep deprived
          b. Telemetered
          c. Chemical activation
   C. Application of international seizure classification
   D. Data base entry of medical problems not directly related to epileptic process

II. To achieve control of seizures
   A. Reliable and accurate record of seizure frequency
   B. Charting of anticonvulsant drug consumption
   C. Periodic anticonvulsant drug levels
   D. Case review
       1. For incompletely controlled patients
          a. Weekly by technical specialist
          b. Monthly by medical specialist
       2. For patients having less than one seizure per month (for patients in community-based living arrangements, periodic review by a physician no fewer than two times per year)

a. Monthly by technical specialist
   b. Quarterly by medical specialist

III. To protect against medical emergency
   A. Appropriate observation by trained attendant or companion
   B. Institution of ongoing and detailed training for families, associates, attendants, or health professionals responsible for the care of patients with epilepsy
   C. Health professional availability on an emergency 24-hour basis
   D. Access to emergency hospital-type care within a time considered reasonable by the standards of care of the community. For persons in institutions, or subject to severe, prolonged or recurrent seizures, such care should be accessible within 20 minutes.

IV. Referral for special study
   Persons with atypical or "focal onset" seizures, or having evidence of underlying neurological disease, or with uncontrolled seizures (more than one per month) should be referred for special evaluation, preferably to a center specializing in epilepsy for special services as follows:
   A. Twenty-four hour video and EEG monitoring
   B. Angiography
   C. Supervised inpatient drug control
   D. Special consideration for surgical intervention

[a] From *Plan For Nationwide Action on Epilepsy*, Vol. 1. U.S. Department of Health, Education, and Welfare: Public Health Service, National Institutes of Health, 1978, DHEW Publication No. (NIH) 78–276.

that the neurologist may not have observed the seizure directly and must rely on a description from a parent, spouse, or teacher. If details are missed or go unreported or are not picked up by other assessment procedures, a less than optimal treatment plan may be instituted. An example would be the treatment of a seizure disorder with and without the knowledge that an aura precedes the main seizure disorder. A patient may describe an aura that precedes the more generalized seizure. The aura itself (which the patient interprets as a warning) may be experienced as distortion of vision, a sudden unprecipitated emotion or reaction, a sensation like cold or heat, or a stomach pain. The aura is currently viewed by neurologists as part of the seizure itself. It is viewed as a partial seizure, and it is thought that the spread of the partial seizure progresses to whatever form of seizure, for example, generalized tonic-clonic or complex partial seizure (psychomotor seizure), is viewed by the client as the chief complaint or main seizure. In such cases, control of the entire seizure complex may be managed by an anticonvulsant medication that is effective in preventing the partial seizure (Cereghino, 1980). Treatment of the main seizure directly without treating the initial seizure (the aura) may not be optimally effective.

Epilepsy and Pregnancy. The monitoring of pregnancy in women with epilepsy requires careful attention to certain risk factors. The anticonvulsant medications of trimethadione (Tridione), phenytoin (Dilantin), and phenobarbital have been associated with mental retardation, growth retardation and other abnormalities including cleft lip and palate (Smith, 1977). In newborns of mothers treated for epilepsy, anticonvulsant drugs may also alter folic acid metabolism during pregnancy, resulting in anemia (Matthews, 1970). Such drugs may also lead to blood coagulation defects in the newborn (Reynolds, 1975). Blood coagulation defects have been identified in a large proportion of newborns of epileptic mothers and are attributed to the effect of anticonvulsant drugs on the immature newborn liver. This problem is managed by administering vitamin K prior to delivery and to the neonate at the time of delivery.

The management of the pregnant woman with epilepsy is compounded by increased seizure susceptibility during pregnancy and possible damage to the newborn resulting from anoxia (should the mother experience prolonged seizures during pregnancy). The problems are minimized in cases in which there is adequate seizure control for at least nine months before pregnancy and in cases where it is possible to reduce, but not eliminate, the amount of anticonvulsant medication required to maintain therapeutic effectiveness.

Table III lists the major anticonvulsant medications and some of the side effects that may be encountered.

Brain Surgery as a Treatment Procedure for the Control of Epilepsy. Aird and Woodbury (1974) report that the percentage of epileptic patients suitable for neurosurgery is less than 2–3% of those with epilepsy. A major reason for this is that the results of neurosurgery (as treatment for epilepsy) seem to be highly dependent upon the complete removal of the epileptogenic lesion. Incomplete removal results in little benefit (Rasmussen, 1969). Since the pathology may involve substantial neuronal tissue, neurosurgery is often ruled out as an option. The very small percentage of cases for whom neurosurgery is a viable treatment choice includes cases in which a brain tumor is involved. Early detection and treatment minimizes risks.

Comprehensive Treatment of Patients with Epilepsy. The treatment of an individual with epilepsy requires considerably more than attention to the seizure disorder itself. Seizure control is important and warrants considerable attention, but other variables are also important. The type of seizures, the age of onset of seizures, the presence of other

TABLE III
Comprehensive List of Drugs Used in Epilepsy[a]

Drug	Indications	Toxicity and precautions
Phenytoin Sodium (Dilantin)	Safest drug for grand mal, some cases of psychomotor epilepsy. May accentuate petit mal.	Gum hypertrophy (dental hygiene); nervousness, rash, ataxia, drowsiness, nystagmus (reduce dosage).
Mephenytoin (Mesantoin)	Grand mal, some cases of psychomotor epilepsy. Effective when grand mal and petit mal coexist.	Nervousness, ataxia, nystagmus (reduce dosage); pancytopenia (frequent blood counts); exfoliative dermatitis (stop drug if severe skin eruption develops).
Ethotoin (Peganone)	Grand mal.	Dizziness, fatigue, skin rash (decrease dose or discontinue).
Trimethadione (Tridone)	Petit mal.	Bone marrow depression, pancytopenia (frequent blood counts); exfoliate dermatitis (as above); photophobia (usually disappears; dark glasses); nephrosis (frequent urinalysis; discontinue if renal lesion develops).
Paramethadione (Paradion)	Petit mal.	Toxic reactions said to be less than with trimethadione. Other remarks as for trimethadione.
Phenacemide (Phenurone)	Psychomotor epilepsy.	Hepatitis (liver function tests at onset; follow urinary urobilinogon at regular intervals); benign proteinuria (stop drug; may continue if patient is having marked relief); dermatitis (stop drug); headache and personality changes (stop drug if severe).

Continued

TABLE III (*Continued*)

Drug	Indications	Toxicity and precautions
Carbamazepine (Tegretol)	Psychomotor epilepsy, grand mal epilepsy.	Diplopia, transient blurred vision, drowsiness, ataxia; bone marrow depression (frequent blood counts).
Phenobarbital	One of the safest drugs for all epilepsies, especially as adjunct. May aggravate psychomotor seizures.	Toxic reactions are rare. Drowsiness (decrease dosage); dermatitis (stop drug and resume later; if dermatitis recurs, stop drug entirely).
Mephobarbital (Mebaral)	As for phenobarbital.	As for phenobarbital. Usually offers no advantage over phenobarbital and must be given in twice the dosage.
Metharbital (Gemonil)	Grand mal. Especially effective in seizures associated with organic brain damage and in infantile myoclonic epilepsy.	Drowsiness (decrease dosage).
Primidone (Mysoline)	Grand mal. Useful in conjunction with other drugs.	Drowsiness (decrease dosage); ataxia (decrease dosage or stop drug).
Phensuximide (Milontin)	Petit mal.	Nausea, ataxia, dizziness (reduce dosage or discontinue); hematuria (discontinue).
Methsuximide (Celontin)	Petit mal, psychomotor epilepsy.	Ataxia, drowsiness (decrease dosage or discontinue).
Ethosuximide (Zarontin)	Petit mal.	Drowsiness, nausea, vomiting (decrease dosage or discontinue).

Drug	Indications	Side Effects
Valproic acid (Depakene)	Petit mal, petit mal variant, myoclonic and akinetic seizures. Larger doses (up to 4 g daily in 3 divided doses) for generalized tonic–clonic and partial seizures.	Nausea and vomiting; drowsiness (decrease dosage or discontinue).
Acetazolamide (Diamox)	Grand mal, petit mal.	Drowsiness, paresthesias (reduce dosage).
Clonazepam (Clonopin)	Petit mal, petit mal variant, myoclonic and akinetic seizures.	Drowsiness, ataxia, agitation (decrease dosage or discontinue).
Chlordiazepoxide (Librium) Diazepam (Valium)	Mixed epilepsies. Useful in patients with behavior disorders; also in status epilepticus (by intravenous infusion of diazepam).	Drowsiness, ataxia, agitation (decrease dosage or discontinue).
Meprobamate (Equanil, Miltown)	Absence attacks, myoclonic seizures.	Drowsiness (decrease dosage or discontinue).
Dextroamphetamine sulfate (Dexedrine)	Absence and akinetic attacks. Counterattacks sleepiness. Useful in narcolepsy.	Anorexia, irritability, insomnia (decrease dosage or discontinue).
Methamphetamine (Desoxyn)		

[a] Reproduced with permission from J.G. Chusid, *Correlative Neuroanatomy and Functional Neurology* (17th ed.). Los Altos, Calif.: Lange, 1979.

physical disabilities, and the presence of psychological problems may have considerable impact on the adjustment of the individual. Ramifications may be felt in home, school, and vocational settings. Problems may impair or distort age-specific development and influence a person's ability to develop role-appropriate behavior. These issues are discussed below in the section on common psychological problems of individuals with epilepsy. The sections on assessment and management provide a framework for ongoing management.

COMMON PSYCHOLOGICAL CHARACTERISTICS AND PROBLEMS

It is difficult to speak of "common" problems associated with epilepsy because the disorder encompasses a heterogenous group of individuals. Of the estimated 2,135,000 Americans with active epilepsy, approximately 7% (or 150,000) have problems so severe that they either require institutional care or broad services covering many aspects of their daily lives. Certainly the needs of the more severely handicapped are vastly different from others with well controlled seizures and no other disabilities. Nevertheless, there are areas in which all those with epilepsy experience problems in common. Epilepsy for most individuals with the disorder represents an episodic disability, with the individual functioning normally almost all of the time with only an occasional occurrence of lack of control. However, seizures have shock value, and the general public does not understand epilepsy. People may experience and express horror and shock when they encounter an individual having a seizure and may attribute unfavorable traits to the individual. This is an example of the phenomenon which Wright (1960) has called *spread* and which is discussed in Chapter 1.

This section will address the issue of common problems in the context of five areas: (1) the initial impact of seizures, (2) problems associated with misunderstanding and/or rejection by family or peers, (3) epilepsy and predicaments, (4) problems in employment, and (5) problems associated with specific forms of epilepsy, for instance, impairments in intellectual and/or personality functioning.

Impact of Seizures

In a carefully conducted retrospective study employing in-depth clinical interviewing techniques, Ward and Bower (1973) interviewed 81 families of children with epilepsy. They sought to assess the impact of seizures themselves and the impact of the diagnosis of epilepsy on these families.

They report that the act of witnessing a seizure evoked fear in virtually all of the parents of children with epilepsy. Some parents reported that they thought the child had died or was dying during their first encounter with a seizure. Many reported heightened anxiety about the child's breathing difficulty during a seizure episode and fear that the child would suffer brain damage or might die. Parents reported concern about the child's losing consciousness and being out of contact, of being unable to be reached, or of being unresponsive. Parents of children with grand mal epilepsy reported feelings of horror and distress at the bodily contortions associated with grand mal seizures and of other aspects of the seizure, including, in some cases, strange noises made by the child, salivation, and unusual eye movements. Concerns about the child's injuring himself during the seizure were often expressed. Ward and Bower state that the onset of epilepsy produces a crisis requiring considerable time for the families to adjust to the diagnosis, to the requirements of medical care, and to the seizures themselves. They specifically probed in their interviews to determine the degree to which parents anticipated problems among the children with epilepsy. A summary of their findings and conclusions is presented below.

Misperceptions or Fears Associated with the Diagnosis of Epilepsy

Ward and Bower report that in their study one half of the parents of children with epilepsy associated some form of personality or behavior problems with epilepsy. They reported that often this was expressed by parents who viewed temper tantrums, acts of noncompliance, or instances of overactivity in a young child as being specifically caused by the epilepsy itself. Similarly, many of the parents in their study reported concern that discipline would evoke a seizure. Although behavior problems may be associated with some forms of epilepsy, Ward and Bower reported that the parents were not making those distinctions. Rather, in a general way, they viewed the child as impaired and assumed that the behavior problems were inescapably associated with epilepsy. Ward and Bower postulated that the tendency of some parents to lump together behavior problems with epilepsy greatly increased their anxiety about epilepsy and created special difficulties in their adjustment to the child with the disorder. Similarly, one may assume that a child's self-concept would be especially vulnerable if all misdeeds and all occasions of not measuring up were interpreted by those around the child as being attributed to the individual's "damaged brain."

Ward and Bower also reported on the perceptions of parents concerning intellectual impairment and epilepsy. Some parents whose children were of normal intelligence reported considerable anxiety that the child might be retarded or might show some signs of reduced school performance. They reflected this concern by interpreting minor lapses, such as one bad score on a test, as a sign of failure resulting from epilepsy. In instances where mental retardation was present, it was often interpreted by parents as simply confirmation of their worst fears about epilepsy.

Remschmidt (1973) studied the predisposition of individuals to view those with epilepsy in a stereotyped way. He administered a questionnaire of 55 personality traits to 300 individuals in West Germany to assess prejudices, stereotypes, or perceptions about individuals with epilepsy. Remschmidt found among his sample of 300 individuals that a number of unfavorable personality traits were indeed attributed to individuals with epilepsy. One half or more of the respondents viewed those with epilepsy as sensitive, irritable, suspicious, solitary, nervous, and moody. Approximately 30% to 40% viewed those with epilepsy as being explosive, dangerous, or aggressive. Most of those who filled out the questionnaires indicated that they knew of no one with epilepsy, but the traits attributed to those with epilepsy were more negative than were the participants' attributions of personality characteristics toward themselves and toward a medically ill comparison group. Furthermore, the negative attributions of traits to those with epilepsy were held independently of whatever kinds of epilepsy were described. The essential conclusion of Remschmidt's study is that many in the general public have unfortunate predispositions to view individuals with epilepsy in a stereotyped and negative way.

Epilepsy and Predicaments

One might assume that most individuals with epilepsy, an episodic disability, are able to function normally. But some people in the community may not understand epilepsy, may experience horror when they encounter an individual having a seizure, and may attribute unfavorable characteristics to the individual with epilepsy. Such reactions will embarrass the individual and family members and may put him in a situation where he fears exposure of his disability. If an individual has a history of occasional seizures that are under control, he may be tempted to withhold information about the diagnosis when applying for a driver's license or applying for a job. This places the individual at risk in the event that a seizure should occur.

In cases where seizures are severe and frequent, major disruptions may occur, severely taxing the individual's and family's ability to cope. About 12% of individuals with epilepsy show no response to anticonvulsant drugs. A child at home having one seizure after another creates stress to a degree seldom matched. Frequent and severe seizures may totally preoccupy and disrupt a family and prevent participation in such everyday activities as having guests over for dinner, taking trips, or eating meals in restaurants.

Anxiety about seizures, which may be reinforced by the considerable fear and dread experienced by concerned parents who may feel unable to cope, may hinder an individual with epilepsy from developing his skills to an optimum level. The handicap shaped by social pressure may be far out of proportion to the medical condition itself.

Employment

The unemployment rate of adults with epilepsy is disproportionately high. Estimates of the unemployment rate are as high as 25%, which is approximately three times as high as the national average. The underemployment rate and the low-skill, dead-end jobs held by individuals with more talent than such jobs require are frequent liabilities among those with epilepsy. The Commission for the Control of Epilepsy and its Consequences (1978) has identified a number of factors that account for the high unemployment rate among adults with epilepsy.

A major problem continues to be widespread fear and misunderstanding on the part of employers, and hiring policies that categorically exclude individuals with epilepsy from certain jobs.

A related problem is the general lack of knowledge among vocational counselors concerning epilepsy and its relationship to employment; this ignorance contributes to less-than-satisfactory placement efforts. In the extreme, these practices may include the dropping of vocational counseling clients from the active list because they are viewed as difficult to place, requiring lengthy follow-up once placement is made, or placing a vocational counseling client at a low priority rating because the individual only has epilepsy—and the seizures are well controlled. Other equally serious problems include placements that do not match the interests or skills of the applicant to job requirements and the failure to consider individual aspects of a client's epilepsy and its relationship to job requirements and safety concerns.

Most states have provisions which permit individuals whose epilepsy is controlled to obtain a driver's license. The most common requirement is a medical statement that the individual has been seizure-free for one year. One state, Kentucky, has recently reduced the requirement from one year to ninety days. This was done in light of the recognition of improved seizure control now possible through anticonvulsant medication. The significance of driving as a psychosocial milestone has been discussed in Chapter 1. Its contribution to independence and personal growth suggests that it should be encouraged wherever feasible, especially in the individual who may be viewed as disabled.

Epilepsy and Intellectual Impairment

Most individuals with epilepsy have normal intelligence, but for some the pathological lesions that cause epilepsy may cause or be associated with other problems—including, in some cases, intellectual impairment. In general, patients with known etiology have mean intelligence test scores that are somewhat lower than patients whose seizures are due to unknown causes (Klove & Matthews, 1966). Individuals with early onset of epilepsy are more likely to have impaired intellectual functioning than patients with relatively late onset (Halstead, 1957; Cooper, 1965). A similar relationship has been observed with respect to brain damage; that which is incurred early in life generally produces more impairment in problem-solving ability and in cognitive skills than does brain damage occurring after a period of normal development and substantial skill development (Boll, 1973).

Impairments in cognitive functioning may be reflected in low IQ scores; in other cases, however, the cognitive deficits may be highly specific and may not be reflected at all, or only minimally, in general measures of intellectual functioning. An individual may perform well on tasks which sample well rehearsed and previously learned material but have substantial difficulty learning new material. Attention deficits, which may be countervailed by an examiner administering an individualized intelligence test in a supportive and structured manner, may severely handicap a child in a classroom setting.

Although early onset of epilepsy has been shown to be associated with greater impairment on psychological test performance than later onset of epilepsy, Dikman, Matthews, and Harley (1975) caution that such differences should not be uncritically attributed entirely to age of onset. Variables such as type and extent of lesion, seizure duration and frequency, type of anticonvulsant medication, and possible deprivation of academic and other learning experience due to inadequate seizure control, should be considered.

Epilepsy and Personality Disorders

It is widely held that a number of factors experienced by individuals with epilepsy may contribute to emotional or personality disorders. These factors include living with the fear of seizures; failing to cope with the rejection, ostracism, or discrimination that may be encountered; and, in some cases, failing to develop adequate competencies in social, self-help, and academic areas because of disruptions or exclusions from school, normal recreational activities, and other normalizing events.

The factors mentioned above are not intrinsically related to epilepsy. They may also be experienced by individuals with other forms of disability, whose disability sets them apart in some way from others and evokes misunderstanding from the general public.

Is there a more direct relationship between epilepsy and certain forms of personality disturbance?

Pincus (1980) reviews some of the difficulties in researching the question of relationships between epilepsy and personality disorders. Apart from separating stress factors associated with epilepsy (as described above) is the difficulty defining "ictal" behavior and "interictal" behavior (seizure-state vs. between–seizure-state behavior), difficulties in defining specific forms of epilepsy, difficulties in defining abnormal behavior, and the tendency in some studies to include the most seriously impaired patients who may have more difficulties in comparison not only with other control groups but perhaps with other individuals with epilepsy as well.

Given the inherent difficulties in conducting research in this area, a number of researchers report results that suggest a relationship between psychomotor epilepsy and rage and other forms of aggressive behavior (Pincus, 1980), between psychomotor epilepsy and violence among delinquents (Lewis, Balla, & Sacks, 1973), and between psychomotor epilepsy and other psychiatric disorders (Glaser, 1964; Aird, 1968; Aird & Woodbury, 1974).

In a recent study, Pritchard, Lombroso, and McIntyre (1980) report a study investigating the relationship between psychomotor epilepsy and psychiatric disorders. They considered as evidence of psychological complications one or more of the following:

1. Psychiatric diagnosis of psychosis or character disorder
2. Admission to an inpatient psychiatric facility
3. History of suicide attempt
4. A recommendation by a psychiatrist for continuing psychotherapy or a major psychotropic medication

5. Behavior disturbances resulting in major confrontation with school authorities, or imprisonment

They found a high incidence of major psychopathology among young adults with psychomotor epilepsy. Specifically, 20 out of 56 individuals demonstrated major problems. Sex differences were not significant. Those for whom onset of epilepsy began between the ages of 5 and 10 were more heavily represented among those with major disturbances than those whose epilepsy began before age 5 or after age 10. The onset of major problems typically began during adolescence. Dominant problems included poor peer relations, outbursts of rage, and firesetting. Five patients had attempted suicide.

Seidel, Chadwick, and Rutter (1975) report a relationship between epilepsy and psychiatric disorders among children and state that it is the combination of epilepsy *and* a history of disturbed family that together places an individual at special risk to develop serious psychiatric disturbances.

EVALUATION OF INDIVIDUALS WITH EPILEPSY

This section will present a framework for viewing assessment issues that may arise in dealing with an individual with epilepsy. It is assumed that the assessment phase of clinical management will represent not merely the routine administration of clinical assessment instruments but also a problem-solving effort to answer specific questions. It is also assumed that assessment will be ongoing and will be tied to treatment or management.

This section will address assessment from the perspective of the following issues: (1) impact of epilepsy on the adjustment of a child, (2) specialized assessment for evaluation of seizure-related transient mental deficits, (3) intellectual and neuropsychological assessment, and (4) assessment of areas relevant to employment.

Impact of Epilepsy on the Adjustment of a Child

In most cases the onset of epilepsy begins before age 20. For many, the onset of epilepsy will begin between the ages of 4 and 10. This section will not address the issue of developmental history or medical history, but rather the issue of changes in style of life that may occur after the onset of epilepsy. The interview format described below is suggested as one to obtain a parent's perception of the child in relation to his adjustment at school, his relationship with peers, his participation in recreational activities, and his response to discipline. It is suggested not as a structured interview, but as a way to draw information about ways in which life-styles may have been influenced by epilepsy (or by the parents' perception of epilepsy) and then to suggest areas in which the family may need either more information or more counseling.

Description of Seizures. I understand that John has epilepsy and that he is under the care of Doctor X for that. Could you tell me what kind of seizures John has? How often do they occur? How long do they last? How many seizures would you say that John has had?

I'd like to get some information from you about how John is doing overall. I'd like to get some information from you about school, home, and play activities.

Adjustment in School. I understand that John is 8 years old and in a regular third grade. What classes is John taking? Who are his teachers? What do you think of John's progress in school? Do the teachers know that John has epilepsy? Have you talked to them about it? As far as you know, have they made any special adjustment in his program in gym, etc? How does he get to school? Has he had any seizures at school? As far as you know, how have they been handled?

Play Activities. Does John participate in any sports, such as soccer, baseball, or football? How often does he participate in these, and how are they set up—are they organized, as opposed to sandlot or child-organized sports activities? Does he enjoy the activities, etc?

What other recreational outlets does he have? Does he ride a bicycle, does he hike, does he ski (downhill or cross-country), does he swim?

Do you feel that he requires any special supervision or protection, or do you have special restrictions for him regarding these activities?

Discipline and Child Behavior. Let us review discipline for a while. How would you describe John as a youngster in your family? Of course, all children will act up at times in some way or another; at those times when John is a behavior problem, how does he show it? What situation seems to bring on the problem behaviors or seems difficult for him? What forms of discipline do you use? How do you feel he responds to you? Is this an area of concern to you? (Note: occasionally a parent will attribute normal behavior problems to epilepsy. It is useful to probe with the parents their perceptions of the child's behavior and the causes which they assign to the problems.)

There may be a relationship between some forms of epilepsy and behavior problems. Aird and Woodbury (1975) suggest that the following factors may indicate a relationship between epilepsy and behavioral problems: (1) temporal lobe foci of EEG abnormal brain waves, (2) behavior problems out of character for the child, and (3) behavioral reaction markedly out of proportion to precipitating factors. Should these factors be present, such a relationship may require investigation.

A clinical interview roughly following the plan described above will often elicit substantial information about specific ways in which epilepsy has made an impact on the family. Epilepsy as an episodic disability will normally require some adjustments in living. Individuals with epilepsy vary tremendously from one to another in terms of type of epilepsy and frequency and severity of seizures. A point to keep in mind is the high degree of stress experienced in some families in which the child showed an early onset of epilepsy *and* did not respond well to anticonvulsant medication *and* also had other impairments (such as intellectual delay). It cannot be a surprise that these factors taken together and over time provide a context for adjustment problems.

In an individual case, it is important to assess the degree to which the adjustment made by the individual and the family is appropriate to the specifics of that individual's epilepsy. If a child with a history of two or three grand mal seizures is driven to and from school by taxi and is not permitted to swim or ride a bike, the environment may be too restrictive. It may not be restrictive enough, however, if the youngster is allowed to swim alone or ride a bike without protective headgear.

The degree to which the family has discussed the issue of epilepsy with the school is important, and may be an area in which the family will need some support. Teachers do not like surprises. They can plan more easily for a child's problems if they are prepared. A parent, on the other hand, may fear that informing the school about the epilepsy may lead to stigmatization and impair the child's progress. Should teachers or school personnel be unfamiliar with epilepsy, there are sources that can be helpful. For example, the School Alert Program is available in many communities under the sponsorship of local and state chapters affiliated with the Epilepsy Foundation of America.

It is valuable to ask the parent what the child has been told about epilepsy and what he understands.

An interview with the child (assuming the child has a sufficient language base to participate in this way) is helpful to review the child's perception about the above areas, including the child's day at school, activities or sports that he participates in, peer relations, and how he feels about any restrictions that are placed on him and about the seizures themselves.

An interview or discussion organized as described above may set the stage for the parents to bring up other areas of concern indirectly related to epilepsy. These may include issues concerning the marriage, which may be affected by the demands of caring for a child with special needs. For example, one parent may feel that he/she is carrying the whole burden and that the other parent is not helping or is withdrawing from involvement with the family. Should problems such as alcoholism in the family, major economic stresses, separation, or failure occur, these factors may add stress beyond the parents' capacity. In addition, as Rutter *et al.* (1975) point out, children with epilepsy who also live in families that are disorganized are the ones who are the most at risk to develop problems in social adjustment. Stressed parents, of course, may also be those who are likely to develop problems in their own relationships.

Specialized Assessment for Evaluation of Seizure-Related Transient Mental Deficits

The child with petit mal seizures may have 50 or 100 or more clinically observable incidents of seizures in a day. A child in a classroom may have major difficulty sustaining attention and task-relevant behavior for the amount of time required to learn complex academic material if these learning sequences are interrupted by petit mal seizures. Recent research has shown that there is wide variation among individuals with petit mal epilepsy in their ability to maintain task-relevant behavior and interactions with the environment *during* a petit mal seizure (Freeman, Douglas, & Penry, 1973). Some individuals show a momentary break in a stream of thought or behavior, but others maintain some degree of effective contact with the environment, even during a seizure itself. In 1969, Penry and Dreifuss reported on a technique of obtaining simultaneous records of a patient's behavior (including performance on mental and motor tests) and electroencephalographic recordings. Typically, a split-screen video recording system is employed through the use of two cameras.

A number of findings have implications for assessment and intervention regarding individuals with epilepsy, particularly petit mal epilepsy:

1. Some individuals may show momentary impairment in performance that is related to EEG changes (particularly wave–spike discharges), even though a seizure was not clinically evident. An individual may show a sudden slowing of response time or make a sudden error. If this occurs during EEG changes (brief wave–spike discharges), it should be interpreted as a seizure (Tizard & Margerison, 1963).
2. Some individuals are able to compensate for errors made during

subclinical seizures (and, for that matter, observable seizures) if they are given time to pace themselves and correct their work (Tizard & Margerison, 1963).
3. The act of engaging in complex mental or motor activity may have the effect of partial suppression of petit mal seizures (Lennox & Lennox, 1961).
4. Some individuals show an increase (or rebound effect) in abnormal EEG waves (and petit mal seizure activity) after testing or other activity requiring sustained attention (Ricci, Berti, & Cherubini, 1972).
5. The more complex and difficult a task, the more interference can be expected from the abnormal spike–wave activity that does occur, even if the seizure activity is subclinical (Hutt & Fairweather, 1975).
6. Impairment in ongoing activity requiring sustained attention is common in petit mal seizures, and the EEG activity is typically a spike–wave pattern. However, impairment may also occur during other EEG patterns such as spike–EEG activity (Rennick, Perez-Borja, & Rodin, 1969).

The above findings have implications for classroom management and also, to some extent, for vocational placement and supervision, although, as we said above, the incidence of petit mal epilepsy among adults is relatively rare. At the least, the child's teacher should be aware that the child may have considerable difficulty sustaining attention. The child must be given a chance to correct errors and pace himself. If it is clear that the child's epilepsy is very severe, it may be wise to recommend that the child be given an opportunity for long-term assessment in a center or program specializing in epilepsy. Continuous monitoring of EEG activity along with ongoing behavioral monitoring may facilitate adjustments in medication and help determine the degree to which the spike–wave activity impairs the child's functioning. Some centers also offer educational assessment and recommendations regarding curriculum and ways of approaching a child in such a way that the child obtains maximum benefit from the educational program.

Intellectual and Cognitive Assessment of Individuals with Epilepsy

An assessment of a child's intellectual functioning is useful in making recommendations about school placement and curriculum. It is known that early onset of epilepsy and epilepsy associated with known etiology are two factors likely to be associated with some impairment in psychological test performance. Furthermore, intelligence test scores in an individual with epilepsy correlate not only with the individual's social and academic adjustment but also with the likelihood of remission of the epilepsy condition itself (Lindsay, Ounsted, & Richards, 1980). Results of an intellectual assessment may yield one among a number of measures that may assist the neurologist in making some estimate of how protracted the seizure disorder may be in considering the outcome.

Specialized Neuropsychological Assessment

Specialized neuropsychological assessment should be considered when an individual with epilepsy is not making an adjustment that seems in line with the general level of intellectual functioning, or if the individual shows a decline in function or performance. There is general agreement that single tests such as the Bender–Gestalt or the commonly used standardized intelligence tests such as the WISC—R, the Stanford–Binet, or the WAIS do not provide sufficient coverage of cognitive and adaptive behavior to form a basis for neuropsychological assessment.

Of a number of assessment strategies for neuropsychological impairment, one approach is represented by the Halstead–Reitan battery, which employs a fixed and extensive battery of tests and involves the processing of scores through scoring keys that have been empirically validated (Reitan & Davison, 1974). An alternate neuropsychological approach is espoused by Lezak (1976), who suggests the flexible application of test procedures guided in part by a knowledge of syndromes. Both approaches share a conceptual framework that many variables, including nature of lesion or insult, locus of insult in the brain, amount of area involved, and age of patient, will all have implications for deficits in intellectual or cognitive skills and in adaptive behavior. Both approaches also assume that deficits will show up in a variety of ways and that no single test or instrument provides a measure of brain impairment. Both approaches require considerable training in clinical testing and interpretation.

Assessment of Issues Pertaining to Epilepsy and Employment

The key to an adequate assessment and placement of individuals with epilepsy requires an understanding of a common misperception about their employability and an understanding of factors related to epilepsy that should be considered in making employment recommendations. This misperception is the view that all individuals with epilepsy are equally disabled. Though seldom directly expressed, such a view is implicit when there are employment policies that have blanket restrictions against hiring individuals with epilepsy to work near machinery or around high places. These rules are too restrictive because they do not take into account individual skills, work history, or individual factors related to epilepsy itself.

As for information about seizures that is relevant for placement, the Commission for Control of Epilepsy (1978) recommends that the following characteristics be assessed and considered regarding job placement:

- Attacks with predictable time of occurrence in relation to hours of work—for example, attacks occurring only at night.
- Attacks occurring without loss of consciousness or loss of voluntary control.
- Attacks preceded by at least 30 seconds of warning prior to unconsciousness or loss of voluntary control.
- Attacks without loss of consciousness but with loss of voluntary control.
- Attacks with loss of consciousness but without associated falling.
- Attacks characterized by falling without warning (with or without convulsions).

Other factors include issues pertaining to the person's work history. Has the person ever been injured on the job? When was the last time a seizure took place? Are the seizures related to or precipitated by known environmental factors such as stress or lights? How reliable is the individual in following an anticonvulsant drug program?

INTERVENTION METHODS

The onset of epilepsy typically brings on a crisis for the individual and family. It represents a time when an individual is most likely to benefit from counseling. Counseling begun early may prevent the development of problems that may be much more difficult to handle at a later time. For example, if parents, in their initial anxiety about epilepsy, become extremely protective of a young child, they may have difficulty undoing such patterns or modifying their approach after their own pattern has been established and the child has begun to adjust to the restrictions imposed by the parents.

Should the onset of epilepsy begin during adolescence, an individual may develop problems in establishing independence. Counseling may be effective in helping the individual gain perspective on his problem and become assertive in everyday situations, so that maximum participation in academic, social, and vocational activities is possible.

With any disorder requiring medical supervision and management for lengthy periods of time, some individuals demonstrate what may be considered noncompliance. An individual's life-style may be incompatible with the management of epilepsy. For example, overusing alcohol, getting too little sleep, or exposing oneself to too much stress may unnecessarily risk an increase in seizure activity. Individuals who find it difficult to follow a particular program for medication also represent an example of noncompliance. Satisfactory control of seizures may be difficult to accomplish after a long period of poor seizure control.

The least intrusive form of counseling for an individual or family coping with epilepsy centers around an explanation of the seizure disorder itself and its implication for the individual. The goals would be to cover all of the following points

1. Explaining epilepsy and the patient's form of epilepsy.
2. Working through the patient's and family's misperceptions of epilepsy.
3. Establishing a working relationship with the family to form a basis for ongoing medical management, even during lengthy periods of freedom from seizures.
4. Discussing with the individual and family the form of adjustments that may be required, minimizing the risks and at the same time allowing for as full a participation in life as possible.
5. Discussing with the individual and family the fact that individuals in our society continue to have misunderstandings about epilepsy and that rejection or discrimination may be encountered, thus enlisting the patient's and family's willingness to be advocates by joining a local or state volunteer organization that seeks to support individuals with epilepsy.

Counseling covering the issues mentioned above should take place over a number of sessions.

TRENDS AND NEEDS

Epilepsy is a disability that has historically taken a heavy toll in the quality of life for a significant number of people. When the misunderstanding, rejection, and exclusion experienced by individuals with epilepsy is considered, the personal toll continues to be high. According to a survey reported in the *National Spokesman,* the newsletter of the Epilepsy Foundation of America, a majority of individuals with epilepsy state that social stresses brought on by reaction of others to seizures were more of a problem to them than the medical condition itself. In many respects, however, the outlook is promising. Most individuals respond to modern anticonvulsant medications and are able to live a life that is seizure-free.

There continues to be a major need to create a favorable climate within society so that individuals with epilepsy do not experience a compounding of social problems, in addition to a medical one. Recent legislation that facilitates mainstreaming for handicapped children in public schools (Public Law 94–142) and Title V of the Vocational Rehabilitation Act of 1973, which has a number of sections designed to guarantee the rights of the handicapped, are a major step in the right direction.

For those individuals with epilepsy whose seizures resist control or who have other impairments as well, our health care programs will need to be increasingly designed for interdisciplinary assessment and treatment over an extended period of time, so that an individual's treatment is not fragmented and is tied to adjustment issues as the person grows, develops, and assumes increasingly complex social roles.

APPENDIX: SOURCES OF INFORMATION

Epilepsy Foundation of America (EFA)
1828 L Street NW, Suite 406
Washington, D.C. 20036
Phone: (202) 293–2930

Also consult state and local chapters of the EFA.

National Epilepsy League
6 Michigan Avenue
Chicago, IL 60602
Phone: (312) 332–6882

REFERENCES

Aird, R. B. Clinical syndromes of the limbic system. *International Journal of Neurology,* 1968, 340–352.

Aird, R. B., & Woodbury, D. M. *The management of epilepsy.* Springfield, Ill.: Charles C Thomas, 1974.

Annegers, J. F., Grabow, J. D., Groover, R. V., Laws, E. R., Elvebeck, L. R., & Kurland, L. T. Seizures after head trauma: A population study. *Neurology,* 1980, *30,* 683–689.

Boll, T. J. The effect of age at onset of brain damage on adaptive abilities in children. Paper presented at the meeting of the American Psychological Association, Montreal, August, 1973.

Cereghino, O. Cited in Aura: A new look at an old phenomenon. *National Spokesman,* July–August, 1980.

Commission For the Control of Epilepsy and its Consequences. *Plan for nationwide action on epilepsy,* Vol. 1. U.S. Department of Health, Education, and Welfare: Public Health Service, National Institutes of Health, 1978, DHEW Publication No. (NIH) 78–276.

Cooper, J. E. Epilepsy in a longitudinal survey of 5,000 children. *British Medical Journal,* 1965, *1,* 1020–1022.

Davison, G. Convulsions in childhood. *Newcastle Medical Journal,* 1970, *31,* 105–112.

Debakan, A. *Neurology of infancy.* Baltimore: Williams & Wilkin, 1959.

Dikmen, S., Matthews, C. G., & Harley, J. P. The effect of early versus late onset of major motor epilepsy upon cognitive–intellectual performance. *Epilepsia,* 1975, *16,* 73–81.

Ford, F. R. *Diseases of the nervous system in infancy, childhood and adolescence* (5th ed.). Springfield, Ill.: Charles C Thomas, 1966.

Freeman, F. R., Douglas, E. F. O, & Penry, J. K. Environmental interaction and memory during petit mal (absence) seizures. *Pediatrica,* 1973, *51*(5), 911–918.

Gastaut, H. Clinical and electroencephalographic classification of epileptic seizures. *Epilepsia,* 1970, *11,* 102–113.

Glaser, G. H. The problem of psychosis in psychomotor temporal lobe epileptics. *Epilepsia.* 1964, *5,* 271–278.

Gloor, P. Generalized spike and wave discharges: A consideration of cortical and subcortical mechanisms of their genesis and synchronization. In H. Petsche & M. A. B. Brazier (Eds.), *Synchronization of EEG activity in epilepsies.* New York: Springer-Verlag, 1972.

Goodglass, H., Folson, A. T., Morgan, M., & Quadfasel, F. A. Epileptic seizure, psychological factors and occupational adjustment. *Epilepsia,* 1963, *4,* 322–341.

Halstead, H. Abilities and behavior of epileptic children. *Journal of Mental Science,* 1957, *103,* 28–47.

Hutt, S. J., & Fairweather, H. Information processing during two types of EEG activity. *Electroencephalography and Clinical Neurophysiology,* 1975, *39,* 43–51.

Klove, H., & Mathews, C. G. Psychometric and adaptive abilities in epilepsy with differential etiology. *Epilepsia,* 1966, *7,* 330–338.

Lennox, W. G., & Lennox, M. A. *Epilepsy and related disorders.* Boston: Little, Brown, 1960.

Lewis, D. O., Balla, D. A., & Sacks, H. C. Psychotic symptomatology in a juvenile court clinic population. *Journal of American Academy of Child Psychiatry,* 1973, *12,* 660–674.

Lezak, M. D. *Neuropsychological assessment.* New York: Oxford University Press, 1976.

Lindsay, J., Ounsted, C., & Richards, P. Long-term outcome in children with temporal lobe seizures. 1: Social outcome and childhood factors. *Developmental Medicine and Child Neurology,* 1979, *21,*(3), 285–298.

Livingston, S. *Comprehensive management of epilepsy in infancy, childhood and adolescence.* Springfield, Ill.: Charles C Thomas, 1972.

Matthews, W. B. *Practical neurology.* Oxford: Blackwell, 1970.

Millichap, J. G. *Febrile convulsions.* New York: Macmillan Company, 1968.

Millon, T. *Modern psychopathology: A biosocial approach to maladaptive learning and functioning.* Philadelphia: Saunders, 1969.

Penry, J. K., & Dreifuss, F. E. Automomatisms associated with the absence of petit mal epilepsy. *Archives of Neurology,* 1969, *21,* 142–149.

Pincus, J. H. Can violence be a manifestation of epilepsy? *Neurology,* 1980, *30,* 304–307.

Pritchard, P. B., Lombroso, C. T., & McIntyre, M. Psychological complications of temporal lobe epilepsy. *Neurology,* 1980, *30,* 227–232.

Rasmussen, T. The role of surgery in the treatment of focal epilepsy. *Clinical Neurosurgery,* 1969, *16,* 288–314.

Reitan, R. M., & Davison, L. A. (Eds.). *Clinical neuropsychology: Current status and applications.* Washington, D.C.: V. H. Winston, 1974.

Remschmidt, H. Psychological studies of parents with epilepsy and popular prejudice. *Epilepsia,* 1973, *14,* 347–356.

Rennick, P. M., Perez-Borja, C., & Rodin, E. A. Transient mental deficits associated with recurrent prolonged epileptic clouded state. *Epilepsia,* 1969, *10,* 397–405.

Reynolds, E. H. Chronic anticipated toxicity: A review. *Epilepsia,* 1975, *16,* 319–352.

Ricci, G., Berti, G., & Cherubini, E. Changes in interictal focal activity and spike-wave paroxyms during motor and mental activity. *Epilepsia,* 1972, *13,* 785–794.

Russell, W. R., & Whitty, C. W. M. Studies in traumatic epilepsy. I. Factors influencing incidence of epilepsy after brain wounds. *Journal of Neurology, Neurosurgery, and Psychiatry,* 1952, *15,* 93–98.

Rutter, M., Graham, P., & Yule, W. *A Neuropsychiatric Study in Childhood.* Clinics in Developmental Medicine, Nos. 35/36. London: SIMP with Heinemann Medical, 1970.

Seidel, V. P., Chadwick, O. F. D., & Rutter, M. Psychological disorders in crippled children. A comparative study of children with and without brain damage. *Developmental Medicine and Child Neurology,* 1975, *17,* 563–573.

Smith, D. W. Teratogenicity of anticonvulsant medicine. *American Journal of Disabled Children,* 1977, *131,* 1337–1339.

Tizard, B., & Margerison, J. H. The relationship between generalized paroxysmal EEG discharges and various test situations in two epileptic patients. *Journal of Neurology, Neurosurgery, and Psychiatry,* 1963, *26,* 308–313.

Ward, F. W., & Bower, B. D. A study of certain social aspects of epilepsy in childhood. Supplement No. 39. *Developmental Medicine and Child Neurology,* 1978, *20,*(1) 1–63.

Wright, B. *Physical disability—A psychological approach.* New York: Harper & Row, 1960.

7

Mental Retardation

LEIF G. TERDAL

Donna L., age 22, was about to buy a cola drink. She stood by the coke machine, looked through the plastic window and tapped it. Her house parent came over and pulled out a handful of change. "Here, Donna, put some money in the machine." Donna picked out one nickel, turned again to the machine. She stared at the machine, making no move to place the coin in the coin slot. The house parent said, "Watch me." The house parent stood in front of the coke machine and, leaning on it with his left hand, tapped the coin slot with his right hand. Donna repeated the sequence. She leaned on the machine and tapped the coin slot. Still no coke. The task was formidable. The house parent took out a coin and then another and placed them in the coin slot. Donna watched. With assistance, she inserted the final nickel. The machine clicked, but still no coke. Donna looked again through the plastic door. The house parent held Donna's hand and placed it over one of the choice buttons and guided it as Donna pushed it. A cup dropped down the slot and coke and ice filled the cup. Donna was excited. When it was filled, Donna bent over and again looked through the plastic door at the cup of coke. She reached for the coke but was blocked by the plastic door. The plastic door had the word "*lift*" on it, but Donna does not read. She has no expressive speech and the problem was another in a series, each too difficult. The house parent held Donna's hand on the glass door and together they raised it. Donna had her coke.

Donna is profoundly retarded. She was recently deinstitutionalized and now lives in a group home for severely and profoundly mentally

The preparation of this chapter was supported in part by the Bureau of Community Health Services, Maternal and Child Health Services Project 920.

retarded adults. The sequence with the coke machine, though an actual experience, is idiosyncratic and is meant only to portray an example of an individual struggling with what seems obvious. Her problems with the machine also illustrate, however, the compounding of problems that may occur with a mentally retarded person. At age 22, she may have had her first exposure to a coke machine. Many mentally retarded individuals have been segregated from the mainstream and have not had their share of opportunities to interact and learn.

The purpose of this chapter is to present a brief framework within which to view mental retardation in terms of its definition and its prevalence, with a focus on assessment and intervention.

THE PHYSICAL DISABILITY

Definition

In the sixth revision of the American Association on Mental Deficiency (AAMD) *Manual on Terminology and Classification in Mental Deficiency,* mental retardation is defined as follows: "Mental retardation refers to significantly subaverage general intellectual functioning existing concurrently with deficits in adaptive behavior, and manifested during the developmental period (to age 18)" (Grossman, 1973, p. 5). The phrase "significantly subaverage" is defined in the manual as two standard deviations below the mean on a standardized instrument and set as the upper limit of mental retardation.

It is important to recognize that a diagnosis of mental retardation requires that two components be identified: (1) significant subaverage intellectual functioning and (2) deficits in adaptive behavior; these factors must be manifested concurrently during the developmental period. An initial diagnosis of mental retardation is not made after the age of 18.

Levels of Mental Retardation

Mental retardation as a diagnostic category covers intellectual impairment and delays or deficits in adaptive behavior that stem from a wide variety of etiological factors. The range of impairment among the mentally retarded is vast. The AAMD Manual recommends that the categories *mild, moderate, severe,* and *profound* be used to indicate the degree or level of mental retardation. The levels are essentially based on performance as measured by standardized intelligence tests. The levels correspond to standard deviation units. The levels of mental retardation when the Stanford–Binet Scale is used (standard deviation = 16) are as follows: mild (IQ range 52–67), moderate (IQ range 36–51), severe (IQ range 20–35) and profound (IQ range 0–19).

Impairment or deficits in adaptive behavior must also be demonstrated to warrant a diagnosis of mental retardation. However, current instruments to assess adaptive behavior are not sufficiently advanced psychometrically to justify cutoff scores to parallel those of the Stanford–Binet or Wechsler Scales. Clinical judgment must be used to make a determination of level of retardation based on scores that are obtained through adaptive behavior scales.

The determination of level of mental retardation is but a part of the task of obtaining information through assessment to plan an individualized program. By themselves, measures of intelligence and adaptive behavior do not specify treatment or disposition.

Mental Retardation as "Reversible"

The term *reversible* is sometimes used in connection with retardation, with the notion increasing that mental retardation be viewed as reversible. For example, Filler, Robinson, Smith, Vincent-Smith, Bricker, and Bricker (1975, p. 28), after reviewing the history of educational efforts on behalf of mentally retarded individuals with an emphasis on the unfortunate effects of labeling, recommend: "Teachers must be trained to deal with categories of behavior, not categories of children, and to view retardation as reversible rather than static." This reflects both the current focus on active intervention in behalf of the mentally retarded and the belief that children should not be burdened with a label that may unfairly stigmatize them as having a condition that will not improve. In our view, mental retardation is used to cover too broad a range of deficits to be considered, categorically, as either reversible or nonreversible. Some children who are diagnosed as mentally retarded will progress and develop to the point that they lose the label. Others, especially many of those who are more severely impaired and who have multiple sensory and physical problems in addition to severe behavioral deficits, will probably never outgrow the label or the need for services. This does not mean they cannot learn or profit from carefully designed interventions, nor does it mean that prediction is a valid function of assessment. But in the area of mental retardation, the range of behavioral deficits is so broad and the etiology so varied that a general statement about the reversibility of mental retardation does not at this time seem useful or valid.

Prevalence

It is commonly stated that 3% of the population is mentally retarded; this indicates that the number of individuals in the United States with mental retardation must be about 6 million. The figure of 3% closely corresponds to a statistical figure that would be obtained if the entire population were tested and all those whose IQ scores were two or more standard deviations below the mean were classified as mentally retarded.

Tarjan, Wright, Eyman, and Keeran (1973) correctly point out that the conclusion that 3% of the population is mentally retarded assumes all of the following: (a) the diagnosis of mental retardation is based essentially on an IQ below 70; (b) mental retardation is identified in infancy; (c) that diagnosis does not change; and (d) the mortality of retarded individuals is similar to that of the general population.

As stated above, impairment both in intellectual functioning and in adaptive behavior must be demonstrated before a diagnosis of mental retardation is established. In cases of mild mental retardation, this is not normally possible until a child reaches school age. The school years create demands for children with impairment in intellectual functioning and in social skills. Tarjan *et al.* (1973) agree that about 3% of the school age population is mentally retarded. After the age of 19, however, a number of individuals lose the label of mental retardation. This occurs because many are able to function adaptively in society without requiring continuing intervention. It would appear that about 3% of the population will at some point be diagnosed as mentally retarded and that this figure is useful for program planning with a major thrust aimed at school and early intervention programs. Regarding the question of prevalence, epidemiological studies consistently show that the proportion of mentally retarded is a good deal less than 3% of the population. Tarjan *et al.* (1973) and Mercer (1975) estimate that the figure of 1% or about two million in the United States is perhaps a realistic figure in terms of overall prevalence.

Etiology

The diagnosis of mental retardation is based on behavioral measures (intelligence test scores and measures of adaptive behavior) rather than on etiology. A current view of mental retardation is that in most cases a number of causal factors interact and that it would be misleading to view either the development or the behavioral patterns of any given child as having been caused by a single factor. Even in cases where a known medical disorder is present, the child's development would be influenced by the care that he receives in his family, by opportunity for schooling and rehabilitation, and by acceptance, ostracism, or stigma.

In cases where there is evidence that psychosocial factors may have contributed to intellectual impairment (e.g., a child born out of wedlock and raised in a disorganized, unstimulating environment), the problem may have been compounded by a variety of biological factors related in part to inadequate prenatal care, poor nutrition, and genetic factors.

It is increasingly common for research in mental retardation to view the question of etiology from a broad perspective which (1) includes measures of biological, psychological, and social variables, (2) evaluates interactions between variables, and (3) assesses the cumulative impact of debilitating factors over a number of developmental periods.

Medical Disorders with Established Risk for Mental Retardation. Approximately 25% of individuals who are mentally retarded have a diagnosis of a medical disorder with known risk for mental retardation. The *International Classification of Diseases,* ninth revision (ICD–9), the American Psychiatric Association's *Diagnostic and Statistical Manual,* third revision (DSM III), and the American Association on Mental Deficiency's *Manual on Terminology and Classification in Mental Retardation* are in essential agreement on the major medical subdivisions or categories of mental retardation associated with known physical disorders. The broad headings include mental retardation associated with infection and intoxication, trauma or physical agent, accompanying disorders of metabolism or nutrition, gross brain disease (postnatal), diseases and conditions due to unknown prenatal influence, chromosomal abnormalities, and gestational disorders (including prematurity).

In all, about 200 syndromes of mental retardation have been identified. Most of the individuals with a definite syndrome eventually function within a moderate to severe or profound range of mental retardation. Because many have a number of associated anomalies, mental retardation is only a part of the picture. Down's Syndrome represents an example of mental retardation associated with chromosomal abnormalities. It is a condition that illustrates the clustering together of a number of anomalies associated with a syndrome. It is the most common malformation associated with chromosome abnormality in humans (Smith, 1976).

Down's Syndrome. Down's Syndrome was described in 1866 by an English physician, J. H. Langdon Down. He felt that it represented a regression from the Caucasian race to an oriental or mongol ethnic group. Later, many disputed his assumptions about the nature of the disorder; however, the cytogenetic discovery of Down's Syndrome as trisomy 21 (three chromosomes instead of two chromosomes in position

21) was not made until 1959, when Lejeune in France and Jacobs in England discovered extra chromosome material on chromosome 21. The following year, Down's Syndrome associated with translocation (transfer of material from one chromosome to a chromosome not of its pair) was identified by Penrose and also by Polani. In 1961, Mosaic Down's Syndrome (some cells have 46 chromosomes and others have 47 chromosomes) was identified by Nichols and Clark.

There is a remarkable relationship between Down's Syndrome and maternal age. The incidence of Down's Syndrome is reported as one in 1,500 for mothers between 15 and 29 years of age, one in 800 for mothers between 30 and 34 years, one in 270 for mothers between 35 and 39 years, one in 100 for mothers between 40 and 44 years, and one in 20 for mothers over 45 years of age (Smith, 1976). While advanced maternal age is associated with the incidence of Down's Syndrome, changes in birth rate among older women and the availability of prenatal diagnosis, for example, amniocentesis, are changing the pattern (Abroms & Bennett, 1980). In a recent review of documents of incidence of Down's Syndrome, Holmes (1978) reports that about 80% of cases are born to women under the age of 35. The relationship between maternal age and Down's Syndrome should not be taken to mean that the extra chromosome material always originates from the mother. It appears to originate from the father at least some of the time, but the exact proportion of maternal to paternal origin is not known (Abroms & Bennett, 1980).

Congenital heart defect is one of a number of associated conditions that may accompany Down's Syndrome. It is a major one, found in about 40% of Down's Syndrome children, whereas fewer than 1% of all newborn infants have such heart defects (Johnson, 1978). These heart defects in Down's Syndrome children may require cardiac surgery. Complications commonly arise in cardiac surgery in patients with Down's Syndrome, related in part to the complexity of their cardiac defects (Shaher, Farina, Porter, & Bishop, 1972), the vulnerability to respiratory infections, and the presence of muscular hypotonia which limits the body's ability to recover from surgery (Johnson, 1978). The mortality rate has been reported to be as high as 26% for open-heart surgery in Down's Syndrome children (Park, Mathews, Zuberbuhler, Rowe, Neches, & Lenox, 1977). Decision-making regarding whether or not to operate is, of course, complicated. Johnson (1978) recommends that a team including the family doctor, the pediatrician, the cardiologist, and the cardiac surgeon work in close cooperation. Early diagnosis of cardiac problems is important and should include an assessment of the distress and functional limitations related to heart defects and an evaluation of the degree to which symptom relief of heart-related problems would enhance the parents' ability to raise the child. Further discussion of congenital heart defect will be found in Chapter 12.

About 40%–50% of Down's Syndrome children have hearing problems. As many as 50% of these children also have visual defects including strabismus, myopia, hyperopia, nystagmus, and cataracts.

The clinical picture of Down's Syndrome is complex with respect to the rate of development. It is common that development often progresses fairly well during infancy and that the gap between Down's Syndrome children and their peers widens during the late preschool and the school-age years. For example, Cornwell and Birch (1968) report that, whereas a mean IQ in the low 50s is common for Down's Syndrome children at 4 years of age, by age 17 the mean IQ is in the low 30s. It is now common practice for children with Down's Syndrome to be enrolled in developmental disability education programs early in life. Initial results are promising, but it is not yet known if the decline in rate of cognitive development will be offset for these individuals who have the opportunity for such early educational interventions.

Biological Risk Factors. While it is beyond the scope of this chapter to present detail on any specific syndrome, there are concepts that have emerged from the treatment of premature infants which illustrate the interplay between biological, social, and psychological variables as related to developmental disorders.

Tjossem (1976) makes a distinction between medical conditions that have an established risk for delayed development (such as Down's Syndrome and also many conditions outlined in the ICD–8 and the AAMD Manual on mental retardation) and what he terms biological risk factors. More specifically: "Biological risk specifies infants presenting a history of prenatal, perinatal, neonatal, and early developmental events suggestive of biological insult(s) to the developing nervous system and which, either singly or collectively, increase the probability of later appearing aberrant development" (Tjossem, 1976, p. 5).

Infants born too early or born too small illustrate this general biological risk factor. Infants of less than 32 weeks' gestation, while accounting for fewer than 1½% of live births, account for nearly one half of all neonatal deaths. A major factor which vastly accentuates the risk for these premature and low weight infants is the presence and severity of hyalene membrane disease, a condition of pulmonary immaturity that interferes with the infants' ability to obtain oxygen (Rantakallo, 1980). The hyalene membrane disease occurs in as many as 75% of infants of less than 28 weeks' gestation. Research in this area suggests the following three points: (1) social and demographic indices are highly predictive of infants who are at risk during the neonatal period; (2) biological risk factors during the neonatal period may contribute to problems of bonding and attachment; and (3) prediction of mental, motor, or sensory handicap from documented biological insults is tenuous.

Social and demographic indices which are predictive of prematurity, but also of fetal and infant mortality (Scurletis & Headrick, 1972) are the following:

1. Maternal age less than 18 years
2. Maternal age more than 34 years
3. Birth order greater than 3
4. Education less than 9th grade
5. Education greater than 9th grade but less than completion of high school
6. Child born out of wedlock
7. Previous fetal death
8. Previous live births now dead

In general, an unwed young mother who obtains poor prenatal care is especially vulnerable to producing a premature infant. The premature infant is likely to be born after a very short labor. Other complications common in these at-risk situations include maternal toxemia, placenta praevia, premature rupture of membrane, and maternal infections (Williams & Scarr, 1971). Thompson and O'Quinn (1979) cite a 1973 study by the National Academy of Sciences to the effect that 19.6% of the infants of at-risk mothers who did not receive adequate prenatal care weighed 5½ pounds or less. The corresponding figure for mothers not at risk was 5.8%. Babson, Benson, Pernoll, and Benda (1975) report that in a study of Oregon farm owners versus farm laborers the latter group had double the incidence of prematurity and triple the incidence of perinatal mortality. Unfortunately, the factors that place the child at risk to be born too early and too small may continue to operate in a detrimental manner during the child's later development.

In addition to the impact of certain neonatal events on the infant, it is possible that the biological factors set a series of events in motion which, taken together, may have a strong impact on the cognitive and emotional development of the child. Brazelton, Koslowski, and Main (1974) have stressed that it is important to evaluate the response of the mother to an infant who has been made vulnerable by a biological insult. If the illness requires separation of the infant from the mother, this could start a scenario in which the infant, when returned to the mother, is perceived by the mother as deviant or as unresponsive to her. If the mother fails to interpret her infant's responses accurately or feels inadequate to respond appropriately, then each may withdraw from the other or develop other coping styles that may impair the relationship.

While issues related to the concepts of bonding and attachment have received considerable attention recently, it is important to maintain a focus on the cumulative effect of the quality of the parent–child relationship and other factors associated with stability of care and adequacy of stimulation.

Parmelee and Haber (1973) state that the prediction of mental, motor, or sensory handicap in later childhood, based on factors determined during pregnancy or surrounding perinatal events, is very weak. Two factors which contribute to the poor predictive relationships between early biological events and later development are the transient nature of many neonatal insults and the "recurrent observation that environmental factors can have a stronger influence on the outcome than can the earlier biological events" (Parmelee, Sigman, Kopp, & Haber, 1976, p. 290).

In order to increase the ability to predict the consequences to the infants, Parmelee, Kopp, and Sigman (1976) developed the cumulative risk index. The index takes into account biological as well as environmental variables and is designed for ongoing assessment and monitoring. The approach takes into account the infant's capacity to recover from the unexpected and to show room to maneuver in development. Furthermore, it reflects a view of development that minimizes the long-term impact of any single biological or environmental event and views cumulative effect over time. Werner, Bierman, and French (1971) report on a study that they conducted among Hawaiian children concerning the relationship between perinatal risk factors and environmental factors in intelligence. They conclude,

> it is quite apparent that the difference in mean IQs between children growing up in the most and least favorable home environments from 2–10 years was much larger than between children from the most and least severely stressed perinatal groups. (Werner et al., 1971, p. 73)

This view most clearly exemplifies the current approach to mental retardation, in which etiology is viewed as an interaction of events, both biological and environmental, which take place over sequential developmental periods.

The Continuum of Environmental Causality

> Environmental risk applies to biologically sound infants for whom early life experiences, including maternal and family care, health care, opportunities for expression for adaptive behavior, and patterns of physical and social stimulation, are sufficiently limiting to the extent that, without corrective intervention, they impart high probability for delayed development. (Tjossem, 1976, p. 6)

According to Tjossem, the majority of children at risk are in this category. These are children without any identifiable syndrome. They generally show normal development during the first 12 to 18 months of life.

The social and demographic variables which are predictive of social–cultural mental retardation are similar to the social and demographic indices which relate to prematurity. The education of the mother, the marital status of the mother, the income level of the family, and the age of the mother are variables associated with mild retardation. Many mental health professionals who quite properly are trained to be nonjudgmental fail to understand the problems that lie beneath rather dull census-type statistics. Why should a young mother (without high school education) who has a child born out of wedlock be so likely to produce a child who by his school age years will be diagnosed, classified, and educated as a mild mentally retarded individual? Those simple indices increase, by up to 15 times, the likelihood of a diagnosis of mild mental retardation as compared with a youngster born to a more advantaged and intact family (President's Panel on Mental Retardation, 1969; Tarjan, Wright, Eyman, & Keeran, 1973).

Current research is beginning to shed light on this continuing problem, which is of significant proportions. A picture unfolds of a young, economically dependent, often isolated parent without a meaningful support group, burdened, despairing, lonely, often unable to view herself as capable of influencing her own life, much less that of her child. From this unsteady base, such a person begins the very long task of being a parent.

Research in this area focuses on attitudes of the mother towards parenting, her self-perception, her perception of the child, characteristics of the mother–child interaction, and social and economic stresses on the family. In a study of mothers considered to be at high risk to produce children with psychosocial retardation, Newman and Ramey (1979) found that such high risk mothers have less positive perceptions of themselves and of their children than a control group of mothers who are not at risk. The dependent measures included the Parental Attitudes Research Instrument, which was designed to assess parental attitude toward self, toward parenting, and toward the child. The investigators also used the Home Observation for the Measurement of the Environment Scale designed by Caldwell, Heider, and Kaplan (1966) and the Coopersmith (1967) Self-Esteem Inventory. The most significant aspect of their findings is that, even within the high risk group, the measures of the mother's attitude toward herself and her role as parent toward her child were related to the child's intelligence at 60 months, with the

Wechsler Preschool and Primary Scale of Intelligence (WPPSI) as the dependent measure.

A study by Engel and Keane (1975) also illustrates the relationship between the perception by high risk mothers of their role in parenting and the subsequent IQ scores of their children. Mothers were rated when their infants were 14 months of age as to the degree to which they perceived their infants' individuality and emotional needs in addition to their physical needs. The ratings were taken in the home and based on observations of parent–child interactions. The rating that the authors obtained at 14 months correlated with the WPPSI at 66 months ($r = .48, p = .05$). That correlation, while not high in an absolute sense, is higher than correlations generally reported between developmental assessments taken during infancy and again at five years of age.

Information such as that a child is born to a single parent who is young, that is, a teenage parent, with limited education, and with limited income should alert practitioners that the child is at risk for biological insults (especially prematurity and associated problems), mental retardation, and child abuse and that the parent is likely to be stressed and may be limited in coping skills. It is assumed that when such major socioeconomic factors are operating, the family is so stressed that a positive, supportive, stimulating, and continuing relationship between the young child and his family is not possible. One American child in seven is born in a situation in which all of the factors listed above are present.

COMMON PSYCHOLOGICAL CHARACTERISTICS AND PROBLEMS

Impact of Diagnosis

The information that a child has a major handicapping condition is usually the first common psychological problem that parents of a mentally retarded child face. Much of the research on parental response to having a mentally retarded child is based on studies conducted with middle-class parents of moderately to severely and profoundly impaired children. In these cases, the mental retardation is pronounced, it may be associated with a number of anomalies in addition to delayed cognitive development, and the evidence of the disorder may be present at birth (or before) or at least during early infancy. Studies characterize parental reactions in terms of a terrible sense of loss, prolonged crises, and lowered self-esteem (Olshansky, 1962; Solnit & Stark, 1961; Fowle, 1968).

Drotar, Baskiewicz, Irvin, Kennel, and Klaus (1975) provide a useful framework for considering the adjustment of parents to the massive crises initiated by the information that a child has a significant disorder of indefinite duration. They list five stages of adjustment in massive crises. The stages are constructed to be dynamic and fluid, not fixed, though partly sequential. Parents may move in and out of a stage, but the process normally takes place over a substantial period of time. Similar stages of reaction to awareness of disability have been discussed in Chapter 1, as well as in several other chapters of this book. Drotar *et al.* list:

Stage 1: *Shock.* The parents may feel overwhelmed at being unprepared. The child is not what they had expected.

Stage 2: *Denial.* "It can not be true." If the defect is not visible, denial may be protracted. Shopping behavior, that is, going from one professional to another, or from one clinic to another, may reflect a rejection of the diagnosis (Anderson & Garner, 1971).

Stage 3: *Sadness, anger and anxiety.* Our society places great value on intelligence and independence. The risk of lifelong dependency may result in the child's being perceived as worthless.

Stage 4: *Adaptation.* The parents feel less emotionally upset and gain confidence in their ability to raise the child and support the child's development.

Stage 5: *Reorganization.* This stage is not reached by all families. It represents acceptance of the child and family members' mutual support of one another as they go about the complex task of rearing the child.

Communication with parents about a significant handicap should take place as soon as possible, when reliable information is available about the disorder. For many of the major medical disorders associated with mental retardation, this will be handled by the physician around the time of birth. Guidelines about how to communicate about major pediatric problems include the following:

1. Parents need an involved physician who will take time to make the diagnosis and to communicate with them.
2. The communication between physician and parents must be interactive, with give-and-take and with ample opportunity for questions.
3. Both parents should be present.
4. Time should be taken to deal with feelings.
5. Assistance about plans for the next action should be provided.
6. A follow-along plan should be initiated to provide continued support and feedback to the family.

Altered Feedback

Parents do not have the luxury of mourning a defective infant. They are faced with the demands of the child's physical care and their own developing relationship with the child. If the infant is only minimally responsive, the parents may have difficulty reading cues and responding appropriately. This constitutes a second area of concern among many parents of mentally retarded children. The concern may be described as anxiety and confusion on the part of the parent as to how to interpret the child's behavior and respond appropriately.

As part of an interdisciplinary evaluation, it is common at the University Affiliated Program in Portland to pay a visit to observe the child and family in the home setting. In one evaluation, a mother of a three-year-old severely retarded child was asked to get some toys together that would be appropriate for her child and then to play with her. The mother was observed sitting in front of her child and holding a toy out to her to engage the child's interest. The child showed no eye contact with mother, did not reach for the toy, but engaged in stereotyped hand-flapping behavior. The mother gave frequent commands to the child and picked up one toy after another to offer to her child. The mother was obviously frustrated by her child's unresponsiveness, and at one point she made a gesture of pounding her child on the head. The mother began making comments: "That kid!" and "She won't respond!"

This mother was well along in assuming a role for which she was unprepared. She will require many visits to clinics for evaluations, recommendations, and assistance in her teaching role, which will involve much more structured effort on her part, more repetition, over more time, for less gain than she had anticipated from parenting.

Some stressed parents become child-abusers. It is now well understood that children with developmental disability are much more vulnerable to abuse than are children who show normal development (Solomons, 1979). Aside from the risk of child abuse, the stress on the family is considerable. The child, like the parent, has to cope with altered feedback. Some parents react to what they perceive as unresponsiveness by being overcontrolling and by paying minimal attention to the cues shown by the child. These interaction patterns may further impede the child's progress.

For example, in a study of parent–child interactions among preschool children of normal development and preschool children with moderate to severe mental retardation, Terdal, Jackson, and Garner (1971) found that in a free play session parents of mentally retarded children were highly directive (gave more commands), their commands were often intrusive, and use of praise and positive interactive behavior on the part of the parent occurred less contingently, when viewed from the perspective of what the child was doing at the time, than was the case in the mother–child interactions in the group of children with normal development. The results were interpreted in terms of altered parental responses in reaction to impaired feedback from the child.

Peer Relations

Preschool will present a developmentally delayed child with ongoing opportunities for peer interaction. If the child is substantially delayed in comparison with other children in the program, this may create a situation in which his peers learn to avoid him. This may occur if the child is perceived by peers as unable to perform the activities, games, or tasks that are preferred by the nonhandicapped children; it may occur if the handicapped child is seen as highly disruptive. Individualized programs within mainstream preschool settings may be necessary to permit optimal participation of the handicapped child, without unnecessarily exposing the child to repeated failure experiences. Current work by Michael Guralnick and Diane Paul-Brown (1980) at the Nisonger Center is encouraging with respect to the ability of nonhandicapped young children to adapt their speech to match the developmental level of moderately and severely handicapped preschool children.

In adolescence, a number of mild and moderately retarded individuals continue in a pattern that isolates them from their peer group. Many young adolescents report that they have no friends; others do not use public transportation, do not shop for family purchases (for groceries for a meal as opposed to candy bars), take no part in community-based recreation programs, and may encounter the police for minor shop lifting. By the time these children arrive at adolescence, many parents are tired and take few risks to expose additional hurt. They may fear rejection or a failure experience if they enroll their teenagers in a scout troop, or send their children to the store to make a significant purchase, or let them take a bus or subway trip alone.

Adult Adjustment

Most studies of graduates of special classes for the mildly mentally retarded (Brolin, 1977; Hoyt, 1975; Razeghi & Davis, 1979) show that they make successful adjustments in the community. Most get jobs in competitive employment in unskilled or semiskilled fields or in service fields. Flynn (1980) states that vocational success of handicapped adults is minimally related to IQ but is more closely related to amount of formal education, occupational knowledge, and personality variables. Parental socioeconomic status is an important contributor but may operate indirectly through such mediating variables as occupational knowledge, educational aspirations, and educational attainment.

EVALUATING PERSONS WITH MENTAL RETARDATION

Recurring Assessment Questions: Infancy, School Years, Adult Years

In a broad sense, two recurring issues represent a focus in the assessment of a mentally retarded individual: (1) How can environmental demands be adjusted to provide opportunity for expression of social, interpersonal, cognitive, and self-help skills on the part of the mentally retarded? and (2) How can a mentally retarded individual be taught those behaviors, skills, and attitudes that will enable him to function in increasingly broad areas of society and assume meaningful roles?

These issues recur at several points in the life of a mentally retarded individual:

- *Infancy.* Is this individual at risk for delayed development? If so, what form of early intervention may facilitate the development of cognitive and interpersonal behavioral skills in the child? Should the main effort of intervention be through a parent-centered approach or a child-centered program (day care or preschool)? How is the family coping with the stresses involved in raising a mentally retarded child?
- *School Years.* Is the child's cognitive functioning sufficiently delayed that he/she will require major adjustments in the school curriculum? Is the child eligible for special services? If major adjustments in school curriculum need to be made, what is the least restrictive program that can facilitate the child's cognitive or social development? Can the child be mainstreamed for much of the curriculum, with access to learning centers or labs for individualized programming in certain subject areas? Is the child so handicapped that a self-contained classroom is necessary? Is the child developing social and interpersonal skills that will maximize the opportunity for independent functioning?
- *Adult Years.* Does the individual have skills that will permit entry into the competitive job market? If not, what level of day program

(sheltered workshop, activity center) is most suitable? Is the individual capable of living independently in the community? If not, what support system would enable the person to function as independently as possible; that is, would the person be able to handle a transition group home, or is relatively permanent care required, such as a total service community-based home, or a residential setting?

Types of Assessment Instruments

The issues related to mental retardation are complex, requiring changing focus as a person goes through developmental sequences. They require attention to risk factors which may make individuals vulnerable to impairment, to individual skills and deficits, to the capacity of the environment to cope with the additional stress of handling the mentally retarded individual, and to the capacity of the environment to facilitate development of a mentally retarded individual. Assessment instruments that are relevant to the mentally retarded are varied and differ from each other on a number of important parameters. Some assessment instruments are criterion-based, others are norm-referenced. Some are direct observation procedures for assessing a person while interacting in the natural environment. Other approaches include demographic data which contribute to risk indices.

The intent of this section is to point out the relevance of selected assessment procedures (including risk indices, developmental screening inventories, intelligence tests, direct observation procedures, and adaptive behavior scales) as to their applicability for answering specific but recurring clinical questions that arise in the management and habilitation of mentally retarded individuals. As in the case of the management of any chronic handicapping condition, it is understood that mental retardation affects the entire family and that the assessment process itself should take into account the resources and capabilities of the people (parent, sibling, teacher, aide) who have most direct contact with the mentally retarded individual. This section will not review the parameters of various assessment procedures (assumptions underlying test construction, norms), for there are excellent sources elsewhere; instead, this section will address the issue of decision-making rules for their application.

Risk Indices. The continued development of risk indices offers the promise of identifying at-risk infants and families who might profit from early and continued intervention programs, with the hope that they may optimize the infant's potential for development and minimize the compounding of problems for those infants who suffer from CNS impairment. Risk indices differ from screening procedures, which assess for highly specific signs of a specific disorder. For example, most states now have programs to screen for a number of metabolic disorders such as phenylketonuria, maple syrup urine disease, hypothyroidism, and others. These cost-effective procedures involve screening every newborn infant to identify the one in 4,000 infants who suffers from one of a number of metabolic disorders that, if undetected, would cause catastrophic damage. Risk indices, on the other hand, bring together a relatively large number of biological and environmental measures that singly or in combination may place the individual at risk for any number of developmental problems.

As we indicated in the section on etiology, the current trend in the development and use of at-risk procedures is away from the concept of static and single prenatal and perinatal events. Instead, the more promising efforts incorporate multiple factors, assess them over time, assume equivalence of heterogeneous factors if weighted scores of numerous items reflecting potential risk factors total the same, and provide a single score which indicates degree of risk.

Current at-risk procedures include the Cumulative Risk Index developed by Parmelee, Kopp, and Sigman (1976). Hobel, Hyvarinen, Okada, and Oh (1973) have identified and provided weighted scores for a number of specific risk factors covering prenatal, intrapartum, and neonatal stages. Again, the potential value of these instruments is that they can identify a youngster and family as being at risk and begin an intervention program before potential debilitating effects accumulate and have further adverse effects on the infant's development.

Developmental Screening Instruments. The child who walks late, who does not say words by age two, who does not relate to peers, or who does not seem to develop self-help skills signals a problem by this developmental delay in one or more areas. It is often such lags in development behind what one assumes to be normal or expected that arouse concern. There are a number of developmental screening instruments designed to assess behavior and skills in four areas of development: (1) gross motor skills, (2) fine motor skills, (3) communication skills, (4) personal–social behavior.

Some of the commonly used instruments are (1) the Denver Developmental Screening Test (Frankenburg & Dodds, 1967), (2) the Headstart Developmental Screening test and Behavior Rating Scale (Dodds, 1967), (3) the Thorpe Developmental Inventory (Thorpe, 1975), and (4) the Boyd Developmental Progress Scale (1974). These instruments have excellent face validity because they quantify many of the developmental stages that alert parents and educators to possible problems. They are designed to measure behavior and skills directly relevant to early education efforts. They are sensitive to growth, experience, and knowledge and can be used to evaluate program effectiveness as well as to appraise the progress of a child in the context of a program. In practice, the instruments are administered by a wide range of individuals within health systems as well as preschool educational programs. Potentially, their use can enhance communication among parents, educators, and health professionals. These instruments provide a brief composite picture of a child's skills and needs. In this way, they can serve as a base line and guide to planning and as a means of evaluating a child's progress during preschool years.

Thorpe (1975) cautions that these instruments require a skilled examiner to make qualitative and quantitative judgments (yes/no) through observation of a child and interview with the parent. Training is, of course, required to ensure that the interpretation of these potentially very practical instruments does not lead to careless mislabeling of youngsters, especially minority or low socioeconomic children, by examiners who do not understand the purpose of the instruments, the assessment procedure itself, the norms, or idiosyncratic behaviors of children.

Intelligence Testing. There is no assessment procedure employed by clinical psychologists in the evaluation of mentally retarded individuals that is under as much fire as is intelligence testing. Intelligence testing for the purpose of determining eligibility for school placement is, in effect, *banned* in California because of an important court decision concerning cultural and ethnic bias. Other states *require* that intelligence tests be used to determine eligibility for school placement.

Intelligence testing has been criticized on a number of grounds. Some of the major criticisms include the assumption of test bias in the practice of using IQ scores to place minority children in classes for the mentally retarded (Hobbs, 1975). Another criticism is that intelligence tests conceptualize individuals in terms of abilities and traits and do not provide answers to such treatment-oriented questions as (1) what specific behaviors or skills would be appropriate goals for this individual? and (2) how is the interplay between this individual and others in the environment maintaining problematic behaviors? A final criticism is that standard IQ scores do not reflect the processes presumed to underlie responses to test items (Sattler, 1974). The concept of intelligence itself continues to change. Obviously, this is a complex issue, but the view that intelligence is a fixed, genotypical function that unfolds over time is being discarded. There are a number of current views of intellectual development that seem to share the view that intelligence consists of a system of somewhat distinct but interrelated abilities (rather than a general fund of abilities) and that intelligence is a product that at any time is a function of "the interactive effects of genotype and environment" (Wachs, 1973, p. 28).

The influence of Jean Piaget is also being strongly felt, especially with respect to the idea that changes in intellectual functioning of a developing child are qualitative as well as quantitative. Coupled with this conception is the idea that as a child develops his intellectual structure becomes increasingly differentiated and able to handle complex constructs in qualitatively different ways.

These assumptions would imply that intelligence tests should depart from the practice of yielding a single score or quotient. For example, the Uzgiris–Hunt ordinal scales (1975), based on Piaget's concepts, provide for measures of early development in six areas interpreted to be related to early intellectual development: (1) visual pursuit and object permanence, (2) means for obtaining environmental events, (3) vocal and gestural imitation, (4) operational causality, (5) object relations, and (6) schemes for relating to objects.

There are a number of situations in which the careful use of norm-referenced standardized intelligence tests can be of substantial clinical use. For example, intelligence tests are useful as part of an assessment procedure for monitoring the progress of a child with a metabolic disorder (such as PKU) who is on a special diet to minimize toxicity to the central nervous system. Intelligence tests are useful as part of an assessment battery to monitor changes in the functioning of an individual who has a known degenerative disease or who has suffered a severe head injury.

Intelligence tests are useful for initial placement in a public school program. A child of five or six years of age, about to begin school and markedly delayed in cognitive development will need special assistance. The school will not have had a chance to compile extensive educational information about the child and his/her readiness for academic and social experiences. A careful psychological assessment, including the use of intelligence test results, can facilitate educational planning and help to identify the strengths and needs of the child in relation to available school resources. Since many parents gauge their expectations for their child by measures of the child's development, measures of a child's intellectual functioning can be useful in counseling.

The Measurement of Adaptive Behavior. The concept of adaptive behavior was implicit in the development of the Vineland Social Maturity Scale by Doll (1947). However, it was not until 1959 that the concept of adaptive behavior became a part of the definition of mental retardation (Heber, 1961). It was not until 1965 that the project to develop the AAMD Adaptive Behavior Scale (ABS) was initiated. In 1969 two scales were published, one designed for children between the ages of 3 and 12, and another for those 13 and over (Nihira, Foster, Shellhaas, & Leland, 1969). The original norms were based on residential populations. For information about a description of validation of the scales, see Nihira (1969a and 1969b). Problems in funding delayed the extension of the scale for use in the community, but recently norms have been published for school-age populations (Lambert & Nicoll, 1976). Currently, a new version of the ABS is being developed for use with infants and young children.

From the creation of the term *adaptive behavior,* the concept has been broadly defined in terms of the ability to adapt to environmental demands. The developers of the ABS viewed this ability as being displayed in three areas: (1) Independent functioning, defined as the ability of the individual to accomplish successfully those tasks or activities demanded of him by the general community, both in terms of the critical survival demands for that community and in terms of the typical expectations for specific ages; (2) Personal responsibility, defined as the willingness of the individual to accomplish those critical tasks he is able to perform (generally under some supervision) and thus to assume individual responsibility for his personal behavior; (3) Social responsibility, defined as the ability of the individual to accept responsibility as a member of a community group and to carry out appropriate behavior in terms of these group expectations. This is reflected in levels of conformity, social adjustment, and emotional maturity. Social responsibility is also reflected in the acceptance of some level of civic responsibility leading to complete or partial economic independence (Leland, Nihira, Foster, Shellhaas, & Kagin, 1968).

The ABS is divided into two sections. Part I includes 10 subscales of (1) independent functioning (eating, toilet use, cleanliness, appearance, care of clothing, dressing, travel); (2) physical development (sensory and motor); (3) economic activity (handling money and budgeting, shopping skills); (4) language development (expression, comprehension, social language development); (5) number and time concepts; (6) domestic activity; (7) vocational activity; (8) self-direction; (9) responsibility; and (10) socialization.

Part II includes an extensive list of items pertaining to behavior disorders that are relevant to mental retardation. The items are grouped into fourteen areas: (1) violent behavior; (2) destructive behavior; (3) antisocial behavior; (4) rebellious behavior; (5) untrustworthy behavior;

(6) withdrawal; (7) stereotyped behavior and odd mannerisms; (8) inappropriate interpersonal manners; (9) unacceptable vocal habits; (10) self-abusive behavior; (11) hyperactive tendencies; (12) sexually aberrant behavior; (13) psychological disturbances; and (14) use of medication. The scale has excellent face validity in the sense of coverage of recurring issues related to mental retardation.

In clinical use of the ABS, it is important to consider: (1) the overall pattern of skills as shown on the various scales in Part I. The information obtained can be used as a guide to indicate the skills that a retarded individual has and what skills may be targeted for intervention. (2) The degree to which the individual normally performs skills that have been developed without extensive supervision. (3) The degree to which the individual has opportunities to interact in social settings in which he could develop and use social skills. (4) The number of problematic behaviors identified as concerns during the administration of Part II of the Scale. Once problematic behaviors have been identified, it is important to follow up the administration of the ABS with a probe to determine information about the situations in which problematic behaviors occur and the ways in which the parents (and significant others) handle them. Furthermore, the type and frequency of problematic behaviors, as determined from the administration of Part II, may be explored from the perspective of a possible mismatch of the skills of the mentally retarded individual and the demands of his environment, which may be chronically frustrating.

Direct Observation Procedure. An assessment strategy that is receiving increasing use in the area of mental retardation is that of direct observation. This approach enables an individual to observe a client as the client interacts in situations that represent his natural environment. Observations are taken directly, whether on film for later analysis or through on-the-spot recording by trained observers. Direct observation offers the potential advantage of providing information about behavior in a context representing the situations in which the behaviors of interest appear and information about how they are handled. Mash and Terdal (1976) provide information about types of direct observation procedures, methods of training observers, reactions to being observed, and methods of assessing agreement in notation.

In this brief section, emphasis will be placed on parent–child interaction in clinic or home settings, although direct observation procedures are clearly applicable to preschool programs, public school programs, and vocational settings, as well as to behavior in stores, restaurants, and public transportation. Assessment data derived from observations of parent–child interactions can provide a base of information from which to give feedback to parents that may contribute toward the habilitation of the handicapped child. Strategies for designing parent-training programs can draw from the now rapidly growing literature on parent–child interaction. While a unified theory does not exist, current efforts share the view that the quality of the interaction sets in motion the cognitive and behavioral development of the infant. The process is complex and is assumed to be reciprocal. Changes in the child's repertoire (due to maturation or learning) evoke changes in the maternal response to the child, which set the stage (along with continued maturation) for an increasingly complex repertoire in the child's response and further changes in maternal responses to the child.

Goldberg (1977) has elaborated on a model of parent–infant interactions that has direct relevance to the area of mental retardation. She views infants as preadapted to be selectively attentive to the kinds of stimulation provided by caretakers. The infant's responses to caretakers elicit their attention and facilitate interactions. These exchanges, to the extent that they are perceived as effective, enhance "feelings of efficacy," a concept elaborated by White (1959).

Infant–adult interactions normally provide the infant with "contingency experiences," in which the infant learns through his or her interactions with significant others that he/she can affect the enviornment. Similarly, the adult may experience "feelings of efficacy" by perceiving that he/she can recognize signals or cues from the infant and respond in a way that is mutually satisfying.

The Impaired Child and Parent–Child Interactions. Terdal, Jackson, and Garner (1976) have studied parent–child interaction patterns among mentally retarded children and their mothers and also interaction patterns among normally developing children and their mothers. Particular attention was paid to the question of gross behavioral deficits on the part of moderately and severely retarded children and the effect of impaired feedback (from child to mother) on the interaction patterns.

Significant behavioral deficits on the part of a mentally retarded child may result in repeated failure experiences for the child. The caretaker may be exposed to repeated lack of feedback and may be uncertain as to how to respond. Much of the continuing anxiety and depression attributed to parents of severely handicapped children may relate not so much to the loss of the idealized child, which has often been reported, as to continuing stress on the mother or caretaker because of ongoing interaction patterns which provide little positive feedback to the parent to indicate that he or she is responding in a way that will facilitate the development and social skills of the child.

The Response Class Matrix. The Response Class Matrix (Mash, Terdal, & Anderson, 1973) was designed to assess parent–child interaction relevant to questions of child management. It is useful for assessing parent–child interactions in situations where the child is between two and eight years of age. The procedure is based on observing parent–child interaction in free play and in a task situation. One assumes that specific management concerns of parents may signal rather general and pervasive problems in the relationship. Therefore, rather than starting out with a highly specific assessment of a target behavior, a broader view of the parent–child interaction is maintained.

The following is a narrative description of one segment of an interaction between a mother and a 4½-year-old moderately retarded boy.

The mother had led the child into the playroom and, holding a red wooden block, was attempting to direct John's attention toward it.

MOTHER: John! What color is this?
JOHN: *(No response.)*
MOTHER: *(Taps the wooden block in an apparent effort to draw John's attention to the wooden block. She repeats the question.)* John! What color is this?
JOHN: *(Taps the wooden block three times, in apparent imitation of the mother's tap, but does not verbalize.)*
MOTHER: No, John! You tell me what color this is!
JOHN: *(Pulls back, does not verbalize.)*
MOTHER: John this block is red. Say red.
JOHN: Red.
MOTHER: *(Holds up a green wooden block.)* John, what color is this?
JOHN: Red.
MOTHER: No. That is not red. This one *(pointing to the red block)* is red. This one *(shaking the green block)* is green.

The mother's behavior in the "free play" segment described above was highly directive. The child was minimally responsive to the mother. More significantly, the task posed by the mother was too difficult for the child. The child imitated the mother's behavior of tapping the block three times. The mother, however, was interested in the child's naming the color of the block. When the mother prompted the child, the child imitated the response and then incorrectly repeated the same answer to the next question. In a post-interaction interview, the mother indicated displeasure with the child and stated that the child "did not mind."

Interpretation of Parent–Child Interaction. It is critical in evaluating a parent–child interaction not to assume that the child's deviant behavior is caused by ineffective parenting. It is also critical not to assume that the behavior shown by the parent represents the caretaker's parenting behavior. The parent may have a broad range of skills and may be very effective in relating to other children. Problems encountered by a parent with a mentally retarded child may reflect the parent's lack of understanding of the child's development, difficulty in reading cues from the child, and difficulty in relating to a child who does not initiate a broad range of behaviors to which the parent can respond. Intervention may start with providing information about the child's developmental level and what his needs are.

Kogan and Tyler (1973) report studies in which parents of handicapped children are shown to employ structure (commands and other directives) at levels much higher than do parents of normally developing children; this is consistent with our own findings. Kogan and Tyler caution that parent-training programs that attempt too much and in which progress is minimal may contribute to increased depression on the part of the parent and greater distance between parent and child.

Post-Interaction Interview. After the session, it is useful to debrief the mother. What were her impressions? Was the child's behavior similar to that which she experiences in other settings? What was her perception of the responsiveness of her child to her behavior, that is, to commands, to attempts on her part to get responses, to questions, and, if applicable, to instances of praise and punishment? How different was her interaction with her child in the observed session from typical ones in other settings? And finally, were problems of concern to her reflected in this session?

This kind of interview can help the parent describe the child's behavior, the situations in which the problematic behaviors occur, and the handling of them. It also provides the therapist with one opportunity to compare his observations of the child's and parent's behavior with the parent's report.

Selection of Assessment Procedure

Psychological evaluation is a complex process. The choices a psychologist must consider will vary according to the referral questions and the use made of the results. Although unnecessary testing is wasteful and intrusive, adequate and ongoing assessment can be very helpful in planning treatment.

Table I provides a matrix organized around persistent questions that arise in rehabilitative work with mentally retarded people and assessment procedures. The boxes are filled in, but individual situations may require a clinician to choose alternative procedures. The table is meant to be heuristic and to permit the reader to consider, depending

TABLE I
Decision-Making Guideline for Matching Assessment Procedure with Assessment Questions

Intervention focus	Assessment procedures							Diagnostic questions
	Risk indices	Developmental inventories	Adaptive behavior scales	Intelligence tests	Direct observation procedures	Interview	Criterion referenced achievement tests	Behavior rating scales	
Eligibility for early intervention	++	+			+	++			Have prenatal, perinatal, or neonatal events placed child at risk for biological insults which may impair development? Does the mother perceive the infant as responsive to her? Are major socioeconomic stresses interfering with the family, providing a supportive environment for child?
Developmental delay (0–6)	+	++			+	++			Is child developing according to expectations? Are vision and hearing normal? Should an intervention plan be instituted?
Monitor progress and goal setting in preschool program		++			++	++			In terms of child's developmental skills, what social, behavioral or cognitive goals would be most relevant? Are adjustments in curriculum required to provide opportunities for child to interact?

Continued

TABLE I (*Continued*)

Intervention focus	Assessment procedures							Diagnostic questions
	Risk indices	Developmental inventories	Adaptive behavior scales	Intelligence tests	Direct observation procedures	Interview	Criterion referenced achievement tests	Behavior rating scales	
Family adjustment to mental retardation			++	++	++	++			Do the parents have an understanding of the child's current level of functioning? If child is severely impaired do the parents perceive themselves as able to support the child's development?
Determine eligibility for special services in school program			++	++	+	++	++		Is the child's level of cognitive skills and adaptive behavior at a level where major adjustments in school programming are required?
Monitor development and behavior patterns of child with metabolic disorder				++	++	++		+	Do parents have a thorough understanding of the metabolic disorder and of diet management requirements? Is the child developing normally in terms of cognitive development and behavior?

Determine or make adjustments in school program.			++	++	+	++		+	Is child coping with curriculum and with peers? Is the program maximizing the child's strengths? Is the focus too narrowly academic?
Behavior management			++	++	++	++		+	Is child developing attitudes and behaviors that will facilitate entry into broader social roles?
Vocational placement			++	+	+	++	+		Is the individual developing social skills and work habits that increase likelihood of competitive employment?
Adult placement			++	+	+	++			Can the individual live independently in the community? If not, what minimum level of support is necessary to permit placement in least restrictive environment?

++ Highly relevant.
+ Potentially relevant.

upon the particular intervention focus and referral questions, what form of assessment strategy might be employed. For example, for questions of child management, the author suggests that an interview with the parents and child (if possible), administration of an adaptive behavior scale, and the use of a direct observation procedure would be highly relevant. For questions pertaining to the school placement of a handicapped child, an intelligence test, an adaptive behavior scale, an achievement test, and an interview would be proper. Depending on time constraints, one should consider observing the child in a classroom setting. For questions about vocational placement of an adult, one might consider an adaptive behavior scale and an interview of the client focused on vocational goals, knowledge of job requirements, expectations about pay, and work history. In this case, to repeat an intellectual assessment would probably not be necessary.

Special Considerations

With a young child, it is important to obtain three kinds of data about the child's functioning, one based on the parent's assessment of the child's functioning, another based on a professional assessment of the child through standardized procedures, and a third through observation of the child interacting with those who are significant to him, for example, a home observation or observation of parent–child interaction in the clinic.

In the interview with the parent(s), it is important to give ample time to their chief complaint, including questions about their observations, when they first noticed the problem, the situations in which the problem occurs, how they are handling the problem, and their estimate of long-term effect if the problem should continue unabated. When a child shows delayed development, it is important to take the time to get a careful appraisal of the parents' perception of the child's functioning. In addition to the information attained by thorough questioning, this technique also directs the parents' attention in behavioral terms to the child's functioning. The author has had the experience of parents' returning a week after a clinic visit to report that they had noticed that their child could not do all the things that they had said he could. "I began to watch him; he does not dress himself. I began to notice that I do more of that for him than I thought. He doesn't eat with a fork," and so forth.

In evaluating a young child with a developmental disability, it is important to obtain some information about the child's current level of functioning that can be communicated to the parents. If the child has no major sensory or motor deficits and is approachable, a developmental test based on the child's performance should not be a problem. A child with major sensory and motor deficits who has not yet developed a base of receptive language can present a real challenge. Consider, however, the impact of telling a parent, "Your child is not testable." If the parent already has grave misconceptions about his/her ability to relate to the child, it can be a severe setback to the parent that others can not relate to the child either. This does not mean that it is necessary to obtain an IQ score, but that *some* assessment of the child's functioning is helpful for communication. It can be a basis for starting the parent on a program.

As soon as possible, the mentally retarded individual should be brought into the evaluation–treatment process as an active participant. This may require an assertive stance on the part of the clinician to protect the right of the client. At times, for example, a parent or a caseworker may answer questions addressed to the mentally retarded client. This implies that the client has nothing of value to say about his situation.

In general, an individual who has a mental age of about 4 or 4½ can usually give a coherent account of his day, covering such things as who lives at home with him, what school he goes to, how his day goes, what he likes to do, what kind of trouble he gets into, and who disciplines him. By the time an individual has a mental age of about 8, it may be possible to administer an adaptive behavior scale with the client as the informant. Obviously there is risk, and some independent sources should be used for verification, but it is a useful approach to engage the client in his own program. Many times, when given a chance, mentally retarded clients will express a concern that reflects their interest in achieving more independence. One, for example (a 15-year-old, brain-injured from an auto accident, and functioning within the mildly retarded range), said in response to a question about concerns or problems, "When my mother is working, I have to be at the house. I can't have any friends over. *(After a long pause)* I get lonely."

INTERVENTION METHODS

Intervention: A Framework

As we have emphasized throughout this chapter, mental retardation encompasses a broad range of impairments resulting from diverse etiologies, some representing largely biological pathology, others largely psychosocial deficits, some with complex interactions between biological and psychosocial factors, and others of unknown etiology. Although there may be no natural way to differentiate among the groups, arbitrary groupings may clarify the directions to be taken in intervention.

Following the framework provided in the section on etiology, intervention strategies will be considered in terms of whether impairment of the child (or risk of impairment) is related to one or more of the following three broad factors: (1) impairment associated with medical factors with established risk for mental retardation, (2) problems associated with high-risk infants, (3) problems associated with inadequate stimulation due to pervasive psychosocial deprivation.

These distinctions follow those suggested by Tjossem (1976). They are arbitrary, and the author recognizes that within the groupings heterogeneity is the norm and that biological and environmental factors will interact over developmental sequences. Distinctions, however, are warranted if they are useful and can guide practitioners in maintaining a focus on likely, profitable strategies in the care and habilitation of mentally retarded individuals and if they can provide a focus for counseling the parents. In general, the distinctions suggested above have most relevance for early intervention programs. By the time an individual is at the age to enter a public school program and as he reaches adulthood, treatment implications based on etiology have progressively less relevance.

Children with Established Risk for Mental Retardation. Diagnosis of impairment in instances in which the child eventually functions in the severe to profound range of mental retardation is generally made in infancy, even when no specific syndrome is evident. When a syndrome, such as Down's Syndrome, is present, diagnosis generally occurs at birth, or before if the mother has undergone amniocentesis. Guidelines for counseling and intervention include continued support and feedback to the parents about the child's condition, with ample time to discuss and share with the family the implications of the disability and their emotional adjustment to the impairment. In general, parents of a child with a major impairment do not find it helpful for professionals to make specific predictions about developmental milestones, but they do find it useful to be oriented to the possibility of their child's being able to live in a sheltered environment with the possibility of a day option, such as a sheltered workshop setting or, in adulthood, an activity center (Springer & Steele, 1980).

It is helpful for the counselor to advise parents about treating their child as normally as possible, to educate them to the wide range of developmental potential, to encourage placement in preschool programs with the possibility of interaction with normally developing children, and to encourage contact with community and state groups associated with mental retardation.

Many parents report that they feel optimistic as they see that the child is developing and making progress. At other times, the same parents may experience extreme fatigue and lack of confidence in their ability to support the child's development. At those times, intervention that is parent–child centered may be helpful to assist the parents in discovering the ways in which the child is responsive to them and what developmental steps may be in prospect.

The Biologically Vulnerable Newborn. In instances in which the child is born too small and too early, a number of risk factors are set into motion. These include separation for extended hospitalization and other factors associated with the care of a biologically vulnerable infant. Intervention must occur at birth. A number of studies have shown that separation of mother and neonate during periods of intensive care places them at risk for developing problems with bonding. Even after hospitalization, some of the patterns persist in the form of altered interactions, with mothers of premature infants engaging in more care-giving behavior, less play, and less frequent smiling (Leifer, Leiderman, Barnett, & Williams, 1972). Other studies report that mothers of high-risk infants are verbally less responsive to their infants as late as nine months following birth (Brown & Bakeman, 1978). High-risk infants are also more likely than normal full-term infants to be battered, abused, and neglected later in childhood (Kline & Stern, 1971; Powell, 1974).

Progressive hospital settings designed to provide comprehensive care for high-risk infants now design their programs to allow as much parent–infant contact as possible, using the parent as a participant in the care and management of the infant. Programmatic evaluations of these settings generally indicate that parents who are permitted and encouraged to have physical contact with their at-risk infants during periods of hospitalization gain in confidence and skill in areas of care and interaction (Seashore, Leifer, Barnett, & Leiderman, 1973) and in improved family adjustment (Leifer *et al.*, 1972).

As we said above in the section on etiology, demographic variables including educational level of the mother, age of mother, income level of family, and marital status are associated with high-risk infants. As a result, a number of variables may interact, and it may be possible to attribute more impact than is warranted to the effect of brief separation between mother and infant and subsequent parent–child relationships with respect to the child's cognitive development. It may be that highly stressful factors associated with low income and a lack of a support group for the mother (especially in the case of a single mother) may continue to operate following departure from the hospital and may substantially affect the child's cognitive development, but that such problems may be incorrectly attributed to a rather brief separation during the stay at the hospital. At any rate, follow-up is warranted to monitor the development of high-risk infants and to give additional assistance and support to the family if it is evident that stresses continue to interfere with parenting or family coping (Leiderman & Seashore, 1975).

Children At Risk for Psychosocial Retardation. The goal of intervention for children at risk for psychosocial retardation is prevention, not amelioration. The current trend continues in a state of flux between programs emphasizing early education for the child and others focusing on parent-centered programs. The stress on the latter is based in part on a belief that the impact of child-centered programs is short-lived (Bronfrenbrenner, 1974), but also on the fear that the child-centered programs may inadvertently detract from the family's role in early childhood care (Bronfrenbrenner, 1974; Shearer & Shearer, 1972). Parent-centered programs for infants at risk for psychosocial mental retardation typically start within the first year of life of the infant, focus on the relationship between the mother and child (rather than on a specific targeted behavior), and build in continuing involvement with the families (Shearer & Shearer, 1972; Ramey & Smith, 1977).

Headstart programs remain a major social experiment in the care of disadvantaged children. Headstart programs stress education of the child *and* parental involvement, as well as nutrition and ongoing health care. Although some early evaluations of the effectiveness of Headstart programs were very pessimistic, a more recent review (Darlington, Royce, Snipper, Murray, & Lazar, 1980) reports that Headstart children perform better in school and require fewer special services than do children of comparable socioeconomic background who did not receive Headstart experience.

Interdisciplinary Care

There is an increasing emphasis on interdisciplinary care in the diagnosis and treatment of mentally retarded individuals. This development reflects the view that mental retardation involves so many areas of functioning, including physical, psychological, social, educational, and vocational, with changing emphases as the individual moves through developmental stages from infancy through adulthood, that no one discipline covers the range of the services required. An interdisciplinary staff may be represented by twelve or more disciplines. Within the staff, one individual may be assigned a case-coordinator role to maintain contact with the family and to ease reentry into the system as needed. Findings from the various disciplines are normally shared in staff meetings, which permit coordination of efforts and facilitate communication with the family about diagnostic findings, including strengths as well as deficits, and recommendations for treatment.

Specialized programs designed to meet specialized needs of some handicapped individuals are a common component of large interdisciplinary service programs. Examples of specialized medically oriented clinics are programs including orthopedics, neonatal intensive care, cardiology, metabolism, neurology, and audiology. Within these clinics, somewhat standardized formats may be developed. For example, a metabolic clinic may have a fairly well established procedure to monitor the diet of PKU children, monitor development, and provide genetic counseling for parents, as well as to provide counseling regarding the need for treated PKU women to return to a low phenylalanine diet prior to and throughout pregnancy to prevent serious central nervous system impairment in the fetus.

Residential Treatment

Without question, there has been a major shift, from about 1960 to the present, toward a major emphasis upon providing care for mentally retarded children in the home with the support of community-based programs. However, residential institutions remain a necessary part of the care of some mentally retarded individuals. Residential institutions have had to change their focus since landmark right-to-treatment judgments were made in cases in Willowbrook (Staten Island) and Pennhurst (in Pennsylvania), and in the Wyatt–Stickney decision in Alabama. As a result of these important legal decisions, custodial care is no longer considered an acceptable option for mentally retarded children. Most institutions now have policies to the effect that (a) a retarded person is admitted only after specific treatment goals are established; (b) residential treatment placement is viewed as time-limited with built-in review procedures to insure that institutionalization does not continue any longer than necessary; (c) contacts with the family and community are maintained; (d) active, planned intervention is assured; and (e) plans for reentry into the community are developed as part of the rehabilitation effort.

At this point, the right-to-treatment movement has not had a general impact on the care of adult residents in mental retardation facilities. In many institutions, once a client reaches 21 years of age, the institution is not required (and not funded) to maintain habilitation efforts.

The population in residential institutions for the retarded is skewed toward those with the most profound impairment. In general, if out-of-home care is required, foster home care should be considered. Parents as well as community agency staff are increasingly aware that institutional placement can further impair a child's development.

With the current trend toward deinstitutionalization, many adults with major impairments in intellectual functioning and adaptive behavior live in the community. Successful adaptation for many of these adults requires group homes and sheltered workshop programs. These requirements strain the resources of many communities and often remain significantly absent in the care of the adult mentally retarded.

TRENDS AND NEEDS

The prevention of mental retardation, when possible, and the care and habilitation of mentally retarded individuals take time and long-term commitment. The problems associated with mental retardation are complex and resist short-term solution. The recent moves toward mainstreaming and normalization certainly offer the potential for providing a more humane life for mentally retarded individuals. On the other hand, these efforts may focus attention on gaps in current knowledge and current treatment programs. One of the needs in the area of mental retardation is a national commitment. Young researchers who begin projects in the field of human development should have some assurance that funding will last beyond a pilot phase of research. Clinicians who plan habilitation programs for the mentally retarded must be assured that the programs will be intact beyond the next national election.

APPENDIX: SOURCES OF INFORMATION

General information for the professional: *Handbook of Mental Deficiency, Psychological Theory and Research,* Second edition, Norman R. Ellis (Editor). Hillsdale, New Jersey: Lawrence Erlbaum Associates, 1979.

Developmental Disabilities, R.J. Thompson and A.N. O'Quinn. New York: Oxford University Press, 1979.

Intervention Strategies for High Risk Infants and Young Children, Theodore D. Tjossem (Editor). Baltimore: University Park Press, 1976.

Information for the family: *The Child with Down's Syndrome*, D.W. Smith and A.A. Wilson. Philadelphia: W.B. Saunders Company, 1974. *Teaching Your Down's Syndrome Infant*, M.J. Hanson. Baltimore: University Park Press, 1977.

REFERENCES

Abroms, K. I., & Bennett, J. W. Current genetic and demographic findings in Down's Syndrome: How are they presented in college text books on exceptionality? *Mental Retardation*, 1980, *18*, 101–118.

Anderson, K. A., & Garner, A. M. Mothers of retarded children: Satisfaction with visits to professional people. *Mental Retardation*, August, 1971, *9*, 3–5.

Babson, S. G., Benson, R. C., Pernoll, M. L., & Benda, G. I. *Management of high risk pregnancy and intensive care of the neonate.* St. Louis: C. V. Mosby, 1975.

Boyd, R. D. *The Boyd Developmental Progress Scale.* San Bernardino, Calif.: Inland Counties Regional Center, 1974.

Brazelton, T. B., Koslowski, B., & Main, M. Origins of reciprocity. In M. Lewis & L. Rosenblum (Eds.) *Origins of behavior* (Vol. 1). New York: Wiley, 1974.

Brazelton, T. B., Parker, W. B., & Zuckerman, B. Importance of behavior assessment in the neonate. In *Current problems in pediatrics.* Chicago: Year Book Medical Publishers, December, 1976.

Brolin, D. E. Career development: A national priority. *Education and Training of the Mentally Retarded*, 1977, *12*, 154–156.

Bronfenbrenner, V. *Is early intervention effective? A report on longitudinal evaluation of preschool programs* (Vol. 2). Department of Health, Education, and Welfare, Office of Human Development, Office of Child Development, Children's Bureau, #(OHD)76–30025. Washington, D.C.: U.S. Government Printing Office, 1974.

Brown, J. V., & Bakeman, R. Relationships of human mothers with their infants during the first year of life: Effects of prematurity. In R. W. Bell & W. P. Smotherman (Eds.), *Maternal influences and early behavior.* Holliswood, N.Y.: Spectrum, 1978.

Caldwell, B., Heider, J., & Kaplan, B. *The inventory of home stimulation.* Paper presented at the annual meeting of the American Psychological Association, New York, September, 1966.

Coopersmith, S. *The antecedents of self-esteem.* San Francisco: W.H. Freeman, 1967.

Cornwell, A., & Birch, H. Psychological and social development in home-reared children with Down's syndrome (mongolism). *American Journal of Mental Deficiency*, 1968, *74*, 341–350.

Darlington, R. B., Royce, J. M., Snipper, A. S., Murray, H. W., & Lazar, I. Preschool programs and later school competence of children from low income families. *Science*, 1980, *208*, 202–208.

Dodds, J. *The Headstart developmental screening test and behavior rating scale*, CAP–16S Form 56, July, 1967, GSA 68, (not copyrighted).

Doll, E. A. *Social Maturity Scale.* Circle Pines, Minn.: American Guidance Service, 1947.

Drotar, D., Baskiewicz, A., Irvin, N., Kennel, J., & Klaus, M. The adaptation of parents to the birth of an infant with a congenital malformation: A hypothetical model. *Pediatrics*, 1975, *56*, 710–717.

Engel, M., & Keane, W. M. *Black mothers and their infant sons: Antecedents, correlates, and predictors of cognitive development in the second and sixth year of life.* Paper presented at the biennial meeting of the Society for Research in Child Development, Denver, 1975.

Filler, J. W., Robinson, C. C., Smith, R. A., Vincent-Smith, L. J., Bricker, D. D., & Bricker, W. A. Mental retardation. In N. Hobbs (Ed.), *Issues in the classification of children* (Vol. 1). Washington, D.C.: Jossey–Bass Publishers, 1975.

Flynn, R. J. Mental ability, schooling and early career achievement of low-IQ and average-IQ young men. *American Journal of Mental Deficiency*, 1980, *84*(5), 431–443.

Fowle, C. The effect of the severely mentally retarded child on his family. *American Journal of Mental Deficiency*, 1968, *73*, 468–473.

Frankenburg, W. K., & Dodds, J. B. The Denver developmental screening test. *Journal of Pediatrics*. 1967, *71*, 181–187.

Goldberg, S. Social competence in infancy: A model of parent–infant interactions. *Merrill–Palmer Quarterly*. 1977, *23*, (3), 163–178.

Grossman, H. J. *Manual on terminology and classification in mental deficiency.* Washington, D.C.: American Association on Mental Deficiency, 1973.

Guralnick, M. J., & Paul-Brown, D. Functional and discourse analyses of nonhandicapped preschool children's speech to handicapped children. *American Journal of Mental Deficiency*, 1980, *84*(5), 444–454.

Heber, R. F. A manual on terminology and classification in mental retardation. *American Journal of Mental Deficiency*, 1961, *61*, Monograph Supplement.

Hobbs, M. (Ed.) *Issues in the classification of children.* San Francisco: Jossey–Bass Publishers, 1975.

Hobel, C. J., Hyvarinen, M. A., Okada, D., & Oh, W. Premature and intrapartum high risk screening. *American Journal of Obstetrics and Gynecology*, 1973, *117*, 1–8.

Holmes, L. B. Genetic counseling for the older pregnant woman: New data and questions. *New England Journal of Medicine*, 1978, *298*, 1419–1421.

Hoyt, K. B. *An introduction to career education.* Washington, D.C.: U.S. Government Printing Office, 1975.

Johnson, A. M. The management of cardiac disease in Down's Syndrome. *Developmental Medicine and Child Neurology*, 1978, *20*(2), 220–223.

Klein, M., & Stern, L. Low birth weight and the battered child syndrome. *American Journal of Diseases of Children*, 1971, *122*, 15–18.

Kogan, K. L., & Tyler, N. Mother–child interaction in young physically handicapped children. *American Journal of Mental Deficiency*, 1973, *77*(5), 492–497.

Lambert, N. M., & Nicoll, R. C. Dimensions of adaptive behavior of retarded and nonretarded public school children. *American Journal of Mental Deficiency*, 1976, *81*, 135–146.

Leiderman, P. H., & Seashore, M. J. Mother–infant neonatal separation: Some delayed consequences. In R. Porter & M. O'Connor (Eds.), *Parent–Infant Interaction*. Ciba Foundation Symposium 33. Amsterdam: Elsevier, 1975.

Leifer, A. D., Leiderman, P. H., Barnett, C. R., & Williams, J. A. Effects of mother–infant separation on maternal attachment behavior. *Child Development*, 1972, *43*, 1203–1218.

Leland, H., Nihira, K., Foster, R., Shellhaas, M., & Kagin, E. *Conference on measurement of adaptive behavior III.* Kansas: Parsons State Hospital and Training Center, 1968.

Manual of the international statistical classification of diseases, injuries and causes of death based on the recommendation of the Ninth Revision Conference, 1975, and adopted by the 29th World Health Assembly (Vols. 1 & 2). Geneva: World Health Organization, 1978.

Mash, E. J., & Terdal, L. G. (Eds.) *Behavior therapy assessment.* New York: Springer Publishing Company, 1976.

Mash, E. J., Terdal, L., & Anderson, K. The response–class matrix: A procedure for recording parent–child interactions. *Journal of Consulting and Clinical Psychology*, 1973, *40*, 163–164.

Mercer, J. R. Sociocultural factors in educational labeling. In M. G. Begob & S. A. Richardson (Eds.), *The mentally retarded and society: A social science perspective.* Baltimore: University Park Press, 1975.

Newman, L. S., & Ramey, C. T. Antecedents and correlates of self-concept, intelligence and school achievement in psychosocially high risk children. Paper presented at the 87th meeting of the American Psychological Association, New York, September, 1979.

Nihira, K. Factorial dimensions of adaptive behavior in adult retardates. *American Journal of Mental Deficiency*, 1969, *73*, 868–878 (a).

Nihira, K. Factorial dimensions of adaptive behavior in mentally retarded children and adolescents. *American Journal of Mental Deficiency*, 1969, *74*, 130–141 (b).

Nihira, K., Foster, R., Shellhaas, M., & Leland, H. *American Association on Mental Deficiency Adaptive Behavior Scale.* Washington, D.C.: American Association on Mental Deficiency, 1969.

Nihira, K., Foster, R., Shellhaas, M., & Leland, H. *American Association on Mental Deficiency Adaptive Behavior Scale, 1975 Revision.* Washington, D.C.: American Association on Mental Deficiency, 1975.

Olshansky, S. Chronic sorrow. A response to having a mentally defective child. *Social Casework*, 1962, *43*, 190–193.

Park, S. C., Mathews, R. A., Zuberbuhler, J. R., Rowe, R. D., Neches, W. H., & Lenox, C. C. Down's Syndrome with congenital heart malformation. *American Journal of Diseases of Children*, 1977, *131*, 29–33.

Parmelee, A. H., & Haber, A. Who is the "risk infant"? In H. J. Osofsky (Ed.), *Clinical obstetrics and gynecology.* New York: Harper & Row, 1973.

Parmelee, A. H., Kopp, C. B., & Sigman, M. Selection of developmental assessment techniques for infants at risk. *Merrill–Palmer Quarterly*, 1976, *22*, 177–199.

Parmelee, A. H., Sigman, M., Kopp, C. B., & Haber, A. Diagnosis of the infant at risk for mental, motor, and sensory handicaps. In T. D. Tjossem (Ed.), *Intervention strategies for high risk infants and young children.* Baltimore: University Park Press, 1976.

Powell, L. F. The effect of extra stimulation and maternal involvement on the development of low birth weight infants and on maternal behavior. *Child Development*, 1974, *45*, 106–113.

President's Panel on Mental Retardation. *A proposed program for national action to combat mental retardation.* Washington, D.C.

Ramey, C. T., & Smith, B. J. Assessing the intellectual consequences of early intervention with high risk infants. *American Journal of Mental Deficiency*, 1977, *81*(4), 318–324.

Rantakallo, P. Predictive indices of neonatal morbidity and mortality. In S. Aladjem, A. K. Brown, & C. Sureau (Eds.), *Clinical perinatology.* St. Louis: The C. V. Mosby Company, 1980.

Razeghi, J. A., & Davis, S. Federal mandates for the handicapped: Vocational education opportunity and employment. *Exceptional Children*, 1979, *45*, 353–359.

Rutter, M., Graham, P., & Yule, W. *Neuropsychiatric study in childhood.* Clinics in Developmental Medicine, Nos. 35/36. London: SIMP with Heinemann Medical, 1970.

Sattler, J. M. *Assessment of children's intelligence.* Philadelphia: W. B. Saunders, 1974.

Scurletis, T. D., & Headrick, M. S. *A system of comprehensive health care screening and service for children.* Paper presented at annual meeting of the American Association of Mental Deficiency, May 15–20, 1972, Minneapolis.

Seashore, M. H., Leifer, A. D., Barnett, C. R., & Leiderman, P. K. The effects of denial of early mother–infant interaction on maternal self-confidence. *Journal of Personality and Social Psychology*, 1975, *26*, 369–378.

Shaher, R. D., Farina, M. A., Porter, I. H., & Bishop, M. Clinical aspects of congenital heart disease in mongolism. *American Journal of Cardiology*, 1972, *29*, 497–503.

Shearer, M., & Shearer, D. The Portage project: A model for early childhood education. *Exceptional Children*, 1972, *36*, 210–217.

Smith, D. W. *Recognizable patterns of human malformation*. Philadelphia: W.B. Saunders Company, 1976.

Solnit, A., & Stark, M. Mourning and the birth of a defective child. *Psychoanalytic Study of the Child*, 1961, *16*, 523–537.

Solomons, G. Child abuse and developmental disabilities. *Developmental Medicine and Child Neurology*, 1979, *21*, 101–106.

Springer, A., & Steele, M. W. Effects of physicians' early parental counseling on rearing of Down's Syndrome children. *American Journal of Mental Deficiency*, 1980, *85*(1), 1–5.

Tarjan, G., Wright, S. W., Eyman, R. K., & Keeran, C. V. Natural history of mental retardation: Some aspects of epidemiology. *American Journal of Mental Deficiency*, 1973, *77*(4), 369–379.

Terdal, L. G., Jackson, R. J., & Garner, A. M. Mother–child interactions: A comparison between normal and developmentally delayed groups. In E. J. Mash, L. A. Hamerlynck, & L. C. Handy (Eds.), *Behavior modification and families*. New York: Bruner/Mazel, 1976.

Thompson, R. J., & O'Quinn, A. N. *Developmental disabilities*. New York: Oxford University Press, 1979.

Thorpe, H. S. Optimal developmental appraisal. *Developmental Medicine and Child Neurology*, 1975, *17*, 481–485.

Tjossem, T. D. Early intervention: Issues and approaches. In T. D. Tjossem (Ed.), *Intervention strategies for high risk infants and young children* Baltimore: University Park Press, 1976.

Uzgiris, I. C., & Hunt, J. McV. *Assessment in infancy: Ordinal scales of psychological development*. Urbana: University of Illinois Press, 1975.

Wachs, T. D. The measurement of early intellectual functioning: Contributions from developmental psychology. In C. Edward Meyers (Ed.), *Monographs of the Association on Mental Deficiency* (No. 1). Sociobehavioral Studies in Mental Retardation, Los Angeles: University of Southern California, 1973.

Werner, E. E., Bierman, J. M., & French, F. E. *The children of Kauai: A longitudinal study from the prenatal period to age ten*. Honolulu: University of Hawaii Press, 1971.

White, R. W. Motivation reconsidered: The concept of competence. *Psychological Review*, 1959, *66*, 297–333.

Williams, M., & Scarr, S. Effects of short-term intervention on performance in low-birth-weight disadvantages children. *Pediatrics*, 1971, *47*, 289–298.

8

Spinal Cord Injury

Traumatic spinal cord injury has been appropriately described as one of the most devastating calamities in human life (Guttman, 1976). It attacks body integrity and threatens life. It rapidly and radically alters the person's mobility, capacity for self-care, self-image, and social role, and requires unparalleled social and psychological adjustment (Burnham & Werner, 1978–1979).

THE PHYSICAL DISABILITY

Incidence

Approximately 10,000 persons per year sustain spinal cord injuries which result in permanent paraplegia or quadriplegia, and there are an estimated 200,000 persons with traumatic paraplegia or quadriplegia in the United States (Pierce, 1977). The ratio of males to females injured is approximately 3:1 (Kraus, Frant, Riggins, Richards, & Borhani, 1975) and the professional literature is heavily weighted with information about the problems of the male patient. Incidence is concentrated in young adults, with a very high proportion in the 15- to 24-year age group (Kraus *et al.*, 1975; Wilcox, Stauffer, & Nickel, 1970). Motor vehicle and sports accidents account for three quarters of the cases (Chiu, 1975). Webb, Berzins, Wingardner, and Lorenzi (1977–1978), reporting on actual costs of 85 spinal cord injured patients, found mean first year hospital costs of $35,676, with home care costs averaging $4,000 per patient per year. The development of new and costly technology plus the impact of inflation insure that these figures are understated.

Acute Care

Pierce (1977) describes the "woefully inadequate" first aid treatment of patients with spinal injuries and cites a proportion in excess of 10% who show a progression in symptomatology between the time of diagnosis at the scene of the accident and the beginning of in-hospital treatment. He stresses the need for careful stabilization and transportation in controlling the sequelae of spinal injury.

The person with spinal cord injury ordinarily requires from one to three months of acute hospital care. In addition to treatment of fractures, hemorrhages, or other injuries associated with the accident, life-sustaining measures may be required to maintain respiration and other vital functions. Treatment of the spinal injury includes alignment of the spine, complete stabilization of the spinal area, decompression of neurologic structures, and early mobilization (Pierce, 1977). Under ideal conditions, the patient would be in a specialized spinal cord injury center with continuity and coordination between the acute and rehabilitative phases of his care. These centers are not available in all areas, however, and care will often include transfer to a general rehabilitation center after acute treatment in a general hospital. Felice, Muthard, and Hamilton (1976) describe a patient who progressed in each phase of his rehabilitation until he would be "dropped" and left on his own. The researchers stress the need for services coordinated by one person over a long period of time.

Injuries at or below the level of the thoracic spine cause paralysis of the lower extremities and trunk (paraplegia), while injuries at the cervical level result in partial or complete paralysis of the upper extremities as well (quadriplegia) (see Figure 1). The designation of the injury is that of the lowest nerve root segment retaining complete function. Spinal shock or swelling will frequently interfere with functioning one or two segments above the level of the actual lesion, but this will ordinarily return within a month or two. Complete lesion at the C4 level is the highest compatible with life unsupported by mechanical respiration, although some patients with incomplete lesions at a higher level can breathe on their own. As we mentioned above, the term *quadriplegia* is applied to patients with partial, as well as complete, paralysis of upper extremities, and many may have considerable use of hands and arms. Although without finger dexterity, some become quite competent in the use of their residual capacities. Judgments about the manual capabilities of patients labeled *quadriplegic* should be made only after direct observation.

SPINAL CORD INJURY

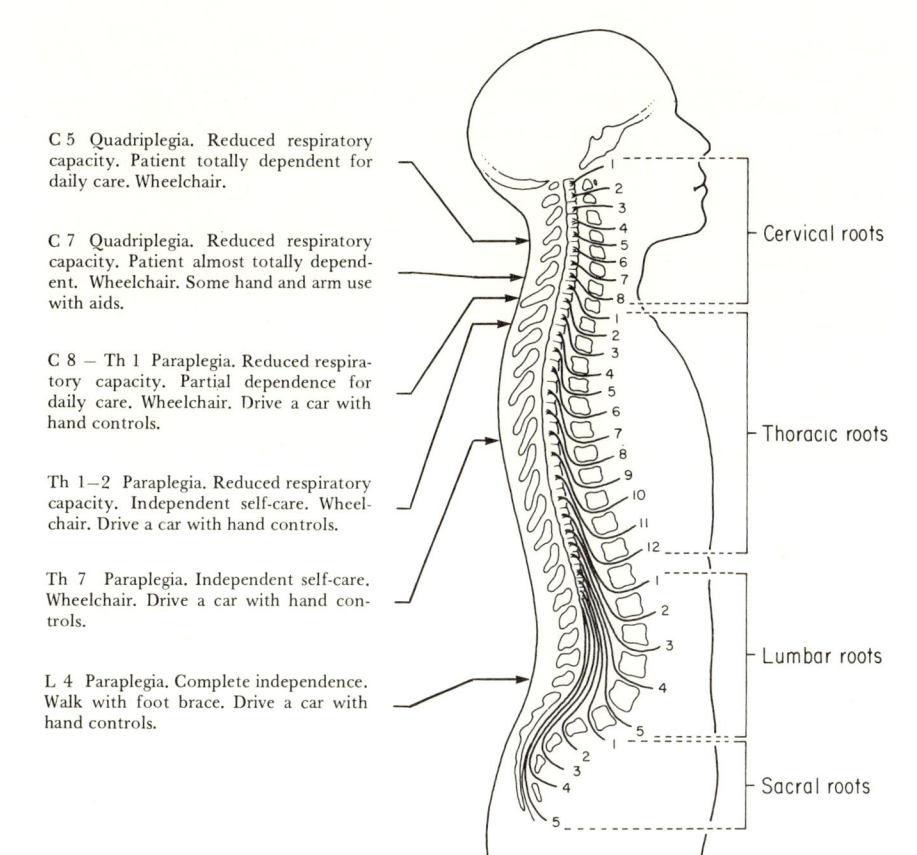

C 5 Quadriplegia. Reduced respiratory capacity. Patient totally dependent for daily care. Wheelchair.

C 7 Quadriplegia. Reduced respiratory capacity. Patient almost totally dependent. Wheelchair. Some hand and arm use with aids.

C 8 – Th 1 Paraplegia. Reduced respiratory capacity. Partial dependence for daily care. Wheelchair. Drive a car with hand controls.

Th 1–2 Paraplegia. Reduced respiratory capacity. Independent self-care. Wheelchair. Drive a car with hand controls.

Th 7 Paraplegia. Independent self-care. Wheelchair. Drive a car with hand controls.

L 4 Paraplegia. Complete independence. Walk with foot brace. Drive a car with hand controls.

FIGURE 1. Spinal cord—level of function.

Rehabilitation Care

At the rehabilitation center, patients with spinal cord injury are trained in mobility and self-care to the optimum level possible for them. Paraplegic patients will be introduced to a wheelchair and trained to propel it. They will learn techniques of transfer from bed to chair to prevent pressure sores. Lack of sensation and mobility make skin care a special problem. A system for proper drainage of urine will be established. The indwelling catheter was extensively used in the past, but more recently intermittent catheterization has been favored because it significantly reduces the incidence of infection, kidney stone development, and erosion of the urethra. Bowel movements are usually accomplished several times a week with proper diet and the use of suppositories or digital assistance. Other activities of daily living, such as dressing and eating, will be taught. As rehabilitation progresses, the patient will be given information regarding possible modes of sexual expression. The feasibility of operating a motor vehicle will be explored.

Many of these problems are more complex for quadriplegic patients, who have a few additional difficulties. The quadriplegic may not be able to propel a wheelchair and may need to learn operation of an electric one. He may not be able to transfer unassisted and may need to learn how to assist others in accomplishing this. Activities such as eating or dressing may be accomplished only partially and may require the use of orthotic devices. Operation of a motor vehicle, if possible, will require power controls. Prompt treatment of respiratory infections is required for the quadriplegic patient, as respiratory failure poses a continuing threat.

Many physical and medical problems remain with spinal cord injured persons throughout their lives. Cleanliness and postural shifting are required for skin care. The urine-disposal system must be maintained carefully, with the periodic consultation of a urologist. Liquid intake needs to be increased and caloric intake adjusted to the level of physical activity of the person. Dysreflexia may cause the body to overreact to signals from internal organs (e.g., distended bladder), resulting in profuse sweating, pounding headache, and increased blood pressure which may, in some cases, cause stroke. The patient has lost voluntary control of muscles but frequently experiences involuntary muscle reflexes mediated by spinal cord centers. At times it is possible to use this reflex activity, for example, to achieve an action or to function sexually. At other times, however, the spasticity and contractures of these muscles may be painful and bothersome. Patients have been known to be thrown out of a bed or wheelchair by the involuntary reflex of a powerful leg muscle. Reflex actions often lead to graphic illustrations of the self-image reconstruction process, when the frustrated and sputtering patient will slap his own limb and shout something like "Down, damn you, down!" with varying degrees of good grace. Muscle relaxants may be helpful for this problem, although they sometimes cause such side effects as sluggishness or drowsiness, which constitute problems in themselves. The patient may also experience tiredness and apathy due to septic conditions, as a result of pressure sores or urinary infection. Table I lists some of the problems of persons with paraplegia or quadriplegia.

TABLE I
Physically Related Problems of Paraplegia and Quadriplegia

1. Mobility	7. Contractures
2. Bladder control	8. Dysreflexia
3. Urinary tract and kidney infections	9. Thermo-regulation
4. Permanent kidney damage	10. Sexuality
5. Bowel control	11. Body image
6. Skin care	12. Respiratory infections (quadriplegia)

COMMON PSYCHOLOGICAL CHARACTERISTICS AND PROBLEMS

Stages of Reaction

The progression of reactions of the spinal cord injured person (and family) has been described by many (Dunn, 1975; Rigoni, 1977; Stewart, 1977–78; Weller & Miller, 1977a,b) using similar terminology and frequently noting the resemblance to the process reported in patients approaching death (Kübler-Ross, 1969). The intensity of response appears to be related to the devastating nature of the injury and the fact that the suddenness of the trauma precludes the opportunity for anticipatory grief, as described by Lindemann (1944). The general process of adaptation to physical disability has been discussed in Chapter 1.

Weller and Miller (1977a,b) describe this progression in terms of shock, denial, anger, depression, and, finally, acceptance or adjustment (sometimes termed adaptation). They note that there may be overlapping or temporary regression to a previous phase of the process and suggest that one to two years post trauma is the typical length of time required for adaptation.

Shock. The stage of shock, for the patient, may be actual physical shock, with speechlessness brought on by trauma as well as by life-saving devices. It is a time of overwhelming anxiety, with fear of the known and unknown, often accompanied by cognitive disorganization. Family members may show the same symptoms, and at times with an intensity that rivals or exceeds that of the patient. It is a time when the patient needs comforting, information about unusual sensations and procedures, and reassurance about his prospects for continued life without mental disturbance. The family needs the same and, if possible, might best be given some part in the action, such as providing information, obtaining insurance papers, or performing other useful support services.

Denial. Denial, or as Rigoni (1977) terms it, defensive retreat, is probably the most helpful adaptive and potentially the most destructive maladaptive psychological mechanism utilized by the spinal cord injured person. Stewart (1977–1978) notes that the reaction allows the gradual introduction into consciousness of the overwhelming implications of the injury and that it is part of a process which aims at maintaining a cohesive sense of self. He describes this as a moratorium in forging a modified (new) identity. Denial may be massive, as in "Nothing has happened, and I'm going to get up and leave this afternoon," or it may be much more subtle. Many, if not most, spinal cord injured persons quietly maintain the dream or the conviction that some day a medical discovery or religious miracle will return them to full function. This hope may be integral to their continued stability. Knowing spinal cord injured persons who live life to the full with apparent self-acceptance may move the therapist to want all such patients to drop all vestiges of denial, but our zeal should not blind us to the fact that this can only be accomplished when the patient's revision of self-concept has reached a point where he is ready. He cannot be coerced.

Denial becomes maladaptive when it becomes an obsessive focus of activity or when it interferes with plans and actions which are a necessary part of treatment or rehabilitation. For example, the patient may see no need to think about a new vocation if he is certain that he will return to work as a longshoreman. A more subtly damaging effect of denial may come from a family's insistence that the patient *must* walk again, a stance that carries with it the message that the patient, as he is now, is not acceptable.

Anger. Anger may be concurrent with denial, or it may appear or be intensified as denial is relinquished. From a simplistic point of view, the cause of anger is straightforward: The patient has sustained a grievous assault upon himself; it hurts physically and psychologically; he feels that this punishment is unearned and unfair, and that makes him angry. The rational expression and direction of the anger is another thing. It is frequently directed at family and professional staff. It may play into family guilt: "I raised him wrong" or "I shouldn't have allowed him to have a motorcycle"; the family may share the anger and join in cursing the staff, road designers, football coaches, swimming pool builders, the fates, or God. The patient can be difficult and ungrateful, and there can be a strong inclination to return the hostility. Expression of anger is to be expected and should be met with much forbearance. It should be tolerated but not shared or otherwise unnecessarily reinforced. If it becomes destructive of others or significantly disruptive, it may be necessary to temper it through counseling and to provide support to its targets in maintaining their objectivity. If it is relatively impunitive in its impact, it should be seen as an inevitable and possibly helpful part of the process of change in identity.

Depression. Depression may occur at any point in the process. It may relate to the sheer fact of disability; it may reflect guilt about the accident, especially if the accident involved others; it may reflect guilt about the irrational expression of anger, especially if the anger has been directed toward those upon whom the patient is dependent; it may reflect a loss of hope. A manifestation of anger–guilt–depression is often identified as shame. The patient will be ashamed of his attempts at feeding himself or of the fact that he cannot have a bowel movement unattended. A common response is to refuse to feed himself and to allow only close family members (to whom he is willing to expose his inability) to feed him. In some instances, only the mother is allowed to help with bowel function. Awareness that this is a perpetuation of dependency begets guilt. Attempts at intervention are typically met with anger, which begets more guilt. All of these feelings add to depression and the continuation of this self-defeating, circular behavior. This pattern ordinarily needs to be interrupted as early as possible, usually vigorously and with provision of support services to patient and family.

Depression in general is usually the signal for supportive counseling from professionals working with the patient; it is also often the appropriate time for referral to a mental health professional for more intensive psychotherapy. Suicidal thinking occurs with some frequency and should be taken seriously. (See "Intervention Methods.") Weller and Miller (1977b) suggest that depression evokes mirror feelings and that the family may also require assistance, relative to their own psychological needs or to their stimulus value for the patient.

Adaptation. Most spinal cord injured persons reach a stage of stability, within one or two years after the injury, which may be called adaptation. This should not be construed as being uniformly optimal or even positive; persons with the same degree of capacity or incapacity may reach adaptations which vary from embittered and passive acceptance of a dependent role in a treatment setting to aggressive and independent pursuit of a social, sexual, and vocational role utilizing all capacities and adding a bit more through innovation.

Personality Patterns

In describing what it means to be a person with spinal cord injury, Morgan, Margolin, St. Pierre, Kruege, and Rynearson (1972, p. 1) say, "There is no such thing as a paraplegic personality, *per se*. The range of personality patterns extends from those who are severely emotionally disturbed to those who are well adjusted." It is true that the spinal cord injured may be male or female, young or old, bright or dull, passive or aggressive, and so on through the lexicon of human traits. Nevertheless, there appear to be certain frequently observed characteristics, and a description of such a modal personality may be useful as a reference point in discussing the disability. In describing the subjects (30 males, 7 females) of their study at New York University Hospital, Weller and Miller (1977a, p. 370) say, "Over half of our patients were young, emotionally immature, in the midst of rebelling or self-destructive acting out, with insecure, poor self-image and low self-esteem; at a peak of physical and sexual activity, with investment in physical prowess far outweighing intellectual interests; with low levels of education and job opportunities; and with troubled families broken through marital discord, death, illness, and other life crises."

These observations parallel those of the present author in working with 82 (63 male, 19 female) spinal cord injured at the Crippled Children's Division of the University of Oregon Health Sciences Center, where the modal patient is a male who has been physically active and motorically oriented, with a corresponding interest in things mechanical and/or athletic and not in things academic. His active life has led him into pursuits in which the risk for serious accident is great.

The self-concept of this person naturally parallels his behavior. His disability places him in a situation which requires a radical revision of self-concept. The activities and vocations for which he now has the capability are generally ones which require him to be sedentary, attentive to detail, reflective, and patient. In order to plan and prepare for such a role, he must be willing to think of himself as such a person. For many spinal cord injured patients the willingness even to think about this kind of radically changed self-concept is the first important step toward rehabilitation—and for many the step is a long time in coming. The new image is incompatible with the old and asks him to subscribe to qualities and values which he may have disdained in the past. Further, the willingness to think about himself in this changed way seems to betray the idea so frequently held (often secretly) that somehow this will all go away, or that great new strides will be made which will restore full physical capacity and obviate the need for this painful psychological adjustment.

Social and Sexual Adjustment

Dunn (1977) has explored some of the social concerns of the male spinal cord injured through a Social Situation Questionnaire which he administered to 40 Veterans Administration (VA) patients. He found that older men (with recent injuries) expressed more social discomfort than younger men and that those patients who could be described as well-adjusted expressed less social discomfort. Highest discomfort ratings were found for bowel or bladder accidents, falling out of a wheelchair, and refusing unwanted help. The twenty items used by Dunn, with the discomfort ratings given by the patients, are shown in Table II.

Kemp and Vash (1971) studied the productivity of 50 spinal cord injured patients (36 male, 14 female) at Ranchos Los Amigos Hospital and found four significant factors: (1) *Goal setting:* The more productive

TABLE II
Twenty Items in Structured Interview with the Mean Rating of the 40 Patients[a]

	Item	Rating
A.	Asking for help up curb	2.5
B.	Lighting cigarette	0.7
C.	Emptying leg bag	2.7
D.	Getting on elevator and young girl pats you on head and says "poor dear"	3.3
E.	Putting wheelchair in car and passerby offers help	2.0
F.	Putting wheelchair in car and passerby insists on helping	4.0
G.	Going into restaurant and hostess asks date/wife, "How many please?"	3.3
H.	Sitting in restaurant and waiter asks wife/date, "What does he want?"	—
I.	At a party, discovering that external catheter has popped out	5.9
J.	At a shopping center where a little child comes up and says, "Why are you in that chair?"	1.3
K.	At a shopping center being stared at by people	3.1
L.	At a bar where a drunk comes up and starts telling you how brave you are	3.8
M.	Meeting someone for the first time who knows nothing about spinal cord injury	2.7
N.	Asking for help in the cafeteria	1.4
O.	Falling out of wheelchair	5.7
P.	Clonus	2.9
Q.	Spasms	3.4
R.	Accidental bowel movement	6.5
S.	People who don't move out of the way	4.5
T.	Offering assistance—in general	2.4

[a] From Dunn, 1977.

were more forward-looking and set more goals for themselves. (2) *Orientation toward loss:* The more productive spoke not in terms of their physical loss, but rather in terms of the activities which it precluded. (3) *Creativity:* The more productive showed more novel and divergent thinking. (4) *Degree of "interpersonal support" received:* This support from the persons around them seemed especially critical for the quadriplegic patients, in contrast to the paraplegics.

Fitting, Salisbury, Davies, and Mayclin (1978) report noteworthy findings in a group of 24 spinal cord injured women who may have been exceptional in that all were high school graduates, with 22 attending college, 11 studying for advanced degrees. These women reported perceiving themselves as "more assertive, more independent, more active as a sexual parther, more intellectual, and more honest with themselves after injury than before." They felt that they had received insufficient sexual counseling and were treated as asexual by health professionals who did not understand their sexual needs.

Women have traditionally been viewed as experiencing less disruption of sexual activity and satisfaction due to spinal cord injury than have men. Weber and Wessman (1971) state that most spinal cord injured women can have coitus, become pregnant, and deliver healthy babies. Fitting *et al.* (1978) point out that emphasis on reproductive capacity ignores the impact of genital sensation on female sexual identity (as well as sexual adjustment). They also, however, stress the continued sexual interest of their subjects. Loss of bowel and bladder control during sexual activity is a concern, an inconvenience, and occasionally an embarrassment to most spinal cord injured men and women.

Weber and Wessman (1971) concluded that 66 to 75% of all spinal cord injured males will have erections, while 5 to 8% will be able to ejaculate, depending upon the level and extent of the injury. Comarr and Hohmann (1972) report that 73% of their patients have reflexogenic erections, while 7% have psychogenic erections. They generalize (p. 14) that

> A substantial number, though not an overwhelming proportion, of SCI patients will have essentially normal functioning. Another group will have an ability to perform sexually but will not experience orgasm or ejaculate. A third group will be unable to do anything as far as genital sexuality is concerned; but this does not mean that sex is a dead issue.

They stress the importance of time in working out a sexual adjustment. (See "Intervention Methods," this chapter.) Hohmann (1972) believes that learning that one can be a meaningful sexual partner leads to general improvement in self-concept. Guttmann (1976) reports that

44.8% of his spinal cord injured patients married, the great majority after injury. This does not, of course, mean that sexual activity is taking place or that it is satisfactory; David, Gur, and Rozin's (1977–78) study of 16 "normal" Israeli women married to paraplegic men suggests that concern about the partner's sexual capability and fertility is a major source of marital dissatisfaction.

EVALUATING PERSONS WITH SPINAL CORD INJURY

Interview

The interview for psychosocial evaluation of a spinal cord injured person will be essentially similar to that required for others. It will cover certain unique areas of physical function, daily activities, and self-concept. A general knowledge of the disability will add significantly to the interviewer's ability to see the person's current status as part of a discernible process, to empathize, and to cover the important aspects of the patient's life. The affect and responsivity of the patient will often differ noticeably with his involvement in the various stages of the shock–denial–anger–depression–adaptation process. An evaluation should frequently involve interview of family members, both separately and with the patient. In so doing, one should avoid dehumanizing or infantilizing the patient by discussing his case in front of him as if he were an inanimate object or a child for whom decisions must be made. It is always important to include the patient as a respected participant in the process; he alone will have the ultimate responsibility for carrying out decisions which will be made.

An approach which manages to combine matter-of-factness about the patient's disability with sensitivity and knowledgeability will ordinarily serve best. Patients will differ in their response to this: Some will be experienced and comfortable with such an approach; some, who are accustomed to having their disability discussed by indirection or not at all, will react with anger or hurt and require very careful handling of their feelings; and some will respond with almost visible relief which seems to convey, "At last, a person with whom I can talk honestly." In taking a personal history, the author has found it useful to discuss activities, interests, and attitudes, prevailing before the accident (sometimes even labeling it *B.A.*) and then after the accident. This technique frequently appears to act as a desensitization exercise for the patient, helping him to think about his current capabilities and prospects. It is apparently important for many patients to establish who they *were* before going on to discuss who they *are* or might become. Stewart (1977) finds it useful to ask patients if they have known others with spinal cord injury; he reports that they usually have, and that they may find it easier at first to say things about others than about themselves. Stewart also feels it is important to inquire about post-injury body image, so that patients can express apparently "crazy" feelings, such as phantom sensations or sensations of impossible body distortions. He makes the distinction between *coping behavior* used to solve problems and reduce stress in the face of drastic change and *defense mechanisms* used to avoid anxiety and pain in longstanding conflicts. He recommends that the mental health professional do an initial interview early, establishing himself as part of the team and not as someone who is called in later to evaluate disturbed behavior. This is one of the desirable effects achieved in the ideal situation in which a specialized team is available for the long-term care of the spinal cord injured person.

Comarr and Hohmann (1972, p. 14) have said: "If you, as a professional, are going to discuss sex with your spinal cord injured patient, it must be done within the context of a meaningful relationship; with gentility and concern as part of the total discussion." They also caution against jumping to conclusions about the possibility of sexual functioning before sufficient time for experimentation has elapsed. The invitation to sex counseling is one which needs to be suggested to the patient frequently over time without any overtones of coercion. The author has found the question, "Do you know as much as you would like to know about your possibilities for sexual functioning?" to be a useful one in this respect.

Rogers and Figone (1978) note a decline in avocational pursuits of cord injured persons, even of things they can do, and express concern about this psychological inertia. An evaluation interview should include assessment of recreational and social functioning as well as activities of daily living. Where there are indications of possible suicide ideation, this should also be explored. (See Chapter 1, as well as the "Intervention Methods" of this chapter.)

Psychological Testing

Psychological testing with spinal cord injured persons requires that the examiner have some general knowledge of the problem, especially the fact that there is no presumption of brain dysfunction unless brain damage was incurred in the accident that injured the spine. Most patients will be in a wheelchair, and it is useful to have available a table, the lower edge of which is three to four inches higher than the standard, so that the patient's knees will fit underneath.

Paraplegics will ordinarily have full upper-limb dexterity and thus the motor ability to do the performance tasks included in many standardized intelligence tests as well as most other motor tests that are carried out on table top. Persons diagnosed as quadriplegic may also be able to manipulate these materials successfully (see "The Physical Disability"), and judgments about their ability to do so should be made only after observation of the subject. Some quadriplegic persons may be able to push blocks around quite successfully but not turn them. They may be told that the examiner will turn any specified block so that the desired color is on top, leaving it to the subject to assemble the design. This may be timed, noting the usual time limits and allowing a reasonable amount of additional time for the cumbersome process. Such measures should not, obviously, be used to compute a traditional IQ, but may provide a quite useful observational basis for estimate of the subject's preinjury ability and possibility of future potential.

A measure of space perception ability (such as block design) may be quite significant, for this will often have been an area of cognitive strength in these frequently motorically oriented individuals (see "Common Psychological Characteristics and Problems"), who may not have developed verbal or numerical skills. Spatial relations ability may give some reflection of future potential as the person modifies self-concept and, one hopes, the direction of skill development.

Oral multiple-choice tests, such as those following the Peabody format, are convenient with subjects who have limited manual dexterity. Since many spinal cord injured persons have not developed their academic skills, the Peabody Individual Achievement Test (Dunn & Markwardt, 1970) is frequently useful. Most portions of the test require a simple response. Similarly, the Peabody Picture Vocabulary Test (Dunn, 1959) may be helpful in obtaining an estimate of verbal skills, although it is a more limited measure than the verbal portions of most standardized intelligence tests, which are often applicable.

Most paraplegic and some quadriplegic persons have sufficient manual skill to mark the answer sheets of paper and pencil tests. In some cases where this is not possible, the patient may be able to operate a tape recorder, dictating by number responses which may later be transcribed to an answer sheet. It is also possible for a second person to mark the sheet for the patient. This is best done by a neutral person, such as a volunteer or aide, although sometimes a family member is the most conveniently available. In any case of second-party assistance, both patient and recorder should be carefully instructed about the avoidance of influence by the recorder, including cues by voice inflection, sighs, groans, and so forth, as well as nonverbal influences such as raised eyebrows or grimaces. Seating for such testing is most effectively arranged so that the participants are not looking directly at each other. Obviously, the participation of a second person will have some influence on responses which cannot be eliminated by any precautions.

Projective tests with oral responses may ordinarily be utilized without any modification in administration. It may be useful to administer a sentence completion test with the examiner recording the oral responses; this may also be accomplished through the use of a tape recorder.

Standardized personality tests may be useful in evaluating the patient's emotional state as well as traits which may have relevance for vocational planning. Kendall, Edinger, and Eberly (1978) followed up a previous study by Taylor (1970) on moderator–variable effects on the MMPI profiles of physically disabled patients. They obtained empirical support for Taylor's correction factor, finding that physical description test items caused spurious profile elevations. They suggest that two profiles be prepared, one using the traditional scales and one deleting items numbered 273, 330, 9, 192, 63, 51, 179, 20 and 62 (old booklet form).

Interest test results may make a significant contribution in vocational planning with the spinal cord injured person, for instance, measuring such differing directions as sales, clerical-accounting, counseling, teaching, science, or manual activities, where it is possible to do so. It may be desirable to repeat these tests as the patient's self-concept is modified, perhaps as often as every 6 to 12 months, or occasionally at even shorter intervals. Patients will frequently inquire about the printed instruction that they not be concerned about *ability* in responding to the items. The author has frequently found it useful to suggest that they *do* take into account limitations imposed by their disability, being liberal in their interpretation of what they might be able to do. This is a transgression of standardized administration and vocational choice theory. It discourages the not infrequent production by the young quadriplegic of a profile which is strictly that of an auto mechanic or a professional athlete. It may also be a useful exercise for the patient in thinking about the self in a new way.

Psychological examiners should be aware of the possibility of slowed responsiveness as well as easy fatigability of some spinal cord injured persons. An attempt should be made to differentiate between this physical slowing down and the apathy of depression. It is often desirable to schedule several testing sessions rather than one prolonged one.

INTERVENTION METHODS

Early Stages

Psychological intervention with the spinal cord injured patient begins as soon as he can consciously hear the words of those working with him, and with his family in the first professional contacts after injury. The patient needs comforting, information about strange sensations and procedures, and any reassurance which can be given about his future. Weller and Miller (1977b), referring to the spinal cord injured patient, say, "The delicate balance between supportive acceptance of his feelings at each state and extension of realistic hope for the future presents an awesome challenge to the professional team." Conroe et al. (1972) say that the patient must have realistic knowledge "but not too bluntly." Stewart (1977–1978) says that the use of denial at this stage allows for the gradual introduction into consciousness of the import of the injury. The personnel who are working with the patient and family during the earliest stages of injury unfortunately may not have the human relations skills and the articulateness to handle this delicate balance. This calls for the utilization of psychosocial members of the treatment team as early in the process as possible and for training in the psychological aspects of disability for all personnel having significant contact with the spinal cord injured, regardless of areas of specialty. Especially useful are just slightly qualified prognostic statements such as, "In my experience, patients with this kind of injury (e.g., have not recovered the use of their legs)" or "The usual course in patients I have known. . . ." After the opinion of the professional has been stated in this fashion a few times, it is often possible to avoid direct refutation of each statement by patient or family implying unrealistic hope, so long as explicit agreement is not expressed. At this point, brief responses such as "We'll see" or "Time will tell" will often suffice. Stewart (1977–1978) makes the point that denial is only maladaptive when it interferes with realistic efforts and plans.

Redden and Jackson (1979) deal at length with the handling of denial, beginning with the distinction that maladaptive (as opposed to adaptive) denial involves refusal of rehabilitation efforts. They view adaptive denial (seeing the disability as temporary but making appropriate rehabilitation efforts in the meantime) as different in that the patient has the opportunity to learn gradually that he has the potential for successful living. They see the goal of intervention in maladaptive denial as one of decreasing the aversiveness of the patient's images and fantasies about his disability. They do this by having the patient set long-term goals (which may be unrealistic) and short-term goals which are broken down into easily attainable units. They then focus the patient's attention on accomplishing these short-term goals (and the satisfaction therein).

The Family

The powerful reactions of families of the spinal cord injured cannot be overstressed. The author has observed an interesting contrast between the parents of chronically disabled (e.g., cerebral-palsied) adolescents and those with traumatic spinal cord injury. In most cases, the parents of the chronically disabled have, over time, developed a certain objectivity, some amount of distance and ability to differentiate themselves from the patient. In contrast, for many parents of spinal cord injured adolescents, the patient is still very much an extension of themselves. In some instances, he may even have been "destined" to do those things and accomplish those goals for which the parent has always longed. The defense of this person becomes exactly the same as the defense of self, with all the intensity of psychological mechanisms.

Conroe *et al.* (1972) suggest that, in general, spouses are more pragmatic and realistic than parents. Kahn (1977) stresses frequency of family visits, the maintenance, where possible, of previous family roles (e.g., father's role in decision-making), and open discussion of changing roles. She points out the many functions that can be assumed by spinal cord injured persons, such as family bookkeeping, maintaining inventory and planning shopping, and helping with housework. These ongoing efforts at maintaining family integrity and functioning may be supplemented at times by more formal family therapy as the various members work through initial grief reactions and then adjust to new roles and relationships.

Independence

Much has been written about the effects of hospitalization. Kahn (1977, p. 310) baldly states, "The prevailing model of organization for medical care is structured so as to gain control over the patient through depersonalization and infantilization. It reinforces the regression in social functioning that seems inherent in any illness experience." Hanson (1974) similarly points to the institutional reinforcement of passive and compliant behavior while assertive behavior is punished. He calls for a "psycho-ecological" approach which takes into account all of the effects of the environment on the patient's behavior. In the author's experience, this problem extends beyond the bounds of the hospital. Appropriately assertive attempts at independence are frequently more trouble for families, as well as for outpatient clinic and agency staffs, than is passive compliance. Assertive behavior is, however, desirable and necessary and to be encouraged wherever possible. The spinal cord injured person is even entitled to make a few mistakes, as most of us do when we try to work into a new role. Whenever exigencies require that something must be done *to* or *for* the patient, it is at a price in his independence and self-esteem. Such actions should always be preceded by the questions, "Is it necessary?" and "Could he do it himself?"

Doing for the patient what he could do for himself is frequently a matter of convenience to the family. "It would take all day for him to dress himself." At times, it may have even greater psychological meaning to the doers and recipients. The author is reminded of the paraplegic young lady who did a creditable job of maintaining the small home in which she lived with her husband. The most difficult times were the biweekly visits of her mother-in-law, who came all day with several other good ladies to help her out. Putting the house in order for those visits and putting things back in place afterward was a considerable chore which she was able to accept only after she conceptualized the whole matter as psychological treatment which she was providing for *them.*

Psychotherapy

As we have suggested throughout this chapter, it is desirable that supportive counseling relationships be maintained throughout the period of the patient's rehabilitation. This may be done by a psychosocial professional who sees the patient periodically as part of a team, or it may be done by almost any member of the team who is sensitive, has some counseling skills, has developed a relationship with the patient, and who has and will take the time to listen to him occasionally, at some length and in privacy when indicated. Ordinarily, quick hallway exchanges of "How are you doing?" are not supportive counseling. This counseling relationship may need to be punctuated at times by more formal and intensive psychotherapy conducted by a mental health professional. These sessions might be during particularly intense identity crises or during periods of serious depression and possible suicidal ideation. Precaution should be taken, however, against premature referral for psychotherapy. Psychotherapy will rarely be useful unless the patient is ready and wants it. The general notion of psychotherapy as a cure-all for any difficult problems fails to take into account the old adage that you can lead a horse to water but you can't make him drink. Premature referral will usually result not only in the failure of the attempt but in increased resistance in the future. Some goals of counseling or psychotherapy may be: (1) to help desensitize the patient to the negative connotations of his appearance, sensations, and dependent needs; (2) to help him learn new social skills such as how to refuse unneeded help and to solicit needed help without feeling inadequate or guilty; and (3) ultimately to help him learn to enjoy being alone, "in his own head," with his inner resources.

Suicide. Thoughts of suicide are a frequent occurrence among spinal cord injured patients. Sometimes they are made quite apparent to families or professionals. Sometimes they will be confided in the context of the professional contact or interview. Sometimes they are suspected (as they always should be during severe depression) but are not openly expressed. (See Chapter 1 for a detailed discussion on approaching the subject of suicidal thoughts with the patient.) When it is known that the spinal cord injured patient may be suicidal, the following actions are suggested: (1) Advise the family (and the patient) to maintain his involvement in daily activities, including recreational and social functions. (2) Have family, friends, and professionals maintain contact and initiate talk about the things that seem to be important to the patient, including suicide, if it is evidently on his mind. (3) Control access to means of self-destruction, such as drugs or revolvers, and make sure that prescription drugs are available only in judicious amounts. (4) Offer referral for psychotherapy and/or psychotropic medication. (5) Consider hospitalization, if necessary, to control suicidal behavior.

Sex and Marital Counseling

Sexual functioning is a major concern for most spinal cord injured persons. Stewart (1977–78) has talked about the moratorium that usually ensues, and this author has noted delay in the development of psychosexual interests among those who had not previously been sexually active. As suggested earlier, the opportunity for sexual counseling should be tactfully offered to patients from time to time, without attempting to coerce but taking into account that some may be too shy or unaware to initiate the request. In an especially helpful descriptive article, Comarr (1973) explains the partial diagnosis of sexual potential through examination for sensation and reflexes but states his preference for carrying on sexual counseling after the patient has had an opportunity for sexual experimentation with a partner. He stresses the importance of time and patience in this process. Hohmann's article (1972) is a good brief guide to sexual counseling. He says (p. 53), "The cord injured person should be encouraged to engage in whatever types of sexual activities are physiologically possible, pleasing, esthetic, gratifying and acceptable to him and his partner." Although a substantial number of spinal cord injured persons will have essentially normal functioning, others will not experience orgasm. Hohmann (1972) describes the "paraorgasm" of spinal cord injured persons who stimulate their mates and says that if they have strong empathy, they will experience many of the psychological and physiological changes associated with a buildup of sexual tension and subsequent release. The book *Sexual Options* by Mooney, Cole, and Chilgren (1975) is especially useful to couples developing a pattern of sexual interaction. It is appropriately explicit narratively and pictorially, and should be introduced carefully, especially to persons whose sense of propriety or religious morality might cause them to view it as offensive. Sex education, in the form of films or lecture–discussion, may be appropriately initiated in a group setting, with further education and counseling on an individual basis.

The wives of spinal cord injured men studied by David *et al.* (1977–78) expressed strong feelings about the absence of premarital counseling and authoritative information about sexual functioning. Considering the large number of patients who get married after injury (Guttman, 1976), more systematic attention might well be paid to this need. Marital counseling will, of course, be frequently appropriate during the spinal cord injured person's rehabilitation, as it relates both to sexual functioning and the assumption of new and altered roles in the marital relationship. That role problems are not always the stereotyped ones we might imagine may be illustrated by the case of a young couple known to the author. The paraplegic man and his normal wife had a conflict about the degree of activity that should characterize their social and recreational life. The young man insisted that the greatest part of their spare time be spent in archery and scuba-diving. His wife found it difficult to keep up with him, became overtired, and strenuously maintained that their time should be spent at bridge and the theater.

Vocation

Most spinal cord injured patients are concerned about their vocational potential from the beginning of the rehabilitation process, and it is important to let them know that many paraplegic and quadriplegic persons are successfully employed. In one sense, the entire process is part of vocational rehabilitation; Hoover (1977) has pointed out the importance of activities of daily living and self-care as preparation for employment. After the patient's physical condition has stabilized, a vocational psychological evaluation should be carried out, and this may need to be repeated, especially as self-concept and interests are modified. Career counseling should be a continuing part of the rehabilitation process and may be carried out by the psychologist or by a vocational rehabilitation counselor. Ultimately, the process of counseling, training, and eventual placement assistance should be carried out on referral by the state vocational rehabilitation division or other analogous agency.

Poor (1975) reviews the professional literature and lists the following factors as significantly affecting vocational outcomes in spinal cord injured persons:

1. Physical ability to work away from home, for example, bowel and bladder management, sitting tolerance
2. Educational level—higher education leads to greater employability
3. Age—younger persons fare better
4. Stability in previous work history
5. Active family support for employment
6. Geographical situation—greater job opportunities in metropolitan areas than in rural areas
7. Availability of economically feasible transportation
8. Proper vocational training
9. Effectiveness of rehabilitation counseling
10. Motivation to work

Insofar as many of these factors may be developed if not already present, they may be looked upon as goals of the rehabilitation process. Poor (1975) also lists jobs held by spinal cord injured persons, as shown in Table III. Vocational functioning rivals sexual functioning in its contribution to the sense of well-being and competence which is indispensable to the overall satisfactory adjustment of the spinal cord injured person.

TRENDS AND NEEDS

The concept of comprehensive care by a specialized interdisciplinary team is one that has been amply demonstrated in some centers and has general acceptance as the desired model for treatment of spinal cord injury. It remains for this model to be made available to patients in all geographic areas; for the various disciplines to refine their contributions to the process; and for all to arrive at a better understanding of the way in which the individual moves through the process. Further understand-

TABLE III
Job Titles of Spinal Cord Injured Clients Texas Institute for Rehabilitation and Research[a]

Traumatic paraplegia	Traumatic quadriplegia
Draftsman, architectural	Civil engineer
Draftsman I	Construction engineer
Design engineer	Tool designer
Draftsman	Petroleum engineer
Project director, business data	Programmer, business
Programmer, technical	Programmer, scientific
Secondary school teacher	Programmer, technical
Tax agent	Psychiatrist
Employment interviewer I	Faculty member, college or university
Controller	Graduate assistant
Store manager I	Secondary school teacher
Secretary	Lawyer, patent
Typist	Feature reporter
Insurance clerk	Employment interviewer I
Stock-control clerk	Underwriter
Clerk	Clerk, general
Telephone operator	Material clerk
Assembler	Inventory clerk
Printed circuit board inspector	Estimator
Electronics assembler	Business service clerk
Mechanical assembler	Central office operator
Stone setter	Telephone operator
Assembler	Order clerk II
Engraver	Advertising salesman
Leathercraftsman	Salesman, farm supplies and equipment
Dispatcher	Salesman, automobile
Dispatcher, motor vehicle	Salesman, general
Service dispatcher	Telephone solicitor
Switchboard operator	Telephone sales clerk
Pantographer	Nurse's aide
	Dry cleaning superintendent
	General machine operator
	Assembler
	Electronic assembler
	Benchworker II
	Grinding-wheel inspector
	Maintenance-man helper
	Photograph finisher I

[a] Adapted from C.R. Poor, 1975.

ing of the response of the individual to catastrophic trauma would be valuable, as would a deeper knowledge of the factors which bring about or facilitate change in self-concept. The trend toward shorter hospital stay and earlier mobilization appears to have physical and psychological, as well as economic, advantages. In the community, the network of financial aids and services (e.g., Social Security, welfare, private agencies) is becoming more attuned to the special needs of the spinal cord injured.

A great deal of research emphasis continues to be placed upon methods to prevent the progressive degeneration of the spinal cord immediately after injury and to stimulate regeneration later (Staff of the U.S. General Accounting Office, 1977). Experimental approaches to the prevention of degeneration include the use of hyperbaric oxygen, cooling of the spinal cord, myelotomy and pharmacological therapy. Research directed toward the possibility of regeneration involves studies of axonal elongation, the biology of neuroglia, and nerve implant techniques. There are also early reports of attempts to develop neurosurgical methods for providing supplementary sources of sensation and voluntary muscle control to paralyzed areas from neurologically intact portions of the body.

Progress in normalizing the functioning of the spinal cord injured is also taking place through social and political action. Goals of such activity include: (1) establishment of residential settings which provide support services without becoming institutions, (2) extension of public transportation services to the handicapped, (3) modification of inappropriate employment criteria, and (4) elimination of architectural barriers. The latter is seen as especially appropriate; the populations studied by Felice, Muthard, and Hamilton (1976) described architectural barriers as a greater hindrance to the mobility of the spinal cord injured than lack of transportation.

APPENDIX: SOURCES OF INFORMATION

General:
National Spinal Cord Injury Foundation
369 Elliot Street
Newton Upper Falls, MA 02164

General information for the patient and his family: *The Source Book for the Disabled*, G. Hale (Ed.). New York: Paddington Press, 1979.
General information for the professional: *The Total Care of Spinal*

Cord Injuries, D. S. Pierce and V. H. Nickel (Eds.). Boston: Little, Brown, 1977.

Sexual counseling guide for the professional: "Considerations in Management of Psychosexual Readjustment in the Cord Injured Male." G. H. Hohmann. *Rehabilitation Psychology,* 1972, *19* (2), 50–58.

Sexual information for the mature patient: *Sexual Options for Paraplegics and Quadriplegics,* T. O. Mooney, T. M. Cole, & R. A. Chilgren. Boston: Little, Brown, 1975.

REFERENCES

Burnham, B. A., & Werner, G. The high-level tetraplegic: Psychological survival and adjustment. *Paraplegia,* 1978–1979, *16,* 184–192.

Chiu, W. S. Life after spinal cord injury. In *Comprehensive vocational rehabilitation for severely disabled persons.* Washington, D. C.: Job Development Laboratory, The George Washington University Medical Center, 1975.

Comarr, A. E. Sex among patients with spinal cord and/or cauda equina injuries. *Medical Aspects of Human Sexuality,* 1973, *7,* 222–238.

Comarr, A. E., & Hohmann, G. W. The sexual function of the SCI patient. In *A source book: Rehabilitating the person with spinal cord injury.* Washington, D.C.: Veterans Administration, 1972.

Conroe, R. M., Hohmann, G. W., Margolin, R. J., Wax, J., Parsons, L. B., Dickman, H., Mayer, S., Dana, B., & Morgan, E. D. The inner man: Social-psychological aspects of rehabilitating the person with SCI. In *A source book: Rehabilitating the person with spinal cord injury.* Washington, D.C.: Veterans Administration, 1972.

David, A., Gur, S., & Rozin, R. Survival in marriage in the paraplegic couple: Psychological study. *Paraplegia,* 1977–78, *15,* 198–201.

Dunn, L. M. *Peabody picture vocabulary test.* Circle Pines, Minn.: American Guidance Service, 1959.

Dunn, L. M., & Markwardt, F. C. Peabody individual achievement test. Circle Pines, Minn.: American Guidance Service, 1970.

Dunn, M. E. Psychological intervention in a spinal cord injury center: An introduction. *Rehabilitation Psychology,* 1975, *22*(4), 165–178.

Dunn, M. E. Social discomfort in the patient with spinal cord injury. *Archives of Physical Medicine and Rehabilitation,* 1977, *58,* 257–260.

Felice, K. A., Muthard, J. E., & Hamilton, L. S. The rehabilitation problems and needs of the spinal-cord injured: A pilot study. *Journal of Applied Rehabilitative Counseling,* 1976, *7*(2), 76–88.

Fitting, M. D., Salisbury, S., Davies, N. H., & Mayclin, D. K. Self-concept and sexuality of spinal cord injured women. *Archives of Sexual Behavior,* 1978, *7*(2), 143–156.

Guttman, L. *Spinal cord injuries: Comprehensive management and research* (2nd ed.). Oxford: Blackwell Scientific Publications, 1976.

Hanson, R. W. The psycho-ecological approach to spinal cord injury rehabilitation: A behavioral perspective. *Rehabilitation Psychology,* 1974, *21*(1), 39–43.

Hohmann, G. W. Considerations in management of psychosexual readjustment in the cord injured male. *Rehabilitation Psychology,* 1972, *19*(2), 50–58.

Hoover, R. M. Vocational rehabilitation of the patient with spinal cord injury. In D. S. Pierce and V. H. Nickel, *The total care of spinal cord injuries*. Boston: Little, Brown, 1977.

Kahn, E. Social functioning of the patient with spinal cord injury. In D. S. Pierce and V. H. Nickel. *The total care of spinal cord injuries*. Boston: Little, Brown, 1977.

Kemp, B. J., & Vash, C. L. Productivity after injury in a sample set of spinal cord injured persons: A pilot study. *Journal of Chronic Diseases*, 1971, *24*, 259–275.

Kendall, P. C., Edinger, J., & Eberly, C. Taylor's MMPI correction factor for spinal cord injury: Empirical endorsement. *Journal of Consulting and Clinical Psychology*, 1978, *46*(2), 370–371.

Kraus, J. F., Frant, C. E., Riggins, R. S., Richards, D. & Borhani, N. O. Incidence of traumatic spinal cord lesions. *Journal of Chronic Diseases*, 1975, **28**, *471–492*.

Kübler-Ross, E. *On death and dying*. New York: Macmillan, 1969.

Lindemann, E. Symptomatology and management of actue grief. *American Journal of Psychiatry*, 1944, *101*, 141–148.

Mooney, T. A., Cole, T. M., & Chilgren, R. A. *Sexual options for paraplegics and quadriplegics*. Boston: Little, Brown, 1975.

Morgan, E. D., Margolin, R. J., St. Pierre, R. G., Krueger, E. G., & Rynearson, R. D. Introduction. In *A source book: Rehabilitating the person with spinal cord injury*. Washington, D. C.: Veterans Administration, 1972.

Pierce, D. S. Acute treatment of spinal cord injuries. In D. S. Pierce and V. H. Nickel, *The total care of spinal cord injuries*. Boston: Little, Brown, 1977.

Poor, C. R. Vocational rehabilitation of persons with spinal cord injuries. In *Comprehensive vocational rehabilitation for severely disabled persons*. Washington, D.C.: Job Development Laboratory, The George Washington University Medical Center, 1975.

Redden, J., & Jackson, D. R. *Denial in spinal cord injured patients: Cognitive behavioral treatment approaches*. In R. C. Grzesiak & P. G. Stenn (Chairs), Rehabilitation of the spinally injured: Contributions from a cognitive-behavioral perspective. Symposium presented at the 87th Annual Convention of the American Psychological Association, New York City, 1979.

Rigoni, H. C. Psychological coping in the patient with spinal cord injury. In D. S. Pierce and V. H. Nickel, *The total care of spinal cord injuries*. Boston: Little, Brown, 1977.

Rogers, J. C., & Figone, J. J. The avocational pursuits of rehabilitants wih traumatic quadriplegia. *American Journal of Occupational Therapy (AJOT)*, 1978, *32*(9), 571–576.

Staff of the U.S. General Accounting Office. *Cost of spinal cord injuries in the United States and progress in spinal cord regeneration*. Study HRD–78–10. Washington: U.S. General Accounting Office, October 14, 1977.

Stewart, T. D. Spinal cord injury: A role for the psychiatrist. *American Journal of Psychiatry*, 1977, *134*(5), 538–541.

Stewart, T. D. Coping behavior and the moratorium following spinal cord injury. *Paraplegia*, 1977–78, *15*, 338–342.

Taylor, G. P. Moderator–variable effects on personality-test-item endorsements of physically disabled patients. *Journal of Consulting and Clinical Psychology*, 1970, *35*, 183–188.

Webb, S. B., Berzins, E., Wingardner, T. S. & Lorenzi, M. E. First year hospitalization costs for the spinal cord injured patient. *Paraplegia*, 1977–78, *15*, 311–318.

Weber, D. K., & Wessman, H. C. A review of sexual function following spinal cord trauma. *Physical Therapy*, 1971, *51*(3), 290–294.

Weller, D. J., & Miller, P. M. Emotional reactions of patient, family and staff in acute-care period of spinal cord injury: 1. *Social Work in Health Care*, 1977, *2*(4), 369–377. (a)

Weller, D. J., & Miller, P. M. Emotional reactions of patient, family and staff in acute-care period of spinal cord injury: 2. *Social Work in Health Care,* 1977, *3*(1), 7–17. (b)

Wilcox, N. E., Stauffer, E. S., & Nickel, V. L. A statistical analysis of 423 consecutive patients admitted to the spinal cord injury center, Rancho Los Amigos Hospital. *Paraplegia,* 1970, *8*(1), 27–35.

9

Myelomeningocele (Spina Bifida)

JAMES E. LINDEMANN AND
ROBERT D. BOYD

Myelomeningocele (or spina bifida), as a medical anomaly, has a long past. Brocklehurst (1976) cites its description by Nicholas Tulp in his *Observations Medicae* of 1652. Effective medical treatment for myelomeningocele has a short history. It begins with the development in the 1950s of new shunting techniques for the hydrocephalus which often accompanies the disorder. Attention to the psychosocial problems of the growing number of persons with myelomeningocele is even more recent. These are problems which become apparent only when a high level of broadly accessible medical care is available, to give an appreciable survival rate beyond infancy.

THE PHYSICAL DISABILITY

Definition

The words *myelomeningocele* and *meningomyelocele* are interchangeable. They refer to a congenital birth defect which involves nonfusion of the dorsal arches of the spine (spina bifida) with a cystic distension of the membranes (meninges) enveloping the spinal cord and some degree of abnormality of the spinal cord itself (myelodysplasia). *Spina bifida* is an older and more inclusive term than myelomeningocele and the one most frequently used in Great Britain, where there is a relatively high incidence of this anomaly. The term *spina bifida occulta* refers to nonfusion of the arches without external manifestations and is rarely, if

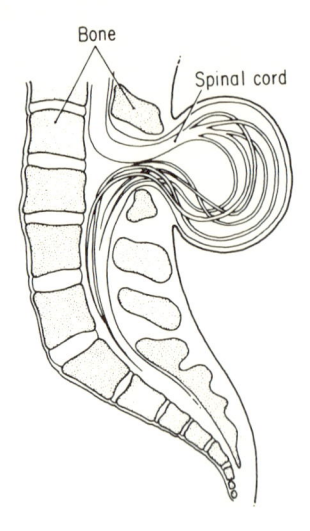

FIGURE 1. Myelomeningocele.

ever, associated with symptoms. The term *spina bifida manifesta* indicates that there are external manifestations which include neurological involvement. The term *meningocele* indicates a cystic protrusion of the meninges only, with intact spinal cord, ordinarily without demonstrable neurological deficit. A prominent American researcher, Shurtleff (1980), prefers to use the general term *myelodysplasia* to include all neural tube disorders that cause loss of muscle and sphincter control with sensory disturbances. This chapter will use myelomeningocele and spina bifida interchangeably, with distinctions in terminology applied only to designate conditions (such as meningocele or spina bifida occulta) which involve lesser degrees of severity.

Figure 1 portrays the distension of the spinal cord and its covering. Depending upon the level at which the lesion occurs in the spinal cord, the patient will suffer weaknesses or paralysis of the legs and problems with bowel and bladder control. About 98% of persons born with myelomeningocele have some degree of hydrocephalus (Shurtleff, 1980), with accumulation of cerebrospinal fluid and enlargement of the head. About 70% of these require treatment through surgical insertion of a shunt to divert excess cerebrospinal fluid from the brain to the bloodstream. Skeletal abnormalities, including kyphosis (humped back or marked increase in the forward curvature of the spine) are frequently present. Finally, other congenital anomalies often co-exist with the disability.

Incidence and Etiology

The incidence of myelomeningocele varies in different parts of the world. Neel (1958) reports an incidence of 0.2 per 1,000 births in Japan, with higher ranges of incidence (about 4 per 1,000) reported in England (Laurence, 1969). The incidence in the United States is generally found to be lower than in Britain, in the range of 1 or 2 per 1,000 live births. Hewitt (1963) reports that mortality from spina bifida is two to three times higher on the Atlantic than on the Pacific coast of the United States. Alter (1962) reports a higher incidence (1.5 per 1,000) among whites than among blacks (0.6 per 1,000). Shurtleff (1980) mentions an increased incidence among Celts.

Various dietary ingredients, such as potatoes, canned meats, and tea, have been investigated as causal elements, with inconclusive results. There appears to be a genetic or familial component in that the birth of a child with myelomeningocele increases the probability of recurrence by a factor variously reported to be from 7 to 40%. Laurence (1969) describes the genetic component as a normally distributed polygenically inherited predisposition.

A controversy exists over two major theories of the pathogenesis of myelomeningocele. In 1886, von Recklinghausen attributed the condition to failure of closure of the neural tube, and his well-stated theory held sway for 75 years. More recently, researchers such as Gardner (1977) and Freeman (1974) have returned to an older theory, that the cause is overdistension and a rupture of the developing neural tube, reasoning that this better explains the defects seen. A potentially significant implication of these theories is that failure to close would take place during the first month of pregnancy, whereas rupture would occur during the second or third month or possibly even later (Warkany, 1977).

The Decision to Treat

The first major problem associated with myelomeningocele is the painful medical-social-ethical decision to apply aggressive treatment or to treat passively, seeing to the comfort of the child without heroic measures to postpone death. Freeman (1974) cites survival figures of 16% prior to the development of early surgical procedures, while 56% survive if operated within the first 24 hours of life. More recently, even higher survival rates have been reported by some centers. Bunch, Cass, Bensman, and Long (1972) ask if, in a world with overpopulation, malnourishment, and inadequate medical care for many, thousands of dollars should be spent if we knew at birth that a child would be nonfunctional, totally dependent on society, and not able to recognize family or surroundings. They go on to observe that a significant number of children born with myelomeningocele *can* function independently, positing this potential for function and the intelligence to reason as justification for treatment. Lorber (1971) has developed criteria for active treatment, which include: (1) degree of paralysis; (2) head circumference; (3) presence of kyphosis; and (4) associated gross congenital anomalies. He recommends that the decision to treat be based on a calculation of a minimum degree of future handicap. He describes selection for treatment as the best but not a good solution to an insoluble problem. Shurtleff (1980) feels that we cannot predict outcome adequately and rejects a mere list of criteria. He advocates basing the decision *only* on what is best for the child; this involves balancing the pain of treatment and interference with parent–child bonding (by lengthy hospitalization) against the ultimate benefits in relief of pain and suffering and improved life.

Opinions vary as to the degree to which parents should participate in the decision to treat. Brocklehurst (1976) points to the difficulty of parents' assimilating a large amount of complex information in time for a rapid decision. Freeman (1974) observes that when a parent strongly desires therapy, no ethical decision is involved. Ellis (1974) states, "Most doctors think they should make the decision themselves," but he himself advocates that parents be given a detailed explanation by the pediatrician and then be involved in the decision. Shurtleff (1980) gives parents a written summary but disagrees with the step of giving them final responsibility for a decision which they may make against the interests of the child. In any event, of course, the parents must give formal, informed consent for any surgery.

Associated Problems

Hydrocephalus is an excessive accumulation of cerebrospinal fluid in the ventricles of the brain, which may cause enlargement of the head and compression of the brain. It is found in about 98% of children born with myelomeningocele and has severe enough symptoms to require treatment in 70%. It is treated by surgical insertion of a shunt, which is indicated if the patient has clinical symptoms or excessive head enlargement (Shurtleff, 1980). The shunt diverts excess cerebrospinal fluid from the ventricles of the brain into other body cavities or the bloodstream.

Installation of a shunt was calculated by Shurtleff (1980) to cost $5,692 in 1978. More recently, it has been estimated that it costs in excess of $100,000 to treat a spina bifida child for the first four years of life and more than $250,000 for a lifetime (Spina Bifida Association of Houston).

Hydrocephalus has a major relationship with intellectual impairment. For example, Tew (1977) studied a myelomeningocele population in South Wales, in which those without hydrocephalus had a mean IQ of 93, with mild hydrocephalus a mean IQ of 88, with moderate hydrocephalus a mean IQ of 78, and with severe hydrocephalus a mean IQ of 58. In general, about 50% of persons with myelomeningocele are found to have some degree of mental retardation. Level of the lesion in the spinal cord also has some relationship to intelligence, and Hunt and Holmes (1975) suggest that the best predictors at birth are the thickness of the cerebral cortex and the sensory level of the lesion.

The ability of the person to ambulate will depend upon the level of the lesion. Shurtleff, Hayden, Chapman, Broy, and Hill (1975) found that those with thoracic and high lumbar lesions (L2 ↑) were confined to wheelchairs (and 52% of the group were retarded). Those with lesions at L3–5 were able to walk with aids. Those with lesions S1 ↓ were fully ambulatory (and only 15% were retarded). A schematic representation of the spinal cord can be found in Chapter 8, Figure 1. Associated deformities are attributed to lack of fetal movement and to the intrauterine position of the child. Ordinarily, intervention to minimize these will consist of surgery, bracing, or physical therapy. In addition to the myelomeningocele, problems of curvature (kyphosis, scoliosis) are commonly found.

Impairment of bowel and bladder functioning is seen in 90% of cases of spina bifida manifesta (Forrest, 1976). This is related in part to loss of sphincter tone or spasticity. A large causal role is also played by the lack of sensation, depriving the person of signals to indicate that elimination is necessary, and of the sensorimotor feedback needed for controlled evacuation or voiding. Incontinence may be managed through intermittent catheterization or by the surgical creation of an ileal loop for urine diversion. Establishment of a regular schedule and diet may help in controlling fecal incontinence. Improper care of appliances and insufficient attention to "accidents" may lead to the chronic odor of urine and feces which Shurtleff (1980) has dubbed the "outhouse syndrome." This will be discussed further in latter parts of this chapter.

Shurtleff (1980) states that most females with myelodysplasia can be fully capable sexual partners; he notes that lack of sensation does not in itself exclude orgasm or sexuality. It is commonly observed that pregnancy may be difficult, especially if an ileal loop is present. Shurtleff also finds that 75% of the males have ejaculation, but not necessarily erection.

Hayden, Davenport, and Campbell (1979) report that myelodysplastic girls have menarche at an average age of 11.4 years, in comparison with 12.7 years for a control group. By contrast, the boys in their group appeared to be slightly behind controls in pubertal stages. The girls were also significantly shorter than their controls and more prone to obesity, unlike the boys, who did not differ from their peers in these characteristics. About 15% of myelodysplastic children are reported to have seizures (Shurtleff, 1980).

Repeated hospitalizations are common for persons with myelomeningocele. Tew and Laurence (1976) studied 43 children ages 8 to 10 and found an average of 11 weeks per year in hospital during the first 2 years of life, 10 weeks per year from ages 2 to 5, and about 9 days per year thereafter. Surgery is typically required to repair the back and relieve the hydrocephalus and is frequently required to correct orthopedic deformities. It will also be necessary if an ileal loop is to be created or if a CSF shunt is in need of revision or repair. Treatment for urinary infection also contributes to the large amount of time in hospital associated with myelomeningocele.

As with most chronic disabilities which have multiple motor, sensory, physiological, and psychological manifestations, the need is for a team of specialists to treat myelomeningocele. When the need for care recurs frequently and is often lengthy, it is imperative that the members of such a team be in close communication and be sensitive to all aspects of the patient's treatment program. In such circumstances, it is especially true that most members of the team, regardless of discipline, will at some time find themselves dealing with the psychosocial aspects of the disability.

COMMON PSYCHOLOGICAL CHARACTERISTICS AND PROBLEMS

Family Impact

The stresses experienced by the new parents of a child with myelomeningocele have been graphically summarized by Freeston (1971, p. 460), who describes

> shock and grief at having an abnormal child . . . anxiety at taking home a child with a large scar on its back and a valve in its head about which they know little. They will endure numerous hospital visits for consultation . . . multiple periods of hospitalization with accompanying strain and upset. The parents' own relationship may deteriorate and other children may react adversely.

All of this has been preceded by the trauma (anguish or indecision) associated with whatever role the parents may have played in deciding to bear the child (whose defect may have been predicted by amniocentesis) and to proceed with aggressive treatment. Parental participation in the latter decision will vary with the philosophy of the physician and the treatment center involved.

Herskowitz and Marks (1977) describe initial parental shock, anger, sadness, and withdrawal, and these reactive stages parallel those associated with the sudden advent of other chronic or traumatic disabilities, as discussed in Chapter 1. They observe that this process may interfere with parent–child bonding and suggest that, once a treatment plan has been evolved, the parents may entrust the defective part to the professional staff and relate to the more normal aspects of the child. Cutright (1977) notes that the discrepancy between the expected, idealized infant and the actual one may interrupt the mother's developing capacity to accept and mother her child. She advocates intensive early intervention to minimize this, feeling that this will reduce maladjustment later in life. Barry (1977) points out that young families with a myelomeningocele child frequently must seek and accept financial aid and frequently will see this as another failure.

The effect on the family can be considerable. Dorner (1973) describes families as suffering major disorganization of their routine, limited social lives (for both patients and family), and maternal psychological stress, especially depression. Tew, Laurence, Payne, and Rawnsley (1977) studied 56 British families with a surviving spina bifida child, finding their divorce rate to be nine times higher than that for the local population and three times higher than for families experiencing the bereavement of their spina bifida child. Marriages which followed a prenuptial conception were especially vulnerable, and the authors concluded that the strain was greatest when the relationship had not been cemented before the arrival of a child. This observation concurs with that of Kolin, Scherzer, New, and Garfield (1971), that parental adaptation is best in those who had a previous stable relationship for at least five years. Kolin *et al.* also observe, as have others, that the degree of disruption does not appear to be directly related to the degree of the child's physical impairment. The findings of Tew *et al.* (1977) in Britain contrast with those of Martin (1975), who found, in the United States, that divorce or separation of parents of spina bifida children did not occur more significantly than in the general population.

In an earlier report, Tew and Laurence (1973) described the siblings of spina bifida children as four times more likely to show evidence of maladjustment than the siblings of a matched control group. The mothers of the spina bifida children also showed higher stress scores than their matched counterparts. The physical and psychological demands encountered in providing care for a disability of this severity are such as to require support, respite, and, perhaps most important, assistance in clarifying the emotional needs and responsibilities of all members of the family.

An important part of the impact on family and patient is the effect of repeated hospitalizations. The interference with parent–child bonding has already been noted, as well as the disruption of family routine. When the child is of school age, there is also disruption of academic activities. Although many hospitals provide schooling for patients with frequent or lengthy hospitalization, it is the observation of the present authors that there is usually insufficient academic demand placed upon the hospital student, in addition to the obvious lack of social stimulation. The cumulative effect of frequent hospitalization can be a significant academic deficit. Varying degrees of severity have been ascribed to the emotional impact of hospitalization. Tew and Laurence (1976) note that children seem to fear orthopedic surgery but welcome shunting (because in the latter case they feel uncomfortable and seek relief). They found increasing resentment of hospitalization after age five, but report that "because of their familiarity with hospital, the emotional hazard associated with frequent admission to hospital seems to have little effect on the behaviour of these children (p. 123)." On the other hand, Harris (1977) decries the regressive aspects of hospitalization, in which the patients are fed, bathed, toileted, and placed in a "crib" (bed with rails). These are aspects which the young patient may often resist or resent. Harris further notes the inconsistency of asking children to be independent in certain ways and at the same time to be totally dependent in others.

Intelligence and Schooling

Despite the adverse effects of hydrocephalus upon the intellectual functioning of a substantial number of persons with myelomeningocele, it should be pointed out that the *range* of intelligence probably parallels that of the general population. Creativity, productivity, and genius may well characterize some afflicted individuals. The relationship with hydrocephalus has been reported earlier in this chapter. Soare and Raimondi (1977) studied 133 children with myelomeningocele and treated (shunted) hydrocephalus and found them to have a mean IQ of 87.7. A group of 40 children with myelomeningocele but *without* hydrocephalus had a mean IQ of 102.3. These authors went on to note that in their shunted group, 63% had IQs above 80, while groups with hydrocephalus before shunting techniques were available had variously been described as including only 10 to 40% with IQs above 80. It appears that hydrocephalus continues to have a damping effect on intellectual effectiveness, although this can be significantly improved through early shunting. In studying a group of young children who were shunted early, Briggs and Marquette (1972) stated their expectation that they will show "close to normal progress."

It is generally reported that persons with myelomeningocele are frequently found to have impaired perceptual-motor functioning associated with hydrocephalus and high spinal cord lesions. Soare and Raimondi (1977) specifically point out that normal IQ does not necessarily indicate normal perceptual-motor function in those with myelomeningocele. Land (1977) questions the general assumption of visual-spatial dysfunction in myelomeningocele persons of normal intelligence. She believes that they do not have dysfunction in visual perception of form and space but that they do have difficulty in planning and executing motor tasks. Sophistication in analyzing the components of perceptual-motor functioning (e.g., perception, motor ability, organization) is becoming increasingly apparent in the neuropsychological literature and should contribute to our knowledge of perceptual-motor functioning as related to many disabilities.

Land (1977) points out that only recently do we have a significant number of survivors in school settings. In reviewing 104 patients who were treated during the last decade, Shurtleff (1980) reports that 59% were in regular school and within two years of their expected grade assignment. Seven percent were in regular schools but over two years behind. Thirty-four percent were in special education. Briggs and Marquette (1972) report that 20% of the group they studied were in special classes, while 20% were two or more years behind in grade placement.

No report has been discovered of the total number of myelomeningocele children to be found in the regular or special classes of public school districts, a number which, because of survival and longevity, should be increasing significantly each year. Dorner (1973) reported that most children who went to residential schools did so because of the lack of appropriate local facilities rather than the inability of the family to care for them at home. Herskowitz and Marks (1977) graphically describe the myelomeningocele child sitting at one end of the room smelling of feces. This is but one of the problems which made the schools, and often the myelomeningocele children themselves, happy to see schooling take place at home or in special facilities. Increased sophistication in dealing with problems of personal hygiene and increased flexibility on the part of the schools (especially as promoted by legislation such as Public Law 94–142) is bringing about almost complete assimilation of this group into the regular school system.

A word should be added about the contribution that can be, and is being, added by improved self-concept of the myelomeningocele patient. The authors have known a person with myelomeningocele who made his way in a wheelchair through three years of education in a high school without an elevator, in which his classes were on two separate floors. He accomplished this by the expedient of going to the closest stairwell when a change of floors was necessary. The first two husky people to come by would carry him up or down. The son of one of the authors was among the carriers and reported, "That guy must have nerves of steel, the way he smiles and chatters while we teeter him up and down the steps." A very positive self-concept, indomitable spirit, and mastery of the necessary self-help and hygiene skills, along with a flexibly tolerant (if not architecturally sophisticated) school district combined to give this young man an emotionally supportive, as well as academically normalized, education.

Emotional Adjustment

No child is born with emotional insecurity or maladjustment. These characteristics are the products of experience. Unfortunately, persons with myelomeningocele are exposed to a series of experiences which increase the probability of developing poor self-esteem, passivity, and dependence. Only a fortunate few are seen, thus far, who escape an exaggerated state of one or more of these characteristics.

The early stress on the family has been described. Early interference with the parent–child bond (through repeated hospitalization or parental rejection) can be expected to promote the kind of insecurity which leads to fearfulness, passive timidity, and withdrawal. Real or perceived neglect of siblings because of the demanding need for care of the disabled child can lead to resentment and destructive rivalry from them. These are forces that may not be evident early in the life of the child. Ellis (1974) has observed that the younger children usually appear to be happy if occupied but that adolescents are acutely (and unhappily) aware of their limitations. It is probably significant that adolescents have also had opportunity to experience the scapegoating and social avoidance which are frequently directed at disabled persons, who develop a sense of insecurity and failure which then compounds the realistic limitations under which they labor. The purpose of intervention (discussed in a later section of this chapter) is to prevent this vicious circle by promoting positive experiences and a positive self-concept from the start, beginning with family life.

Shurtleff (1980) believes that the chronic smell of urine and feces, or "outhouse syndrome," contributes significantly to the poor social adjustment of the myelomeningocele child. This is hard to control, accidents will happen, and the child tends to make an olfactory accommodation so that he is no longer bothered, or perhaps even aware. Shurtleff believes that, while carefully avoiding the imputation of guilt, the child should be taught that such odors are absolutely unacceptable to others (regardless of whether they give overt indication) and that they are, for the most part, avoidable. The importance of this factor is borne out by Kolin, Scherzer, New, and Garfield (1971), who found bowel and bladder incontinence a major concern of children and by Hayden, Davenport, and Campbell (1979), who found it one of the greatest impediments to emotional growth. Control of this problem will be discussed further in the "Intervention" section of this chapter.

In his study of 104 patients during the past ten years, Shurtleff (1980) described 70% of those with normal intelligence as having a "happy" adjustment, in contrast with 39% of those who were mentally retarded. Perhaps significantly, 63% of those with normal intelligence were capable of independent daily living, in contrast with 29% of those who were retarded. Although it is commonly observed that emotional adjustment does not seem to be directly related to degree of impairment, perhaps this is more true of physical than intellectual impairment.

In an intensive study of 20 adolescents with IQ over 80, Hayden, Davenport, and Campbell (1979) found that young girls in the myelodysplasia group showed the most emotional disturbance, while older girls expressed more social concerns, particularly isolation and loneliness. Boys were more concerned about sexuality and mastery of the environment. Tew and Laurence (1976) also note that girls with spina bifida appear to have greater physical and mental handicaps than boys, and Anderson (1979) found spina bifida girls to have the highest rate of psychological disorder in the subjects she studied.

Hayden *et al.* (1979) report that their myelodysplastic subjects see being different as a negative attribute, while their controls see it as positive. The myelodysplastic group participated in fewer team sports and group and extracurricular activities, and had far fewer close friends than their control counterparts. In an interesting example of Wright's (1960) "spread" concept, the parents of adolescents with myelodysplasia thought their teenagers had fewer, and the control parents, more, extracurricular activities than the teenagers themselves reported. Because of lengthy hospitalization and failure to remain in school grade, many of the myelodysplastic children had most of their social contacts with younger individuals. A large percentage of teenagers in both groups reported feeling sad more often than once a month, and neither group of parents appeared to be aware of this sadness. Although the myelodysplastic adolescents were physically able to handle many chores at home, only half had appropriate chores assigned, whereas virtually all members of the control group had appropriate chore assignments. Anderson (1979) also found that the mothers of disabled teenagers thought that they did not demand enough of their children and that this was especially true of the mothers of boys.

The contributions of ignorance, expedience, psychological self-protection, and unsophisticated benevolence to the adjustment difficulties of the seriously physically disabled have been discussed in Chapter 1. Some of the unusual characteristics of myelomeningocele (e.g., hydrocephalus, spinal lesion) make it difficult for parents and others to know how much to expect or demand, and experienced professional consultation can be invaluable in that respect. These young people, usually with visible difficulties, are especially subject to unsophisticated benevolence in the form of sympathy, overprotection, and unrealistic feedback which leads to unrealistic self-appraisal. The social isolation in which they so frequently exist lends itself to maintaining unrealistic self-appraisal in fantasy, without the leavening that comes from actual experience. Those in contact with them need to practice praising them when they use their capacities effectively, without creating inflated images of their comparative strength in the world at large.

Studies of the adults with myelomeningocele are few, due to the limited number of survivors in the past. Shurtleff *et al.* (1975) report on 34 persons over age 19, with IQ above 70. Of these, 38% were fully employed or housewives with complete self-help skills. Twenty-nine percent were involved in education or training. Thirty-two percent were in custodial care or at home with no program. Evans, Hickman, and Carter (1974) report on 202 adults born from 1940 through 1953. Ninety-three of these, mostly with meningocele only, were mildly impaired, lived essentially normal lives, and were employed. Half of them were married. Of the 106 described as having serious disability, 58 worked regularly, 17 worked periodically, and 31 were never employed. About one fourth were married. The fact that only three of those with serious disability were mentally retarded suggests that this group, which survived before the advent of cerebrospinal shunting, was probably less severely disabled than many who are now living.

Adolescents and adults with myelomeningocele frequently present the problem described by Nigro (1976) of lacking the kind of meaningful personal relationships which might go on to become sexual. This social lack is frequently a product of the stigma of having a visible disability, overprotection, poor self-esteem, shyness, and consequent failure to develop social skills. To these difficulties may be added confusion on the part of patients, family, and even some professionals about the sexual possibilities or normality. Most frequent are unfounded doubts about the patients' ability to function sexually in any capacity. The result is that competent and attractive persons with myelomeningocele who are functioning successfully in a number of life spheres (e.g., academic, vocational) will frequently have great ambivalence about sex and marriage, perhaps rationalizing that this is a part of life that is "not for me."

Dorner (1977) studied 63 adolescents with spina bifida and found that only 15% learned about sexuality from their peers, in contrast to about 50% of normal teenagers. Only 11% were going out on dates, while 80% were definitely interested in doing so, citing lack of peer contacts as a limiting factor. In describing the social isolation and feelings of misery of the spina bifida group, Dorner mentioned ordinary adolescent worries (am I attractive enough?) as well as special ones (incontinence—how and when to tell about it). Shurtleff et al. (1975) found in a group of 51 patients over 16 years of age that about one third were participating in some kind of sexual activity. In the group of 93 described by Evans, Hickman, and Carter (1974) as "living essentially normal lives," only 47 were married, while of 109 with "serious disability," only 24 were married.

Vocation

Hayden, Davenport, and Campbell (1979) found that realistic ideas about the training requirements for jobs in which they were interested were held by twice as many controls as by myelodysplasic adolescents. This may well reflect the limited social experience and reduced family "chore" expectancy of this same group. James (1975) reports that individual factors such as achievement of mobility, sitting tolerance, and self-care are of prognostic importance in determining the level of rehabilitation possible. Lawrence and Beresford (1976) note that problems of mobility are greater for adults than for children. James (1975) states that ability to drive a car should receive high priority, citing a study in which only those who could drive had been able to become self-sufficient or complete college. The signal position of driving in relation to motivation and independence has already been discussed in Chapter 1.

Statistics on employment vary widely among the groups which have been studied. Evans, Hickman, and Carter (1974) reported that all of

93 persons with mild disability were employed, along with 58 of 109 with severe disability. Shurtleff *et al.* (1975) found, in a group over 19 years of age and having IQs above 70, that 67% were either employed or in training. Lorber (1975), in a study of 96 young adults with myelomeningocele, predicts that 20 will achieve competitive employment and another 20 or 30 sheltered employment. He forecasts pessimistically, "No person severely handicapped by myelomeningocele who also has an IQ below 100 is likely to earn a living in competitive employment." A somewhat more hopeful prognostication may be made from reference to Chapter 1 of this book, using Table III, *Minimum Requirements for Competitive Employment*. Laurence and Beresford (1976) studied 51 adults with spina bifida and found 36 of them in normal occupation. Of those employed, 23% were in managerial/technical positions, 45% in clerical, 26% in light manual, and 6% in heavy manual. They noted that positions as telex or telephone operators were frequently occupied by people who were wheelchair-bound and incontinent.

This somewhat poor overall record of employment should be interpreted, of course, in view of the entire range of abilities and achievements of the myelomeningocele group, some of whom may be found to have outstanding records. As treatment methods, both physical and psychological, become more sophisticated, the resultant competence, self-esteem, and achievement of this burgeoning group can be expected to rise.

EVALUATING PERSONS WITH MYELOMENINGOCELE

Evaluation of the Environment

It is difficult to determine which is more important and which should take precedence—evaluation of the person who carries the diagnosis of myelomeningocele or evaluation of the interpersonal environment which responds to the condition and further shapes the patient, both behaviorally and emotionally. Our society is yet learning about persons with myelomeningocele, if only because, as previously indicated, survival figures as recent as 1974 (Freeman, 1974) suggested that approximately only one of six lives to adulthood. Even though these figures have greatly improved, the number of adults with myelomeningocele is so small that, especially in the United States, the general public has neither sufficient current exposure to them nor sufficient experience with them to respond to them in constructively meaningful and growth-producing ways.

Reference has already been made to the impact of a birth of a myelomeningocele child on a family, particularly if it is a firstborn. The stage is all too easily set, particularly with the reported frequency of hospitalizations, for excessive care and possible overprotection. Parents provide physical care and protection from hurt; nurses frequently give extra attention to these often attractive and sharp, but obviously handicapped children; schools may exclude them because of the "outhouse syndrome" (previously described) and recommend special education in the home away from normal school and peer experiences. If one is to understand the myelomeningocele patient, one needs to look carefully at the growth milieu which nurtures and shapes him or her.

Parents exert the first impact on the child and thus merit evaluation consideration. Parents may be evaluated in two ways: by interview, to elicit their feelings and reactions to their child, and by actual observation of parent–child interactions. Both are important. In interviewing parents, the approach must be developmentally planned and chronologically followed to bring out the natural sequences of training experiences to which the child has been exposed—feeding, locomotion, toileting, dressing, and other self-help skills. The interviewer should be interested not only in parental descriptions of training methods but also in direct or indirect expressions of feeling about the comparative adequacy of their child. Particular attention should be paid to any tendency to do for the child what the child might actually be able to do without help.

An evaluation technique which may be used for exploring parent attitudes is the semantic differential scale by Osgood, Suci, and Tannenbaum (1957). This approach asks the person taking the scale to react to a number of paired antonyms on a seven-point scale and can be tailored to fit a condition such as myelomeningocele, as well as to measure specific areas of feeling and reaction, such as dependent-independent, capable-incapable, happy-sad. Thus, parents can be asked to describe their perception of myelomeningocele patients in general, of physically disabled persons in general, and of normal persons. While this technique does not provide a precise score and is not a single standardized test, its adaptability and practical usefulness for evaluating parental feelings, for comparing attitudes of one parent with the other, and, by readministration over time, changes in feelings, argue for including it in one's battery of useful instruments.

Some will argue that feelings have little importance as compared with behavior and that the major way of changing feelings and attitudes is to change behavior. This need not, however, be an "either–or" matter. We are inclined to stress the usefulness of both and to suggest that to do one without the other may be doing only half a job. Therefore, some consideration should be given to observation of natural or specifically contrived situations to bring out parent–child and interpersonal factors which train both behaviors and attitudes.

A procedure for measuring dyadic interactions between parent and child which makes available immediate information about behavior, its antecedents, and its consequences, is described by Mash, Terdal, and Anderson (1976). Recorders, observing, for example, mother–child interactions, attend to the behavior of each participant, such as mother's command, child's compliance, and mother's praise or, conversely, mother's command, child's failure to respond, and mother's failure to respond. An added advantage to this approach is the reversibility of the process, enabling observation of one participant's behavior as either an antecedent or a consequence. Similar procedures have been developed for coding discrete behaviors in the classroom by Cobb and Ray (1972). Variations of these approaches could conceivably be adapted to the behavioral study of other interpersonal interactions such as nurse–child, which may be particularly important for the myelomeningocele child who spends so much time in hospitals and who, because of this, may be especially vulnerable to learning to be cared for by others. Such information can be particularly helpful in planning treatment, for by changing antecedent (training) behavior, consequent behavior may be changed as well.

Evaluation of the Person

Thus far, our discussion has focused on the child's environment and the behavior of significant people in it whose feelings, especially fears and anxieties, may influence the child. Now we shall look more specifically at evaluation of the person, through observation, interview, and psychological tests.

Self-Concept and Adaptive Behavior. Because the patient has physical limitations from the time of birth, yet usually possesses reasonably adequate intellectual abilities, the self-concept or self-image becomes most important to the effective use of those abilities. If one sees oneself as negatively different or inadequate, if one has been taught to be dependent, and if one has learned substitute means of achieving recognition, conditions are nearly perfect for continuing inadequate behavior, frequently adaptively well below measures of cognitive skill. One child observed in his school setting consistently failed to exert effort or initiative academically and persistently asked for help. He went to great lengths, however, to entertain his classmates on the playground by performing "wheelies" (precariously balancing his wheelchair on the rear wheels only). Several older adolescents with myelomeningocele have made statements in interview such as "I guess I could do it, but someone will have to help me." These attitudes, which poorly camouflage underlying feelings reflective of a negative self-image, can best be evaluated through observation or play, especially with younger children.

Often it is of value to compare observed behavior, especially behavior which can be directly measured, such as cognitive or motor skills, with typical day-to-day behavior reported by a knowledgeable informant. With younger children, use of the Boyd Developmental Progress Scale (Boyd, 1974) enables comparison of tested motor and communication (cognitive) skills with reports of self-sufficiency skills derived from interview with the parents. The Vineland Social Maturity Scale (Doll, 1965) specifically measures social or adaptive behavior, again from information elicited by interview with a knowledgeable informant. Both of these procedures, however, require expert interviewing, with open questions and emphasis on eliciting description of typical behavior, in order to avoid "haloing" on the part of the parents.

Adolescence has been described as a time for reality testing and search for ego identity in the normally developing adolescent. There is no reason to believe that this is not equally true, and perhaps even more crucial, for the teenager with myelomeningocele. The interview should probe perceptions of the past ("What were your major strengths?" "What brought you your greatest recognition?" "How did you feel about your relationship with your peers?"), perceptions of the present ("What do you most enjoy doing now?" "What causes you the most difficulty at the present time?" "What kind of people do you most enjoy being with?"), and hopes and expectations for the future ("What do you expect to be doing ten years from now?" "What occupational choices have you been considering?" "How do you feel about marrying and having children?"). The derived information may be of value in planning psychotherapeutic procedures and in beginning to define goals, not only to identify and modify disabling feelings, but also to develop existing skills and to adapt them to appropriate vocational choices.

Evaluation of Personality. Measurement of attitudes through the use of psychological tests includes the usual spectrum of tests and scales available to normal persons, since the major limitations of the myelomeningocele group (motor limitations, bowel and bladder control) do not directly limit ability to read, to understand, to respond to such scales. An excellent example of the use of such measures is the study by Hayden, Davenport, and Campbell (1979), in which myelodysplasic adolescents and a control group were administered the Offer Self-Image Questionnaire, the Tennessee Self Concept Scale, the Wahler Self-Description Inventory, and the Rotter Incomplete Sentences Blank, together with selected cards from the Michigan Picture Test and the Symonds Picture-Story Test. Results (described earlier in this chapter) were consistent with much of what might be expected from the symptoms of the condition.

Additional measures of emotional attitudes, especially with adults, include objective personality measures such as the Minnesota Multiphasic Personality Inventory (Hathaway & McKinley, 1948) and the Edwards Personal Preference Record (Edwards, 1959), as well as projective measures such as the Thematic Apperception Test (Murray, 1943), or the Rorschach technique (Rorschach, 1948).

Evaluation of Perceptual-Motor Skills. Although there is controversy as to whether the myelomeningocele population does or does not show evidence of true perceptual-motor problems separate from IQ or motor limitations, it would appear injudicious to ignore this area in conducting a complete evaluation. Evaluation procedures available to the clinician range from the complete Halstead–Reitan battery (Reitan, 1966) to short visual–motor tests such as the Benton Visual Memory Test (Benton, 1955) or the Bender–Gestalt test (Bender, 1946). A strong bias of one of the authors, however, is that the results must be viewed not only as reflections of perceptual-motor or central nervous system dysfunction but as possible artifacts. These may reflect the way in which the stimulus materials were presented in relation to the drawing paper, how the pencil was grasped (certain ways of holding the pencil may impair the patient's ability to see what he is drawing), or left/right hand dominance, which may determine direction of movement. Knowledge of the presence of any of the latter factors may be as important in planning future educational or training programs as knowledge of the presence of central nervous system dysfunction.

Evaluation of Intelligence. Measurement of intellectual or cognitive ability can follow traditional procedures, since the myelomeningocele child is not typically limited in vision, hearing, speech, or motor skills of the upper extremity. Early screening can use the Denver Developmental Screening Test (Frankenburg, Dodds, & Fandal, 1970) or the Boyd Developmental Progress Scale (Boyd, 1974), both of which offer comparison between motor, cognitive, and adaptive behaviors. For more precise measurement, the Bayley Scales of Infant Development (Bayley, 1969), which offer both motor and cognitive measures, may be used. The Stanford–Binet (Terman & Merrill, 1960), with its long history of clinical use, remains as a major measure of intellectual functioning, especially from approximately two to eight years of age. The Wechsler Intelligence Scale for Children—Revised Form (Wechsler, 1974) and the Wechsler Adult Intelligence Scale (Wechsler, 1955) come into greater usefulness beyond eight years of age. The Wechsler scales are particularly useful, since their subtests offer a comparison of different mental functions which may be helpful in predicting and planning not only academic, but also later occupational directions.

Evaluation of Interests. If the major focus is on vocational or career planning, measures of interest need to be included. The major instruments include the Kuder Preference Record (Kuder, 1960), which furnishes a general reflection of degree of interest in occupational areas, and the Strong–Campbell Interest Inventory (Campbell, 1974), which makes available not only measures of degree of interest in broad vocational areas but also comparison with interest patterns of successful individuals in a large number of professions and occupations. These instruments may be useful in calling to the attention of the maturing myelomeningocele patient the broad spectrum of occupations which can be considered, notwithstanding motor or possible intellectual–academic limitations.

INTERVENTION METHODS

Intervention Goals

The primary goal of intervention procedures involving the person who has myelomeningocele (and his family) is to produce a productive and happy adult in spite of limitations imposed by the condition. To accomplish this goal, an environment which establishes and maintains realistic expectations consistent with ability levels and which rewards effort and achievement rather than dependence needs to be established and maintained over time. Such an environment requires focusing not only on the external environment of home and school, which enhances or limits growth and development, but also on the internal environment of the individual who has reacted to, and learned from, the environment as he has perceived it. Under positive conditions one might expect increased effort, increased success, and an emerging positive, yet realistic, self-image; under less positive or less desirable conditions, one may see avoidance of effort, development of substitute attention-seeking behavior, and an increasingly negative and unrealistic self-image.

Intervention with Parents

As previously discussed, the impact on the family of the birth of a child with myelomeningocele may constitute a threat to family solidarity, especially in view of the limited knowledge most parents have about the condition. Especially at this time, transmission of information regarding what the disease is and is not, what treatment possibilities exist and what their limitations are, and what the future may realistically bring, are exceedingly important. To bring the most useful information to the parents, the professional must rely not only on his general knowledge of the disease but also specific knowledge of the patient derived from the complete initial examination. Armed with knowledge accumulated over the years about the outcome of those born with myelomeningocele, together with specific knowledge about the newborn child, such as level of the lesion, the professional team is ready to start the process of intervention with an informed consent conference with the parents, primarily to discuss treatment.

Shurtleff (1980) recognizes the complexity of making a decision regarding treatment or nontreatment and suggests that the decision should be based on the value of treatment to the infant rather than on "selection criteria for nontreatment." He does not, however, overlook recognition of the extent to which frequent, long, and sometimes painful hospitalizations make normal parent–child bonding more difficult for the child and also for the mother, who may already find it difficult to accept her malformed child comfortably. Finally, while appreciating that the parents' wishes, after communication and discussion of the physician's findings and recommendations, should be understood and followed whenever possible, other steps may be necessary, such as voluntary or court-ordered relinquishment of the child, if "the parents' decision is based on their own interests at the expense of the child" (Shurtleff, 1980, p. 29). Shurtleff further stresses (1980, p. 29) that, while some mothers can adequately care for their children in spite of the deformity, care should be taken "to protect mothers from being required to care for infants at the insistence of a non-supportive spouse or a society."

Shock, confusion, grief, and guilt make the parents more dependent on recommendations of the physician. Shaw (1973), Stark (1977), and Shurtleff (1980) recognize and elaborate this situation. Shurtleff (1980) has developed a rather elaborate and complete procedure which makes available to the parents information regarding the most significant problems, possible treatment, and management techniques, with indications as well as contraindications for treatment. Although discussion of possible outcomes may be difficult at the beginning, long-term effects may be positive, especially since the evaluative framework is established for later revised decisions based on changes in conditions, such as worsening of an infection, the prognosis or return of neuromuscular function improving chances for ambulation. Families frequently will need emotional support through periods of guilt or ambivalence, whether their decision has been to treat passively or aggressively.

Once early decisions regarding treatment have been made, the process has only begun. There must be a constant monitoring of conditions and reaction to treatment of the family as well as the child. McGill (1980), a social worker connected with the myelomeningocele clinic of the University of Oregon Health Sciences Center, reflects her belief that parental tendency to foster dependency seems to come from two sources: "lack of knowledge about the defect and the loving desire to help the helpless." To meet these needs, McGill stresses continuing parent education by a medical–social team of professionals who are familiar with the defect and in good communication with each other. They will be able to speak with confidence and elicit confidence from the parents. The matter of communication is especially important in order to avoid contradictory or conflicting advice. Frequent staff conferences may alleviate the problem in part. Parent groups may permit easier expression and exchange of current feelings, as well as clarification of specific problems of communication. A technique used by this clinic is to furnish a room, coffee and cookies, and a professional social worker to meet in a casual atmosphere with parents while their children are being seen by various professionals. Barry (1977) has stressed the value of getting the new parents of a myelomeningocele child in touch with the parents of older ones.

A more formal series of parent sessions has been described by Cutright (1977), who met with a group twice monthly for twelve months. She describes a progression beginning with charged discussion of emotions such as anger at health professionals, pessimism, confusion, problems of separation, and fear of mental retardation. This was followed by a period of dealing with factual topics and acquiring information. The group then returned to feeling-toned discussion at a more mature and informed level.

Intervention with School Personnel

As with the beginning parent, what the educator knows about the student with myelomeningocele may be little and/or erroneous. As a person who spends much time with the growing child, the educator needs to know much more than the fact that the child may be intellectually slower, may be crippled and confined to a wheelchair, and may have bowel and/or bladder problems which make smells. Most of all, the educator must know what can be accomplished when suitable training opportunities are established and firm and reasonable expectations of performance are set and adhered to.

Normally, toilet training, even for the child with myelomeningocele, will have been initiated and to some extent achieved prior to regular school attendance. The teacher can do much, however, to reinforce child behavior which leads to avoidance of the "outhouse syndrome" previously discussed, particularly through stressing personal responsibility for hygienic care and regularity of defecation and urination. The teacher or principal who assumes that the child is incapable of achieving any degree of control or personal responsibility may be teaching the child exactly that; conversely, the teacher who expects and anticipates some accidents, yet also expects success, may reinforce the likelihood of success.

Some school administrators have, largely through lack of knowledge and possibly through pressure from parents, assumed that the child was incapable of school attendance and have recommended home tutoring. In such instances, the child needs an advocate who can intervene on behalf of the child, one who appreciates the child's capabilities and potentials as well as his right, as much as that of any other student, to achieve as normal an education as possible. Although information is limited regarding differences in effectiveness between public schools and special classes or special schools, Tew and Laurence (1975) studied spina bifida children in Wales and found that those receiving a normal school education demonstrated an ability to read up to the level expected on the basis of measures of intelligence. Those in special schools (admittedly, this group suffered from greater physical handicaps) showed significantly lower reading scores. Tew and Laurence concluded that the teacher's expectations were a crucial variable in school achievement.

One of the authors had opportunity several years ago to observe the introduction of a four-year-old spina bifida child to a special class for the physically handicapped. The first day the child was brought in his wheelchair to the classroom and observed the other children enjoying the activities, but he was told that wheelchairs were not allowed in the room. When the child complained that he could not leave his chair, he was permitted to watch from the door while remaining in his chair. Everyone was friendly with him, but no one took him into the room. After several days, he expressed willingness to leave his chair and sit on a blanket in one corner of the room. This brought him into some of the activities, but he still could not be a part of all that went on in the room unless, as he learned in a few days more, he assumed the responsibility for moving himself, literally by dragging himself to where the action was. In the relatively short period of a few weeks, he changed from a passive, dependent, and whimpering child to a participating, relatively independent, and happy child.

This same hospital and school in Scotland furnished one author opportunity to evaluate and follow three preschool-age spina bifida children, all of whom came from impoverished homes. Two children had the advantage of attending the previously described school class for physically handicapped children. One child, however, was not exposed to these training resources because those responsible for her care believed the expectations of the teacher would be too difficult for her; the hospital care personnel, therefore, continued to bathe her, dress her, and feed her. Two years later, this girl was found in another hospital and reevaluated. She was still markedly dependent, with essentially no change in knowledge or skill. The other two children had the benefit of two years of training in the special preschool before starting regular public school. One child went to a school which prided itself on its students' academic achievement; after two years, he was reevaluated and found to have grade-level academic skills but a marked regression in self-help skills. The remaining child, after the same preschool training, entered a school headed by a principal who firmly believed that overall achievement, both academic and social, was the responsibility of the school—its teachers and students—and that the degree of learning achieved was related to expectations. The child, two years later, was doing well, not only academically but also in terms of independent functioning and social interactions.

Much of the preceding discussion might imply that schools need only *expect* and achievement will result. This is hardly the case, for some children with myelomeningocele, for example, those who were not shunted early enough or successfully enough, do show less than average ability to learn. It has also been pointed out that perceptual-motor problems may exist, either related to a generalized delay or specific in nature. Those who may be intellectually delayed will need special resources in the school, such as classes for the retarded or, at the least, special room facilities to augment their otherwise normal or mainstreamed program. For those with perceptual-motor deficiencies, expectations must be realistic, and care must be taken to utilize appropriate teaching methods. Controversy still exists over whether one should, in these situations, teach to the weaknesses, hoping to bring up overall performance, or whether one should teach to the strengths on the assumption that the weaknesses can be bypassed and that motivation will be increased by earlier success. The writers favor emphasis on strengths, but each case should be approached in terms of individual findings. Whatever approach is used, it should always be reviewed regularly to determine whether good progress is being made or whether revisions of teaching methods are indicated.

Direct Intervention with the Myelomeningocele Patient

Thus far we have discussed the environment of the home and the school. The person who has myelomeningocele needs direct intervention in a number of additional areas. Especially important are those areas which relate, behaviorally and/or attitudinally, to independent functioning, social acceptance, and a positive self-image.

Considerable emphasis has already been given to the importance of attaining as much bowel and bladder control as possible. This aspect of intervention should begin as early as other developed skills (such as sitting) permit, usually beginning with bowel training since this normally is achieved earlier and since it can usually be achieved with greater ease. One of the first steps is to train the child that the responsibility is his but that others will share satisfaction in achievement of cleanliness and whatever control is possible. Shurtleff (1980) advocates aggressively teaching the child at an early age that the odor of feces and urine is unacceptable to others and that consistent self-care and rapid cleanup of accidents is mandatory for social acceptance. He has a number of specific recommendations, including: (1) dietary management for small stool bulk; (2) regular daily evacuation schedule; (3) evacuation before strenuous effort; (4) the use of paper tape with or without tampon; (5) staying at home during gastrointestinal upsets if necessary; and (6) timed voiding for urine control. This management of personal hygiene, with associated habits and attitudes, is learned most readily when the patient is young. Nevertheless, there are occasions when responsible professionals may, and should, choose to point out the necessity to their adult patients and help them to learn more effective methods.

Peer acceptance is an important desired achievement, especially during the formative years, and especially for a person with handicaps which prohibit successful performance in activities normally enjoyed by others. Thus, to achieve as much of the normal life as possible helps to develop a positive self-image—a sense of being liked and, therefore, of belonging. This concept is no better portrayed than by the myelomeningocele child who, upon getting braces which made it possible for him to be in the upright position for the first time in his life, said "Now I can stand up just like everybody."

With so many body-image damages to the ego from the combined defects of myelomeningocele, it is logical that medical treatment and environmental manipulation alone will not be sufficient to achieve the ideally positive self-concept and psychological well-being. Counseling and psychotherapy may additionally be required, both for prophylactic and therapeutic reasons. These two purposes can frequently meld into the same process.

Essentially, three major functions may be elaborated for counseling the myelomeningocele patient: (1) making information available regarding not only disease-imposed limitations but also remaining capabilities and potential; (2) providing receptive environment for expression and resolution of negative feelings, especially anger and frustration; and (3) furnishing an arena for determination of constructive actions, together with opportunities to test them in real situations.

One of the best times to conduct counseling or psychotherapy, especially group therapy, is during adolescence, when the myelomeningocele child approaches the age when society more firmly expects independent behavior and when the adolescent both wants to assume the rights, privileges, and responsibilities of adult life and doubts his or her ability to do so. Emerging sexuality, for example, can be dealt with by dispensing general information (as with the normal person), while also dealing with personal doubts associated with the condition. At this time, again, the importance of personal hygiene can be stressed.

Dorner (1977) recommends that sexual counseling in these cases be done only by persons who know sex education, spina bifida, genetic counseling, and the psychological aspects of physical handicap in adolescence. Shurtleff *et al.* (1975) suggest that the following points be included in reproductive counseling: (1) both male and female myelomeningocele patients state that they experience sexual gratification; (2) myelomeningocele females can usually conceive and men are fertile if they can ejaculate; (3) three percent of the children born of myelodysplasic parents are born with a neural tube defect; (4) amniocentesis can identify affected fetuses; and (5) a paralyzed female patient with an ileal inversion has a difficult and hazardous third trimester of pregnancy. Elsewhere, Shurtleff (1980) has suggested assuring the patient that sex and urine control are separate functions.

One of the final, critical steps in the long preparation for full adult responsibility is career planning. Here the patient needs ongoing guidance from persons particularly trained to evaluate capabilities and interests and to merge these with occupational requirements. This process requires a full partnership of counselor and client, with the counselor being most sensitive to the personal feelings and needs of his client. In a study of adults with spina bifida in New South Wales, Laurence and Beresford (1976) found over two thirds in normal occupation (some in school); of those actually employed, 23% were in managerial/technical occupations, 45% in clerical occupations, 26% in light manual occupations, and 6% in heavy manual occupations. Kolin *et al.* (1971) noted that many myelomeningocele patients aspire to work in health fields, probably influenced by the exposure they have had in their own treatment.

It is especially important to realize the ongoing nature of career planning, not only in the evaluation process but also through supportive follow-up as job training or advanced education proceed. The central theme underlying this process must be an extension of the theme with which this section began: In spite of physical limitations and in spite of the dangers of developed dependency, the person with myelomeningocele can usually attain a happy and productive life—to assume otherwise would only increase the probability of failure.

TRENDS AND NEEDS

Training of Professional Care Personnel

Medical science has only recently developed the skills and knowledge to keep those afflicted with myelomeningocele alive to adult life. Unfortunately, many of those responsible for their care have functioned within the previous belief that these people would not live long or that they were essentially helpless and to be pitied. The result has too often been the "help the helpless" approach which has created dependency.

To change these attitudes, a concerted program of education and reeducation may be needed. Nurses, because of frequent hospitalizations of these children, might benefit from workshops or continuing education programs which focus on ways of developing independence while still giving adequate medical care. Teachers might also benefit from similar in service training in building academic motivation in children who, without such attention, may be vulnerable to the "I can't" or "You help me" attitude. Vocational counselors, particularly those who deal with the physically handicapped, might be able to use updated information regarding not only limitations but also capabilities and potential of their myelomeningocele clients.

APPENDIX: SOURCES OF INFORMATION

General:

Spina Bifida Association of America
343 South Dearborn Street
Chicago, Il 60604

General information for the professional: D. B. Shurtleff, "Myelodysplasia: Management and Treatment." *Current Problems in Pediatrics,* January, 1980, *10*(3).

REFERENCES

Alter, M. Anencephalus, hydrocephalus and spina bifida. Epidemiology, with special reference to a survey in Charleston, S. C. *Archives of Neurology*, 1962, 7, 411–422.
Anderson, E. The psychological and social adjustment of adolescents with cerebral palsy or spina bifida and hydrocephalus. *International Journal of Rehabilitation Research*, 1979, 2(2), 245–247 (Research Abstract).
Barry, M. A. Myelomeningocele as a family problem: A developmental task model. In R. L. McLaurin (Ed.), *Myelomeningocele*. New York: Grune & Stratton, 1977.
Bayley, N. *Bayley scales of infant development*. New York: The Psychological Corporation, 1969.
Bender, L. *Visual motor gestalt test*. American Orthopsychiatric Association, 1946.
Benton, A. L. *The revised visual retention test*. New York: Psychological Corporation, 1955.
Boyd, R. D. *Boyd developmental progress scale*. San Bernardino: Inland Counties Regional Center, 1974.
Briggs, P. F., & Marquette, C. H. Intellectual and emotional development. In W. H. Bunch, A. S. Cass, A. S. Bensman, & D. M. Long, *Modern management of myelomeningocele*. St. Louis: Warren H. Green, 1972.
Brocklehurst, G. Spina bifida for the clinician. *Clinics in developmental medicine No. 57*. London: Spastics International Medical Publications, 1976.
Bundh, W. H., Cass, A. S., Bensman, A. S., & Long, D. M. *Modern management of myelomeningocele*. St. Louis: Warren H. Green, 1972.
Campbell, D. P. *Manual for the Strong–Campbell interest inventory*. Stanford, Calif: Stanford University Press, 1974.
Cobb, J. A., and Ray, R. S. Manual for coding discrete behaviors in the school setting. In T. W. Clark, D. R. Evans, & L. A. Hamerlynck (Eds.), *Implementing behavioral programs for schools and clinics*. Champaign, Ill.: Research Press, 1972.
Cutright, A. S. Foundations of parental adjustment—early intervention, crisis intervention. In R. L. McLaurin (Ed.), *Myelomeningocele*. New York: Grune & Stratton, 1977.
Doll, E. A. Vineland social maturity scale. Circle Pines, Minnesota: American Guidance Service, 1965.
Dorner, S. Psychological and social problems of families of adolescent spina bifida patients: A preliminary report. *Developmental Medicine and Child Neurology* (Supplement No. 29), 1973, 15(6), 24–26.
Dorner, S. Sexual interest and activity in adolescents with spina bifida. *Journal of Child Psychology and Psychiatry*, 1977, 18, 229–237.
Edwards, A. L. *Edwards personal preference schedule*. New York: Psychological Corporation, 1959.
Ellis, H. L. Parental involvement in the decision to treat spina bifida cystica. *British Medical Journal*, 1974, 1, 369–372.
Evans, K., Hickman, V., & Carter, C. D. Handicap and social status of adults with spina bifida cystica. *British Journal of Preventive and Social Medicine*, 1974, 28, 85–92.
Frankenburg, W. K., Dodds, J. B., & Fandal, A. W. *Denver developmental screening test*, University of Colorado Medical Center, 1970.
Forrest, D. Management of bowel and bladder in spina bifida. In G. Brocklehurst, *Spina bifida for the clinician*: Clinics in Developmental Medicine No. 57, 1976.
Freeman, J. *Practical management of meningomyelocele*. Baltimore: University Park Press, 1974.
Freeston, B. M. An enquiry into the effect of a spina bifida child upon family life. *Developmental Medicine and Child Neurology*, 1971, 13, 456–461.

Gardner, W. J. Etiology and pathogenesis of the development of myelomeningocele. In R. L. McLaurin (Ed.), *Myelomeningocele*. New York: Grune & Stratton, 1977.

Harris, L. Hospitalization. In R. L. McLaurin (Ed.), *Myelomeningocele*. New York: Grune & Stratton, 1977.

Hathaway, S. R., & McKinley, J. C. *Minnesota multiphasic personality inventory*. New York: Psychological Corporation, 1948.

Hayden, P. W., Davenport, S. L. H., & Campbell, M. M. Adolescents with myelodysplasia: Impact of physical disability on emotional maturation. *Pediatrics*, 1979, *1*(64), 53–59.

Herskowitz, J., & Marks, A. N. The spina bifida patient as a person. *Developmental Medicine and Child Neurology*, 1977, *19*, 413–417.

Hewitt, D. Geographic variations in the mortality attributed to spina bifida and other congenital malformations. *British Journal of Preventive and Social Medicine*, 1963, *17*, 13.

Hunt, G. M., & Holmes, A. E. Some factors relating to intelligence in treated children with spina bifida cystica. *Developmental Medicine and Child Neurology* (Supplement No. 35), 1975, *6*, 65–70.

James, J. A. Faulty management limits myelomeningocele. *Pediatric News*, 1975, *9*(10),

Kolin, I. S., Scherzer, A. L., New, B., & Garfield, M. Studies of the school-age child with meningomyelocele: Social and emotional adaptation. *Journal of Pediatrics*, 1971, *78*, 1013–1019.

Kuder, G. F. *Kuder Preference Record—Form C*. Chicago: Science Research Associates, 1960.

Land, L. C. A study of the sensory integration of children with myelomeningocele. In R. L. McLaurin (Ed.), *Myelomeningocele*. New York: Grune & Stratton, 1977.

Laurence, K. M. The recurrence risk in spina bifida cystica and anencephaly. *Developmental Medicine and Child Neurology* (Supplement No. 20), 1969, 23–30.

Laurence, K. M., & Beresford, A. Degree of physical handicap, education, and occupation of 51 adults with spina bifida. *British Journal of Preventive and Social Medicine*, 1979, *30*(3), 197–202.

Lorber, J. Results of treatment of myelomeningocele. *Developmental Medicine and Child Neurology*, 1971, *13*, 279–303.

Lorber, J. Faulty management limits myelomeningocele. *Pediatric News*, 1976, *9*(10),

Martin, P. Marital breakdown in families of patients with spina bifida cystica. *Developmental Medicine and Child Neurology*, 1975, *17*, 757–764.

Mash, E., Terdal, L., & Anderson, K. The response class matrix: A procedure for recording parent-child interactions. In E. J. Mash & L. G. Terdal (Eds.), *Behavior therapy assessment*. New York: Springer Publishing Company, 1976.

McGill, M., Coordinator of Myelomeningocele Clinic, Crippled Children's Division, University of Oregon Health Sciences Center, Personal communication, 1980.

Murray, H. A. *Manual for the thematic apperception test*. Cambridge: Harvard University Press, 1943.

Neel, J. V. A study of major congenital defects in Japanese infants. *American Journal of Human Genetics*, 1958, *10*, 398–445.

Nigro, G. Some observations on personal relationships and sexual relationships among lifelong disabled Americans. *Rehabilitation Literature*, 1976, *37*, 328–330, 334.

Osgood, C. E., Suci, G. J., & Tannenbaum, P. H. *The measurement of meaning*. Urbana: University of Illinois Press, 1957.

Reitan, R. A research program on the psychological effects of brain lesions in human beings. In M. R. Ellis (Ed.), *International review in mental retardation*. (Vol. 1). New York: Academic Press, 1966.

Rorschach, H. *Rorschach psychodiagnostics*. New York: Grune & Stratton, 1948.

Shaw, A. Dilemmas of "informed consent" in children. *New England Journal of Medicine,* 1973, *289,* 890.
Shurtleff, D. B. Myelodysplasia: Management and treatment. *Current Problems in Pediatrics,* 1980, *10*(3),
Shurtleff, D. B., Hayden, P. W., Chapman, W. H., Broy, A. B., & Hill, M. L. Myelodysplasia problems of long-term survival and social function. *Western Journal of Medicine,* 1975, *122,* 199–205.
Soare, P. L., & Raimondi, A. J. Intellectual and perceptual-motor characteristics of treated myelomeningocele children. *American Journal of Diseases of Children,* 1977, *131,* 199–204.
Spina Bifida Association of Houston. *Spina bifida: The second most common major birth defect* (pamphlet). Houston, Texas: Spina Bifida Association.
Stark, D. G. (Ed.). *Spina bifida: Problems and management.* London: Blackwell Scientific Publications, 1977.
Terman, L. M., & Merrill, M. A. *Stanford–Binet Intelligence Scale—Form LM,* Boston: Houghton Mifflin, 1960.
Tew, B. Spina bifida children's scores on the Wechsler intelligence scale for children. *Perceptual and Motor Skills,* 1977, *44,* 381–382.
Tew, B., & Laurence, K. M. Mothers, brothers and sisters of patients with spina bifida. *Developmental Medicine and Child Neurology* (Supplement No. 29), 1973, *15*(6), 69–76.
Tew, B. J., & Laurence, K. M. The effects of admission to hospital and surgery on children with spina bifida. *Developmental Medicine and Child Neurology* (Supplement No. 37), 1976, *18*(6), 119–125.
Tew, B. J., Laurence, K. M., Payne, H., & Rawnsley, K. Marital stability following the birth of a child with spina bifida. *British Journal of Psychiatry,* 1977, *131,* 79–82.
von Recklinghausen, F. Untersuchungen über die spina bifida. *Archiv für Pathologische Anatomie und Physiologie,* 1886, *105,* 243–330.
Warkany, J. Morphogenesis of spina bifida. In R. L. McLaurin (Ed.), *Myelomeningocele.* New York: Grune & Stratton, 1977.
Wechsler, D. *Wechsler Adult Intelligence Scale.* New York: The Psychological Corporation, 1955.
Wechsler, D. *Wechsler Intelligence Scale for Children—Revised.* New York: The Psychological Corporation, 1974.
Wright, B. *Physical disability—A psychological approach.* New York: Harper & Row, 1960.

10

Progressive Muscle Disorders

JAMES E. LINDEMANN AND
MARY ELLEN STANGER

Toward the closing months of his life, 19-year-old Michael philosophically discussed the impact that Duchenne muscular dystrophy had had on his life. He said, "I think I would like a total body transplant. I'd like to keep my brain and my memories and all that is 'me', but I wish I could trade in the rest for something that works."

Bodies that don't work are all too familiar to people with progressive muscle disorders, and those so afflicted cling to the hope that the not-yet-discovered "cure" will come in time to benefit them or fantasize about a "trade-in."

THE PHYSICAL DISABILITY

The progressive muscle disorders are associated with increasing muscle weakness and usually with associated muscle atrophy or wasting. In some of these disorders, the muscle itself is considered to be the site of the disease process; these are termed *myopathic.* In other progressive muscle disorders, the disease process affects the muscle only secondarily, while the primary problem occurs along the motor unit prior to the level of the muscle; these muscle disorders are called *neuropathic* or *neurogenic.*

The motor unit is composed of the *lower motor neuron* (the motor neuron of the anterior, or ventral, horn of the spinal cord), the axon (the nerve fiber that leaves the neuron), and its continued course as the nerve root and peripheral nerve, the neuromuscular (myoneural) junction, and the muscle (see Figure 1). The muscle disorders are often classified by their location along the sites of the motor unit.

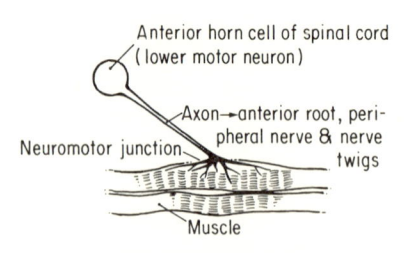

FIGURE 1. Motor unit.

This chapter presents those muscle diseases which tend to be treated from the standpoint of the muscle weakness, namely, anterior horn cell disease, hereditary peripheral neuropathy, myasthenia gravis, and muscular dystrophies. Other muscle diseases, such as those which are infectious, inflammatory, toxic, or hormone-related in etiology, will not be included in this discussion.

Diagnostic Methods

Not always does the patient with progressive muscle weakness come to the physician with the complaint of weakness. Often the weakness has been present for quite some time and has been considered to be an individual characteristic—"That's just the way I am." When the patient is a child, a number of other concerns may provide the impetus for an evaluation; these concerns could include developmental delay, academic problems, poor performance in physical education or loss of previous PE skills, hypernasal speech, "mushy" speech, droopy eyelids, double vision (diplopia), curvature of the spine (scoliosis), flat feet, high arches, or clumsiness and frequent falls. Occasionally, but rarely, pain is the main complaint. In one of the disorders (myotonic dystrophy), muscle stiffness or cramps may bother the patient more than his weakness.

Thus, *history* is very important in sorting out just what is meant by the patient's complaint; it is critical to know when the problem was first noted by the patient or family. Often the patient or family can realize in retrospect, after attention is brought to certain aspects of the history, that earlier, but unrecognized, problems had occurred. The history of which motor tasks are functionally impaired can provide clues as to the distribution and severity of the weakness. It is quite important to obtain *family history* in the evaluation of muscle weakness, for many of the entities described in this chapter are hereditary. In fact, some patients seek medical attention because of recognition or fear that they have inherited the weakness and wasting that limited or destroyed the lives of their relatives.

Physical examination should include both a general and a neurological examination; the former may provide clues that the problem lies elsewhere than along the motor unit and that the muscle weakness is a manifestation of some other primary disease, or it may yield some muscle disease-related clues (such as cataract, testicular atrophy, and early frontal balding in the patient with myotonic dystrophy). The neurological examination should attend to areas such as weakness, muscle wasting, or atrophy, muscle pseudohypertrophy (muscles that look big and bulky but which really represent affected muscle infiltrated with fatty tissue and partly replaced by connective tissue), muscle tone, deep tendon reflexes, joint contractures or deformity, sensation, cerebellar function, and involvement of muscles innervated by the cranial nerves.

Laboratory studies by means of *enzyme* testing, especially creatine phosphokinase (CPK), can be helpful. CPK is markedly elevated in Duchenne and Becker muscular dystrophy, often 50 or more times the normal value. In Duchenne dystrophy, the levels of CPK are most elevated in the early stages; by the time there is very little muscle left to degenerate, the enzyme level can be normal. In the neurogenic atrophies and in the other muscular dystrophies, the CPK levels are either normal or somewhat—but not exceedingly—elevated.

Electrodiagnostic studies used in evaluating the patient with muscle weakness include electromyography and nerve conduction velocity determination. Electromyography (EMG) uses a needle electrode to pick up the electrical activity of a muscle at rest and during contraction. Normally, muscle is electrically silent at rest but produces motor unit potentials during muscle contraction. The EMG may enable the examiner to differentiate between whether the electrical pattern of a muscle is normal or whether it is characteristic of anterior horn cell disease, of peripheral nerve disease, or of muscle disease; again, it helps to sort out the neurogenic from the myopathic disorders.

Nerve conduction studies measure the speed with which a nerve impulse is transmitted along the nerve. The velocity is normal in anterior horn cell disease (except in the very severe form of Werdnig–Hoffman Disease) and in the myopathic disorders. It is much slowed in the peripheral neuropathies which show demyelinization or loss of the myelin sheath around the nerves and can be normal or slightly slow in the neuropathies which involve the nerve fiber (axon) itself.

Muscle biopsy, performed either as an open, surgical procedure or as a closed, needle procedure, provides actual muscle tissue for histological examination by light microscopy and by electron microscopy. Just in the past decade or so, histochemical staining techniques have added greatly to the information obtainable by microscopy; now, in addition to general information about muscle microscopic structure, the muscle pathologist can distinguish two main muscle fiber types (and subdivisions) and can note whether the pathological process generally or selectively involves the various fiber types. Some of the non-dystrophy types of myopathies (e.g., nemaline myopathy) have abnormalities of structure demonstrable by histochemical stains.

Nerve biopsy is sometimes needed for diagnostic information. For this study, the sural nerve, located in the foot, is chosen, since the loss of this nerve is of minimal significance. If the nerve is abnormal, the important feature is whether the nerve shows changes which are axonal (of the nerve fiber itself) or demyelinating (loss of the protective myelin sheath).

The Anterior Horn Cell or Lower Motor Neuron

The spinal muscular atrophies involve degeneration of the anterior horn cell (see Figure 1). Infantile spinal muscular atrophy, also called *Werdnig–Hoffman Disease,* is a hereditary, autosomal recessive condition in which a progressive degeneration of tbe anterior horn cell occurs, often ominously involving some of the brain stem nuclei as well. The severe form of Werdnig–Hoffman Disease (type 1) may start in fetal life, but more often the baby appears normal at birth and then develops rapidly progressive weakness in the first weeks or months of life. The infant becomes quite flaccid or "floppy," lies in frog-leg position, has no head and neck control, and has very little movement of the extremities other than slight wiggling movements of the hands and feet. Because of weakness of muscles of respiration, with use mainly of the diaphragmatic muscle, the chest develops a typical deformity, with pectus excavatum ("funnel chest") and flare of the lower rib cage. There often is mild facial weakness, weakness and fasciculations (involuntary, wormy-looking movements) of the tongue, and increasing difficulties in sucking and swallowing. Death usually occurs within the first six months of life, but occasionally the child survives for two or three years.

In the milder form of Werdnig–Hoffman Disease (type 2), the onset of weakness often—but not always—is later than in type 1. More typically, the milder form starts in the latter half of the first year or in the second year of life. The child usually achieves the motor landmark of sitting unsupported but rarely achieves independent or aided ambulation. Since the arms are less severely involved than the legs, the child may have some degree of self-sufficiency in skills involving the upper extremities. As time goes on, these children develop joint contractures and scoliosis.

The outlook for longevity corresponds to the severity of respiratory muscle involvement; some of these children experience repeated episodes of respiratory infection and succumb by the age of 10 or so, while others have only mildly limited vital capacity, are not victims of frequent infection, and go on to live into their twenties or beyond. Some develop cardiac failure secondary to chronic pulmonary disease (cor pulmonale).

The juvenile form of progressive spinal muscular atrophy is called Wohlfart–Kugelberg–Welander Disease, or more commonly just *Kugelberg–Welander Disease.* It usually becomes manifest in mid- to late childhood or early adolescence. Although inheritance is usually as an autosomal recessive condition, in some families the inheritance seems to be autosomal dominant. The involved children initially seem normal in motor abilities and then gradually begin to manifest a somewhat waddling gait and some difficulty using stairs or arising from the floor. Progression varies in rate and degree; most patients remain ambulatory, while others will become wheelchair-bound; some will develop disabling upper extremity weakness and others will be only mildly weak in the arms; some develop scoliosis, others do not. Some authorities include the milder form of Werdnig–Hoffman Disease in the category of Kugelberg–Welander Disease; and the difference between these two diseases has become blurred.

Amyotrophic lateral sclerosis (ALS), also called motor neuron disease, involves the anterior horn cell, but it also involves the upper motor neuron of the cerebral cortex (and subsequently the cortico-spinal tract of the spinal cord) as well as the nuclei of the lower brain stem. There seem to be several different entities included in this category, most of which are not inherited. Amyotrophic lateral sclerosis has often been called "Lou Gehrig's disease" after the legendary first baseman of the New York Yankees. His futile battle with the disease made the tragic progression and fatal outcome a well publicized piece of medical information, and many a physician, groping to inform the patient about his disease, would mention Lou Gehrig's disease, aware that the patient then knew the worst. Depending upon which site is earliest or most involved, the initial complaint may vary. However, most patients will show fasciculations (involuntary muscle wormy or twitching movements) and weakness and wasting, but with spasticity and brisk deep tendon reflexes (as opposed to decreased or absent reflexes in diseases with only lower motor neuron involvement), and sooner or later difficulty in swallowing, talking, and breathing. ALS tends to be a disease of middle life, with most patients being in the 40–70-year-old group. Bobowick and Brody (1973) estimate the prevalence to be 2–7/100,000. For reasons unknown, men are affected more than women, 2:1. The average survival is about 3 years (Kurland, Choi, & Sayre, 1969; Mulder & Espinosa, 1969), but some patients have a much longer course.

Progressive Peripheral Neuropathies. The most common peripheral neuropathy seen in muscle disorder clinics is the hereditary hypertrophic peripheral neuropathy known as peroneal muscular atrophy or Charcot–Marie–Tooth disease. Newer terminology for this disease is *hereditary motor and sensory neuropathy (HMSN), type 1*. This entity is usually inherited as an autosomal dominant disorder. Severity can vary. Very mildly involved persons may have only high arches and little if any weaknesses of the feet. More typically, however, patients have more serious problems which become apparent in late childhood or early teens. The feet, because of weakness of peroneal muscles and intrinsic foot muscles, develop a *pes cavus* deformity with high arches and hammertoe. The ankles become unstable, and the gait may sometimes be of the footdrop type. Distal wasting of the leg muscles gradually occurs, producing a mild "stork leg" appearance. Weakness and wasting of the hands and distal arms may occur, but upper extremity involvement tends to occur later and to be milder. Most patients remain ambulatory. In this entity, the nerve conduction velocity is quite slow, even in persons who are still asymptomatic. Demyelination is seen on nerve biopsy.

Type 2 HMSN is also inherited in autosomal dominant fashion but involves neuronal atrophy rather than demyelination. It tends to occur somewhat later than the demyelinating form. The "stork leg" deformity of distal leg muscle wasting is much more prominent. Nerve conduction studies are normal or just slightly slow.

Type 3 HMSN is a hypertrophic demyelinating hereditary neuropathy, also called Dejerine–Sottas disease or severe demyelinating Charcot–Marie–Tooth disease, which occurs in infancy and is notable for its extremely slow nerve conduction velocities. This condition usually has an autosomal recessive pattern of inheritance. The involved children tend to be hypotonic and delayed in motor landmarks; they do achieve ambulation but then lose ambulatory abilities earlier in life than do patients with HMSN type 1. Scoliosis may be seen in the hereditary neuropathies.

Myasthenia Gravis. *Myasthenia gravis*, with weakness and abnormal fatigability of muscle after sustained or repetitive activity, is a disease involving the neuromuscular junction. There is failure of transmission of the nerve impulse across the junction; this now appears to be an immunological abnormality, in which antibodies block the acetylcholine receptor of the motor endplate. In young adults, the disease shows a female:male predilection of 2:1 or 3:1, while in middle life the sexes are about equally involved. In women, peak onset is in the third decade, while for men it is in the fifth and sixth decades. Incidence has been said to be about 1/20,000 (Osserman & Genkins, 1971), and occurrence is usually sporadic. In about 3.5–5% of cases, there seems to be a family history, yet without a definite pattern of inheritance.

The disease may present with weakness of eye muscles, manifested by diplopia (double vision) or ptosis (droopy eyelids); or by weakness of the bulbar muscles of face, tongue, palate, mouth, and pharynx causing loss of facial expression and atrophy of muscles of trunk and extremities. Sometimes all three groups of muscles are involved. The course is variable and somewhat unpredictable. Weakness may vary at different times of the day, or variations may be spread over much longer periods of time. In some patients, a spontaneous improvement or recovery occurs, while others have serious or life-threatening periods of exacerbation. Some patients stabilize and continue to do well with drug treatment, while still others show gradually progressive weakness. Those with only eye muscle involvement have the best prognosis, while those with bulbar and respiratory involvement can die despite the modern support systems of intensive care facilities. In the young adult female, thymoma (benign tumor of the thymus) is associated with myasthenia gravis in about 10% of the cases.

In this disease, the diagnostic methods described earlier are less helpful. Electrodiagnosis, using a technique of repetitive stimulation of the intramuscular nerve, may demonstrate reduction of endplate potentials leading to transmission failure. More commonly, diagnosis can be made by use of anticholinesterase drugs, either Edrophonium (Tensilon), or prostigmin.

Myasthenia gravis can be seen in the newborn babies of myasthenic mothers. The babies may be extremely floppy and may have quite serious difficulties with sucking, swallowing, and breathing. However, this condition is transient, lasting days to several months. There is another condition, called *congenital myasthenia gravis,* in which quite mild symptoms occur within the first year or so of life and which in retrospect probably were present as early as the newborn period. The course tends to be very mild and nonprogressive.

Myopathies. In this section, one type of myopathy will be discussed—the muscular dystrophies. The muscular dystrophies are myopathies which are set aside from other myopathies because of common features that include hereditary nature, muscle wasting, and progressive nature. Some of the other myopathies, those categorized as congenital myopathies, can share some of the characteristics and may, indeed, someday be viewed as belonging to the same group of diseases.

The best known of the muscular dystrophies is *Duchenne type*, probably because it is the most tragic of the dystrophies, running a relentless, almost stereotyped, rapidly progressive course with a fatal outcome. It has also been called by two other names, *pseudohypertrophic muscular dystrophy* and *progressive muscular dystrophy*. The first name relates to the common finding of large bulky calves (and sometimes other muscles). The seemingly large muscle is not actually a well developed muscle; on the contrary, it is a wasting muscle in which degenerating muscle fibers are replaced by adipose tissue and connective tissue. The latter name is based on the much more rapid rate of progression in this type of dystrophy.

Duchenne muscular dystrophy is inherited as a sex(X)-linked recessive condition. Each son of a carrier mother has a 50% chance of inheriting the abnormal gene and having Duchenne dystrophy, while each daughter has a 50% chance of being a carrier also. (See Chapter 4 for a further discussion of genetic patterns.) The exact incidence of Duchenne dystrophy is not known; but, as noted by Dubowitz (1978), various reports suggest a range from 13 per 100,000 to 33 per 100,000 live male births. There is thought to be a high mutation rate for this gene, but the estimated rate may be falsely high because of inability to accurately detect all carriers. So far, the CPK enzyme test has been the most useful in detecting carrier status and identifies about 70% of carrier women.

Research attempts to identify the involved male fetus by intrauterine fetal blood sampling for CPK testing gave early promise of providing early detection and option for elective abortion of a dystrophied male fetus; however, the test did not prove adequately reliable. At present, the only available choice for parents of a fetus at risk for Duchenne dystrophy is amniocentesis for chromosome study to determine the sex of the unborn child. If the fetus is male, the parents have the option of elective abortion of the possibly involved, but also possibly normal, fetus.

A newborn screening test has become available but produces some ethical dilemmas. Early detection contributes statistical information, as well as early information for genetic counseling of the parents. On the other hand, early knowledge of the condition—especially in families without a known history of the diesase—wipes out the "ignorance is bliss" of the early years, when the child appears normal or very near normal. Some authorities question whether it is then fair to try to make an early diagnosis in this condition, for which there is not any specific treatment available.

Although the involved boys have abnormal CPK studies, they appear clinically normal for the first year of life and often for the second year.

Some do have delay in the motor landmark for walking. Subtle differences then begin to occur, which can easily be missed by parents who are inexperienced in normal child development or who are unfamiliar with this entity and thus do not look for signs of weakness. The boys do not run normally, have difficulty with stairs, and rise from the floor by "climbing up their legs" (termed the Gowers maneuver). They are hypotonic in the shoulder girdle. Initially somewhat flat-footed in appearance, the boys later begin to toe-walk at about 5–7 years of age. They tend to waddle and have lordotic (swayback) posture. As weakness progresses, falls become more frequent and the boys no longer can use the Gowers maneuver; for a while, they can struggle to rise from the floor if there is some heavy, stable furniture to pull up on, but soon it is impossible for them to pick themselves up.

At about 10–12 years of age, the boys with Duchenne dystrophy will require use of a wheelchair; a few require a chair as early as 8 years, and a few can persist in walking precariously until about 14 years. Often a wheelchair is used for fast or long-distance travel about a year before the child becomes permanently wheelchair-bound. Once the boy is confined to the chair, the combination of weakness and chronic sitting posture leads to joint contractures of the extremities and to curvature of the spine. By mid- to late teens, respiratory muscles become weak enough to create hazards of frequent respiratory infections and of difficulty in handling the secretions of even a mild cold or bronchitis. Cardiac muscle also becomes involved by the dystrophic process. Death usually occurs in late teens or early twenties (occasionally in early or mid teens or as late as the mid twenties) due to either respiratory infection, respiratory muscle failure, or cardiac involvement.

Becker-type muscular dystrophy tends to have high CPK values. It usually, but not always, shows similar pattern of inheritance as Duchenne muscular dystrophy. However, it has a milder course and longer survival.

Limb–girdle type of muscular dystrophy is usually autosomal recessive in its inheritance (each parent carries the abnormal gene). Its distribution of weakness is similar to that of Duchenne dystrophy, mainly hip and shoulder girdles and proximal limbs. CPK values can be either normal or slightly elevated in the patient and are not helpful in detecting carriers (although some known carrier parents do have mildly elevated enzyme values). The age of onset is usually later than for Duchenne muscular dystrophy, but this is not always so. The course of the disease is milder, and most patients are still ambulatory in middle age. Life span may be shortened.

Facioscapulohumeral muscular dystrophy is inherited as an autosomal dominant disease, in which either parent is involved and in which each offspring has a 50% chance of having muscular dystrophy. As might be guessed by the name (*facio*-face, *scapulo*-scapula or the "wing bone" of the back, humeral-upper arm bone), the disease affects the muscles of the face, shoulder, and upper arms. The facial weakness occurs early but often goes unrecognized and is considered to be a manifestation of the patient's individual characteristics (such as "funny smile") and lack of talent for whistling or blowing up balloons. The amount of muscle wasting often seems more marked than expected for the degree of muscle weakness. The age at which the disease is recognized can vary, but most patients are identified during the teen years. The course can vary, even within the same family group. Most patients are ambulatory in middle life, while a few go into the wheelchair in late teens or early twenties. Life span is usually normal.

Although previously listed in texts and articles under the muscular dystrophies, *myotonic dystrophy* is now usually discussed under the myotonic conditions. It differs from the other muscular dystrophies in being quite clearly a *multi-system* disorder, of which the muscle involvement represents just one of the systems involved. This entity is inherited as an autosomal dominant condition. Other names for this disease are dystrophia myotonica, myotonia dystrophica, myotonia atrophica, and Steinert's disease. This type of muscular dystrophy varies greatly in age of onset and in severity. Harper (1979) reviewed various reports of prevalence rates and notes that 4.9 per 100,000 population is probably most accurate. The more typical history is of onset of symptoms in the late teens or twenties. However, the disease may occur as early as the newborn period or may be so mild as to go unrecognized until old age; the latter, very mild cases sometimes are discovered only when one routinely tests relatives of a known patient. In adolescent or adult onset of symptoms, the initial problem may relate to weakness or it may relate to the myotonia, which is delay in relaxation of a muscle that has contracted. Many patients use the terms "stiff" or "cramping" to describe their perception of the symptoms of myotonia, which they usually note first in the hands. In this muscular dystrophy, muscle weakness and wasting tend to occur in face, neck, and distal extremities. In families where the disease has been identified, diagnosis in symptomatic children is often made within the first decade by parents who recognize the myopathic face and the slow release of hand grip. Because there is an increased occurrence of mental retardation in myotonic dystrophy, some children's mild weakness and myotonia go unrecognized and they are initially evaluated from the standpoint of developmental delay or academic difficulties. Other children are referred by the school because of speech problems, including poor articulation and/or hypernasality. Still other children may present first to an orthopedist because of scoliosis, or perhaps even earlier because of flat feet.

It is just within the past few years that congenital myotonic dystrophy (presentation of this entity at birth) has been recognized. The involved infant is very flaccid or "floppy," may have severe difficulties with feeding and respiration, and may die in the newborn period. This infant does not yet show clinical or electrical myotonia; the distribution of weakness is diffuse rather than distal. It has been of interest that the infant with congenital myotonic dystrophy is usually the offspring of a myotonic mother with mild (sometimes not even yet diagnosed) disease. It is suspected that the fetus of such a mother has something different in the intrauterine milieu. The what and why of that difference is not yet known.

Cardiac arrhythmias are not uncommon in myotonic dystrophy and can lead to a shortened life span, as can respiratory insufficiency. However, as we noted previously, patients without these complications can live a normal life-span.

Treatment. There is no specific treatment for most of the muscle diseases. Treatment is aimed at prevention of or minimizing deformities, such as joint contractures and scoliosis (the former by braces, splints, tendon surgery, passive range of motion, and proper positioning; the latter by proper positioning, bracing, or spinal fusion). For those conditions that are rapidly progressive, medical philosophy varies; some treatment programs aggressively work to maintain ambulation or even assisted standing for as long as possible, while other treatment centers "don't fight it" and acquiesce in the inevitable transition to the wheelchair.

Much treatment aims at adjusting the environment to the patient, when it is impossible for the patient to cope with his usual environment. Adaptive equipment, such as elevated toilet seats, toilet or bathtub rails, use of a bar-type chair instead of a chair of regular height, portable lifts with various slings for transfers, and clothing adaptations (loose-necked undershirts, button-front shirts, velcro fasteners, for example) are some of the personal environmental changes which can be quite helpful. On a larger scale, elimination of architectural barriers, ramps instead of stairs, bathrooms and toilet stalls which can accommodate a wheel chair, automatic door-openers for public buildings, drinking fountains, sinks, paper towels at a level accessible to the person in a wheelchair illustrate some of the improvements.

For those persons whose muscle disease leads to wheelchair existence, the motorized wheelchair has become a welcome—cherished, perhaps—liberator. With such a chair to substitute for useless legs, the patient can travel about the home, neighborhood, school, stores, place of employment, parks, bike trails—with no need to wait for someone else to have the time or willingness to push a manual wheelchair. Ah, freedom! (well, relatively at least). In fairly widespread use for less than a decade, the power wheelchair does present some new challenges; the battery needs regular recharging, and the more powerful chairs do not fold down for easy transport but require use of a van equipped with ramps or use of public lift-type bus.

For children with Werdnig–Hoffman Disease or Duchenne muscular dystrophy, use of postural drainage and chest percussion to help with the raising of secretions can mean the difference between remaining at home and entering a hospital, or the difference between a mild respiratory infection and a severe one. The availability of this important service may mean the difference between a child's attendance at school and the necessity of remaining at home.

Treatment of cardiac arrhythmias plays a role in some of the muscle diseases, such as myotonic dystrophy or Duchenne muscular dystrophy. The outlook for treatment results is certainly good in the latter condition, since there can be quite extensive underlying degeneration and fibrosis of heart muscle.

Cor pulmonale responds poorly to the usual treatment programs for heart failure, and some patients with Werdnig–Hoffman Disease or Duchenne dystrophy will succumb to the cardiac complications of their chronic pulmonary disease.

Although mechanical respiratory assistance can be offered to patients with critical respiratory muscle weakness, this treatment is most effectively used in patients with myasthenia gravis in crisis; for them, the respirator or ventilator is an acute, relatively short-term need. For long-term need, the patients often make the decision regarding aggressive attempts to prolong life when there is no hope of being weaned from the respirator.

Of the muscle disorders discussed in this chapter, only two lend themselves to medical treatment. For one, myotonic dystrophy, there is no treatment to reverse or retard the progression of muscle weakness and wasting but there are available medications to treat the myotonia if this aspect of the disease is really disabling to the patient. Quinine, procaineamide, and Dilantin (phenytoin) are the most common drugs used; each has potential side effects which must be considered in deciding whether the myotonia is disabling or merely bothersome. The other treatable muscle disorder discussed here is myasthenia gravis, which most often is treated with anticholinesterase drugs, usually with either neostigmine bromide (Prostigmin) or longer-acting pyridostigmine bromide (Mestinon). Each patient responds in individual fashion to the drugs; dose and time schedule for drug administration, therefore, must also be individualized. In young women, as we have seen, myasthenia gravis is associated with thymoma, a benign tumor of the thymus gland; removal of the thymoma may result in marked improvement of the myasthenic symptoms. Steroid therapy is sometimes indicated in patients who are not responding well to the anticholinesterase therapy. A very recent treatment, plasmapheresis, has become available for those patients who are refractory to all other treatments; this technique attempts to remove abnormal immune factors from the blood stream and has had some dramatic successes.

COMMON PSYCHOLOGICAL CHARACTERISTICS AND PROBLEMS

The most common characteristic of persons with muscle disorder is some degree of muscle weakness. Consequently, the most common psychological problem of the group is some degree of dependence on others. This dependence, albeit forced, comes with the usual attendant difficulties.

The problems caused by dependency are in large part determined by the established personality pattern. People who have been excessively dependent typically do well in the early phases of illness and poorly when the time comes, if the illness permits, for rehabilitation. Their very independent counterparts do the converse. The dependent person typically is a "good patient" who conforms well to treatment regimes and restrictions and may even appear to enjoy them. Passivity and lack of initiative may hinder efforts to return him or her to an active life role. Conversely, the very independent person may chafe at restrictions or bothersome treatments but may be eager to use his or her available strengths and abilities in a rehabilitation effort.

Muscle weakness has certain other ramifications. It frequently results in a very specific loss of physical mobility, which in turn may play a large role in bringing about the social isolation which so often characterizes persons with muscle disorder. Social isolation results not only from the inability to get around, but from more specifically psychological causes. The anxious parent may wish to protect the child from the unfair competition or thoughtless teasing of his peers, and the child may concur. Where weakness affects facial muscles, the person may become painfully self-conscious or embarrassed at the inability to smile or give other appropriate facial response. This characteristic may cause persons with muscle disorder to be diagnosed as depressed or rejected as unfriendly. Where progressive debility reaches moderate or severe proportions, the person is forced to depend upon others for necessary daily functions. Much of the impact of this may fall on the mother, who may already labor under guilt if she feels responsible for genetic inheritance. In addition, she must balance her responsibility for the patient with that which she feels toward the rest of the family. Besides feeling neglect, siblings may be trapped between wishing to restrict themselves in order to minimize the discrepancy between their own abilities and the patient's and enduring the anger and frustration when the affected sibling is unable to keep up.

When debility progresses to the point where a wheelchair is required, this is usually a significant milestone and often brings with it important changes in personal orientation. For some it may represent the point at which they seriously reconceptualize themselves and their lives, abandoning the self-concept of the athlete, the mechanic, or the dancer, and beginning to think of themselves and their lives within the limits of their muscular condition. This may include giving up the idea that, somehow, the condition will be reversed, although the hope should not be confronted unless the person indicates willingness to relinquish it or unless it interferes with needed treatment. This particular aspect of adjusting to and accepting disability has been discussed in Chapter 1 and in Chapter 8.

For the person who is aware that his illness is progressive and carries with it a prognosis for limited life span, the wheelchair may mark a turn inward. Such persons often become stoic and quietly depressed, preferring to avoid discussion of the inevitable outcome and not to dwell on signs of progression. Their adjustment obviously includes elements of denial, repression, and suppression which may have a necessary role in allowing the individual to maintain ordinary daily relationships. Such individuals generally need at least one person in their lives with whom they can fully share all their hopes and fears. Families may need help in handling their own feelings and communicating with the patient through this process (see "Intervention Methods").

Coping with the prospect of death is a common feature in many muscle disorders. It may be the prospect of nearly certain death, when the disease characteristically progresses to termination within known time limits. Or it may be the ever present threat of death due to respiratory weakness, which occurs in many illnesses that may otherwise have a nearly normal life expectancy. Vital dependence on others is never more dramatically illustrated, nor the uncertainty and fragility of life more apparent, than in the terrifying experience frequently recounted

(Sneddon, 1980) by muscle disorder patients, of being hospitalized for an unrelated condition requiring a respirator, under emergency conditions, and having a person inexperienced with the equipment set it up while someone else reads the instructions from a book.

The remainder of this section is organized in a general way around certain specific muscle disease entities. There is a sequence of concepts, and in order to be adequately informed, one should read the section in its entirety.

Childhood Onset

Werdnig–Hoffman Disease. In the acute form of Werdnig–Hoffman Disease (infantile spinal muscular atrophy), death is almost certain by three years of age, while in the chronic form the patient may live to early adult years or longer. In each case there is progressive deterioration. Each demonstrates, during the first few years of life, the point so frequently made about muscle disorders, that *the family is the patient.*

As might be expected, parents have a great deal of difficulty in receiving, comprehending, and accepting the finality of the disease, no matter how gently (or explicitly) it is described. Denial is common, frequently in the form of the quest for additional diagnostic opinions and then for a solution or cure. Denial may also be seen in the families who decline to return for follow-up services, not wishing to know about the signs which mark the progression of the disease. Such families need access to professionals for information about the disease, treatment to keep the patient comfortable, and help in handling their grief.

In the chronic form of this disease, as in others to be discussed later (e.g., Duchenne's), some parents cannot get past the certainty of death if they do come to accept it. They may be quietly resigned or loudly weeping and in either case do little to contribute to the psychosocial growth and stimulation of their child. Matters of discipline or expectation may be met with "How can I be hard on her?" The problem is not made easier by the fact that these children are commonly observed (clinically) to be of average or higher-than-average intelligence.

Duchenne's Muscular Dystrophy. Boys with this disease are usually asymptomatic until 3–5 years of age, followed by progressive weakness eventually necessitating a wheelchair and death in the late teen years or early twenties. Here the mechanism of denial is more evident, probably because there is a long period in which the boy looks and acts normal, and denial is generally not obstructive. The impact is especially hard on parents with no family history, and therefore no prior warning about the illness. Buchanan, LaBarbera, Roelofs, and Olson (1979) describe extreme reactions in some such parents, including suicide attempts, abandonment, and the need for sedation and psychotherapy. They describe denial in the form of disbelief or magical thinking, for example, "This child is different and the disease will not progress." Kornfeld and Siegel (1979) found that families in group therapy tended to isolate themselves from reminders of the future, and Buchanan *et al.* (1979) similarly observed that focus on past accomplishments or on the future brought gloom.

In the 25 families studied by Buchanan *et al.* (1979), divorce (28%) was not higher than the national average, but an additional 27% had significant marital problems. Sixty percent of the siblings also experienced some degree of emotional distress, with older sisters defensive about their protective role and brothers guilty about what would ordinarily be considered normal competitiveness. Siegel and Kornfeld (1980) studied dystrophic boys and their siblings through drawings and similarly describe the unaffected siblings as harboring feelings of competitiveness, anger, and guilt without a viable mode of expression available to them. At the same time, they note that the siblings distance themselves from their handicapped brother for fear of hurting him and show a special respect for the close relationship between him and his mother. They also note that the affected boy's identification with the father is weak.

Buchanan *et al.* (1979) found that 76% of their families identified some psychological problems, but the majority were related to some future stressor, such as becoming bedridden. Some mentioned mothers' guilt and some sibling rivalry, but only one (of 25) identified an emotional problem of the patient (loneliness and depression). Similarly, Holroyd and Guthrie (1979) found that the children with neuromuscular disease whom they studied were not considered by their families to be more socially obtrusive or difficult as personalities than other children. These findings may be consonant with Mearig's (1973) observation that most personality problems in boys with Duchenne's are part of attempts to adjust rather than inherent parts of the disability. Mearig points out the implicit conflict in the boy's being forced by the disease to become more dependent upon his mother just at a time (that is, early school age) when he should be becoming more independent.

A degree of overprotectiveness and, especially, difficulty in punishment is reported by many observers (Kornfeld & Siegel, 1979; Buchanan *et al.*, 1979; Mearig, 1973). This will create serious problems when no attempt is made to impose discipline and limits on the developing child, or when social isolation is increased through mechanisms such as protecting him from competitive peers, withdrawing him from school, and providing him with an all-sufficient home environment, with facilities for entertainment and recreation which preclude the need for searching elsewhere. Failure to discipline is seen by Kornfeld and Siegel (1979) as retarding development of social responsibility, control of impulses, and consideration for the needs and feelings of others.

The early school years are often an especially traumatic time. As with any child at that age, the boy with Duchenne's must learn to accommodate an authority other than his parents' and, especially, must learn to cope with peers. Buchanan et al. (1979) point out that school involves more social peer contact than the child has ever had, presenting him with peer differences and self-perceived inadequacies. They also note that those children with emotional or behavioral difficulties were those without information about their disease.

Some of the implications of confinement to the wheelchair have been discussed previously. This is especially traumatic in that it is an unignorable sign of progressing weakness, as well as a barrier to mobility. The trauma has been only slightly relieved by the tendency in recent years to put almost all boys into motorized wheel chairs, giving them an immediate boost in mobility, and introducing them to the joys of "hotrodding." It is at this stage that boys often welcome the company of others with the same illness. A fortunate concomitant of frequent clinic or hospital visits is that Duchenne's boys become acquainted with, and may act as a source of information and support for each other. In this way they learn many details about the progression (and the prognosis) of their disease in bits and pieces which may be more readily accepted than if the information were presented formally all at once. While the period of grief on going into the chair may be met in many ways, passive or aggressive, most of the boys eventually become quiet, often rather stoic and philosophical. Frequently, they become solicitous toward the significant people in their lives, as if they were seeking to have each one taken care of and things put in order before their departure.

Sedentary pursuits such as reading, conversation, or art work become important both for diversion and for a sense of productivity or achievement. Many teenage boys have utilized career counseling as a source of direction for leisure pursuits and also for setting educational (and occasionally employment) goals which may be achieved in their lifetimes.

Intelligence. It is a commonly held assumption that some degree of impaired intelligence is a concomitant of Duchenne's muscular dystrophy. Marsh and Munsat (1974) tested 16 boys at age 7.9, finding a verbal IQ of 85.3 and performance IQ of 97.6. In a somewhat older group (age 10.8), in which muscle weakness had progressed, they found a verbal IQ of 87.6 and performance IQ of 89.7. From this and previous studies, they infer that intellectual impairment in Duchenne's is amply documented, that it consists of an early, nonprogressive verbal deficit and that it is genetically determined. Karagan and Zellweger (1978) support this finding in a study of 53 boys who achieved a mean verbal IQ of 80 and performance IQ of 88. It is generally held that performance IQ scores will decline with age due to progressive physical disability.

Mearig (1979) vigorously contests the above conclusions regarding Duchenne's and intelligence. She cites some studies (with small numbers) which found average IQ. She criticizes other studies in terms of sampling and design. She marshals traditional arguments about the influence of learning and environment on IQ and about inconsistent definitions of retardation. She points out that Duchenne's boys experience emotional disequilibrium at important stages in cognitive development. Finally, she presents data based on a study which is at least as erratic in methodology and sampling as those she reviewed, in which she finds no verbal deficit. She states (Mearig, 1979, p. 272), "Many researchers who believe an intellectual deficit is an inherent part of Duchenne dystrophy now talk in terms of one standard deviation below average rather than the more serious retardation often claimed in earlier studies. If this amount of deficit is found, it would be parsimonious to hold in reserve, for the present, genetic or central nervous system dysfunction explanations until all other possibilities have been carefully studied and eliminated." Mearig raises a question which cannot be ignored, and which makes critical her agreement with Karagan and Zellweger (1978) in calling for longitudinal rather than cross-sectional designs for the study of intellectual functioning in this group and for careful analysis which takes into account the interaction of factors which could influence the results.

Adolescent and Early Adult Onset

Myotonic Dystrophy. Myotonic dystrophy is most often diagnosed in adolescence or early adult life, and life-span may be somewhat diminished, with death often occurring in the fifth or sixth decade. Ambrosini and Nurnberg (1979) believe that altered mental functioning is a basic feature of the disease and that this alteration is not reactive or secondary. From their review of the literature, they list the following characteristics as having been observed: confusion, brooding, deviant behavior, "inferiority of ethical concepts," indolence, moodiness, suspicious attitudes, dull intellect, disagreeableness, apathy, and indifference. While emotional disturbance and impaired intellect are observed by virtually all who describe the disease, it should be pointed out that these are clinical observations which warrant more systematic documentation and description. This is especially true in that these patients develop physical manifestations such as ptosis, facial weakness, and peculiar gait, which cause them to look different and may contribute to the impression (or even self-concept) of being strange or dull. Ambrosini and Nurnberg believe that the etiology of neuropsychopathological changes in myotonic dystrophy may be thalamic dysfunction and that this needs to be considered in the differential diagnosis of conditions producing altered states of mental functioning.

Lynch, Roberts, and Ounsted (1979) write about the bonding failure in myotonic dystrophy and observe that children who have the disease at birth and who survive the neonatal period are likely to have accumulated a number of features commonly associated with child abuse. These include neonatal separation, early ill health, and maternal physical and mental illness. They note that a mother and child are further handicapped by an inability to use facial expression as a means of communication.

It appears that the range of intelligence in myotonic dystrophy may parallel that of the normal population but that a significant number will have impaired intellect, producing a reduced mean intelligence. This appears to be more prominent when the disease manifests itself in the neonatal period, and Harper (1975) found one such group of 70 patients to include 48 who were considered to be retarded. Of those on whom testing was available (number unspecified), the mean IQ was 66. Intellectual impairment, when present, does not appear to be progressive.

Maturing persons with myotonic dystrophy typically are frustrated by inability to participate in active sports such as football or baseball and in social activities such as dancing. Ultimately, they may have difficulty with stairs, and mobility is impaired. Ordinarily there is little physical problem with sexual function, but difficulty in attracting a mate. Vocational potential may be severely impaired by the combination of muscle weakness, intellectual deficit, and lack of social skills.

Adult Onset

Myasthenia Gravis. The onset of myasthenia gravis may be any time, but the peak age of onset for women is 30 to 40 and for men 50 to 70 years. Because it is characterized by progressive muscle weakness upon exertion, and also because weakness appears to be triggered by emotional episodes, it is often confused with hysterical neurosis. Sneddon (1980) reports that one third of the patients she studied had initially been given psychiatric diagnoses because physical signs fluctuated so much that often there were no abnormalities on examination, especially in the morning. Schwartz and Cahill (1971) estimated that 20–50% of myasthenia gravis patients have had previous emotional difficulties. Martin and Flegenheimer (1971) state that the impression persists that emotional stress may be related to the onset of the disease. It is commonly reported that emotional conflict brings on episodes of weakness. Brolley and Hollender's (1955) subjects attributed episodes of weakness to anger or envy. Of Sneddon's (1980) 26 patients, 16 mentioned anger, 12 frustration, 11 anxiety, 9 depression, and 8 infection. Eleven of 14 women mentioned that menstrual periods seemed to produce episodes of weakness.

Martin and Flegenheimer (1971) report that many patients show relief at the diagnosis of myasthenia gravis, having been seeking an explanation for a long time. They observe that those who are dependent may accept it too fully. They note that there is no single myasthenic personality, and Schwartz and Cahill (1971) report that myasthenia gravis patients have an MMPI profile similar to that of patients with other medical illnesses.

Schwartz and Cahill (1971) describe the most important psychological configurations seen in their myasthenia gravis groups as coping with pressing dependency needs. These will vary with the course of the disease and exacerbations, which may occur erratically. The ultimate difficulty, of course, is the myasthenic crisis which may threaten life through respiratory failure. The kind of frightening experience which may occur when the patient must depend on others to operate the respirator has already been described. Myasthenia gravis like, for example, hemophilia (see Chapter 2), is one of those diseases of which the patient may have more knowledge than those providing emergency care, and the patient should be seen as a valuable source of information in such situations.

Sneddon (1980) reports that one half of the married women in her study said that myasthenia gravis put a strain on their marriage, although none said that sexual activity produced weakness. Seven of her 26 patients wished that their illness had more obvious symptoms. The majority of her patients anticipated meeting strangers with embarrassment, in case they were unable to smile. Social contacts posed threats such as slurred speech and inability to chew at a business dinner, which could be interpreted as drunkenness.

The manner in which medication is handled may have psychological significance in myasthenia gravis patients. Denial may be exhibited by the patient who doesn't take medication "because it isn't really necessary." Some may be quite punctilious in their self-medication, including making adjustments in relation to circumstances such as social pressure. Some are described by Brolley and Hollender (1955) as making a compulsive life focus of their medication.

Amyotrophic Lateral Sclerosis. Amyotrophic lateral sclerosis is a catastrophic disease of unknown etiology which is two to three times as common in men as in women and which generally has its onset after 40. With rare exceptions, it progresses rapidly to death in several months to several years. DeLisa, Mikulic, Miller, and Melrich (1979) note that establishing the diagnosis is often a lengthy process which may cause considerable anxiety and sometimes situational reactive depression. Depressive reactions may recur as the disease progresses, although they are apt to be time-limited and controlled by these patients, who are also known for fierce attempts to hold on and to keep on functioning until the end. Brown and Mueller (1970), in fact, see these patients as chronically excluding dysphoric effect, as well as displaying a high degree of active, masterful behavior. Their study also found amyotrophic lateral sclerosis patients to have primarily an internal locus of control, that is, to be motivated by events within themselves rather than in the environment. They were also seen as independent and highly competent.

Speech in amyotrophic lateral sclerosis often becomes dysarthric and slow and eventually may be lost entirely. In addition to using language boards, patients are often quite ingenious in devising ways to communicate, as well as to carry on other activities. Cognitive dysfunction and sensory impairment is almost never present. In the latter stages of the illness, uncontrolled outbursts of laughing or crying may occur, usually on a neurological basis. Despite the relentless progression and dire prognosis, suicide is rare.

Peters, Swenson, and Mulder (1978) did not find a characteristic profile on the MMPI, although many of their patients showed a slight increase in neuroticism and in thought disturbance. Brown and Mueller (1970) similarly noted higher scores on the neurotic triad of the MMPI.

EVALUATION OF PATIENTS WITH PROGRESSIVE MUSCLE DISORDER

Interview

As with many physical disabilities, it is the case in progressive muscle disorders that the interviewer who may wish to evaluate social, emotional, or behavioral status should have a working knowledge of the various diseases, their characteristics, typical progression, and prognoses. In addition, it is extremely important to have current medical information about the particular patient being interviewed, including diagnosis and, especially, best estimate of prognosis, if known. The combination of gravity of prognosis and frequent use of denial and repression by the patient will often pose challenges for the most skilled and informed of interviewers, and lack of information may result in an interview which produces meaningless, erroneous, or even destructive results.

Slowness and fatigability are characteristic of many muscle disorder patients and must be taken into consideration in setting the length and frequency of interviews. Often it is desirable to schedule them in the morning, when the patient is fresh (although not too early, for it takes time to get ready). Sneddon (1980) says that the voice of many of her myasthenia gravis patients faded after 15 or 20 minutes of interview. The vulnerability to stress of myasthenia gravis patients should also be taken into consideration. Dwelling on past accomplishments or brooding about threats is unproductive for muscle disorder patients in general and, while discussion of past and future may be a necessary and justified part of an interview, decisions about such potential sources of stress should be knowledgeable ones which weigh advantage against potential detriment.

While interview or psychological testing alone is never sufficient to make a differential diagnosis between physical disability and hysteria or hypochondriasis, both are useful in helping to establish that the patient has, or has not, those traits which are compatible with either diagnosis and which make it likely. In this evaluation, it is useful to know some of the features (e.g., nasal reflux and regurgitation, difficulty in climbing stairs or arising from a chair) which usually characterize neuromuscular diseases as contrasted with those which usually characterize hysterical reactions (e.g., diplopia which cannot be corrected by covering an eye, or globus hystericus). In relation to this phenomenon, Schwartz and Cahill (1971) note that patients with pseudomyasthenia frequently have a previous history of conversion reaction, as well as other hysterical symptoms.

Psychological Testing

Scheduling for psychological testing should take into consideration the factors of fatigability and slowness as mentioned above. Evaluation might need to be done in several sessions, rather than one longer one. Where the subject is in a wheelchair, it may be desirable to use a testing table which has a few inches more clearance than the ordinary.

Verbal tests of ability may usually be administered without modification, unless the patient has significant loss of speech. Where speech and motor ability are impaired, tests such as the Peabody Picture Vocabulary Test (Dunn, 1959) or the Columbia Mental Maturity Scale (Burgemeister, 1972) may be utilized. In using instruments such as the Wechsler Adult Intelligence Scale (Wechsler, 1955) or Wechsler Intelligence Scale for Children—Revised (Wechsler, 1974), the verbal portions may generally be administered without difficulty. Some modification of performance scales may be utilized, such as aligning the Picture Arrangement cards or turning up specified blocks at the direction of the subject. Results under such modified conditions must be evaluated against a backdrop of standardized administration and standard norms and require the skills of the fully trained psychologist for interpretation.

Paper and pencil tests may frequently be administered without modification, although their length may require several sessions. Tape-recording of responses may be helpful if the patient does not have sufficient strength to mark the paper. Previously mentioned results with the Minnesota Multiphasic Personality Inventory (Hathaway & McKinley, 1948) suggested that muscle disorder patients will have elevated scores on the neurotic triad (hypochondriasis, depression, and hysteria scales).

Holroyd (1974) has constructed and described a Questionnaire on Resources and Stress, which is an instrument to measure family response to a handicapped family member. While currently available only as a research instrument, it appears to have utility in appraising family response to muscle disorder. Holroyd and Guthrie (1979), for example, used it to contrast the responses of parents of children with neuromuscular disease with those of parents of children with psychiatric diagnoses, and also to contrast children whose disease was more advanced (in a wheelchair) with those who remained ambulatory. Parents of children in wheelchairs reported excessive time demands, more overcommitment, and martyrdom, more limits on family opportunity, and greater physical and occupational limitation.

Various studies report the use of drawings in evaluating personality and interpersonal relationship characteristics of persons with muscle disorders. Siegel and Kornfeld (1980) describe the use of the Kinetic Family Drawing technique (Burns & Kaufman, 1972) and conclude that this is a valuable diagnostic adjunct. They report a number of inferences about the self-concept and family relationships of boys with Duchenne's muscular dystrophy, most of which have been reported in earlier sections of this chapter. Brumback, Bertorini, and Liberman (1978) had 50 adult patients with neuromuscular disease make inside-of-the-body drawings. They noted that patients will draw prominently their diseased body structures, and also observed that there seems to be increased body self-awareness in patients with medical disease, relative to that of 20 years ago.

The use of interest tests has been mentioned previously, as guides to leisure pursuits of persons with progressive muscle disease, as well as for their vocational implications. Patients with these disorders frequently have special need of interest, ability, and other testing in order to select vocations which are compatible with their motor limitations.

INTERVENTION METHODS

In no disability is the need greater than in progressive muscle disorders for psychosocial intervention to include the whole family. This typically begins with the physician at the time of diagnosis, and much can be accomplished, as suggested by Brolley and Hollender (1955), by a clear and thorough discussion of the disease with the patient and family, in a manner that not only informs, but models openness. Buchanan *et al.* (1979) suggest especially that the physician help to foster open and frank communication between father and mother. They also note that families, especially those with no previous history of the disease, may misinterpret information during the initial stages of diagnosis, partially because of information overload. They recommend going over such information repeatedly.

Successful use of group counseling or psychotherapy has been described for the patient (Schwartz & Cahill, 1971) and for the family (Kornfeld & Siegel, 1979). Buchanan *et al.* (1979) recommend that families be encouraged to utilize outside support systems such as religious groups, medical staff personnel, community agencies, the extended family, or neighbors. They also recommend that parents of muscle disorder patients systematically schedule one day or night per week for their own recreation.

Lynch, Roberts, and Ounsted (1979) have expressed concern about the effect on early bonding of lack of facial expression between mother and child with myotonic dystrophy. They describe success in teaching both mother and child to respond to subtle facial clues and sounds. Flynn, Schwetz, and Williams (1979) suggest that it is useful for young persons with progressive muscle disease to focus initially on reading and creative, rather than physical, activities. They, as does Mearig (1973), recommend remaining in school as long as possible, in order to retain resistance to respiratory infection, as well as for the obvious social and academic advantages. Mearig also recommends keeping the patient out of the wheelchair as long as possible, seeing its use as prematurely limiting life space and curtailing independence.

In working with amyotrophic lateral sclerosis patients, Blount, Bratton, and Luttrell (1979) suggest the value of energy conservation and work simplification methods, citing, for example, the use of the waterpicks or electric toothbrush as a means of sustaining one small bit of independence. They recommend a home visit by a professional to evaluate architectural barriers, inefficient work-flow patterns, and other impediments to independence. They point out that the choice of foods such as casseroles will allow for greater sustained independence than meats which are difficult to manage.

In view of the special role of emotional stress that is described, especially by patients with myasthenia gravis, therapy or counseling directed toward the handling of stress and anger-provoking situations may be useful. This might include mechanisms for responding to provocative stimuli, development of more relaxed or detached attitudes, or methods of effective functioning which avoid such stimuli. In general, an emphasis on the present (rather than past or future) and on near goals appears to be appropriate.

Leisure or recreational pursuits can be important in helping the muscle disorder patient to maintain social, cognitive and, to some degree, physical skills. While such activities may be sedentary, they can involve interaction with others, such as attending meetings of organizations or engaging in games (cards, chess, table games). Reading, puzzles, and cultural interests may help to retain intellectual alertness, even when pursued alone. Some degree of physical activity may be involved, as in crafts, to maintain manual skills. Many muscle disorder patients, even with limited life span, have been able to keep direction and order in their lives by engaging in programs of education or training.

Martin and Flegenheimer (1971) note recurrent depression in myasthenia gravis patients when the condition worsens. They describe as unimpressive results with tranquilizers (which may also have unfortunate side effects) and recommend supportive psychotherapy as well as an open line of communication with the physician. While suicide has not been reported to occur with unusually high incidence in muscle disorder patients, it will, at times, become a possible threat and a matter of concern. An approach to the subject of suicidal thought and suggestions for working with suicidal persons have been discussed in Chapter 1.

In recent years, much attention has been paid to counseling with patients and families who are coping with approaching death. This has been stimulated by the work of Kübler-Ross (1969) and has resulted in the development of helpful techniques and approaches. There are times when it is very useful to approach patients and families to determine their readiness and willingness to discuss impending death. It may even be useful to tactfully describe the advantages that such discussion might offer, such as opening communication, relieving tension, and putting relationships in order before a final separation. Currently, however, there are so many persons from so many different disciplines who are attuned to death-and-dying counseling that there is a danger that the patient or family may feel harassed by numerous well-meaning approaches. Counselors are cautioned to coordinate such approaches with other involved professionals. Also to be avoided is a mechanistic approach to this counseling, which stresses stages and implies that one should experience them in proper order.

TRENDS AND NEEDS

As in many areas of chronic physical disability, there is the need with progressive muscle disorders for consistent application of the psychosocial principles and methods which are already available. Geist (1979, p. 5) has said, "In a setting where life and death often depend on technical competence, the application of psychological knowledge to the care of the total child can for years remain subservient to the application of new advances in physical treatment." He goes on to point out that psychosocial intervention is typically relegated to the period following the incipient stages of the illness, fostering the false belief that such intervention is not necessary unless and until acute behavioral symptoms occur. There is a need to work with patient and family from the beginning, to inform accurately, open lines of communication, foster positive and realistic self-concepts, and maximize functioning in all spheres, physical, social, recreational, and vocational.

There appears to be a specific need to clarify the relationship between intellectual capacity and Duchenne's muscular dystrophy. It is clearly possible to do so within the bounds of present psychological technology. It requires only the resources to design and gather data for a longitudinal study with a carefully chosen representative sample, analyzing results to determine the effect of relevant environmental influence (e.g., age of onset, socioeconomic level of family, school attendance). An accurate knowledge of the empirical relationship between the disease and intellectual capacity could then serve as a marker in the further quest for knowledge of any possible genetic linkage.

APPENDIX: SOURCES OF INFORMATION

Muscular Dystrophy Association
810 Seventh Avenue
New York, NY 10019
212-586-0808

The Myasthenia Gravis Foundation
15 E. 26 Street
New York NY 10010

A Clinician's View of Neuromuscular Diseases, Michael H. Brooke. Baltimore: Williams & Wilkins, 1977.

Muscle Disorders in Childhood, Victor Dubowitz. Philadelphia: W. B. Saunders, 1978.

Disorders of Voluntary Muscle, John N. Walton (Ed.). Edinburgh and London: Churchill Livingstone, 1974.

REFERENCES

Ambrosini, P., & Nurnberg, H. Psychopathology: A primary feature of myotonic dystrophy. *Psychosomatics,* 1979, *20*(6), 393–395, 398–399.

Blount, M., Bratton, C., & Luttrell, N. Management of the patient with amyotropic lateral sclerosis. *The Nursing Clinics of North America,* 1979, *14*(1), 157–171.

Bobowick, A., & Brody, J. Epidemiology of motor-neuron diseases. *New England Journal of Medicine,* 1973, *288,* 1051.

Brolley, M., & Hollender, M. Psychological problems of patients with myasthenia gravis. *Journal of Nervous and Mental Diseases,* 1955, *122,* 178–184.

Brown, W., & Mueller, P. Psychological function in individuals with amyotrophic lateral sclerosis. *Psychosomatic Medicine,* 1970, *32,* 141–152.

Brumback, R., Bertorini, T., & Liberman, J. Inside-of-the-body test drawings performed by patients with neuromuscular diseases: A preliminary report. *Perceptual and Motor Skills,* 1978, *47,* 155–160.

Buchanan, D., LaBarbera, C., Roelofs, R., & Olson, W. Reactions of families with children with Duchenne muscular dystrophy. *General Hospital Psychiatry,* 1979, *1*(3), 262–269.

Burgemeister, B., Blum, L., & Lorge, I. *Columbia mental maturity scale.* New York: Harcourt Brace Jovanovich, 1972.

Burns, R., & Kaufman, H. *Actions, styles and symbols in Kinetic Family Drawings (K-F-D): An interpretive manual.* New York: Bruner/Mazel, 1972.

DeLisa, J., Mikulic, M., Miller, R., & Melnick, R. Amyotrophic lateral sclerosis: Comprehensive management. *American Family Physician,* March, 1979, 137–142.

Dubowitz, V. *Muscle disorders in childhood.* Philadelphia: W. B. Saunders, 1978.

Dunn, L.M. *Peabody picture vocabulary test.* Circle Pines, Minn.: American Guidance Service, 1959.

Flynn, I., Schwetz, K., & Williams, D. Muscular dystrophy: Comprehensive nursing care. *The Nursing Clinics of North America,* 1979, *14*(1), 123–132.

Geist, R. Onset of chronic illness in children and adolescents: Psychotherapeutic and consultative intervention. *American Journal of Orthopsychiatry,* 1979, *49*(1), 4–23.
Harper, P. Congenital myotonic dystrophy in Britain. I. Clinical aspects. *Archives of Disease in Childhood,* 1975, *50,* 505–513.
Harper, P. *Myotonic Dystrophy.* Philadelphia: W. B. Saunders, 1979.
Hathaway, S., & McKinley, J. *Minnesota Multiphasic Personality Inventory.* New York: The Psychological Corporation, 1948.
Holroyd, J. The Questionnaire on Resources and Stress: An instrument to measure family response to a handicapped family member. *Journal of Community Psychology,* 1974, *2,* 92–94.
Holroyd, J., & Guthrie, D. Stress in families of children with neuromuscular disease. *Journal of Clinical Psychology,* 1979, *35*(4), 734–739.
Karagan, J., & Zellweger, H. Early verbal disability in children with Duchenne muscular dystrophy. *Developmental Medicine and Child Neurology,* 1978, *20,* 435–441.
Kornfeld, M., & Siegel, I. Parental group therapy in the management of a fatal childhood disease. *Health and Social Work,* 1979, *4,* 99–118.
Kübler-Ross, E. *On death and dying.* New York: Macmillan, 1969.
Kurland, L., Choi, N., & Sayre, G. Implications of incidence and geographic patterns on the classification of amyotrophic lateral sclerosis. In F. H. Norris, Jr., & L. Kurland (Eds.), *Motor neuron disease.* New York: Grune & Stratton, 1969.
Lynch, M., Roberts, J., & Ounsted, C. Myotonic dystrophy and bonding failure: letter. *Archives of Disease in Childhood,* 1979, *54,* 807–808.
Marsh, G. G., & Munsat, T. Evidence of early impairment of verbal intelligence in Duchenne muscular dystrophy. *Archives of Disease in Childhood,* 1974, *49,* 118–122.
Martin, R., & Flegenheimer, W. Psychiatric aspects of the management of the myasthenic patient. *The Mount Sinai Journal of Medicine,* 1971, *38*(6), 594–601.
Mearig, J. Some dynamics of personality development in boys suffering from muscular dystrophy. *Rehabilitation Literature,* 1973, *34*(8), 226–230, 243.
Mearig, J. The assessment of intelligence in boys with muscular dystrophy. *Rehabilitation Literature,* 1979, *40*(9), 262–274.
Mulder, D., & Espinosa, R. Amyotrophic lateral sclerosis: Comparison of the clinical syndrome in Guam and the United States. In F. Norris, Jr., & L. Kurland (Eds.), *Motor neuron diseases.* New York: Grune & Stratton, 1969.
Osserman, K., & Genkins, G. Studies in myasthenia gravis: A review of a 20-year experience in over 1,200 patients. *Mt. Sinai Journal of Medicine,* 1971, 497–537.
Peters, P., Swenson, W., & Mulder, D. Is there a characteristic personality in amyotrophic lateral sclerosis? *Archives of Neurology,* 1978, *35,* 321–322.
Schwartz, M., & Cahill, R. Psychopathology associated with myasthenia gravis and its treatment by psychotherapeutically oriented group counseling. *Journal of Chronic Diseases,* 1971, *24,* 543–552.
Siegel, I., & Kornfeld, M. Kinetic family drawing test for evaluating families having children with muscular dystrophy. *Physical Therapy,* 1980, *60*(3), 293–298.
Sneddon, J. Myasthenia gravis: A study of social, medical and emotional problems in 26 patients. *The Lancet,* 1980, Mar 8, *1*(8167), 526–528.
Wechsler, D. *Wechsler adult intelligence scale.* New York: The Psychological Corporation, 1955.
Wechsler, D. *Wechsler intelligence scale for children - Revised.* New York: The Psychological Corporation, 1974.

11

Congenital Heart Defects

The symbolism associated with the heart in human thought and literature suggests that its function and its impairment will have psychological meaning that transcends the physiological. The heart has variously been seen as the seat of the emotions and the *situs* of the self. Aristotle thought of the brain as the cooling system for the heart. Affairs of the heart defy categorization into mind and body.

This chapter will consider primarily those conditions known as congenital heart defects. Since they are usually discovered and treated in childhood, the emphasis will be on that period of life. The available findings regarding congenital heart defects in adults will be noted, and mention will also be made of some acquired conditions (e.g., rheumatic heart disease) which are primarily associated with the childhood years. Coronary heart disease, which is primarily found in adults, will be the topic of Chapter Twelve.

THE PHYSICAL DISABILITY

Definition and Incidence

Congenital heart defect is frequently, but less accurately, called congenital heart disease. It is a structural abnormality of the heart which is usually present at birth, although most abnormalities do not assume pathognomic characteristics until months or years later.

Embryologically, most congenital heart defects occur during intrauterine development when the primitive straight cardiac tube undergoes looping and differentiation which ultimately transforms it into the four-chambered, four-valved heart. The *left atrium* receives oxygenated blood from the lungs and passes it through the *mitral valve* to the *left ventricle*. This blood departs the heart via the *aortic valve* and passes by way of the aorta and arteries to carry oxygen throughout the body tissues. After the blood has passed through the capillaries and lost much of its oxygen, it returns via the veins to the *right atrium* and through the *tricuspid valve* to the *right ventricle*, from which it passes through the *pulmonary valve* to the lungs for reoxygenation (see Figure 1). Congenital heart defects ordinarily involve abnormal flow between the circuits serving the body and the lungs, lesions in valves or vessels, or transposition of great arteries, veins, or cardiac chambers.

Keith (1978, p. 6) reports that nine common defects comprise 85% of congenital heart defects. Table I contains a listing and brief description of each of these, with the approximate frequencies of occurrence reported by Keith.

The overall incidence of congenital heart defect is eight per 1,000 with about 25,000 affected infants born each year and 6,445 deaths in 1977, as reported by the American Heart Association (1979). Kitchen (1978) summarizes current opinion as holding that these cardiovascular malformations result from a complex interaction among genetic and

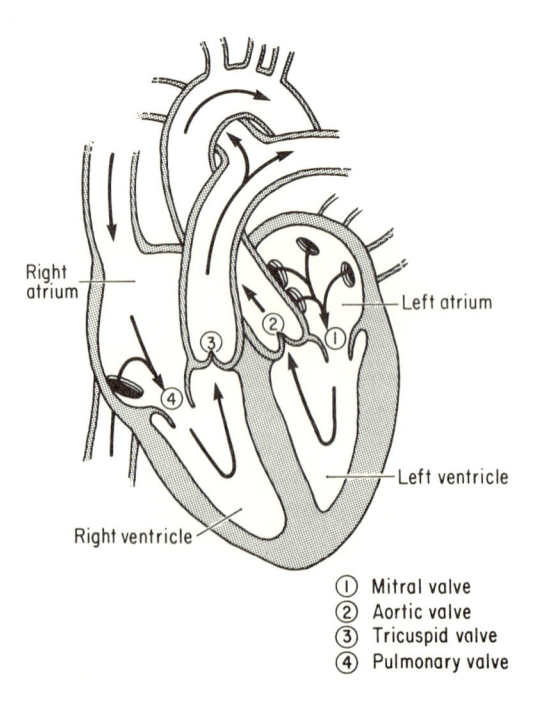

FIGURE 1. Schematic representation of the heart.

TABLE I
Common Congenital Heart Defects

Defect	Description	Approximate frequency per live birth[a]
Bicuspid aortic valve	Common defect in which the aortic valve has two cusps (flaps) rather than three. Compatible with normal functioning if uncomplicated.	1 in 78
Ventricular septal defect	Hole in septum (wall) between ventricles (lower chambers). If large, requires correction by open-heart surgery. Long-term outlook excellent.	1 in 532
Patent ductus arteriosis	Duct between aorta and pulmonary artery has failed to close. Correctible by closed heart surgery. Long-term outlook excellent.	1 in 1,340
Pulmonary stenosis	Narrowing of the pulmonary valve. May cause enlargement of right ventricle or atrium and increased pressure, requiring surgery. Long-term outlook excellent.	1 in 1,620
Atrial septal defect	Hole in septum between atria (upper chambers). If large, requires correction by open-heart surgery. Long-term outlook excellent.	1 in 1,548
Tetralogy of Fallot	Combination of ventricular septal defect and stenosis (narrowing) of pulmonary valve. Causes cyanosis (blueness) due to lack of oxygen in blood. Should be corrected by open-heart surgery before teen years. Ninety percent may then engage in normal activity.	1 in 1,834
Coarctation of the aorta	Constriction of the aorta. Requires correction by removal of the constricted portion. Long-term outlook very favorable.	1 in 2,323
Aortic stenosis	Narrowing due to improper formation of the aortic valve. Often requires cardiac catheterization for diagnosis. Some cases may be fully correctable; in others, long-term outlook uncertain.	1 in 2,787
Transposition of the great arteries	Transposition of pulmonary artery and aorta. Survival occurs only when other abnormal passageways allow oxygenated blood to reach the aorta. Functioning may be improved through surgery. Outlook uncertain.	1 in 3,319

[a] From Keith, 1978.

environmental (e.g., rubella) factors. The incidence is reported as 2% among the siblings and 3–4% among the children of persons with congenital heart defects (Nadas & Fyler, 1972). Congenital heart defect is now clearly more prominent than rheumatic heart disease, in part because children with these defects are now being sought out, treated, and saved and also because widespread use of antibiotics has reduced the incidence of rheumatic fever and consequently of rheumatic heart disease.

Rheumatic heart disease is caused by rheumatic fever, which is always preceded by streptococcal infection. Rheumatic heart disease may occasionally also be caused by other viral infections. It occurs most often in children between ages 5 and 15. Prior to the development of antibiotic therapy, the disease was apt to recur and eventually to result in inflammation (carditis), with the potential for serious impairment of heart function. While declining in incidence, this now preventable illness affected 100,000 children and 1,750,000 adults and resulted in 12,770 deaths in 1977 (American Heart Association, 1979).

Fisher, Wilson, and Theilen (1962) studied adults with congenital heart defect at a time when many of the surgical intervention techniques were newly developed and few such patients had survived the childhood years. In reviewing 50 adult patients over 40 years of age, they found atrial septal defect to be the most common, representing about half the cases. They concluded that the defect could be compatible with long life, although rapidly progressive if symptoms did occur. Higgins and Mulder (1972) found that adults with tetralogy of Fallot ordinarily have had palliative or totally corrective surgery, although they estimated that nearly 10% survive until age 21 without surgery. They note that surgical correction can be accomplished in adults with an acceptable degree of risk and with considerable improvement. Fisher *et al.* (1962) also point out the possibly advantageous use of surgery with adults and stress differential diagnosis in adults with heart conditions, so that these defects may be accurately identified.

Associated Conditions

Among other pathological conditions, those with the greatest association with congenital heart defect are the chromosomal abnormalities. Perhaps the best known associated condition is Down's Syndrome, which involves mental retardation and other characteristics (see Chapter 7). After reviewing studies reporting a range of frequencies, Rowe, Uchida, and Char (1978) conclude that approximately 40% of persons with Down's Syndrome also have heart defects, with about three quarters of these septal defects. Down's Syndrome may occur in either sex, as may

Marfan's Syndrome, which is also associated with heart malformation. Among sex-related disorders associated with heart defect are Turner's (female only) and Klinefelter's (male only) Syndromes. See Chapter 4 for a discussion of these and other genetic disorders. Nadas and Fyler (1972) also report the clinical observation that mental retardation and cleft palate are more common in children with heart defect, but without statistical verification.

Manifestations

The common physiological effects of congenital heart defect are exercise intolerance and/or cyanosis (blueness), although many children with congenital heart defects will have no discernible symptoms.

Children with congenital heart defects are usually classified as having *cyanotic* or *acyanotic* heart disease. Acyanotic heart disease is more common and would include (see Table I) atrial septal defect, ventricular septal defect, patent ductus arteriosis, aortic stenosis, pulmonary stenosis, coarctation of the aorta, and bicuspid aortic valve. Most of these children are discovered to have heart defects by the incidental finding of a heart murmur during a physical exam, though some may be discovered in infancy with the manifestation of heart failure.

Cyanotic heart diseases listed in Table I are tetralogy of Fallot and transposition of the great arteries. Children with tetralogy of Fallot may experience hypoxic (anoxic) spells manifested by paroxysms of dyspnea (shortness of breath) and increased cyanosis, and sometimes unconsciousness or convulsions. These are not always associated with exertion. Lambert, Menon, Wagner, and Vlad (1974) point out that, in contrast with adult cardiac patients in whom sudden death is common and largely due to a few causes, sudden death from cardiovascular disease in children is rare and due to many causes. They note that most are at rest when sudden death occurs, indicating that avoidance of strenuous activity seldom prevents this catastrophe. They hasten to add, however, that those with severe aortic stenosis or obstructive cardiomyopathy *are* at risk from strenuous activity.

A secondary manifestation of congenital heart defect may be failure to grow in height or, especially, in weight. This is particularly true of infants who are cyanotic. A spurt in growth, again especially in weight, may sometimes be seen following corrective surgery in cases where there has been previous heart failure.

Diagnosis and Treatment

The use of the chest X-ray and electrocardiogram are well known in the diagnosis of heart disorder. To these has been added echocardiography, involving ultrasound, as a means of evaluating heart function and anatomy noninvasively (without entering the body). Common invasive tests for evaluating congenital heart defects are cardiac catheterization and angiocardiography. To perform these tests, a catheter (a thin plastic tube) is introduced into an artery or vein and subsequently into the heart chambers. By sampling of blood and recording of intracavity pressures, information about physiological function can be obtained. By injection of contrast material and by recording with cine X-rays (angiocardiography), detail about cardiac anatomy is outlined. These refinements of diagnostic accuracy are associated with dramatic advances in surgical technique.

Possibilities for repair of congenital defect through closed- or open-heart surgery are indicated in Table I. Such surgery, especially in very young children, may be palliative, a temporary measure to allow adequate circulation until the child grows to the point where corrective surgery is possible. Bonchek, Starr, Sunderland, and Menashe (1973) generally favor early corrective surgery, stating, "The early and late results of this approach compare very favorably with the traditional policy of early shunt procedures and delayed corrective operations." They go on to say that the approach should not be assessed in terms of survival rate alone, noting serious problems of behavior and physical development which may accompany delayed corrective surgery. They add that this retarded physical growth and social development may never be completely overcome when such delay has occurred.

The necessity for surgery for certain forms of congenital heart defect is evident when one studies the survival figures in its absence. For example, Bertranou, Blackstone, Hazelrig, Turner, and Kirklin (1978) report that, of patients with tetralogy of Fallot who are not treated surgically, 65% live to one year, 49% to three years and 24% to ten years. Congenital heart defect, then, is often a severe condition for which, with appropriate surgical intervention, the word *cure* may be used appropriately. This combination of serious threat and almost total cure is not without its significant psychological effects, as will be seen in the next section of this chapter.

COMMON PSYCHOLOGICAL CHARACTERISTICS AND PROBLEMS

Emotional

In an early classic study, Green and Levitt (1962) found that children (age 8–16) with congenital heart defect tended to depict themselves graphically as smaller than normal. They inferred that these children had a constricted view of their bodies. One could also speculate about their restricted activity and the possibility that their bodies were, in fact, smaller than those of their peers. There is a consistency in the findings and the description of personality traits attributed to persons with congenital heart defect. Linde, Rasof, and Dunn (1967) described children they studied as less self-confident, less socially confident, and exhibiting a lower degree of cooperation. In a study of 37 young adults, utilizing the Cattell 16PF Personality Inventory, Garson, Williams, and Reckless (1974) concluded that 22 of them could be defined as neurotic and described them with such terms as weak superego, self-indulgent, overprotected, lack of ambition, conservative, less well informed, using feelings over thought, and dependent. In a later study, Garson, Benson, Ivler, and Patton (1978) described children as responding with overactive destructiveness or clinging dependency. Similarly, Glazer, Harrison, and Lynn (1964), describing children ages five to eleven, saw some adjusted, some depressed and withdrawn, and some angry and aggressive.

The point must be emphasized that not *all* children or adults with congenital heart defect are emotionally maladjusted. When they are, however, a principal dimension is one of passiveness and dependence, with a secondary dimension of angry and petulant misbehavior. Descriptions of parental attitudes and relationships with children run to words like overprotected and pampered—in popular language, "spoiled." Difficulties with discipline are common. Bonchek *et al.* (1973) suggest that parental oversolicitousness is often a misinformed attempt to prevent hypoxic spells or episodes of severe cyanosis.

The kind of aggressive behavior shown by the congenital heart population is in contrast with that of some other disability groups (e.g., hemophilia—see Chapter 2), for whom aggressiveness, when displayed, will often take the form of risk-taking behavior calculated to test the limits of and, essentially, to deny the effects of the illness. It should be noted that this latter behavior *is* displayed by some congenital heart patients. The tendency to show aggression through passive demanding rather than risk-taking may have several possible explanations: (1) congenital heart patients typically have the severest disability early in life, and the condition is frequently resolved (through surgical intervention) before they enter the more rebellious stage of adolescence; (2) the uncertain outcome of this potentially fatal condition may cause a greater feeling of threat and vulnerability that discourages testing behavior; and (3) easy fatigability may encourage passive, rather than active, aggression.

Numerous observers (Garson *et al.*, 1974; Linde, Rasof, Dunn, & Rabb, 1966; Garson *et al.*, 1978) have noted that the fact of the diagnosis of congenital heart defect appears to have greater importance in the development of secondary emotional problems than does its severity. Attempts to relate severity of physical illness with severity of emotional maladjustment have been unsuccessful. Garson *et al.* (1978), in fact, go on to state, "If anything, children with less severe defects are at a higher risk for the development of psychological disability because their parents frequently receive less support than they need." Linde *et al.* (1966) similarly state that poorer adjustment and anxiety in the cardiac child are related more highly to maternal anxiety and pampering than to degree of incapacity and that maternal anxiety is related to the presence rather than the severity of the heart condition.

Garson *et al.* (1978) have listed some concerns parents have but rarely discuss fully with their physicians. These include:

1. The etiology of the defect—was mother to blame, or a history of myocardial infarction elsewhere in the family?
2. Why did it take weeks or months to make the diagnosis? Did the physician act competently?
3. Inability to understand the explanation of the diagnosis.
4. What symptoms to expect—a heart attack perhaps?
5. What to tell the child.
6. How to treat a child with congenital heart defect normally.

They concluded that a small proportion of parents have an adequate understanding of the child's illness. In cases in which children with an operable defect had symptoms (e.g., cyanosis), the parents readily oriented to preparation for surgery. Where children with an operable defect were asymptomatic, there was often resistance to surgery. When the child had a serious, nonoperable defect, parents had feelings of helplessness and anger, to the degree that some were unable to hear an accurate prognosis and some withdrew from the child, as if in anticipatory grief. (Others have noted that parents in this situation may direct their ire toward the professional staff.) When children had a nonoperable benign defect, the parents were told to treat the child normally and thereafter were given little staff attention. This is a group which is productive of considerable unnecessary psychological maladjustment, because many of these parents continued to worry and overprotect their children.

Thus, it can be seen that the family will initially have difficulty in accepting the threatening or presumably threatening fact of congenital heart defect and providing the special care and protection that may be required. Similarly, but perhaps more surprisingly, it is reported that many parents have difficulty in accepting the fact that their child has been cured and in changing their protective attitudes. It is as if they had difficulty in giving up the impaired child equal to their original difficulty in giving up the normal child.

Linde *et al.* (1966) report that the siblings of cardiac patients receive treatment different than from that afforded other well children, noting that they are pampered less, probably because of the excessive demands on the mother in the care of the sick child. This may result in resentment directed at the sick child, causing further anxiety and lowered self-esteem. Such attitudes and behavior patterns may persist even after corrective treatment and may result in long-term adjustment problems in the absence of intervention.

In general, younger children with congenital heart defect self-limit their activities because of easy fatigability. This is a concept which is often difficult for parents to grasp and accept. Older children, especially adolescents, are more susceptible to social pressures which may lead them to push themselves beyond their capacities. This is especially true if they engage in competitive sports.

Cognitive

Findings with regard to intellectual development of children with congenital heart defect have tended to be equivocal when based on a broad and undifferentiated spectrum of defects and significant if refined, for example, comparing cyanotic and acyanotic children. Honzik, Collart, Robinson, and Finley (1969) studied congenital heart children in San Francisco and found normal IQ in the boys and reduced verbal IQ in the girls. In contrast, Cravioto, Lindoro, and Birch (1971) studied Mexican children with congenital heart defect and found males to have significantly lower verbal, performance and full scale IQs than their normal counterparts, while girls did not differ significantly. Studies taking into account cyanosis have been more consistent. Feldt, Ewert, Stickler, and Weidman (1969) studied 34 cyanotic children (mean IQ 95.7) and 44 acyanotic children (mean IQ 103.6), while Linde *et al.* (1967) studied 98 cyanotic children (mean IQ 96) and 100 acynotic children (mean IQ 104). Thus, there appears to be reason to believe that cyanosis will, in some instances, cause delayed intellectual development. Mitigating this circumstance is the fact that the range of intelligence in both cyanotic and acyanotic groups was about the same, including children with superior intelligence, and that Linde, Rasof, and Dunn (1970), reporting on the same group of subjects as in their 1967 publication, observed that cyanotic children displayed an increase in IQ after surgery. Another factor to be considered is that many of the subjects of these studies were quite young, of an age where motor skills represent a large component of intelligence test items, and that delay in motor development is observed in patients with congenital heart defect (Feldt *et al.*, 1969).

Cayler, Lynn, and Stein (1973) took into account the effect of diagnosis *per se* and restriction *per se* on intellectual development. They studied 34 children mistakenly diagnosed as having heart defects, 9 of whom had been placed on restricted activity. They found both groups at intellectual development levels lower than controls, with the restricted group lower. They concluded that the accumulated emotional impact of the diagnosis, especially if accompanied by physical restriction, is detrimental to intellectual development. Myers-Vando, Steward, Folkins, and Hines (1979) also concluded that restriction on interacting with the environment impedes cognitive development; they based this conclusion on a Piagetian measure of cognitive development on which 12 children with congenital heart defect were at a lower level than a healthy control group.

Finley, Buse, Popper, Honzik, and Collart (1974) studied the influence of early palliative surgery and open-heart surgery on children with tetralogy of Fallot. They report a mean IQ of 106 in a group who had palliative surgery and a mean IQ of 96 in a corresponding group who had not. They add that the hypothesis that children undergoing open-heart surgery suffer minimal brain damage was not proved by their study. Also measuring the effects of surgery, Haka-Ikse, Blackwood, and Steward (1978) studied children who had the surgery under the effects of profound hypothermia. They found this group to have a mean developmental quotient (Revised Yale Developmental Scale) of 92.5, lower than their control group but comparable to other children with cyanotic congenital heart defect. They conclude that profound hypothermia may be used without fear of gross neurological sequelae or retarded psychomotor development.

EVALUATING PERSONS WITH CONGENITAL HEART DEFECT

As with most disabling conditions, effective evaluation of the person with congenital heart defect should be carried out by a person with a background of knowledge and experience in the field, including a general knowledge of congenital heart defects, the limitations they impose, and the outlook for surgical correction. It is especially important, with any given individual, to have information from cardiologists, surgeons, and others involved about the outlook and limitations imposed by that particular person's condition.

Interviews should, of course, be directed to the feelings and attitudes of the patient and significant others such as parents or spouse. In addition, however, it is often extremely important to get an extensive behaviorally oriented description of the patient's activities. When such explicit descriptions are contrasted with what the patient or family may label "normal activity," for example, it may well emerge that the definition used was a highly restricted one or, in some instances, a very permissive one. In gathering such information, it is often useful to supplement the interview with a structured instrument such as the Adaptive Behavior Scale (Nihira, Foster, Shellhaas, & Leland, 1974) or the Vineland Social Maturity Scale (Doll, 1965).

Because congenital heart defect is ordinarily found and treated in childhood, interview is apt to involve both parent and child. In seeking to learn the patient's understanding of the condition, the limits it imposes, the outlook, and his/her feelings about self and the future, it is well to accord the dignity of a private interview to all patients who are reasonably self-aware and reasonably capable of self-report. In the absence of special limitations, this will be at about school age or slightly earlier. Concurrent information may also be obtained from parents or spouse, who may well give a differing and more or less objective account than the patient.

Psychological testing with congenital heart patients will ordinarily include no demands or constraints that differ significantly from the general population, since major sensory or motor deficits are found in about the same proportion as the general population. Because the testing will often be with children, it will be useful to carry it out with dispatch in view of limited concentration span. Should testing be of extraordinary length, consideration must also be paid to the fatigability of the subject.

INTERVENTION METHODS

Some of the best psychological intervention in congenital heart defect can be done by the physician and other personnel, who initially provide information about the condition to the patient and his family and who later determine the restriction of activity, if any, which is required. Glazer *et al.* (1964) suggest that physicians give neither bland reassurances about outgrowing the condition nor dire predictions about its negative consequences. The findings of Garson *et al.* (1978) suggest the need for extended communication and discussion if patient and family are to bring forth their questions and doubts and finally achieve a realistic grasp of the situation. This function can be served by the physician if he/she realistically has the time and the capacity for carrying out this kind of counseling. It can also be served by psychosocial personnel who are well informed about congenital heart defect and who have ready access to the medical personnel involved in each case. Naive and uninformed psychosocial personnel and hurried, insensitive, and/or inarticulate physicians will be equally ineffective in carrying out the function.

It is apparent that there is a particular need for intervention during the period after the major medical and surgical services have been rendered. This is the case in the family which cannot accept the fact that the condition has been corrected and that restrictions are no longer required. It is also the case when the condition has been pronounced benign and the parents told to treat the child normally but when this message has not really been understood. These require follow-up evaluation of the patient's psychosocial functioning after an appropriate interval, with counseling where indicated.

Kupst, Blatterbauer, Westman, Schulman, and Paul (1977) contrasted the effectiveness of informing the parents of congenital heart patients through the following approaches: (1) medical information, (2) psychosocial intervention, (3) medical and psychological information-intervention, and (4) no intervention. They found that all three intervention groups did well in acquiring increased medical information. The intervention was well received, with most parents expressing satisfaction.

In addition to the promotion of full understanding of the condition, a second area of major psychological significance is the minimization of restrictions. In a policy statement on cardiac evaluation for participation in sports, the American Academy of Pediatrics (1977) said, "Whenever possible, allow participation rather than to arbitrarily impose restrictions which might predispose to all of the problems attendant with 'cardiac crippling.' " They advised consultation with a cardiologist prior to complete exclusion from competition. In a similar vein, Ongley and DuShane (1961) say, "Undue restriction or overindulgence because of physical disability tends to divorce the child from the realities of everyday life and to make him less well prepared to cope with problems in the future." Finally, in talking about adolescents and young adults, Nadas and Fyler (1972, p. 311) say, "Their work capacity ... is conditioned at least as much by extracardiac (psychosocial) as by cardiac factors."

Thus, as the person with congenital heart defect contemplates the social, recreational, or vocational aspects of his future, the objective fact of any required limitations (or the absence of them) is merely a start. Equally important is the understanding of the defect and its implications acquired by the patient and the significant others in his/her life (parents, teachers, spouse), the self-concept developed by the patient, especially prior to correction of the defect, and the ability of patient and family to understand, accept, and act upon the liberating effects of corrective treatment.

The emphasis here is upon prevention of problems through thorough communication and enlightened application of restrictions. There is no question that some patients and families, even with the most appropriate treatment, will, either through predisposition or the effect of these stresses, become entrenched in symbiotic relationships which combine anxious oversolicitousness and cardiac invalidism. These people will require the skills of a psychotherapist trained to work with individuals and families, who has sophisticated knowledge about congenital heart defect and who is in close touch with the medical facts of the case. While the literature has little to say about the effectiveness of group psychotherapy in such cases, it would seem that this could be useful, especially in later stages, when patients have begun to move toward a normal existence.

Vocational evaluation and career counseling are effective forms of intervention for any individual who has questions about his/her abilities, interests, and potential for the future. Where the congenital heart patient *does* have objective limitations on his/her activities, a detailed assessment of abilities and the knowledge of a vocational counselor skilled in working with handicapping conditions become imperative. This point is made by Manning and Hutchinson (1977) in a report on insurability and employability of young cardiac patients from a conference of cardiac specialists and representatives of life insurance companies. They make several additional points: (1) that innocent (functional) heart murmurs should not be cause for insurance restriction; (2) that large companies are more likely to hire a young person with a cardiac lesion than small companies; and (3) that "second injury" laws in many states protect employers from any liability which may be incurred when an existing condition is aggravated.

TRENDS AND NEEDS

There is a fortunate trend in the field of congenital heart defect to pay attention to the psychological consequences of the condition. More must be learned about effective ways of explaining to families and patients, especially young patients, the meaning and implications of their condition. More sophistication is required in helping families and patients make the necessary changes when restriction of activity is no longer required because the condition has either been corrected or been diagnosed as benign. More attention must be paid to serving patients with a combination of counseling skills and medical knowledge, either through development of greater counseling skills in physicians, more sophistication of psychosocial personnel, or a much closer integration of the services of both.

There is a need for further definition of whatever effect congenital heart defect of any kind may have on intellectual development. Such research would require considerable investment of time and effort but should certainly be feasible at our present level of research knowledge. In need of careful control and analysis would be: (1) socioeconomic and cultural background of subjects; (2) presence of cyanosis; (3) degree of restriction of activity; (4) differentiation of development, for example, motor, verbal, etc.; and (5) type and timing of palliative or corrective surgery.

APPENDIX: SOURCES OF INFORMATION

General:

American Heart Association
7320 Greenville Avenue
Dallas, TX 75231

General for the professional: *Heart Disease in Infancy and Childhood*, J. D. Keith, R. D. Rowe and P. Vlad. New York: Macmillan, 1978.

Pediatric Cardiology, A. S. Nadas and D. C. Fyler. Philadelphia: Saunders, 1972.

For the patient and family: *If Your Child Has a Congenital Heart Defect*, American Heart Association. 7320 Greenville Avenue, Dallas, TX 75231.

REFERENCES

American Academy of Pediatrics. *Policy statement: Cardiac evaluation for participation in sports*. April, 1977.

American Heart Association. *Heart facts 1980*. Dallas: American Heart Association, 1979.

Bertranou, E. G., Blackstone, E. H., Hazelrig, J. B., Turner, M. E., & Kirklin, J. W. Life expectancy without surgery in tetralogy of Fallot. *The American Journal of Cardiology*, 1978, *42*, 458–466.

Bonchek, L. I., Starr, A., Sunderland, C. O., & Menashe, V. D. Natural history of tetralogy of Fallot in infancy. *Circulation*, 1973, *48*, 392–397.

Cayler, G. C., Lynn, D. B., & Stein, E. M. Effect of cardiac 'non-disease' on intellectual and perceptual motor development. *British Heart Journal,* 1973, *35,* 543–547.

Cravioto, J., Lindoro, M., & Birch, H. G. Sex differences in IQ pattern of children with congenital heart defects. *Science,* 1971, *174,* 1042–1044.

Doll, E. A. *Vineland social maturity scale.* Circle Pines, Minn.: American Guidance Service, 1965.

Feldt, R. H., Ewert, J. C., Stickler, G. B., & Weidman, W. H. Children with congenital heart disease. *American Journal of Diseases of Children,* 1969, *117,* 281–287.

Finley, K. H., Buse, S. T., Popper, R. W., Honzik, M. P., & Collart, D. S. Intellectual functioning of children with tetralogy of Fallot: Influence of open heart surgery and earlier palliative operations. *The Journal of Pediatrics,* 1974, *85,* 318–323.

Fisher, J. M., Wilson, W. R., & Theilen, E. O. Recognition of congenital heart disease in the fifth to eighth decades of life. *Circulation,* 1962, *25,* 821–826.

Garson, A., Williams, R. B., & Reckless, J. Long-term follow-up of patients with tetralogy of Fallot: Physical health and psychopathology. *The Journal of Pediatrics,* 1974, *85*(3), 429–433.

Garson, A., Benson, R. S., Ivler, L., & Patton, C. Parental reactions to children with congenital heart disease. *Child Psychiatry and Human Development,* 1978, *9*(2), 86–94.

Glazer, H. H., Harrison, G. S., & Lynn, D. B. Emotional implications of heart disease in children. *Pediatrics,* 1964, *33,* 367–379.

Green, M., & Levitt, E. E. Constriction of body image in children with congenital heart disease. *Pediatrics,* 1962, *29,* 438–441.

Haka-Ikse, K., Blackwood, M. J., & Steward, D. J. Psychomotor development of infants and children after profound hypothermia during surgery for congenital heart disease. *Developmental Medicine and Child Neurology,* 1978, *20*(1), 62–70.

Higgins, C. B., & Mulder, D. G. Tetralogy of Fallot in the adult. *The American Journal of Cardiology,* 1972, *29,* 837–846.

Honzik, M. P., Collart, D. S., Robinson, S. J., & Finley, K. H. Sex differences in verbal and performance IQs of children undergoing open heart surgery. *Science,* 1969, *164,* 445–557.

Keith, J. D. Prevalence, incidence and epidemiology. In J. D. Keith, R. D. Rowe, & P. Vlad, *Heart disease in infancy and childhood.* New York: Macmillan, 1978.

Kitchen, L. W. Psychological factors in congenital heart disease in children. *Journal of Family Practice,* 1978, *6*(4), 777–783.

Kupst, M. J., Blatterbauer, S., Westman, J., Schulman, J. L., & Paul, M. H. Helping parents cope with the diagnosis of congenital heart defect. *Pediatrics,* 1977, *59,* 266–272.

Lambert, E. C., Menon, V. A., Wagner, H. R., & Vlad, P. Sudden unexpected death from cardiovascular disease in children. *The American Journal of Cardiology,* 1974, *34,* 89–96.

Linde, L. M., Rasof, B., & Dunn, O. J. Mental development in congenital heart disease. *Journal of Pediatrics,* 1967, *71,* 198–203.

Linde, L. M., Rasof, B., & Dunn, O. J. Longitudinal studies of intellectual and behavioral development in children with congenital heart disease. *Acta Paediatrica Scandinavia,* 1970, *59,* 169–176.

Linde, L. M., Rasof, B., Dunn, O. J., & Rabb, E. Attitudinal factors in congenital heart disease. *Pediatrics,* 1966, *38,* 92–101.

Manning, J. A., & Hutchinson, J. J. Insurability and employability of young cardiacs. *Circulation,* 1977, *56*(2), 335A–337A.

Myers-Vando, R., Steward, M. S., Folkins, C. H., & Hines, P. The effects of congenital heart disease on cognitive development, illness causality concepts, and vulnerability. *American Journal of Orthopsychiatry,* 1979, *49*(4), 617–625.

Nadas, A. S., & Fyler, D. C. *Pediatric Cardiology.* Philadelphia: W. B. Saunders, 1972.
Nihira, K., Foster, R., Shellhaas, M., Leland, H. *AAMD Adaptive Behavior Scale.* Washington: American Association on Mental Deficiency, 1974.
Ongley, P. A., & DuShane, J. W. Rehabilitation of the child with congenital heart disease. *The American Journal of Cardiology,* 1961, 7(3), 335–339.
Rowe, R. D., Uchida, I. A., & Char, F. Heart disease associated with chromosomal abnormalities. In J. D. Keith, R. D. Rowe, & P. Vlad, *Heart disease in infancy and childhood.* New York: Macmillan, 1978.

12

Coronary Heart Disease

If the heart has a special symbolism in human affairs, as we suggested in Chapter 11, then coronary heart disease may be seen as a signal pointing insistently to patterns that are destructive in human affairs. The significance of behavior and life style in many risk factors associated with this leading cause of death in the United States is a compelling reason for attention from a wide range of health practitioners.

This chapter will be principally involved with coronary heart disease and related phenomena such as hypertension and angina pectoris. They are primarily manifested in adults. Congenital heart defects, which are ordinarily discovered and treated in childhood, are the subject of Chapter 11. An illustration, with brief explanation of the heart's circulatory function, will be found in that chapter.

THE PHYSICAL DISABILITY

Definition and Incidence

Coronary heart disease is sometimes known as coronary artery disease and, perhaps most precisely, as ischemic heart disease. Ischemia means deficient blood supply, in this case insufficient to meet the metabolic (energy) needs of the heart's work load. A primary cause of this condition is coronary atherosclerosis, in which plaques or thickenings occlude the vessels which supply the heart muscle. This is a degenerative process which ordinarily begins early in life and progresses gradually throughout life. As the blood supply is decreased, the individual may experience arrhythmia, angina pectoris (chest discomfort described as heaviness, pressure), myocardial infarction (heart attack, severe deep chest pain), or cardiac failure. Myocardial infarction occurs when one or more of the three coronary arteries which supply the heart muscle (myocardium) become blocked, causing the muscle tissue nourished by that vessel to become damaged or destroyed. This may result in impaired heart function or in a disturbance of the heart rhythm. If these disturbances are not controlled, death may ensue.

It is estimated that 40,810,000 Americans have some major form of heart or blood vessel disease. This number includes 34,290,000 with hypertension and 4,240,000 with a history of heart attack and/or angina pectoris. Heart attack (otherwise described as myocardial infarction, coronary thrombosis, or coronary occlusion) was responsible for 638,427 deaths in 1977 (American Heart Association, 1979). Fox (1979) cites a National Heart and Lung Institute report: "Each year more than 670,000 U.S. citizens survive an episode of acute myocardial infarction." He notes that to a large number of health professionals the greatest impairment is psychological, noting the effects of depression, the difficult path of psychological recovery, and the need for adequate rehabilitation programs.

Internationally, heart and vascular disease accounts for 40% of all deaths and, in the United States, for 50%. Mason (1979) points out that this is true despite unprecedented progress that has seen a 30% reduction in deaths due to heart and vascular disease during the past 30 years. He views this progress as having been spearheaded by use of the method of cardiac catheterization to obtain accurate diagnostic knowledge which made possible operative techniques such as valve replacement, as well as the development of devices such as heart–lung machines and pacemakers. In the reduction of coronary heart disease mortality, he singles out the contributions of delineation of risk factors, physical fitness programs, comprehensive rehabilitation programs, more efficacious drugs for angina pectoris, coronary care units, coronary bypass surgery, and potentially effective antiarrhythmic modalities.

Risk Factors

A major source of knowledge of risk factors in coronary heart disease has been the Framingham study, which began in 1948 and followed for over 20 years a sample of 5,209 men and women, originally within the ages of 30–62 years and free of coronary heart disease. Kannel (1971), one of the investigators in the Framingham study, describes the "prime candidate for a coronary attack" (PCCA) as overweight, with high blood pressure, elevated blood lipids, abnormal EKGs, a cigarette smoker, physically indolent yet tense, and a heavy sugar user, with a preference for foods that are rich in animal fat. He dubs the atherosclerotic disease "the disease of living" and suggests that our way of life and way of dying are interrelated.

In addition to age and male sex, the three major risk factors are serum cholesterol (hypercholesterolemia), hypertension, and cigarette smoking. Multiple risk factors enhance the probability of a cardiovascular event; for instance, in the Framingham study the probability of such an event within eight years increased from 2% for patients with no risk factor to 49% for those with five risk factors (Kannel, McGee, & Gordon, 1976). Despite this amplification of risk, however, Byington, Dyer, Garside, Liu, Moss, Stamler, and Tsong (1978) point out that coronary heart disease occurs in populations at all levels of risk and that even modest decreases in the prevalence of major risk factors in the general population will reduce coronary heart disease among low risk as well as high risk populations.

In addition to the factors already named (age, male sex, hypertension, hypercholesterolemia, cigarette smoking), Sokolow and McIlroy (1979) list the following: diabetes, family history of coronary deaths, physical inactivity, personality factors (discussed later in this chapter), prostaglandins (which affect the aggregation of platelets), and estrogen.

Diagnosis

The beginning of coronary heart disease may be considered to be the gradual buildup of atherosclerotic plaques in the artery walls, which appears to be a normal life process. *Angina pectoris* occurs when the coronary arteries are unable to provide a blood supply sufficient for the needs of the heart muscle. This insufficiency frequently becomes apparent with exertion and may also be precipitated by emotional stress. The major symptom is heavy, tight pain in the chest, which may also radiate to the left arm and shoulder.

Hypertension is a distinct condition with its own etiology. It may not manifest itself in subjective symptoms. It increases the work load of the heart, aggravating even mild coronary narrowing and increasing the risk of myocardial infarction. It is diagnosed rather simply and accurately through standard procedures for measuring blood pressure. It is usually controllable through sodium restriction in diet, weight loss, and the use of appropriate drugs.

While 15 to 20% of the instances of *myocardial infarction* may be "silent" or painless (Ross, 1970), most of them are experienced as severe, deep chest pain which is described as heavy and crushing. About one third of myocardial infarcts result in death, and most of these victims die before reaching the hospital. About two thirds of those who do reach the hospital have a benign and uncomplicated course of treatment, in which the problems of psychological rehabilitation may loom as large as those of physical rehabilitation.

Perhaps the best known approach to the diagnosis of heart function or malfunction is the electrocardiogram (ECG or EKG), which measures the electric impulses generated by the heart. This may be combined with various degrees of exercise (e.g., on a treadmill or cycle) as a stress tolerance test to measure functional capacity or latent heart disease. The electrocardiogram may now be done in stereo (vectorcardiography), recording the electrical impulse in three dimensions, or in conjunction with recording of heart sounds (phonocardiography) for more accurate information about heart function and/or injury. Echocardiography aims ultrahigh frequency sound waves through the chest wall to the heart and records the echoes returning from the surfaces of the heart, measuring wall thickness as well as degree of velocity of contraction. All of these techniques are noninvasive, requiring no penetration of the patient's body.

In angiocardiography, X-ray-opaque material is injected into a heart chamber or through a blood vessel while high speed X-ray photography records its course. In cardiac catheterization, a thin plastic tube is passed through artery or vein into heart chambers, allowing for measurement of pressure and injection of opaque dyes to reveal irregularities.

Increased precision in reading the variety of cardiographic records is being achieved by the programming of computers for this purpose. An added diagnostic dimension is the measure of enzymes in the blood, which may reveal tissue damage in heart muscle.

Treatment

In addition to the treatment of hypertension through drugs, sodium restriction, or weight loss, the recommendation of moderate physical exercise, diet low in saturated fat, and nonsmoking is standard for those who are, or may become, at risk for coronary heart disease. Where coronary heart disease is known to exist, other measures may be used: Diuretics may be prescribed to reduce fluid in body tissue; anticoagulant drugs may be used to reduce the possibility of blood clotting; digitalis or antiarrhythmic drugs may be used to increase heart function or control irregularities of heart rhythm.

A variety of surgical procedures have been made possible by development of the heart–lung machine, which allows the heart to be exposed and repaired while its function is assumed by the machine. In coronary bypass surgery, a vein taken from the leg may be used to construct a detour around an occluded coronary artery. Major arteries (e.g., those which supply the brain or kidneys) may be replaced by transplanted or synthetic vessels. Heart valves may be replaced. Artificial pacemakers may be implanted to control irregular rhythms through a small electrical impulse.

The multidisciplinary nature of the diagnosis, treatment, and, especially, the rehabilitation of the coronary heart patient is apparent in the fact that Fox (1979, p. 5–6) lists no fewer than 16 specialists as comprising the ideal treatment team.

COMMON PSYCHOLOGICAL CHARACTERISTICS AND PROBLEMS

Type A Personality

The psychological literature of coronary heart disease is dominated by discussion and study of the Type A personality as described by Friedman and Rosenman (1974) and measured by investigators such as Jenkins and others (Jenkins, Zyzanski, & Rosenman, 1978). This concept will serve as a starting point for discussion of psychosocial factors, with note of some dissenting points of view.

Gentry (1979) characterizes individuals with Type A or coronary-prone personality as having: (a) a sense of time urgency; (b) an exaggerated sense of involvement; and (c) hostile, competitive, and hard-driving tendencies in their relationships with the environment. He notes evidence that links this behavior pattern with a higher risk of initial coronary heart disease, a higher incidence of fatality, and a greater risk of recurrence.

Haynes, Feinleib, and Kannel (1980), using a measure of Type A obtained from the Framingham data, found it a significant risk factor in men and women under 65. Women who developed coronary heart disease were higher on Framingham Type A as well as suppressed hostility, tension, and anxiety. Men who developed coronary heart disease were higher on Framingham Type A and also work overload, suppressed hostility, and frequent job promotions. Interestingly, these results were found only among white-collar workers. Matthews (1979) found that Type A male children and adults made more vigorous efforts to control a situation where the potential for loss of control was quite salient. She linked the effect of saliency to the Type A characteristic of attending only to central aspects of the environment. The fact that boys paralleled men in this respect suggests to her that this behavior may originate in childhood and be maintained into adulthood. Suls, Gastorf, and Witenberg (1979) also pursued the idea that Type A persons were concerned about a sense of control over life and, conversely, that the feeling of helplessness would cause them considerable stress. They found that Type A personalities experienced more life changes (events) than Type Bs and that ambiguity of causation bothered them most. They were apparently not distressed by events that were either within their control or clearly out of their control.

Jenkins (1979, p. 8) cites reports indicating that men with Type A behavior "incurred 1.7 to 4.5 times the rate of new coronary disease as men judged to possess the converse, relaxed, easy-going Type B pattern." He sees coronary-prone behavior as a style of life rather than a response to stress and posits psychic exhaustion and emotional drain as prodromal to myocardial infarction.

Jenkins elaborates the Type A characteristics as follows:

1. *Values*—responsible; seeks respect for achievement; inner directed
2. *Style of thought*—several unrelated lines simultaneously; anticipated; poor causal observer
3. *Interpersonal relationships*—self-centered; easily angered, impatient; expresses overt bravado; aggressive sexually
4. *Response style*—rapid; certain
5. *Gestures and movements*—tense; energetic
6. *Facial expressions*—tense, brief smiles
7. *Breathing*—irregular; expiratory sighing

Jenkins notes that knowledge of which aspects of Type A behavior are most strongly associated with coronary heart disease would be helpful in intervention programs.

While numerous cross-cultural studies have supported the concept of the relationship between Type A behavior and coronary heart disease, these findings have not been consistently positive nor have they uniformly supported all aspects of the construct. For example, Cohen, Matthews, and Waldron (1978) review a study of Japanese–Americans living in Hawaii in which only one factor, "hard-driving and competitive," was associated with coronary heart disease, while the total behavior pattern was not. Since "hard-driving and competitive behavior" is not culturally compatible for the Japanese, this characteristic was rarely found. Reasoning from this finding, they speculate about the possible development of environmental settings (e.g., business organizations) which might cultivate a hard-working disposition without encouraging the participants to be hard-driving and competitive.

Morgan (1979) cites the research of Eden, Shiron, Kellerman, Aronson, and French (1977), who studied 35–60 year old male managers of kibbutzim and found stress factors negatively correlated with coronary risk: "The greater the overload, conflict and social pressure, the less the risk" (p. 106). He interprets this in the light of Selye's (Selye, 1976; Selye & Cherry, 1978) view of the potentially positive value of stress and reiterates that it may be more stressful for some individuals to cut back on their work schedules than to maintain their current load. Eden et al. suggested that such persons might represent Type C personality. Morgan goes on to raise serious question about the validity of the Type A construct, objecting to it as a "simplistic and unitary approach" and advocating a model which stresses interaction between characteristics of the individual and the environment. He proposes an exercise model based on the assumption that physical activity is "good stress" under normal conditions and that, up to a point it "provokes decrements in state anxiety."

Dimsdale, Hackett, Hutter, and Block (1980) also call into question the generality of previously reported associations between Type A and extent of coronary heart disease, after finding it unrelated to membership in three ethnic groups (Irish Catholic, Italian Catholic, and white Anglo–Saxon Protestant), to cardiac symptomatology, or to depression or anxiety in individuals.

While controversy and research refinements continue, it is important to observe that: (a) Type A and Type B behavior patterns are defined in the extreme, and individuals rarely conform to all aspects of the model; (b) many persons with Type A behavior patterns do not develop coronary heart disease and, conversely, some Type B persons do; and (c) Type A behavior is a multidimensional construct, the refinement of which may lead to greater predictive accuracy and/or therapeutically significant implications.

Post-Coronary

Gulledge (1979) points out that the post-coronary patient, often an aggressive, impatient person, returns home to: (a) problems of home routine; (b) an oversolicitous, anxious spouse; (c) the noise and conflict of children; and (d) a multitude of instructions regarding medicine, diet, and physical activity.

The role of the spouse in coronary rehabilitation is a critical and difficult one. It requires coming to grips with many of the problems (e.g., protection-overprotection) that are encountered in other disabilities and which are discussed in Chapter 1 and elsewhere in this book. This adjustment must occur in a brief time span and is imposed upon a previous relationship often quite at variance with the current one. Oversolicitousness is branded as such and resented. Lack of expression or failure to extend elaborate care may be seen by the patient or, especially by relatives and friends, as lack of concern. Skelton and Dominian (1973) studied 65 wives of myocardial infarction patients and determined that 38% of them found the convalescence period very stressful because of fear of a recurrent infarct and increased irritability and dependence on the part of the patient. The spouses commonly felt loss, depression (as reflected in appetite and sleep disturbance), and guilt ("I ought not to have let him do so much").

Patient responses to myocardial infarction (or cardiac surgery) may be described differently depending upon the point in the process being observed or the amount of the process included. For example, Fox (1979) describes depression in nearly all post-coronary patients, taking approximately three months to resolve in a healthy personality. Depression and anxiety are undoubtedly common phenomena in the coronary care unit. Many patients will maintain an anxious adjustment which may result in overdependence and feelings of helplessness, the classic "coronary invalid." On the other hand, Gentry (1979) points out that many of these patients are Type A personalities who may actually increase their activity after the crisis is past so as to demonstrate that they have not been slowed down. Gentry describes other patients who rely heavily on denial as a psychological mechanism and may deny that they have ever had a serious disability. He points out that little attention has been paid to the rehabilitation of those groups who overdo following coronary problems because so much emphasis has been placed upon increasing function and preventing invalidism.

Gentry (1979) attempts to put psychological problems in some perspective with regard to their effect on return to function. He notes that 80% of coronary heart disease patients resume their pre-illness work status within the first year, 60% of them within three to four months. He notes the considerable impact of age (virtually all patients under 45 return to some employment), severity of illness (54% of severely impaired patients return to work, as opposed to 86% less severely impaired) and pre-illness level of physical activity (compared to sedentary persons, twice as many highly active persons resumed work by the end of one year). He summarizes (p. 692), "One can easily see that the psychological problems of most persons experiencing an episode of CHD are not sufficient to lead to a failure to return to work; i.e., they may be the reason for only 3–12% of the patients not returning to work." He does note that psychological problems may cause some delay in return to work.

Stages of reaction to myocardial infarction have been described by Lambert and Lambert (1979) as repudiation, recognition, and reconciliation. Their description parallels the shock–denial–anger–depression–adaptation progression which has been seen in a number of other disabilities (e.g., spinal cord injury) and which has been discussed in Chapter 1. They observe the need to allow the patient to deny the loss of good health during the repudiation stage, which they describe as usually very early in the illness. In the stage of recognition, they mention depression, overt anger, and negotiation, noting an increased likelihood of depression in patients 50 to 60 years of age. As with other illnesses, anger may be directed toward professional staff as well as relatives. Negotiation is seen as the patient's attempt to handle feelings of guilt about the possibility that some of his/her actions may have helped to cause the disability. They recommend that patients be allowed to express these feelings of guilt, and suggest that this negotiation will end when the patient accepts his condition.

Return to sexual function is a matter of considerable concern for many patients with coronary heart disease. Skinner (1979) cites numerous studies which found a significant drop in the frequency of intercourse following myocardial infarction. He points out that a combination of age, compromised cardiovascular system, and anxiety make many of these patients doubt their ability to do normal physical activity, much less to perform sexually on demand. This despite the fact, he notes, that "sexual activity, at least as practiced by the majority of middle-aged and older men and women, is not a major problem in terms of increased risk of morbidity or mortality from cardiovascular disease. Except for those patients who are limited by the severity of their disease to low-intensity activities, most patients should be able to perform sexually." Similarly, Gulledge (1979) says that the usual demands of sex are well within the range of physical capability of 70 to 80% of middle-aged men who recover from an uncomplicated myocardial infarction.

Reasons given for decreased sexual activity include loss of desire, depression and anxiety, spouse's anxiety, impotence, and physical symptoms such as angina. Problems in returning to sexual activity may be increased when physical deconditioning has taken place as a consequence of prolonged rest and inactivity and also when side effects of medication may contribute to impotence.

Despite apprehension about coital death, Skinner (1979) concludes that sexual intercourse does not appear to be a high-risk activity for the majority of the population. Such deaths are more likely to be associated with extramarital sex which involves: (1) an unfamiliar partner, (2) guilt and anxiety about discovery, and (3) excessive intake of food and drink.

Mitchell (1979) suggests that there are two major areas of concern regarding the coronary patient's return to work. One of these includes traditional factors such as: (1) severity of cardiopathology, (2) age, (3) stressfulness of occupation, (4) prior work record, (5) family instability, and (6) negative employer attitudes. To these he adds such factors as: (a) chronic negative emotional outlook, (depression, anxiety); (b) the patient's attribution of the infarction (i.e., was it attributed to the job); (c) the patient's sense of health and well-being; and (d) need level—that is, patients who return to work tend to show high need for autonomy and introspection, low need for change. In general, it should also be noted that white-collar and high skill level persons tend to return to a work role sooner than their blue collar or low skill level counterparts.

EVALUATING PERSONS WITH CORONARY HEART DISEASE

As with any significant disability, the effective interview evaluation of persons with coronary heart disease requires that the interviewer have a reasonable level of sophistication about the disease process. Although the psychosocial interview will typically be aimed at evaluation of the whole person (not just the illness), nevertheless, it will be important to have some understanding of terminology and the significance of various symptoms and medical procedures. In the case of coronary heart disease, it is also especially important to have current medical information about the status and outlook for this particular person, to avoid the pitfalls of inappropriately exaggerating or minimizing the significance of the illness or allowing the patient to do so.

Coronary heart disease patients will frequently be interviewed during the convalescent period, and it will be necessary to tailor the length and intensity of interview to the tolerance of the patient. Shorter and more frequent interviews may be desirable. If it is in the hospital setting, arrangements should be made for as much privacy as possible. If only limited privacy is possible, the interviewer should take this, and the patient's reaction to it, into account in directing the interview, both in terms of subject matter and depth of probing. As in most areas, when an accurate picture of the patient's activities is desired, a clear-cut behavioral description should be obtained. It is often desirable to get collaborating information about the patient's activities from other family members, especially the spouse. This should be done only with the patient's knowledge, and care should be taken not to discuss the patient as if he/she were an inanimate or incompetent object. This is of particular importance since the patient is likely to have Type A personality characteristics, and control may be an important issue to him/her. At some point, joint interviewing may be appropriate. This may be especially helpful in identifying psychological and interpersonal issues before the patient returns to regular functioning. Mitchell (1979) has emphasized the need for identification of such issues before returning to a work setting which may cause their exacerbation.

The original measure of the coronary-prone Type A behavior pattern was accomplished through the Structured Interview developed for that purpose by Rosenman, Friedman, Straus, Wurm, Kositchek, Hahn, and Werthessen (1964). It is brief (10–20 minutes) and easily conducted, although it requires the services of a trained interviewer. It is considered by many as *the* criterion of Type A behavior. The Jenkins Activity Survey (Jenkins, Zyzanski, & Rosenman, 1978) utilized many of the same subjects (Western Collaborative Group Study) as the Structured Interview and was developed to measure the Type A personality and subsequently three components of it, *speed and impatience, job involvement*, and *hard-driving and competitive*. It has the advantage of being self-administered. It is commonly used as a measure of Type A personality, although Rosenman (1978, p. 58) believes that its predictive ability is weaker and that it should not be used to replace the interview method of assessment.

Bortner (1969) has developed a measure of the Type A behavior pattern utilizing 14 semantic differential rating scales representing contrasting dimensions of behavior. This has the advantage of brevity and criterion-related scoring but has yet to receive extensive use. Price (1979) found it only moderately correlated with the Jenkins Activity Survey and expresses concern about this.

Where there is concern about serious psychopathology, traditional measures such as the MMPI (Hathaway & McKinley, 1948) may be used, although Gillum, Leon, Kamp, and Becera-Aldama (1980) report a lack of success in predicting onset of cardiovascular disease from MMPI data. The coronary heart disease patient does not ordinarily have motor or perceptual problems beyond those found in the general population and, other than concern for length of testing session in those who have severe coronary impairment or who are early in their convalescence, standard tests and procedures may be utilized for psychological evaluation.

INTERVENTION METHODS

Fox (1979) suggests that "a reassuring message of appropriate optimistic tenor provided by the ambulance and rescue personnel will enhance the probabilities of survival" (p. 4). He further recommends a simple but meaningful statement of what is being done to help protect the patient and his/her heart from further damage—the reasons for continued monitoring and frequent visits by ward personnel in the acute care facility. A personal validation of the latter recommendation may be found in the description by a gynecologist of his own cardiac valve replacement (Anonymous, 1969). He believes that he was psychologically less scathed, partly because he knew what to expect. He states flatly, "The more the patient knows about the details, why and wherefore of his operation the better" (p. 1129). This knowledge of what to expect, and why, would appear to be especially important to the coronary heart disease patient who may be very competent and in whose life control is often a very important issue. Many of these patients will especially resent the implication that they could not understand what is going on or that they could not handle the knowledge. The life-threatening possibilities which most patients know to exist in the situation may also lead to overinterpretation of pains or procedures which are actually routine and to be expected. The coronary heart disease patient is apt to be especially vulnerable to anxiety and emotional stress at a time when hospitalization is required.

The author has had the opportunity to compare the recent experiences of two acquaintances in cardiac surgery. One was introduced to the personnel, equipment, and procedures of the coronary care unit the day before surgery and found this extremely helpful in tolerating his later experiences there. The other had only a friendly word of reassurance before surgery and found himself bewildered by the procedures as they were applied. This led to anxiety and resentment which subsided only as he recovered sufficiently to develop, on his own, a rational understanding of the treatment program.

Skelton and Dominian (1973), finding that wives of myocardial infarction patients commonly felt loss, depression, and guilt, concluded that increased support and information were required from physicians and hospital staff. Gulledge (1979) emphasizes the need to prepare both patient and spouse for the return home and the fact that to know what is normal and when to expect it is useful information for both. In providing information, physician and staff have the delicate task of balancing hope and realism; this was discussed in Chapters 1 and 8. Information should be given in such a way as not to dash hope, which may be necessary to the motivation and sense of well-being of the patient. All predictions, especially negative ones, should be given with appropriate tentativeness. Unrealistic hopes should not be reinforced, but neither must they be confronted each time they appear, if they are not interfering with the treatment process. The goal is for the family to be supportive but not overprotective and for the patient to have realistic self-expectations. Education to reassure family members will frequently result in their reassuring the patient.

Gentry (1979) suggests that early mobilization and exercise combat depression and enhance self-esteem, and Gulledge (1979) notes that progressive physical activity with self-monitoring will help the patient to regain the idea of self-control and thus will reduce depression. He cautions against vague generalizations which cause confusion and conflict and may add to depression. In general, heavy emphasis is *not* put on diet modification and smoking cessation during the immediate post-coronary period, because of the additional stress this places on the patient, with consequent increase in risk of further myocardial episodes.

Gruen (1975) cites impressive gains in providing brief psychotherapy to myocardial patients during the hospitalization period. He saw 35 such patients for one-half hour sessions five or six times per week during the hospital stay. Compared with an appropriate control group, these patients spent 1.2 fewer days in intensive care and 2.5 fewer days in total hospitalization. They showed less anxiety and depression, as well as a reduced incidence of arrhythmia and congestive heart failure. He recommends individual psychotherapy on a systematic basis for the management of myocardial infarction patients. He states that one of the most useful psychological effects of the treatment was to make the patient aware of the positive aspects (prospects for a different, satisfying life) which he had been ignoring because of a narrowly restricted self-concept. It should be noted that in this approach the therapist was conversant with the problems of coronary heart disease, and the sessions were not labeled "psychotherapy" at the start, so as to avoid initial resistance.

Authorities discuss the notion of modifying Type A behavior in order to reduce the risk factor with varying degrees of enthusiasm. Morgan (1979) feels that it is at least premature to recommend that individuals alter their life style to avoid stress to prevent hypertension. He calls on the writings of Selye (1978) and the findings of Eden *et al.* (1977) to question a causal relationship and even to suggest that to change might be more stressful to Type A personalities. Leventhal and Cleary (1979) take the position that the evidence for causation is sufficiently strong to investigate causal mechanisms and see if their modification will reduce the incidence of disease. Hartman (1978, p. 599) concludes, "Type A behavior and stress contribute substantially to the pathogenesis of cardiovascular disease." He calculates that eliminating Type A behavior could reduce ischemic heart disease by 31% and proposes that we test more vigorous behavioral intervention as a possible means of reducing psychosocial risk factors.

Gentry (1978), while cautioning that we should not naively presume that survival and freedom from coronary heart disease are more potent reinforcers than the other consequences of coronary-prone behavior, such as higher status and more money, describes some of the applications of behavior modification to the change of such behavior: (1) positive reinforcement, as in scheduling longer appointments with supportive persons following brief appointments with stress-eliciting ones; (2) avoidance responding, such as having the secretary not interrupt appointments; (3) response–cost techniques, such as penalizing oneself for speeding to make yellow traffic lights by turning right and circling the block; (4) thought-stopping of stress-inducing themes, such as overcommitment or time limitations; (5) relaxation procedures; and (6) cognitive behavior modification, such as "My anger is a signal of the need for problem-solving."

Inclusion of spouse or other family members in psychological intervention with the coronary heart disease patient is consistently recommended. The spouse may share the anxiety and/or depression of the patient and may be equally in need of brief psychotherapy. Reluctance about participation in sex may be shared by, or even originate with, the spouse, who fears the possibility of an exacerbation. Sexual counseling should, at some point, always include the spouse. A frequent cause of problems is failure to understand directions for medications and instructions about activity. Again, the understanding and cooperation of the spouse is critical.

Mitchell (1979) states that approximately 40% of coronary patients attempt to return to work within 8 to 12 weeks following an infarction, and 85% to 95% are reported to have returned by one year. Success rates, however, vary from 80% to 85% initially but fall to 60% to 65% in follow-up studies a year later. The need for vocational counseling for coronary patients cannot be overemphasized. This should be based upon a realistic medical appraisal of the patient's functional capacity and limitations, if any, as well as an analysis of the demands of the patient's employment. If the patient indicates that his employment has been a source of dissatisfaction or stress, or if new limitations are imposed, it will be important to get a thorough evaluation of his skills, abilities, and interests. This vocational rehabilitation effort should be concurrent with the patient's gradual return to physical activity. The patient should, early on, get the sense that he will continue to have useful employment capacities, before the notion of the "cardiac invalid" can begin to develop.

Demonstrating that intervention in coronary heart disease can be done at many levels, Meyer, Nash, McAlister, Maccoby, and Farquhar (1980) carried on a community-wide education program via mass media in a number of small towns in California. They tried to reduce risk of heart disease by increasing knowledge of risk factors and modifying dietary, smoking, and exercise behaviors in groups with higher than average risk. One group was also given face-to-face instruction. Some significant risk reduction and increase in knowledge was found in all treated groups, and some measures indicated greater and longer lasting change in the group that received both mass media and face-to-face instruction. Education via the media appears to be a useful supplement to individual intervention techniques.

TRENDS AND NEEDS

There is a trend toward the study of psychological factors as they affect the coronary heart disease patient and his response to treatment. The need is for application of what is already known about psychological preparation of patients for surgery; explanation of the treatment process, medication and prognosis; and effectiveness of brief psychotherapy for patient and spouse. It appears that enough is known so that such support services should be standard procedure for all patients who enter the treatment system.

Further research into whatever causal relationships may exist between behavior and coronary heart disease appears to be a continuing need. Knowledge of the dimensions of Type A behavior needs to be refined. A set of questions in particular need of answers is: (1) Is it possible to effectively modify the behavior of Type A individuals?; (2) If Type A behavior is modified, does the risk factor actually decrease for those individuals?; and (3) Assuming positive answers to questions 1 and 2, what are the most effective ways of bringing about such changes?

APPENDIX: SOURCES OF INFORMATION

Psychological Aspects of Myocardial Infarction and Coronary Care, W. Doyle Gentry and Redford B. Williams, Jr. (Eds.). St. Louis: Mosby, 1979.

Coronary-Prone Behavior, T. M. Dembroski, S. M. Weiss, J. L. Shields, S. G. Haynes, & M. Feinleib (Eds.). New York: Springer-Verlag, 1978.

Heart Disease and Rehabilitation, Michael L. Pollock and Donald H. Schmidt (Eds.). Boston: Houghton Mifflin, 1979.

Clinical Cardiology, Maurice Sokolow and Malcolm B. McIlroy. Los Altos: Lange, 1979.

REFERENCES

American Heart Association. *Heart facts, 1980.* Dallas: American Heart Association, 1979.

Anonymous. At the receiving end: A doctor's personal recollections of cardiac-valve replacement. *The Lancet,* 1969, Nov., 1129–1131.

Bortner, R. W. A short rating scale as a potential measure of pattern A behavior. *Journal of Chronic Diseases,* 1969, *22,* 87–91.

Byington, R., Dyer, A. R., Garside, D., Liu, K., Moss, D., Stamler, J., & Tsong, Y. Recent trends of major coronary risk factors and CHD mortality in the U.S. and other industrialized countries. In R. J. Havlik & M. Feinleib (Eds.), *Proceedings of the conference on the decline in coronary heart disease mortality.* Bethesda, Md.: NIH Publication No. 79-1610. May, 1979.

Cohen, J. B., Matthews, K. A., & Waldron, I, Coronary-prone behavior: Developmental and cultural considerations. In T. M. Dembroski, S. M. Weiss, J. L. Shields, S. G. Haynes, & M. Feinleib, *Coronary-prone behavior.* New York: Springer-Verlag, 1978.

Dimsdale, J. E., Hackett, T. P., Hutter, A. M., & Block, P. C. The risk of type A mediated coronary artery disease in different populations. *Psychosomatic Medicine,* 1980, *42*(1), 55–62.

Eden, D., Shiron, A., Kellerman, J. J., Aronson, J., & French, J. R. P. Stress, anxiety and coronary risk in a supportive society. In C. D. Spielberger & I. G. Sarason (Eds.), *Stress and anxiety.* New York: Wiley, 1977.

Fox, S. M. Heart disease and rehabilitation: Scope of the problem. In M. L. Pollock & D. H. Schmidt (Eds.), *Heart disease and rehabilitation.* Boston: Houghton Mifflin, 1979.

Friedman, M., & Rosenman, R. H. *Type A behavior and your heart.* Greenwich, Conn.: Fawcett, 1974.

Gentry, W. D. Behavior modification of the coronary-prone behavior pattern. In T. M. Dembroski, S. M. Weiss, J. L. Shields, S. G. Haynes, & M. Feinleib, *Coronary-prone behavior.* New York: Springer-Verlag, 1978.

Gentry, W. D. Psychosocial concerns and benefits in cardiac rehabilitation. In M. L. Pollock & D. H. Schmidt (Eds.), *Heart disease and rehabilitation.* Boston: Houghton Mifflin, 1979.

Gillum, R., Leon, G. R., Kamp, J., & Becerra-Aldama, J. Prediction of cardiovascular and other disease onset and mortality from 30-year longitudinal MMPI data. *Journal of Consulting and Clinical Psychology,* 1980, *48*(3), 405–406.

Gruen, W. Effects of brief psychotherapy during the hospitalization period on the recovery process in heart attacks. *Journal of Consulting and Clinical Psychology,* 1975, *43*(2), 223–232.

Gulledge, A. D. Psychological aftermaths of myocardial infarction. In W. D. Gentry & R. B. Williams (Eds.), *Psychological aspects of myocardial infarction and coronary care.* St. Louis: C. V. Mosby, 1979.

Hartman, L. M. Behavioral prevention of ischemic heart disease. *Canadian Medical Association Journal,* 1978, *119,* 599–604.

Hathaway, S. R., & McKinley, J. C. *Minnesota Multiphasic Personality Inventory.* New York: Psychological Corporation, 1948.

Haynes, S. G., Feinleib, M., & Kannel, W. B. The relationship of psychosocial factors to coronary heart disease in the Framingham study. III. Eight-year incidence of coronary heart disease. *American Journal of Epidemiology,* 1980, *111,* 37–58.

Jenkins, C. D. The coronary-prone personality. In W. D. Gentry & R. B. Williams (Eds.), *Psychological aspects of myocardial infarction and coronary care.* St. Louis: C. V. Mosby, 1979.

Jenkins, C. D., Zyzanski, S. J., & Rosenman, R. H. *Manual for the Jenkins activity survey.* New York: Psychological Corporation, 1978.

Kannel, W. B. The disease of living. *Nutrition Today,* 1979, *6*(3), 2–11.

Kannel, W. B., McGee, D., & Gordon, T. A general cardiovascular risk profile: The Framingham study. *American Journal of Cardiology,* 1976, *38,* 46–51.

Lambert, V. A., & Lambert, C. E. *The impact of physical illness.* Englewood Cliffs, N.J.: Prentice–Hall, 1979.

Leventhal, H., & Cleary, P. D. Behavioral modification of risk factors: Technology or science? In M. L. Pollock & D. H. Schmidt (Eds.), *Heart disease and rehabilitation.* Boston: Houghton Mifflin, 1979.

Mason, D. T. Foreword. In M. L. Pollock & D. H. Schmidt (Eds.), *Heart disease and rehabilitation.* Boston: Houghton Mifflin, 1979.

Matthews, K. A. Efforts to control children and adults with the type A coronary-prone behavior pattern. *Child Development,* 1979, *50*(3), 842–847.

Meyer, A. J., Nash, J. D., McAlister, A. L., Maccoby, N., & Farquhar, J. W. Skills training in a cardiovascular health education campaign. *Journal of Consulting and Clinical Psychology,* 1980, *48*(2), 129–142.

Mitchell, D. K. Vocational rehabilitation and the coronary patient. In W. D. Gentry & R. B. Williams (Eds.), *Psychological aspects of myocardial infarction and coronary care.* St. Louis: C. V. Mosby, 1979.

Morgan, W. P. Psychologic aspects of heart disease. In M. L. Pollock & D. H. Schmidt (Eds.), *Heart Disease and Rehabilitation,* Boston: Houghton Mifflin, 1979.

Pollock, M. L., & Schmidt, D. H. (Eds.), *Heart disease and rehabilitation.* Boston: Houghton Mifflin, 1979.

Price, K. P. Reliability of assessment of coronary-prone behavior with special reference to the Bortner Rating Scale. *Journal of Psychosomatic Research,* 1979, *23,* 45–47.

Rosenman, R. H. The interview method of assessment of the coronary-prone behavior pattern. In T. M. Dembroski, S. M. Weiss, J. L. Shields, S. G. Haynes, & M. Feinleib, *Coronary-prone behavior.* New York: Springer-Verlag, 1978.

Rosenman, R. H., Friedman, M., Straus, R., Wurm, M., Kositchek, R., Hahn, W., & Werthessen, N. T. A predictive study of coronary heart disease: The Western Collaborative Group Study. *Journal of the American Medical Association,* 1964, *189,* 15–22.

Ross, R. S. Ischemic heart disease. In *Harrison's principles of internal medicine* (6th ed.). New York: McGraw-Hill, 1970.

Selye, H. *The stress of life.* New York: McGraw-Hill, 1976.

Selye, H., & Cherry, L. On the real benefits of eustress. *Psychology Today,* March, 1978, *11,* 60–70.

Skelton, M., & Dominian, J. Psychological stress in wives of patients with myocardial infarction. *British Medical Journal,* 1973, *2,* 101–103.

Skinner, J. S. Sexual relations and the cardiac patient. In M. L. Pollock & D. H. Schmidt (Eds.), *Heart disease and rehabilitation.* Boston: Houghton Mifflin, 1979.

Sokolow, M., & McIlroy, M. B. *Clinical cardiology.* Los Altos, Calif. Lange, 1979.

Suls, J., Gastorf, J. W., & Witenberg, S. H. Life events, psychological distress and the type A coronary-prone behavior pattern. *Journal of Psychosomatic Research,* 1979, *23,* 315–319.

13

Visual Handicaps

ROBERT D. BOYD AND
MAURINE OTOS

THE PHYSICAL DISABILITY

Overview

As with the ability to hear, the ability to see may vary in degree of impairment from minor anomalies of sight which impose, especially with the use of corrective lens, little or no inconvenience, to complete blindness which, especially when present from birth, significantly changes life experiences and imposes major problems of adjustment in a seeing world. This chapter will focus primarily on those who are blind or partially blind rather than with those who are partially sighted or have a minor visual impairment.

To acquire some feeling for what it might be like to be blind, imagine for a moment what your world would be like without vision: a world limited to what you hear, touch, and taste; a world differing from that of those who can see, whose perceptions and explanations are not always perceived or understood in the same way by those who cannot. Imagine a world in which you cannot find the person who angers you; you cannot attack him except with words, and even then, you cannot see his response. Imagine a world that will not let you know a puzzled look, a scowl or a smile, or truly share, even with language, the full beauty of a flower garden, a painting, or a sunset.

Incidence and Causation

There are at least 10 million totally blind people in the world today; the number is much larger if one includes the partially blind. World

Health Organization (WHO) estimates (Vaughan & Asbury, 1977) show significant differences in incidence among different countries, ranging from a high incidence of 300 blind per 10,000 population in Saudi Arabia to a low incidence of 51 blind per 100,000 population in Belgium. England and the United States report approximately 20 blind per 10,000 population, or nearly 500,000 people in the United States (*Vision Problems in the United States*, 1980). Sorsby (1972) found little variation from year to year in the blind population in England and Wales, although he also reported increasingly greater incidence among the older population, who have become blind, and also among women, who also show a higher incidence of diabetic retinopathy (see the discussion later in the chapter). These results appear to be consistent with those in other Western countries, where medical and social services are widely available.

Blindness in the United States is to a great extent related to the aging process, with approximately half of the legally blind population being over 65 years of age (Vaughan & Asbury, 1977). By way of contrast, there are 42 per 100,000 blind children under the age of 5, compared to 3,003/100,000 blind persons 85 and over. Fifty-five percent of the *newly blinded* are 65 and older (*Vision Problems in the United States*, 1980). An estimated 47,000 become blind each year in the United States, one person every eleven minutes *(Vision Problems in the United States,* 1980).

Sorsby (1972) organizes the causes of blindness into four categories: (1) congenital and prenatal influences, (2) systemic diseases, (3) optic atrophy, and (4) glaucoma and cataracts. Congenital defects and prenatal influences are largely genetically determined but may also include transmission of maternal infection such as syphilis or rubella. Gardiner (1979) specifies the major antenatal and perinatal causes of blindness as intrauterine rubella (producing cataracts), excessive oxygen administered at the time of birth (retrolental fibroplasia), and low birthweight. Congenital and prenatal influences, with emphasis on genetic conditions, account for approximately 70% of all causes of blindness appearing in the first four years of life. Systemic diseases include vascular disease, and various neurological disorders such as tumors and diabetes.

Vaughan and Asbury (1977) state that the three major causes of blindness in the world today are trachoma, onchocerciasis, and xerophthalmia, all of which could be prevented with adequate health measures. These conditions exist largely in underdeveloped countries where health standards are low and together account for the fact that the frequency of blindness in countries such as Saudi Arabia, Uganda, and Pakistan averages approximately 30 times that of England, Italy, and the United States. Beyond these more unusual and esoteric (to the average

Westerner) etiologies, there are conditions existing worldwide which account for a significant incidence of blindness. Vaughan and Asbury (1977) specifically name glaucoma, cataracts, retinal detachment, and diabetic retinopathy. They further suggest that, taken together, these four conditions may account for more cases of blindness than any condition other than trachoma and that they are less easily prevented or treated.

The National Society to Prevent Blindness (*Vision Problems in the United States,* 1980) reports that in the United States the principal causes of blindness in the order of frequency are glaucoma, macular degeneration, senile cataract, and optic nerve atrophy. Diabetic retinopathy is the leading cause of *new blindness* for ages 20–75.

Glaucoma, a significant increase in intraocular pressure, which reduces blood supply to the retina and destroys nerve cells, causes blindness if it is not identified and treated early. It is especially important that infantile glaucoma be identified and treated surgically, while glaucoma in late life may be treated medically but may also require surgery. Glaucoma is usually a slowly progressing condition with acuity unaffected in the earlier stages, except for peripheral vision. Advanced glaucoma becomes very painful. The goal of treatment is to reduce the pressure and halt possible permanent eye damage. With current medical knowledge and skill, blindness need not result. It is also noted that the earlier infantile glaucoma is manifest, the greater the permanent damage and the poorer the prognosis.

Cataracts, a lens opacity which clouds and eventually blocks vision if left untreated, occurs principally in older people but may also occur early in life due to such factors as genetic inheritance, maternal rubella in the first trimester of gestation, or traumatic conditions caused by impact of foreign bodies (such as BB shot) striking the lens. Prior to treatment, the opacity of the lens can in some respects be compared to the image seen when one looks through a piece of cloudy plasticized material. Treatment is surgical removal of the opaque lens with an expected success rate of 90–95%. If the lens has been surgically removed, special cataract (framed or contact) lenses are needed to compensate for the extracted lens. A reading lens may be required for close work and a telescopic device for distance. With available treatment, this condition probably will no longer need to be a cause of blindness.

Retinal detachment, a separation of the retina from the wall of the eyeball, is the result of a small hole (or holes) in the retina which allows fluid to collect and, under pressure, to separate the retina from its usual attachment. Treatment is surgical closure of the leakage holes and reattachment of the retina to the wall. With the improved surgical techniques now available, Vaughan and Asbury (1977) estimate that 90% of retinal detachments can be corrected with one surgical procedure and an additional 6% corrected by a second procedure, with little probability of later separation.

Diabetic retinopathy, a disease affecting the retinal blood vessel has become a major cause of blindness in the Western world. (See also Chapter 3.) Incidence of blindness as a result of diabetes is higher when onset is during childhood (Coughlin & Patz, 1978). Blindness occurs as a result of unchecked blockage and hemorrhage of retinal capillaries which leak fluid, thickening and blocking the retina. If the diabetic condition is diagnosed and controlled early in life, the retinopathy may at least be deferred or delayed, but once the progress is started, day-to-day control of the diabetes has little effect. It is difficult to predict in individual cases what the course of the disease may bring.

Macular degeneration is a retinal disorder, a disease that causes damage to the blood vessels in the macular area, the specialized section of the retina responsible for sharpest and clearest vision. Both eyes are affected, and the individual has difficulty seeing into the distance, performing close work, and distinguishing faces and objects. The disease is a condition of aging affecting more females than males (*Vision Problems in the United States,* 1980).

Optic atrophy, diminution or wasting away of the optic nerve, may occur for various reasons including degenerative diseases. It may appear at almost any age, but it is more frequent in youth and middle age, when it may set the stage for problems of life readjustment.

Definition of Blindness

It is interesting to note that governmental bureaus and industry have probably had more influence on the definition of blindness than the medical profession which diagnoses and treats the condition. For example, in the United States determination and degree of blindness become important in establishing eligibility for income tax deductions. Thus, it is the Internal Revenue Service which specifies that "legal blindness" exists when a person demonstrates no better than "visual acuity for distant vision of 20/200 or less in the better eye with best correction, or widest diameter of visual field subtending an angle of less than 20 degrees." It will be noted that this definition, which is probably the most widely used in the United States, says nothing about the degree of handicap imposed on the individual or the psychological or occupational adjustment to visual limitations. It states only that a blind person cannot see at 20 feet what the person with normal vision could correctly identify at 200 feet and that peripheral vision does not extend more than 20 degrees from central gaze; it says nothing about near vision.

The same definition of legal blindness makes it possible for the blind individual to receive financial benefits such as Supplemental Security Income (SSI) at a rate higher than would be received by persons with different disabling conditions, as well as earned income exclusions and special transportation benefits. The Veterans Administration has historically been charged with actively seeking out and extending services to blinded veterans, while those with other disabilities are expected to apply for care. These special benefits peculiar only to blindness may have emerged because of the emotional overtones in the historical reaction of society to blindness, resulting in special supportive legislation for the blind. Unfortunately, these special benefits often serve to extend society's reaction to blindness to the blind person, thus increasing dependency (Carroll, 1961; Cholden, 1958; Cutsforth, 1951).

A slightly broader, but equally legalistic definition is the one used to determine *industrial* visual efficiency, frequently demanded in legal and industrial cases to determine compensation for injury. This approach uses a rather complicated mathematical system to calculate visual efficiency based on three factors which are presumed to be of equal importance: percentage loss of visual acuity, percentage loss of visual field, and percentage loss of coordinated ocular movements (Vaughan & Asbury, 1977).

Measurement of industrial visual efficiency of visual acuity gives equal weight to near and distance vision. *Near visual acuity* is based on the size of Jaeger Test Type which the person can read when the type is presented at a normal reading distance from the eye. *Distance visual acuity* is based on the size of letters the person can read when the material is presented from a distance of 20 feet. Measurement of *visual field* involves use of a perimeter mechanism which records the field position based on a signal when the person first sees a test object brought in from the side at 15-degree intervals until the entire 360-degree field has been plotted. Measurement of *coordinated ocular movements* is determined by the extent to which diplopia (seeing one object as two) is described by the person under certain positions of gaze and at certain distances. Visual efficiency can be measured for one eye only or for both eyes. In the latter case, the efficiency of the better eye is weighted three times that of the poorer eye; this weighting takes into consideration that one can still function reasonably well with only one good eye. Having one blind eye and one normal eye would result in a binocular visual efficiency score of 75%. Failure to meet industrial visual efficiency standards might be called "industrial" blindness.

The armed forces specify visual acuity requirements which vary according to type of service and according to differing standards for officers and enlisted personnel. Failure to meet these requirements might be called "military" blindness.

States have varying visual standards for persons wishing to apply for a driver's license. Failure to meet state standards could be called "automobile" blindness.

Standards of visual efficiency for children are established by state and federal legislation regulating eligibility for special education. The major criterion for legal blindness is visual acuity corrected to no better than 20/200 vision, although a national trend appears under way to change the criterion to a more functional definition. Children with this degree of visual limitation require either special resource material or placement in special classes for the blind. Those placed in this category could be called educationally blind.

It may be seen from the preceding material that defining blindness is not simple, that meaningful standards may vary according to the situation in which a person with limited vision may be placed, and that emphasis on measurement by numbers may, therefore, frequently result in meaningless labeling. Vaughan and Asbury (1977) favor a functional definition which specifies blindness as existing when loss of vision prevents an individual from supporting himself or when limited vision makes him or her dependent on others. The positive aspect of this definition is that the key variable becomes *reaction to* the visual deficiency rather than simple *measurement of* visual loss. The negative aspect of this definition is a possible overemphasis on dependency.

Colenbrander (1976) suggests a system for describing and classifying low vision. This approach begins with the concept that three conditions may cause human physical limitation: a disease, an injury, or a physical anomaly. When any of these conditions exists a *disorder* is said to exist, defined only as a deviation from normal structure or function and not necessarily resulting in any inconvenience or loss of ability. If, however, the result of the disorder interferes with organ function, the condition would be classified as an *impairment;* but even this might not necessarily result in significant loss of ability to perform tasks—that is, the organ might not function, but the person still could. If the impairment results in a lack, loss, or reduction of a person's ability to perform certain tasks, the condition would be classified as a *disability,* with major emphasis placed on the person rather than on an organ of the body. Colenbrander further suggests that a disorder, an impairment, or a disability can directly become a *handicap* when the condition places the person at a perceived or actual disadvantage in respect to social expectations. Thus, one moves from medical conditions to structural limitation, to organ dysfunction, to personal dysfunction and, eventually, to psychosocial problems. A person with a *disorder* or an *impairment* may need medical treatment or no treatment at all; when a *disability* exists, the person may need not only medical treatment but also psychological help and educational training to overcome the inability to perform tasks which he or she previously could perform. Most significantly, when a *handicap* exists, one moves into a realm combining medical needs, psychological needs, and social expectations. The person with sufficient visual deficiency to prevent independent functioning as expected by the society in which he or she lives may be defined as functionally blind and will require services which, as much as possible, will increase ability to function, improve attitudinal well-being, and modify environmental and social expectations. The result of successful services should reduce the degree of dependency to realistic limits.

It is perhaps appropriate that we move from emphasis on the physical disability to psychological characteristics and problems of the blind, focusing on social, developmental, and psychological factors which contribute to the ability or inability to meet social expectations. Through understanding these mechanisms, we may more meaningfully approach the study of intervention techniques and procedures which might reduce a *handicap* to a *disability* or a *disability* to an *impairment*.

COMMON PSYCHOLOGICAL CHARACTERISTICS AND PROBLEMS

Parent–Child Interactions

The initial psychological impact relative to congenital or early blindness is on the family, particularly the parents when they first become aware of the fact that their child cannot—and possibly will never—see. Parents may react in a variety of ways which, in turn, may be picked up by the child. Parental reactions may include denial ("It can't be true!"), guilt ("What did I do to cause this to happen?"), withdrawal ("There's no use trying, my baby can't respond"), and depression ("I give up!").

Wills (1979b) states that it is extremely difficult for a new mother to "fall in love" with a blind baby, but he suggests that a meaningful and positive relationship between mother and baby can develop if the parents are given immediate and ongoing support and information.

Als, Tromick, and Brazelton (1980) specify that "with support, resourceful parents can from the beginning understand the distorted signals their infant displays as part of his grappling to realize normal developmental goals" (p. 22). Wills (1979b) stresses that the positive mother–child relationship which is necessary for growth and development is made possible and enhanced when the mother is furnished with information regarding what is *normal* behavior for a *blind* child.

Marcy (1975) describes a blind child who ceased to use old words or acquire new ones between 16 and 20 months of age, a period during which his mother was experiencing a severe depression because of her child's blindness. The child's language progressed again, however, when the mother received treatment for her depression. Als *et al.* (1980) studied the development of autonomy in a blind child and the relationship between this growing independence and parental reactions. They described the tendency of a father to interpret his baby's "stilling response" to auditory stimuli as unavailability and a lack of desire to respond. They also described the mother's depression and suddenly expressed concern about possible additional neurological damage to her baby when the baby went through a normal period of regression in learning prior to advancing to another developmental stage. But they also indicated that with continued help both mother and child recovered and progressed.

In spite of all of the emphasis on the importance of positive maternal attitudes, Cowen, Underberg, Verrillo, and Benham (1961), studying adjustment of adolescents to blindness, found little relationship between expressed attitudes regarding child-rearing and later positive adjustment to visual disability in adolescence. They did find, however, a strong relationship between maternal understanding (ability to predict accurately her child's response on a wide variety of variables) and adjustment of the child. This finding would certainly underscore the importance of "knowing" typical behavior at almost any stage of development. Such knowledge may permit greater interpersonal closeness and also a more realistic set of expectations.

Early Development and Learning

It is generally accepted that a child learns about his environment from his own perceptions and experiences. In the case of the congenitally blind, as with the congenitally deaf, one major avenue of communication is cut off, affecting both quantitatively and qualitatively the perception of the environment and the acquisition of coping methods.

Als *et al.* (1980) speak of affective reciprocity between a blind child and the caring parent which, when present, results in the development of autonomy. They suggest that the normal process of autonomy development in the blind child requires the consistent and persistent intervention of the mother, who teaches the child to go to the environment rather than waiting for the unknown environment to come to him. They suggest that five steps or stages of developmental learning can be posited. First is a period of *immobility,* with the body essentially in a closed-in posture, defined as a "stilling" reaction as the child attends auditorily to his world. Second is a period of *attentive stillness,* but with more openness and a gradually increasing expression of awareness of the environment by facial expressions. The authors point out that these two periods may be easily perceived by anxious parents as unavailability rather than attentive readiness. In confirmation of this observation, Burlingham (1979) describes blind babies as lacking or avoiding extensive muscular activity; this is a natural avoidance of danger but can be easily perceived as slow, clumsy, and awkward behavior. This perception may all too easily lead to the assumption of lack of inherent ability not only to respond but also to understand.

After these two initial stages which deal primarily with attention and initial response, Als *et al.* (1980) describe the child's third stage as *reciprocity,* primarily with the mother. Then the child can begin the fourth stage of *object manipulation and interaction with others,* with the mother serving as the introducer and intermediary. Finally, the fifth and final step of *infant-initiated interaction with people and objects* emerges. The main thrust of this developmental description is the importance of parental awareness of normal stages of growth in a blind baby and appropriate response to the blind child's messages of developmental readiness. The ideal attitude of this last stage is perhaps best summarized by the mother quoted as saying: "If I wait long enough and don't leap to her aid, she can generally find something—if it's anywhere in her reach" (p. 34).

"If it's anywhere in her reach" clearly points to the real limitations affecting the blind child's early learning. It is not surprising, therefore, to find, according to Reynell (1978), that while language development, largely dependent on auditory stimulation, may not be significantly delayed in blind babies, it takes a blind child at least a year longer to acquire concepts of concrete objects. In like manner, Sonksen (1979) stresses the importance of moving the child's hand *to* the object, rather than bringing the object to the child, in order to enhance self-initiated environmental interaction as well as the idea of object permanence.

The necessity of this intervention is again stressed by Fraiberg (1977), who points out that a five- to eight-month-old blind child's failure to reach for a toy removed from his grasp even if the toy is still making noise suggests that the object no longer exists for him when lost from physical contact. Fraiberg, Siegel, and Gibson (1966) and Fraiberg (1968) suggest that sound and tactile perceptions do not integrate and become characteristics of the same object until the infant is around 9 to 11 months old. Not until this integration of properties is accomplished will an infant reach on a sound cue alone. Fraiberg further states that blind children do not begin searching movements on their own until approximately 8 ½ months, as compared with the sighted baby, who begins the same activity at approximately 4 ½ months.

These conditions may help to explain why, according to Burlingham (1979), the blind child finds it extremely difficult to gauge space and distance; even with good training experience the blind child must rely in large measure on *past* experiences and *memory* of those experiences, without the added check of vision available to the sighted child. Millar (1979) also stresses that the blind child tends to use *previous* movement and self-reference in learning. Wills (1979a) puts it well in stressing that parental intervention is most important in order to teach the child to *act on* the environment.

The importance of parental intervention cannot be overstressed. The child's development of locomotion may be delayed until he or she has realized that objects and people continue to exist when physical contact is lost (Warren, 1977). It is not until the child begins to reach out and search for objects that a reason is established (moving about in the environment). The incentive to search for and locate a desired person or toy produces the first steps toward mobility. This is a critical time in the child's development as locomotion (creeping, crawling, walking) becomes the child's vehicle for development of the self as separate from the other. Self, objects, and other persons achieve separate identity, function, and place in relationship to space through exploration of the environment.

Fraiberg (1968) states that it is not blindness alone that "imperils development, but the absence of vision as an organizer of experience." For sighted children, vision facilitates gross motor developmental milestones leading the child to expanding environments experienced first hand. In both the blind and the sighted child, locomotion serves to expand knowledge of the existence of objects and people, but their mental representation differs with the absence or presence of sight.

Cratty (1971) posits that the blind child gains body image awareness if provided with the opportunity for direct contact with the bodies of other people. Tactual exploration, when appropriate, and comparison of his or her own body surface with those of family members teach relative size and shape. Cratty describes lack of vision and its relationship to spatial awareness as "the absence of efficient space organizers (the eyes)" and feels that it is unrealistic to expect a blind child to function in space if he has not learned about the "nature of the space he occupies, the manner in which he can move and the names given to his body and its parts" (p. 37).

Even when the blind child is taught to initiate his or her own environmental investigations, there are obvious limitations in learning because certain objects or experiences cannot be tactilely experienced. Even those which can, such as one's own body parts, may not be accurately perceived when there is no visual input. Kinsbourne and Lempert (1980) compared the abilities of congenitally blind and sighted children of 7 to 13 years of age to make human figures with plasticine. They found that sighted children, whether blindfolded or not, performed more accurately than the blind with respect to body parts. They conclude that tactile–kinesthetic information cannot take the place of visual experience in learning body awareness.

Development of Communication Skills

The foundation for communication is coexistent with the opportunity to acquire body image through physical contact with the mother during infancy. When the mother holds her child, communication by touch takes place. The infant hears mother's voice. The sighted infant sees the mother's face and her expressions but the child without sight is unable to form a visual conception of people and objects or to gain communicative information from facial expressions and body movement. Warren (1977) cites studies indicating that blind infants show less facial expression than sighted children and that adults blind from early childhood show decreased appropriate facial expression. According to Kastein, Spaulding, and Scharf (1980), the child is *not* attracted to people and objects unless guided and motivated to explore and experience through touch, sound, or taste.

As the child gains awareness of and familiarity with objects and people in the environment through touch, sound, and smell, the concepts required for recognition and discrimination develop. When the function of an object becomes evident, and the child knows of its existence and wants it even when it is out of reach, then the child has reached the stage at which he *needs* a name or label so he can *ask* for it—the beginning of language.

With increased experience beyond this point, the child will want to interact and communicate not only personal needs but a description of the objects' characteristics which can be *shared*. Now words are needed: they serve a purpose.

Although language development does not appear to be delayed by lack of sight, studies indicate differences in word meaning, association, and usage between blind and sighted children (Warren, 1977). The term *verbalism* is sometimes used to describe the language used by blind children and adults. Verbalism is defined by Cutsforth (1951) as the words used to describe situations not experienced. Content must be derived from the experience of others. Cutsforth (1951) states, "Socially and educationally, the blind are expected to appreciate things not as they themselves experience them, but as they are taught others experience them" (p. 51).

However, more recent studies cited by Warren (1977) indicate that "verbalisms" may have diminished since Cutsforth's study. The reduction is credited to changes in educational approach and the child's increased interaction with the environment.

As the child grows older, there is increased desire to be part of the peer group. Social interaction with a group may again involve, to a large extent, language that contains words which have little meaning in terms of actual experience. Burlingham (1965) refers to two sets of vocabulary used by blind children and adults, one based on actual experience and the other on "borrowed" experience.

Psychological and Behavioral Reactions to Blindness

Under ideal conditions of learning, a blind person's perception of the environment and his or her reactions to it will still be different from those of a sighted person, a difference of which the blind cannot help but be aware. Burlingham (1979) gives examples of statements made by blind children exemplifying their partially, or differently, perceived world and their feelings relative to their comparative limitations. Consider the implications of some of their statements: "How do you know my sock is down?" "You do it, you do it so much faster." "When the lights are put out, who will look after us?" "It's all dark in here—you know, cold and rainy." "It's the nicest school I ever heard." "If I had been more careful, this wouldn't have happened" (after walking off a platform). After lack of success in putting a puzzle together—"I can't walk; I can't see; I can't do nothing."

Burlingham (1979) suggests that most blind children are painfully aware of their differences and limitations in comparison with the sighted ("You can do it so much faster"). Because the world is aware of their limitations, it is prone to protect them from hurt, frequently reminding them by warnings to be careful. Burlingham suggests that this situation sets the stage for feelings of inadequacy and guilt ("If I had been more careful, this wouldn't have happened") which can lead to further withdrawal unless counterbalanced by successful attempts to perform with relative independence.

The independence–dependence conflict may be intensified in the blind child because many needs and desires are fulfilled only with assistance from a sighted person. The child learns from experience how dependent he or she must sometimes be, which can easily lead to unnecessary dependence. At times he expresses anger at how much he needs the sighted person. Part of the anger may result from the ongoing struggle to accomplish competency skills and self-reliance. Part may reflect the family's inability to help the blind child to develop independence while still helping him to realize appropriate times to seek assistance. The child must learn that opportunities to gain independence are enhanced by asking for and accepting help, information, and instruction: "I want to do it myself and I can if you'll show me how."

Burlingham (1965) observed that the blind child's effective orientation depended upon emotional equilibrium and "any unexpected happening, any increase of stress, excitement or anxiety can overthrow balance and result in complete lack of orientation" (p. 200). Self-orientation in the environment depends upon memory, concentration, and self-control. Stress situations interfere with concentration. The blind child learns early in life that what is easily accomplished by the sighted because of visual cues always requires more effort and concentration for him. The blind child needs to work harder than the sighted child to "master new and different experiences" (Burlingham, 1965).

Young sighted children are in continuous motion, running and jumping and content to stay in one place for only short periods of time before moving on to something else. Constant movement is a natural expression of energy and is required for acting on and learning about the environment. The young child naturally checks himself while running quickly to avoid tripping and getting hurt. Parents may, out of desire to protect from physical injury, overly restrict the young blind child's movement. The child's fear, produced by lack of successful experience or parental overprotectiveness, can result in the child's sitting quietly with head down on a table or engaging in rhythmical repetitive movement as an outlet for energy.

Sighted children deprived of free movement because of hospitalization or parental restriction develop similar movement patterns that include head rocking, swaying from one foot to another, or twisting. For the young blind child, the movement may provide pleasure and a sense of safety and security. Burlingham (1965) observed young blind children left on their own engaging in repetitive play such as opening and shutting doors, turning switches off and on, and filling and emptying containers. When offered a new toy, the blind child would tend to reject it unless individualized assistance and guidance were provided to demonstrate how the toy operated. Thus, repeated indulgence in repetitive behavior may prevent the child from learning new skills and concepts and will certainly serve to set him apart.

The blind child, and the blind adult to some degree, depending on several variables, are in a constant conflict between the desire for independence and the realistic need for dependence in certain situations. Burlingham (1961) notes that sighted children go through a phase in which they have an apparent need to receive assistance in doing things they are perfectly capable of doing independently. She observes that for the blind child this stage is "prolonged and enlarged."

It is logical to ask next what happens to these children, in terms of attitude and function, when they become adults. These authors are unaware of any longitudinal studies demonstrating any direct causal relationship between specific training of blind children and their adult behavior. However, one study (Joffe & Bast, 1978) examining personality characteristics of different categories of blind persons merits special attention. They studied congenitally totally blind, congenitally partially blind, and acquired totally blind persons. They divided those studied into (1) those who were employed compared with those who were unemployed and showed a history of unemployment and (2) those who showed a high mobility level as compared with those who showed a low mobility level. All were tested using the California Personality Inventory (Gough, 1957), an objective personality test usually administered by having the subjects read the items and respond by marking an answer sheet. In this instance, however, the items were presented by a recorded tape and the subjects were asked to respond by placing a card for each item as it was heard on the tape into either a *false* or *true* pile. Joffe and Bast reported few significant differences between those born with severe visual deficit and those who had acquired their visual deficiency later in life. It was noted, however, that those born with partial but significantly limited sight appeared to have experienced more situational press over time; essentially, the message which they had received was, "He can still see, he is not totally helpless, he can still work and travel" (p. 544). By contrast, those who had acquired total or partial blindness later in life appeared to have experienced less situational press and to have received a different message: "You are blind, helpless, not expected to. . . ." Those who received less situational press (i.e., were totally blind) appeared to be less aggressive and more dependent, while those receiving a message of greater environmental expectations (i.e., had partial sight) tended to divide into some who had fought back with renewed effort and some who had capitulated and surrendered to dependency and defensive strategies to explain their lack of accomplishment.

The most significant findings in the Joffe and Bast study related to the personality differences between those who were employed contrasted with those who were unemployed and not particularly mobile. Those who were employed and mobile showed personality profiles suggesting better ability to cope and less dependence on defense mechanisms; those with history of unemployment and low mobility showed personality characteristics suggesting poor ability to cope and greater dependence on defense mechanisms. More specifically, those with better employment records and better demonstrated mobility produced scores suggesting better ability to integrate material; better ability to articulate; less distractibility; more capability in making impartial, objective decisions; and less need to utilize pathological defense mechanisms of doubt, projection, regression, and rationalization.

Rehabilitation counselors for the blind describe the congenitally blind as having more difficulty in making abstractions about the route of travel while traveling. If an obstacle is in the path of travel or if a change from a familiar route becomes necessary, the congenitally blind person has more difficulty reorienting himself than does the acquired blind person, who retains the ability to perceive the environment based on visual terms and memory.

The above findings make several general conclusions possible: First, there may well be no single profile to describe personality characteristics of the blind; variations in reactions may be a result of the degree of visual loss, the point in life at which the loss occurred, early training experiences, basic characterological makeup, societal images and expectations, or other factors not yet fully known or understood. Second, personality tests may be useful in selecting those most ready to accept training and benefit from it (employability). Third, such tests may identify those who need treatment and suggest the nature of the treatment necessary before training or occupational placement can proceed.

Professionals working with the blind are in agreement about observable differences between partially sighted and totally blind individuals. A person with residual vision often suffers an identity problem—"Am I sighted or am I blind?" In some situations, the person can see well enough to function, and residual vision provides access to information and the ability to be independently mobile in situations where a totally blind person could not function. However, if one "passes for sighted," there is pressure to behave as one thinks a sighted person would. At times a partially sighted but legally blind person needs assistance to cross a street or read a bus destination, a street sign, or written directions on a package. Repeated negative reactions to one's requests for assistance can cause the partially sighted person to withdraw and to deny himself participation in experiences otherwise quite available to him.

The partially sighted person does not look blind, since he moves more freely and obviously uses vision to a degree. This may confuse the sighted and cause them to question the reality of the partially sighted person's visual limitations. Little public information is available about the partially sighted which may contribute to their identity struggle. Monroe (1978) indicates that the term *degree of impairment* is not clearly understood by the general public or the affected person. Some partially sighted adults and even, although less often, totally blind adults, make the effort to excel in activities engaged in by the sighted. Such overcompensation can result in an increased state of stress and tension.

Differences have also been observed between the congenitally blind and those with acquired blindness. The person who loses sight in late childhood or during adult years tends to retain a better sense of personal appearance, orientation in space, and interpersonal relations. However, the congenitally blind person may need special instruction about use of facial expressions, style of dress, and grooming in order not to be conspicuous. Spatial awareness and relativity are based almost entirely on experience. Without the benefit of sight to maintain and utilize a sense of orientation, continuous concentration to remember and sequence appropriately is necessary. This is also true for those who become blind, but to a lesser degree, since they may retain visual concepts and imagery.

It is difficult to imagine how one would react to suddenly being told that blindness was inevitable. From those who have experienced this situation, however, we may derive some clues about adjustment to blindness. Fitzgerald (1970) studied adults with recent loss of sight and found that shock, denial, anger, and depression were the most frequent reactions; of these, depression was the most common, occurring in 8 or 9 of every 10 adults studied.

Adjustment to blindness, or recovery from these reactions, is apparently a somewhat predictable phenomenon according to Greenough, Keegan, and Ash (1978) who found, using the Sixteen Personality Factor Questionnaire (Cattell, Eber, & Talsuokos, 1970), an objective personality test, that those who adjusted well to recent blindness showed minimal depression scores and high social independence, while those who adjusted poorly to their new handicap demonstrated high depression scores and low scores in social independence. Tendencies toward depression following loss of sight appear related to personality characteristics prior to blindness. Those who were assertive, aggressive, independent, and uninhibited suffered less depression than those who were by nature shy, conforming, conservative, humble, and obedient.

Lukoff and Whiteman (1972), approaching the problem more on an historical or case-study basis, found that those who lost their sight earlier in life were found to be more socially independent. The higher the level of prior educational attainment, the greater the problem of readjustment and adaptation. These findings suggest that the less one's life has become dependent on visual acuity prior to visual loss the less there is to overcome—all other things being equal, which, of course, they never are.

Ash, Keegan, and Greenough (1978) studied 114 blind adults to elicit those factors which contribute to good and poor adjustment. Their findings indicated that, while greater disturbance occurs at the onset of blindness, there is, in general, little relationship between psychological and social adjustment and length of time from onset of blindness. They also found that glaucoma patients had the poorest social adjustment, perhaps because of the presence of partial sight and the resultant continuing hope of regaining sight. Similarly, those with total blindness were found to adjust better than the partially blind who continued to try to function as if sighted, but failed. These findings underline the importance of the acceptance of real limitations.

Those who are blind may become victims not only of their own internal feelings but also of the treatment society gives them as blind people. Society and the significant others in the blind person's life play a dynamic role in the reactions and degrees of adjustment to loss of sight. Generally speaking, when people are asked to name the disability most feared, the most frequent response (next to death or cancer) is blindness.

Blind persons' perceptions of expectations of others and of their own self-concepts were studied by Mayadas and Duehn (1976). They found a significant correlation between the expectations of significant others and the role assumed by the blind patient. Carroll (1961) observes that previous beliefs and attitudes about being blind once held by the person carry over. On the positive side, Carroll reports that the public image of blindness as insurmountable and hopeless has gradually decreased and become more realistic, probably due to more accurate public information and the gradual integration of the blind into the mainstream of life.

Cholden (1958) describes one cultural stereotype of the "blind beggar," socially inferior and completely dependent on the kindness of the sighted person for financial assistance and care. This cultural set may make the giver feel good for what he or she has done for a less fortunate person but also, unfortunately, may reinforce the blind person's belief that such care is necessary. Monroe (1978) refers to families which "perpetuate and aggravate" negative and dependent behaviors. Carroll (1961) notes that some people seem to *need* to have another person dependent on them in order to gain or maintain feelings of power, strength, or security, or to alleviate guilt. Cholden further describes another cultural stereotype of the "blind genius," a person who has been able to overcome great odds, at great personal expense, and who therefore has almost magical powers.

Needham and Ehmer (1980), in an article describing irrational thinking related to the myths associated with blindness, discuss the belief of visually impaired persons that the degree of possible happiness and life satisfaction is related to the amount of residual vision. The implication of such a belief is that improvement of vision will bring proportionate gain in life satisfaction and the reverse, that loss of vision will decrease opportunity to experience enjoyment in life.

Well-intentioned but uninformed people express amazement when a blind person is able to perform ordinary everyday tasks. Many endorse the widely held belief that the blind have unusual perceptual skills. It is not uncommon for the sighted to assume extraordinary auditory and tactile powers in the blind.

It is generally accepted that vision is the most efficient means of acquiring and processing information and that when sight is absent there is a necessary reliance on the other senses—touch, hearing, smell. The newly blinded have lost their primary mode of providing confirmation for what is heard, felt, smelled, or tasted. According to Carroll (1961), the newly blinded, as with the congenitally blind infant, need to develop trust in the information provided by remaining avenues of information. Prior to blindness, vision was used to confirm and integrate the combinations of information simultaneously provided by the other senses. Loss of sight requires the person to reorient himself and learn over a period of time how to use new cues to gain and confirm information. However, nature does not compensate for loss of vision by providing extraordinary power, nor are the blind any more accurate than the sighted in the ability to make distinctions using auditory and tactile cues. A study reported by Cobb, Lawrence, and Nelson (1979) demonstrated that the blind do not have a greater ability than the sighted to identify new objects or sounds not previously experienced. Bernard (1979) found that blind adolescents are not significantly superior to their sighted peers in auditory reaction time.

Smithdas (1980), a man who is both deaf and blind, says that the question asked of him most often is, "If a person loses both sight and hearing, do you develop another sense to make up for them?" His responses confirm not only the devastating impact of the loss, but also the position that a person eventually learns to *concentrate* on his remaining senses to provide information. People with intact sight and hearing rarely develop to the fullest extent possible the sensitivity possible from touch, taste, or smell, nor do they develop to the degree possible kinesthetic awareness or muscle sense. Observation, concentration, and memory developed over a period of time serve to allow touch, smell, and taste to become provinces of information previously acquired through sight (Smithdas, 1980).

A myth sometimes perpetuated by education and rehabilitation is that the blind can become completely independent of sighted people. Accepting this myth too often results in feelings of failure and inadequacy when one is unable to function totally without help from the sighted (Needham & Ehmer, 1980). The blind individual needs to know that it is only reasonable to ask for assistance in some situations and that not to do so will result in placing limitations on experiences and could, over time, increase dependency. It may be reasonable to ask for directions when lost, to have the menu read in a restaurant, and to ask where the restroom is whether one is blind or sighted. The blind person must learn that seeking assistance does not necessarily decrease his adequacy nor his esteem in the eyes of others.

It may be difficult for the blind to accept how slowly most things change. It is difficult to sit patiently while the waitress asks your dinner partner in a louder than usual voice what *you* would like to order. According to Cutsforth (1951), the fear of being watched or being conspicuous not only causes annoyance but also contributes to fear and stress. Some blind persons use substitute behaviors to avoid public attention which may cause additional stress. For instance, to avoid undue attention, the blind person might risk pouring liquid into a glass to overflowing by relying on his memory of the time it usually takes or the sound made by a full glass instead of using the more certain method of placing his finger just inside the glass to indicate when the liquid has reached the top.

Carroll (1961) discusses the fears and concerns most often related by a newly blinded person. These are supported and confirmed by others who are blind or who are in frequent contact with the blind. Some of these fears are social isolation, financial insecurity (loss of job), immobility, dependence, fear of becoming physically injured, and the unknown. Initially, a newly blinded person may have difficulty making decisions because of uncertainty, may experience loss of sleep due to tension, and, if totally blind, may require time to reorient to day and night. A newly blinded person may also experience loss of physical vitality (feelings of tiredness) due to tension and reduction of the accustomed physical activity. When the new reaction and the processing of information in new ways become more habitual, the strain and subsequent fatigue will diminish.

The confused perceptions of blindness lead to the basic psychological problem for the blind—the battle between succumbing to complete dependence and the desire to achieve at an unrealistically high level. The problem is one of balance, of being able to accept the need for some dependence (as all humans must) while striving for reasonable independence. All the responsibility for resolution of this problem cannot be assigned to the blind person; the general public must also balance its actions between realistic support and realistic expectations if good adjustment is to occur.

Fitting (1954) also stresses the importance of balanced adjustment, which he defines as encompassing six areas: morale, attitude toward sighted people, outlook on blindness, family relationships, attitude toward training, and occupational outlook. According to Fitting, a well-adjusted blind person should be neither too optimistic nor too pessimistic, neither reject help nor become too dependent, consider blindness as neither inconsequential nor totally incapacitating, neither require special services from the family nor permit them to dominate him, neither reject training nor expect it to be a cure-all, and recognize that blindness does impose vocational limitations but does not "excuse" mediocre performance. At the least, this entails a phenomenal balancing act!

EVALUATING THE BLIND

Parental and Environmental Evaluation

So much depends on the interpersonal environment in which the blind child lives and grows that it would be an error not to start any evaluation process with consideration of the parents—their feelings, knowledge, and readiness to take on the difficult, but potentially rewarding, challenge of training a blind child.

We are unaware of any scale or procedure, constructed and standardized, which accurately measures parental attitudes and knowledge of the blind, specifically blind children. Yet, good counsel cannot be given parents unless such information is available. Probably the most efficient way of acquiring such information is by interview, utilizing content-structuring and proceeding in an open and flexible manner. The interview may also offer the most compassionate method of acquiring necessary information at a time when parents are vulnerable to shock and depression. The interviewer can offer understanding and support in a nonthreatening way. In fact, the initial exploratory interview should also constitute the beginning of a therapeutic relationship.

Two major areas of information need to be covered in the initial parent interview: first, what the parents already know—or perhaps falsely believe—about blindness as a physical and psychological disability, including limitations of both function and potential abilities; and second, prevailing feelings and attitudes which may reflect parental ability to provide the consistent, supportive, yet realistic training necessary for optimal development of their blind child or, conversely, those attitudes which might render good training impossible. It is important, in particular, to evaluate the attitudes of *both* parents. It has been our experience that when parents have very different beliefs about child-rearing, particularly what should be *expected* of a child, the child suffers, even without the burden of physical or sensory limitation. If one parent demands and the other protects, the child's training is inconsistent at best; such conflict of parenting attitudes may also make it too easy for the child to play one parent against the other, thus holding the power to cause parental disagreement. This the blind child, especially, cannot afford.

Once the initial interview is completed and a positive relationship has been established, personality and parent attitude scales may be administered to add supplemental and possible corroborative information to what has been learned from the interview. Such scales might include attitude measures such as the Osgood semantic differential scale (Osgood, 1957), described in Chapter 9, or published or self-constructed measures of attitudes about how children, in general, should be raised. One author uses a self-constructed measure in which each parent is asked to respond to a number of statements about child-rearing by agreeing or disagreeing; each parent is then asked to take the scale again, answering as he or she believes his or her spouse to have answered. This gives some measure of how much demand, protection, indulgence, or neglect each parent reflects and also of how far apart they are in belief and how accurately each perceives the other.

Frequently, the initial contact occurs long after the birth of the child. In such cases, one may assume that the initial state of shock is over and plunge more directly into behavioral questioning and administration of those personality scales or inventories which seem clinically most suitable. With increased age, and especially in the preschool years, it becomes increasingly important to evaluate actual parent–child interactions to determine the extent to which a parent may be demanding more than the child can do, may be capitulating to demands and doing things for the child which might be done without help, or may be setting up inappropriate contingencies by reinforcing undesirable behaviors (e.g., holding and comforting principally when the child cries). Norris, Spaulding, and Brodie (1957) suggest that these "qualitative observations" may often have more significance than responses to test items.

Actual parent–child observations may follow a prescribed format such as that developed by Mash, Terdal, and Anderson (1976) (see Chapter 9 for a description) or may be done on a naturalistic observation basis by observing interactions where and how they occur. In view of the previously reported data regarding the importance of fostering searching behavior in the blind child, one can examine, for example, the extent to which the parent brings the child to the object rather than the object to the child.

Evaluation of Development and Intelligence

Almost any measure of growth and development of blind children must, if it is to be individually accurate and meaningful, take into consideration the fact that absence of vision imposes a limitation on the immediate, as well as the predictive, applicability of norms. What is normal for blind children may not match what is normal for children with a full complement of senses. This results in discrepancies if one attempts to compare norms for the blind with norms for children without sensory deficit. For example, Reynell (1978) reports that, while blind babies appear not to be significantly delayed in language development in the first 8 to 10 months of life, it takes a blind child at least a year longer to acquire concepts of concrete objects. In like manner, Als *et al.* (1980) report that under almost ideal parent-training conditions, the blind infant they studied, while showing "appropriate or advanced" developmental activities in many areas, was not yet walking at 15 ½ months, the average for sighted children.

Cobb, Lawrence, and Nelson (1979) report that accuracy of memory for material presented by tactile and auditory stimulation is no better for the blind child than for the child with vision. Similarly, Liddle (1969) reports that the reaction time in response to auditory stimuli is no better for the blind than for the sighted. There is, however, agreement (Hill & Bliss, 1968) that the *amount* of tactile sensory information which can be retained by the blind is greater than for the sighted. On the other hand, Swanson (1979) generalizes that, while the visually handicapped may lag in cognitive skills, they go "through the same developmental sequence but at a slower rate" than sighted children do.

Kastein, Spaulding, and Scharf (1980) warn against too quickly attributing observed deviations in the development of a blind child to the lack of vision. Some of the symptoms that could indicate problems not due to blindness during infancy included "failure to smile back when talked to, excessive irritability, inability to adjust to changes in position, environment, or feeding, failure to respond and turn to sound or touch, failure to grasp . . . to roll over, sit up or pull to standing or walk at expected age, or to imitate simple activities . . . absence of vocalizing . . . excessive rocking, intolerance of cuddling" (p. 195).

There also appear to be discrepancies between different developmental scales for blind children, probably due to variations in sampling procedures. Two scales known to these authors purport to measure normal development of blind children. The Maxfield-Fjeld scale reported by Norris *et al.* (1957) gives a breakdown of blind developmental norms; Maxfield and Buchholz (1957) contribute the Social Maturity Scale for Blind Pre-School Children, following the model of the Vineland Social Maturity Scale (Doll, 1935) and standardized on blind children. This scale also gives developmental norms, but there is some disagreement between the two scales as to what is "normal" at a given time. These scales, therefore, probably should be considered only as screening devices until more generally agreed–upon and up-to-date norms are available.

As early as 1942, the Interim Hayes-Binet Intelligence Tests for the Blind (Hayes, 1942) were developed. These tests were an attempt to adapt Form L and Form M of the Stanford-Binet Intelligence Scales (Terman & Merrill, 1937) for use with blind children. The method of adaptation was to select those items from both forms which did not require vision, thus limiting items to auditorily presented questions. The so-called Hayes-Binet probably now should be considered only of historical significance because of its date of construction, especially since later revisions of Stanford-Binet scales have demonstrated change in age assignment of selected items. It appears that the preschool child of today is able to perform much better on the average, if judged by the 1937 revision from which Hayes selected items. The technique used by Hayes, however, may still be useful. These authors are still inclined to use, as one measuring instrument, the current Stanford-Binet Intelligence Scale, Form LM (Terman & Merrill, 1972), with blind preschool and primary children. At the risk of reducing accuracy by reducing the number of items, only those items which do not require vision are administered and scored. These are prorated to achieve a *blind* mental age. This, in turn, can be used to derive, using the current 1972 normative IQ tables, an estimate of intelligence which does not penalize for lack of sight.

The Perkins-Binet appears to be the most recent test which attempts to measure learning ability and which has been standardized on the legally blind population. There are two forms combining a blend of verbal and nonverbal Binet items: Form N for persons with no usable vision and Form U for those with usable vision (*The Lantern,* 1980).

Another approach developed by the author to measuring the intelligence of legally blind and partially sighted children has been to enlarge photographically the materials from the Leiter International Performance Scale (Leiter, 1969). Enlarged to 16 times their usual size (4" × 4"), the materials can be used effectively. Although this approach has its limitations and risks, it is particularly useful for children whose speech is not intelligible or who may have a significant hearing loss. It should be noted, however, that if a person is *both* deaf and blind, there are no normed or standardized tests known to us which permit measurement of intellectual ability; the only possible sense modality which might be utilized is tactual or kinesthetic. The sense of touch can sometimes be used (such as the ability to learn the pattern of an elevated wire maze), but only to acquire a clinical estimate of the ability to learn, or to eliminate a presumed erroneous label of retardation.

The Callier-Azuza Scale (Stillman, 1978) is a developmental scale often used to assess deaf and blind children who are functioning at low developmental levels. The child's developmental progress may also be evaluated if the same edition of the scale is repeated over time. The authors of the scale are careful to emphasize that it will most accurately reflect the child's level of development when used by persons having extended contact involving daily observation over a two-week period. The scales, intended to evaluate spontaneous behavior, contain age equivalencies from birth to six years.

A major problem in measuring intellectual ability of blind people is to avoid those instruments which present material visually. The various Wechsler Scales, the Wechsler Pre-school and Primary Scale of Intelligence (1967), the Wechsler Intelligence Scale for Children (1974), and the Wechsler Adult Intelligence Scale (1955) are often used. Their major advantage is that each scale separately measures verbal (nonvisual) intelligence and performance (visual) intelligence. Thus, for the blind, one may administer only the verbal materials and eliminate the performance tasks which would penalize and lower the IQ score of those who are blind.

Even though the verbal measures of intelligence of the Wechsler scales may be considered fair and valid reflections of the intellectual abilities of the blind without penalizing them for lack of visual acuity, there has been the temptation to try, in addition, to translate the performance section of the Wechsler scales into test material which can be used with the blind. Shurrager and Shurrager (1964) studied 399 subjects of varying visual skill, including the blind, and published the Haptic Intelligence Scale for Adult Blind. They indicated that there was no intention that the Haptic Intelligence Scale (HIS) used with the blind measure the same factors as the Wechsler Adult Intelligence Scale (WAIS) performance tests with the sighted. They also observed that it was reasonable to suppose that the two scales do assess the same abilities to some extent. This is most apparent when one notes, as reported by Jordan (1978), that the HIS has taken four subtests of the WAIS (Digit Symbol, Object Assembly, Block Design and Picture Arrangement) and modified them to tactual and kinesthetic presentation. Only Picture Arrangement was not copied, but two new tests were substituted—Pattern Board (copying peg board arrangements) and Bead Arithmetic (a modification of the abacus). Jordan believes that the Haptic test measures ability to use touch and kinesis without visual clues and may reveal how a subject has compensated for the loss of sight. Jordan concludes that the HIS might best be used in addition to standardized tests such as the WAIS, largely for clinical purposes such as reflection of learning styles and modes of coping with, or adjusting to, emotionally laden or stress-producing situations.

Because of all the points made about possible unfairness of quantified developmental and intellectual tests for the blind, questions have arisen as to whether such tests should be used in conjunction with natural observation or should be eliminated entirely. Diebold, Curtis, and DuBose (1978) compared the nature of data derived from developmental scales and from observation and concluded that, while there is some overlap, there is also sufficient difference to conclude that both approaches should be used. Bennett, Hughes, and Hughes (1979) confirm their findings and conclude that both quantified scales and behavioral observations are necessary in accomplishing a complete and comprehensive evaluation of exceptional children.

Evaluation of Personality

Measurement of personality characteristics, personality deviations, and psychological adjustment of the blind or partially blind is obviously limited to those procedures which are not dependent on vision. This immediately eliminates the usual projective personality tests such as the Rorschach technique (Rorschach, 1948), the Thematic Apperception Test (Murray, 1943), the Visual Motor Gestalt Test (Bender, 1946) or the Draw-a-Person Test (Machover, 1949). The latter test, however, might be utilized in modified form as adapted by Kinsbourne and Lempert (1980), who instructed their subjects to make a human figure using plasticine. One projective instrument which can easily be administered by reading is the Incomplete Sentences Blank (Rotter and Rafferty, 1950). For the most part, however, useful measures of personality characteristics of the blind are limited to those which can be presented auditorily.

There are three major ways of presenting these test materials: (1) by reading each test item to the subject, as done by Greenough, Keegan, and Ash (1978) using the 16PF Scale; (2) recording the items on tape as previously reported in the work of Joffe and Bast (1978), using the California Personality Inventory (Gough, 1957); or (3) administering the scale printed in Braille. Which approach is used will depend on personal choice, the skills of the subject, and available materials. For those who have learned Braille, there is a form of the Minnesota Multiphasic Personality Inventory (Cross, 1947).

One warning should be given regarding interpretation of personality scales which require the subject to respond to specific items: Some items will be inappropriate for the blind, for example, items such as: "I like movie love scenes," "The only interesting part of the newspaper is the 'funnies,' " or "In walking, I am very careful to step over sidewalk cracks." When the blind subject responds to such items as a blind person, the response may inappropriately contribute to an increased measure of a specific personality trait. Therefore, any scale should be screened to determine "false-blind" items in advance or, even more appropriately, any deviant personality measure should be examined to determine how many false-blind items contributed to the measure. This approach should enable correction of false high scores by eliminating those items which, in truth, were measuring the effect of blindness rather than personality deviation.

In preparation for occupational selection and training, one usually administers tests which measure degree of interest and similarity of interest patterns to successful practitioners in those occupations. These authors are not aware of special tests of interest which can easily be administered to the blind. The usual tests, such as the Kuder Preference Record (1960) and the Strong-Campbell Interest Inventory (Campbell, 1974), can be administered by reading the items to the subject, but only with considerable use of time. Care must be taken that the length and format of these scales do not confuse the subject, and more than one session may be necessary for administration in order to hold interest and effort. Even then, these instruments may need to be supplemented by history and open interview.

Bauman and Yoder (1966) refer to a "unifying formula," originated by J.R. Roberts, for the organization of information which globally describes strengths and weaknesses and which, if well used, should lead to responsible intervention. This formula specifies that adjustment to blindness is a function of the interplay of measured competency, internal and external stimulation, physical and environmental handicaps, and distracting emotions such as anxieties, conflicts, and irritations. This formula, while not capable of numerical solution, does pertinently stress the importance of viewing the blind from multiple perspectives and should ultimately be of use to the counselor planning a rehabilitation program for a blind client.

After careful and extended evaluation, including developmental history, background training experiences, current occupational and intellectual skills and interest, and personality characteristics, including coping skills as well as weaknesses, one should be ready to undertake the appropriate intervention procedures.

INTERVENTION METHODS

Positive intervention procedures with the blind appear to us to center on four different areas: (1) medical intervention to correct as much of the physical limitation as possible, (2) prophylactic training of the parents to eliminate unsalutary behavior patterns and inappropriate or inadequate coping mechanisms, (3) specific training of blind persons to realize as much of their potential as possible, and (4) application of corrective, rehabilitative, or psychotherapeutic procedures to the blind to modify those behaviors and attitudes which, if left uncorrected and untreated, would minimize productive and satisfying living.

Medical Intervention

Obviously the most rewarding medical intervention would be prevention rather than treatment. Vaughan and Asbury (1977) indicate that modest outlay of funds, assuming adequate distribution and political cooperation, could rather easily prevent much blindness in the world today. Remedies are known but are not being used. Vaughan and Asbury state that to cure one person of trachoma in Saudi Arabia would cost

$0.50, to restore vision to one person with cataracts in Pakistan would cost $10, and to prevent blindness due to xerophthalmia in one infant in Java would cost $0.12. Hereditary conditions causing blindness should decrease in incidence in response to increased knowledge and efforts of genetic counselors.

But, as we noted above, many of the causes of blindness in the Western world, especially those related to aging, will not so easily respond to preventive measures. In the absence of possible preventive procedures, one turns next to medical treatment of existing conditions. It is obvious that whatever medical or surgical treatment may be of value in improving vision should be made available. Vaughan and Asbury (1977) suggest the establishment and easy availability of low-vision aid clinics where, especially for the partially sighted, optical aids can be prescribed. Low-vision aids are capable of assisting people who might otherwise be blind to use their residual vision to perform many activities of daily living. Specially designed glasses and various types of magnifiers allow many legally blind persons to read print. Commercially available enlarging machines magnify anything placed under the lens of the machines and project the image onto a screen. Machines such as these open up employment opportunities and allow students to read print at home and in school instead of Braille.

Care must be taken not to assign greater medical importance to functional vision than can be defended. Mallison (1976) reports that only 3 of 96 patients with subnormal vision and learning problems who were referred for examination were found to have sufficient visual impairment to *cause* a learning disability. She stresses that learning to read, for example, is a *brain function* rather than an *eye function* and even with only minimal vision one can learn to read. Finally, she tackles the controversial subject of problems of fusion and depth perception, indicating that if these problems were truly crucial to learning to read, "no one-eyed or low-vision patient could learn to read—and they do."

Parent Training and Child Training

Emphasis on therapeutic intervention with parents of blind children is at once both therapeutic for the parents and prophylactic or preventive for children. The work of Wills (1979), Sonksen (1979), Curson (1979), Marcy (1975), Burlingham (1979), and others have stressed the importance of developing an ongoing positive relationship between a mother and her blind child—as important for one as for the other. A mother cannot adequately train her child if she is puzzled, shocked, and possibly depressed. She needs help to free her from binding and uncomfortable feelings. The question is, "What kind of help?"

Vaughan and Asbury (1977) stress the importance of giving parents the information they need and want even though they may fear asking for it directly. They further point out the fallacy of offering false hopes if blindness is inevitable, but they also warn that the news should be broken to the parents in an atmosphere of "warmth, understanding, encouragement and assistance." This usually cannot be accomplished in one meeting, and therefore it becomes important for the professional to take the responsibility for maintaining contact by arranging for at least a second appointment. The professional should remain particularly alert to severe depressive reactions. Additional support can come from those who have successfully gone through the experience of having a blind baby. Somehow the same words which the professional might use seem to have more validity if they come from someone who has had the actual experience. An additional supportive step can come from referral to parent groups or to organizations such as the American Foundation for the Blind, where much useful information can be found.

Warmth and supportive understanding will not be enough unless backed by specific help in training the blind child. If such help is already available through existing agency resources within a community, referral to that agency may be sufficient to engage an ongoing training program for the parent. If such help is not available, it can be created by pulling together professional resources in the community, including psychologists, educators, and social workers. The curriculum for parents should include knowledge regarding normal blind behavior and development, establishing communication with the blind baby, involving the child with his environment, shaping desired behaviors and extinguishing undesirable ones, and initiating and developing the use of the other senses as substitutes for vision.

Training the Blind Person

Training the blind covers a broad age span and variety of functions. Although early home training has been effective, a blind child may continue to need special educational services, and a blind person, whether child or adult, will need additional help to acquire orientation and mobility skills, to learn Braille or other adaptive systems for reading, typing, and writing, and to acquire other skills for daily living, according to interests and eventual vocational choice.

Training children from birth through age 21 is the major responsibility of the educational system, backed by state and federally supported programs which can furnish additional adaptive teaching materials equipment, other resources for those whose vision is minimal, and special schools for the blind. While in the past the blind typically were placed in special schools, usually operated by the state, the trend has developed during the past two decades to mainstream these children into regular schools so that the child need not be deprived of all contact with sighted persons of his own age. This approach retains the opportunity to grow up at home, benefit from family living, and be part of the neighborhood and community. Thus, the special programs and resource materials are brought to the blind student in his own regular school or resource rooms rather than necessarily sending him to a residential school for the blind. In some instances, more complete services may be made available only by utilizing residential training.

Burlingham (1979) stresses the importance of assimilation into sighted programs rather than segregation, especially during adolescence. She cites case studies showing improved attitude and motivation when the blind adolescent can join sighted adolescents; as one blind teenager put it, "I am a changed person; I am happy; I have friends, sighted friends" (p. 29). However, additional training beyond that provided in the regular school is required for developing home living skills, grooming, and at times physical education. Summer school and after-school sessions may be necessary for the blind student to acquire adequate competencies to maintain his own home by adulthood.

Simon and Gillman (1979) offer a word of warning regarding mainstreaming young blind children in regular classrooms. They observed blind preschool children placed in a regular classroom and reported a general lack of acceptance of the blind children, shown by exclusion from games, infantilizing, and taunting. There was evidence of increased anxiety on the part of both students and staff, which appeared to worsen during the year. The authors stress the importance of careful preparation of the staff prior to integration. Special education teachers for the visually handicapped can reduce staff anxiety by working closely with the school, the teacher, the family, and the child prior to placement in school. This holds true for a child of any age who will be attending a regular public school.

Anyone working with the blind should learn what educational resources are available, should establish contact, and should maintain a working relationship with those support resources and specialized programs in order to increase the opportunity for successful adjustment and total development to continue. A team effort could help the blind child and the family avoid unsuccessful educational experiences.

Mobility training is a crucial training need for those whose degree of visual loss prohibits them from moving about with freedom and safety within their home and community. Many state commissions offer a variety of programs for providing mobility and independent living training to blind adults, with curricula usually centering on self-care, skills of daily living, and mobility within the community, including to and from the job and school.

When the sighted public visualizes the method of mobility of a blind person, images come to mind of a tapping white cane, or a seeing-eye dog and perhaps a sighted guide. The proficient and well-taught cane traveler has learned to use his cane in a regular side-to-side sweeping pattern which need not result in the tapping sound so often associated with cane travel. Use of a sighted guide is the least conspicuous form of mobility, and the wise blind person will inform the guide about appropriate sighted-guide techniques.

Actually, only about 2% of blind people in the United States use guide dogs (Vaughan & Asbury, 1977), and it is quite possible that functional use of this method of mobility has been exaggerated in the general public's mind because of admiration for the animal. There are some realistic limitations which argue against rapid expansion of this approach to mobility: first, the dog does not think and does not make decisions in a strange world but must rely on familiarity with the environment and competence of his blind master to plan and give appropriate commands; second, the dog may be difficult for older people to control physically; third, the cost and availability may be limiting factors. Guide dogs have been found to be most useful for students and professional people in good health and for those who lead well organized lives.

In view of the limitations of guide dogs, one may well ask, "Does this mean that a blind person must rely on a cane?" The answer is both yes and no—yes in that a cane may still be useful but no in terms of the usual cane. Vaughan and Asbury (1977) state that a cane using a sonar electronic system may ultimately be the best answer; others question this conclusion.

Braille has been historically perceived as the major means of communication for the blind, both for reading and writing. There is no doubt that this method of reading has been remarkably effective. A blind child who has mastered reading readiness concepts and skills can usually learn to read Braille easily and, in fact, usually learns the system much more quickly than the newly blind adult; good readers can read Braille as fast as they can talk, but below the speed of visual reading. A good Braille reader can read about 150 to 200 words a minute, while the speed of visual readers is two or three times that (Lowenfeld, 1971). But even this efficient system with its long history (it was originally developed in 1825) may be doomed to gradually less use with the development of electronic devices which permit the blind to "read" by listening to an increasingly greater number of talking books and the advent of an electronic device which directly converts visual printed letters into tactile forms which, with little additional electronic development, may be converted into audible sounds.

Sighted people in the blind person's environment have responsibilities to assist the blind to function with optimum independence. It is a source of annoyance and frustration and a reminder of blindness to have to ask continually where things are or to bump into furniture. The sighted person should inform the blind person when furniture has been moved, clothes shifted in drawers and closets, and food items rearranged in the cupboard or refrigerator. It is helpful to inform the blind person about current clothing and hair styles as well as pleasing color combinations flattering to the person. It is courteous for the sighted to state his name when talking to a blind person and to inform him or her when leaving the room.

Those working directly with rehabilitation and education of the blind should be aware of the International Catalog issued by the American Foundation for the Blind (see Appendix) containing over 200 pages of descriptions of electronic devices available to the blind, including enlargers, talking calculators, printed material converters, and many others which can be used for either occupational or recreational purposes.

The blind person may help in his own readjustment by an increasing awareness of how his blindness affects the sighted and by helping make the sighted person more comfortable. For example, when assistance is offered, the blind person should tell the person *how* to provide it. A blind person who develops many interests and acquires general information about current events, sports, the weather, and other subjects of common interest will, through easy conversation, put the sighted at ease and help establish normal relationships. Each blind individual can contribute to the collective well-being of the blind in general by creating a good image. Grooming and appearance, courteous behavior, and pleasant bearing increase the likelihood of a positive image. To behave otherwise thwarts opportunities and reduces the effect provided by the well adjusted.

Rehabilitative and Therapeutic Intervention

The type and extent of rehabilitation of blind individuals will vary markedly according to age of onset, among other factors. Those who are born blind must have available to them a long period of training to *habilitate* them a world of sight which they have never experienced. Those who become blind in late childhood or early adulthood require different services to *rehabilitate* them to compensate for loss of familiar methods of environmental coping and to learn how to deal with a different world without visual cues. Such persons may well need a gamut of services, including educational assessment, vocational and career planning, and psychological counseling. Those who lose their sight late in life may need only mobility and home living training, access to talking books, and help in sustaining social interaction with others.

Those who are born blind, although their habilitation is highly dependent on skill training, do still normally require some psychological help. Care must be taken to avoid loading demands and expectations beyond what can reasonably be assimilated and, at the same time, to persist in requiring acquisition of new skills. Even with appropriate training, blind children must experience some confusion about their disability and their place among their sighted peers. Curson (1979) stresses the importance of talking about blindness, beginning in preschool and kindergarten years, to expose and clarify confused expectations.

Those who have lost vision may require much more psychological intervention. They are particularly vulnerable to depressed feelings which can be dealt with through supportive counseling. This does more than allow release of feelings and offer sympathy to the patient; it also offers a sound reality-based proving ground for current conduct and conflicts as well as a planning forum for future actions.

Cholden (1958) stresses the importance of recognizing and accepting any depression prior to attempts to rehabilitate. He cites the example of a blind patient who had come to grips with her blindness and the resultant feeling of depression only to regress when "comforted" by a well meaning professional who hinted, in an effort to "brace the patient up," that there was a strong possibility that vision might return. This well-meant effort only confused the patient and caused her to go through another period of depression before proceeding with her rehabilitation. Thus, two of the most important contributions the professional can give to the newly blind person are (1) permission and acceptance of the need to grieve and be depressed and (2) firmness in stating the realities of the blindness.

The authors of this chapter strongly support a therapeutic approach which begins with cathartic feeling release and acceptance of those feelings as typical but temporary reactions and expands to practical discussion of what *can* be done. Vocational or career planning offers an excellent example. One cannot forever persist in talking about negative feelings if one wishes to progress, for to do so only reinforces their importance. One must consider the remaining available skills and how they might or might not fit with previous vocational plans or vocational accomplishments. Therapeutic interviews must eventually examine the strengths and weaknesses of suggested solutions.

Monroe (1978) believes that limitations to adjustment result from the blind person's not knowing *how* to adapt to new and different situations and his unfamiliarity with resources or equipment, including how to obtain them and how to use them. Thus, giving specific and practical information serves an important function during the therapeutic process and creates knowledge about the range of possibilities. Most states have vocational rehabilitation agencies with rehabilitation teachers and counselors on the staff who can provide such training and information.

A therapeutic tool which these authors believe may be useful is the Interpersonal Cognitive Problem Solving approach (Spivak, Platt, & Shure, 1976), which stresses the importance of having the client think of as many behavioral reactions as possible which might be used to solve conflict situations on the premise that the greater the number of solutions generated, the greater the possibility that the client will use *some* which bring positive results. Thus, the counselor serves a multiple function: an understanding listener, a facilitator of ideas, and a reality-based but supportive sounding board for the development of constructive behavior which will lead not only to productive results but to personal satisfaction and an improved self-image.

Needham and Ehmer (1980) emphasize that it is almost as important for a therapist to know about blindness as it is for him to know about psychological functioning. Our society holds many myths about blindness, and therapeutic assistance will be less effective if the therapist holds to these myths. It is important to know not only about existing techniques and equipment but also about their limitations. The counselor must be cognizant of actual possibilities for daily living and employment and must transmit this information to the client.

There are currently some blind psychologists who, with this unique background (life experience as well as training) may be especially valuable in habilitating and rehabilitating other blind people. These professionals not only should bring a wealth of background experience to the problem but also should meet acceptance by the blind person as "one who knows, who has experienced what I am experiencing."

Perhaps the best summary of the traumatic reaction to loss of vision and, with appropriate intervention, its possible outcome is expressed by Sorsby (1972): "If it is true that no one has ever become blind without crying—need the tears be as bitter as they are?"

TRENDS AND NEEDS

Although trends in resources for the blind are somewhat consistent with resource needs expressed by the adult blind, there is some variance in the priority of needs between blind clients and vocational rehabilitation agencies. Delaney and Nuttal (1978) surveyed 1,050 blind adults regarding their perceived needs. The most frequent need expressed by the blind was for equipment specifically designed for the blind; agency professionals, on the other hand, rated vocational services as the greatest need. Blind clients, it appeared, placed more emphasis on meeting practical and basic needs. One cannot argue that either group is correct while the other is not, but one can emphasize the importance of not overlooking needs expressed by those who are experiencing the need.

Probably the most positive of the trends, other than prevention, is the development of electronic devices which may open new vistas for the blind, and the current emphasis on normalizing or mainstreaming the handicapped into as full a membership as possible in the sighted world. These positive trends do not, however, come without problems. Availability and cost are still deterring factors against wide usage of the new electronic devices; and, while mainstreaming the handicapped is, without doubt, a worthy aim and one with which few people quarrel in principle, it is one for which our communities may not be well prepared. There still lurks the stereotyped image of the blind person as one who cannot share the world of the sighted, who requires special and separate training, and who does not "belong in my normal class." Much education of the general public remains to be done.

APPENDIX: SOURCES OF INFORMATION

American Association of Workers
for the Blind, Inc.
1511 K Street, N.W.
Washington, DC 20005

Membership organization that operates a job exchange and reference information center and certifies habilitation teachers and orientation and mobility specialists.

American Foundation for the Blind
15 West 16 Street
New York, NY 10011

National clearing house for information about blindness and publisher of *Directory of Agencies Serving the Visually Handicapped in the United States*.

American Printing House for the Blind
P.O. Box 6085
Louisville, KY 40206

Develops and provides textbooks and educational aids; publishes Braille books, music, and magazines; conducts research in educational procedures.

Association for the Education of
the Visually Handicapped
919 Walnut Street, 4th Floor
Philadelphia, PA 19107

Professional organization for educators; publishes books, periodicals, bibliographies.

Better Vision Institute
230 Park Avenue
New York, NY 10017

List of available large-print material.

Library of Congress
Division for the Blind and
Physically Handicapped
1291 Taylor Street, N.W.
Washington, DC 20542

Provides free reading material, tapes, Braille, and talking book machines; conducts national correspondence course to train Braille transcribers.

National Retinitis Pigmentosa Foundation
Rawling Park Building
8391 Wandull Circle
Baltimore, MD 21207

A research, information, and advocacy organization.

National Society for the Prevention of Blindness
16 East 40 Street
New York, NY 10016

Publisher of *Directory of Low Vision Clinics*, Sloan's *Recommended Aids for the Partially Sighted*, catalogue of publications.

The Lighthouse
New York Association for the Blind
111 East 59 Street
New York, NY 10022

Publisher of *Catalog of Opitcal Aids,* books, films, nonoptical aids, referral services.
Rehabilitation Services Administration Office for
the Blind and
Visually Handicapped
330 C Street, S.W.
Washington, DC 20201
Develops methods, standards, and procedures to assist state agencies in the rehabilitation of blind persons.

REFERENCES

Als, H., Tromick, E., & Brazelton, T. B. Affective reciprocity and the development of autonomy: The study of a blind infant. *Journal of the American Academy of Child Psychiatry,* 1980, *19,* 22–40.

Ash, D. D., Keegan, D. L., & Greenough, T. Factors in adjustment to blindness. *Canadian Journal of Ophthalmology,* 1978, *13,* 15–21.

Bauman, M. K., & Yoder, N. M. *Adjustment to blindness—Re-viewed.* Springfield, Ill.: Charles C Thomas, 1966.

Bender, L. *Visual motor gestalt test.* New York: American Orthopsychiatric Association, 1946.

Bennett, F., Hughes, A., & Hughes, H. Assessment techniques for deaf-blind children. *Exceptional Children,* 1979, *45,* 287–289.

Bernard, John. Simple auditory reaction time in blind and sighted adolescents. *Perceptual and Motor Skills,* 1979, *48,* 465–466.

Burlingham, D. Some notes on the development of the blind. *The Psychoanalytic Study of the Child,* 1961, *16,* 121–145.

Burlingham, D. Some problems of ego development in blind children. *The Psychoanalytic Study of the Child,* 1965, *20,* 194–208.

Burlingham, D. To be blind in a sighted world. *The Psychoanalytic Study of the Child,* 1979, *34,* 5–30.

Campbell, D. P. *Manual for the Strong-Campbell Interest Inventory.* Palo Alto: Stanford University Press, 1974.

Carroll, T. J. *Blindness: What is is, what it does, and how to live with it.* Boston: Little, Brown, 1961.

Cattell, R. B., Eber, H. J., & Talsuokos, M. *The sixteen personality factor questionnaire* (3rd ed.). Champaign, Ill.: Institute for Personality and Ability Testing, 1970.

Cholden, L. S. *A psychiatrist works with blindness.* New York: American Foundation for the Blind, 1958.

Cobb, N. J., Lawrence, D. M., & Nelson, N. D. Report on blind subjects' tactile and auditory recognition for environmental stimuli. *Perception and Motor Skills,* 1979, *48,* 363–366.

Colenbrander, A. Low vision: Definition and classification. In E. E. Faye (Ed.), *Clinical low vision.* Boston: Little, Brown, 1976.

Coughlin, W. R., & Patz, A. Diabetic retinopathy: Nature and extent. *Journal of Vision Impairment and Blindness,* 1978, *72*(8), 343–347.

Cowen, E. L., Underberg, R. P., Verrillo, R. F., & Benham, F. G. *Adjustment to visual disability in adolescence.* New York: American Foundation for the Blind, 1961.

Cratty, B. T. *Movement and spatial awareness in blind children and youth.* Springfield, Ill.: Charles C Thomas, 1971.
Cross, O. H. Braille edition of the Minnesota Multiphasic Personality Inventory for use with the blind. *Journal of Applied Psychology,* 1947, *31,* 189–198.
Curson, A. The blind nursery school child. *The Psychoanalytic Study of the Child,* 1979, *34,* 51–83.
Cutsforth, T. D. *The blind in school and society.* New York: American Foundation for the Blind, 1951.
Delaney, A. M., & Nuttal, R. L. Assessing the needs of a blind client population. *Journal of Visual Impairment and Blindness,* 1978, *72*(2), 46–54.
Diebold, M. H., Curtis, W. S., & DuBose, R. F. Developmental scales versus observational measures for deaf-blind children. *Exceptional Children,* 1978, *44,* 275–278.
Doll, E. A. *The Vineland social maturity scale—Manual of directions.* Vineland, N.J.: The Training School, 1935.
Fitting, E. A. *Evaluation of adjustment to blindness.* New York: American Foundation for the Blind, 1954.
Fitzgerald, R. G. Reactions to blindness: An exploratory study of adults with recent loss of sight. *Archives of General Psychiatry,* 1970, *20,* 370–379.
Fraiberg, S. Parallel and divergent patterns in blind and sighted infants. *The Psychoanalytic Study of the Child,* 1968, *23,* 264–300.
Fraiberg, S. *Insights from the blind.* London: Souvenir Press, 1977.
Fraiberg, S., Siegel, B. L., & Gibson, R. The role of sound in the speech behavior of a blind infant. *The Psychoanalytic Study of the Child,* 1966, *21,* 327–357.
Gardiner, P. A. *ABC of ophthalmology.* London: British Medical Journal, 1979.
Gough, H. G. *California personality inventory.* Los Angeles: Western Psychological Services, 1957.
Greenough, T. J., Keegan, D. L., & Ash, D. G. Psychological and social adjustment of blind subjects and the 16PF. *Journal of Clinical Psychology,* 1978, *34,* 84–87.
Hayes, S. P. *Interim Hayes-Binet intelligence tests for the blind, 1942.* Watertown, Mass.: Perkins School for the Blind, 1942.
Hill, J. W., & Bliss, J. C. Modeling a tactile sensory register. *Perception and Psychophysics,* 1968, *4,* 91–101.
Joffe, P. E., & Bast, B. A. Coping and defense in relation to accommodation among a sample of blind men. *The Journal of Nervous and Mental Disease,* 1978, *166,* 537–552.
Jordon, S. Some clinical interpretations of the Haptic Intelligence Scale for Adult Blind. *Perceptual and Motor Skills,* 1978, *47,* 213–222.
Kastein, S., Spaulding, I., & Scharf, *Raising the young blind child.* New York: Human Sciences Press, 1980.
Kinsbourne, M., & Lempert, H. Human figure representation by blind children. *The Journal of General Psychology,* 1980, *102,* 33–37.
Kuder, G. *Kuder preference record—Form C.* Chicago: Science Research Associates, 1960.
The Lantern. Watertown, Mass.: Perkins School for the Blind, Fall, 1980.
Leiter, R. *Examiner's manual for the Leiter international performance scale.* Chicago: C. H. Stoelting, 1969.
Liddle, D. The effects of signal strength on reaction time to auditory signals in noise. *American Foundation for the Blind Research Bulletin,* 1969, *19,* 129–190.
Lowenfeld, B. *Our blind children: Growing and learning with them.* Springfield, Ill.: Charles C Thomas, 1971.

Lukoff, I., & Whiteman, M. *Social sources of adjustment to blindness* (Research Series 21). New York: American Foundation for the Blind, 1972.
Machover, K. *Personality projection in the drawing of the human figure: A method of personality investigation.* Springfield, Ill.: Charles C Thomas, 1949.
Mallison, R. Learning problems in the child with low vision. In E. E. Faye (Ed.), *Clinical low vision.* Boston: Little, Brown, 1976.
Marcy, T. G. Sensory and perceptual dysfunctioning in early childhood. Read at Symposium on Guidance Program to Maximize Sensorimotor Development of Blind Infants. University of Southern California, 1975.
Mash, E., Terdal, L., & Anderson, K. The response class matrix: A procedure for recording parent-child interactions. In E. J. Mash & L. G. Terdal (Eds.), *Behavior Therapy Assessment.* New York: Springer Publishing Company, 1976.
Maxfield, K. E., & Buchholz, S. *A social maturity scale for blind children.* New York: American Foundation for the Blind, 1957.
Mayadas, N. S., & Duehn, W. D. The impact of significant adults' expectations on the life style of visually impaired children. *The New Outlook for the Blind,* 1976, *70*(7), 286–290.
Millar, S. The utilization of external and movement clues in simple spatial tasks by the blind and sighted children. *Perception,* 1979, *8,* 11–20.
Monroe, C. H., Jr. Adjustment services for the blind. *Journal of Rehabilitation,* 1978, *44*(1), 30–34.
Murray, H. *Manual for the thematic apperception test.* Cambridge: Harvard University Press, 1943.
Needham, W. E., & Ehmer, M. N. Irrational thinking and adjustment to loss of vision. *Journal of Vision Impairments and Blindness,* 1980, *74*(2), 57–61.
Norris, M., Spaulding, P., & Brodie, F. *Blindness in children.* Chicago: University of Chicago Press, 1957.
Osgood, C. E., Suci, G. J., & Tannenbaum, P H. *The measurement of meaning.* Urbana, Ill.: University of Illinois Press, 1957.
Reynell, J. K. Developmental patterns of visually handicapped children. *Child: Care, Health and Development,* 1978, *4,* 291–303.
Rorschach, H. *Rorschach psychodiagnostics.* New York: Grune & Stratton, 1948.
Rotter, J., & Rafferty, J. E. *Manual for the Rotter incomplete sentences blank.* New York: The Psychological Corporation, 1950.
Shurrager, H. C., & Shurrager, P. S. *Manual for the Haptic intelligence scale for adult blind.* Chicago: Psychology Research, 1964.
Simon, E. R., & Gillman, A. E. Mainstreaming visually handicapped preschoolers. *Exceptional Children,* 1979, *45,* 463–464.
Smithdas, R. T. Sense about sensitivity. *Nat-Cent News,* July, 1980, *10,* 4.
Sonksen, P. M. Sound and the visually handicapped baby. *Child: Care, Health and Development,* 1979, *5,* 413–420.
Sorsby, A. *The incidence and causes of blindness in England and Wales 1963-68.* London: Her Majesty's Stationery Office, 1972.
Spivak, G., Platt, J. J., & Shure, M. B. *The problem solving approach to adjustment.* San Francisco: Jossey-Bass, 1976.
Stillman, R. (Ed.). *The Callier-Azuza Scale (G).* Dallas: Callier Center for Communication Disorders, 1978.
Swanson, L. Partially sighted children's conservation development. *Journal of Genetic Psychology,* 1979, *135,* 153–154.

Terman, L., & Merrill, M. *Measuring intelligence.* Boston: Houghton Mifflin, 1937.
Terman, L., & Merrill, M. *Stanford-Binet intelligence scale—Form LM.* Boston: Houghton Mifflin, 1972.
Vaughan, D., & Asbury, T. *General ophthalmology.* Los Altos, Calif.: Lange Medical Publications, 1977.
Vision Problems in the U.S.: Highlights, Facts & Figures. National Society to Prevent Blindness, 1980.
Warren, D. H. *Blindness and early childhood development.* New York: American Foundation for the Blind, 1977.
Wechsler, D. *Wechsler adult intelligence scale.* New York: The Psychological Corporation, 1955.
Wechsler, D. *Wechsler intelligence scale for children—Revised.* New York: The Psychological Corporation, 1974.
Wechsler, D. *Wechsler pre-school and primary scale of intelligence.* New York: The Psychological Corporation, 1967.
Wills, D. M. Early speech development in blind children. *The Psychoanalytic Study of the Child,* 1979, *34,* 85–117(a).
Wills, D. M. "The ordinary devoted mother" and her blind baby. *The Psychoanalytic Study of the Child,* 1979, *34,* 31–49(b).

14

Hearing Disorders

ROBERT D. BOYD AND
NORTON B. YOUNG

THE PHYSICAL DISABILITY

Definition and Incidence

Hearing loss which affects the quality of life is a concomitant of our industrialized society and its increasing urban noise. Nearly every individual beyond late childhood will develop increasing hearing loss for high frequencies to the point of handicap by middle or old age. This is the norm for our industrialized society and does not take into consideration those individuals who either are born with hearing impairment or develop hearing loss due to disease or injury. It may be said that the incidence of hearing impairment is essentially 100% for our society when one includes the effect of aging and environment on the hearing function coupled with the effect of increased life span.

Because hearing disorders are not medically reportable conditions, their incidence can only be estimated. Approximately 20 million people in the United States are thought to have some degree of hearing loss, according to Chalfant and Scheffelin (1969). Binnie (1976) reports that approximately 8.5 million persons in the United States seek medical attention for hearing loss; 3 million of these people have major hearing defects, and about 250,000 deaf persons are unable to detect even loud speech.

Probably more important than incidence estimates is the economic impact of hearing loss on our society and on the individual. The Department of Health, Education and Welfare (Carhart, 1967–68) estimates the cost of coping with hearing disorders, which includes special public and private schools, preparation of special teachers, vocational rehabilitation, compensation for disability, audiological services for veterans, hearing aids and their maintenance, and many other direct and indirect services, at $410,445,000 *per year!* Shein and Delk (1974) highlight the economic impact on the educationally deaf individual by comparing the average income of the deaf ($5,915) with that of the normal hearing population ($8,188). While not all of the difference is necessarily due to deafness alone, one cannot overlook the $2,273 per year lesser income for the deaf. Northern and Downs (1978) multiply this by the estimated number of deaf in the U.S. and calculate the loss to be *$4 billion per year* to society.

Hearing impairment is often classified into *hard of hearing* (those in whom the sense of hearing, although defective, is functional with or without a hearing aid) and *deaf* (those in whom the sense of hearing is nonfunctional for ordinary purposes of life). The deaf are separated into pre- and postlingually deaf. The dichotomy of *hard of hearing* and *deaf*, as defined, is both misleading and a gross oversimplification of the problem.

The impact of hearing loss which affects learning, communication, and social and vocational functioning is tied to a number of variables which may have differential effects. Some of the most important variables, although certainly not all, are as follows: (1) The severity of the hearing loss in decibel level. Table I details the handicapping effect of hearing loss by decibel range. (2) The age at the time of the loss and the age of diagnosis. In general, the earlier in a child's life a permanent hearing loss is acquired, the greater the delay in communication skills and the greater the barriers to learning. Even mild hearing loss can cause significant delay in speech and language development, particularly if it is not discovered in the first year of life and treated by early training and the use of hearing aids. (3) The audiometric frequency loss pattern. Hearing losses involving the high frequencies of 1,000–4,000 result in low speech discrimination ability even with properly selected hearing aids. Losses which are approximately equal at each audiometric frequency benefit most by amplification with hearing aids. (4) Accompanying vision problem. Speech reception for the hearing-impaired is improved by good vision, which allows for the development of speech (lip) reading. Poor vision, especially in the elderly, increases the hearing handicap. (5) The course of the loss. A stable hearing loss allows for better adjustment to the handicap than either a gradually progressive or fluctuating hearing level. (6) The presence of a central auditory processing problem or organic language problems accompanying a peripheral hearing loss. Acquired brain injury or faulty central nervous system development, when coupled with a hearing sensitivity problem, can be improved with hearing aids.

While not representing *physical* variables, the following highly important additional factors must not be overlooked: (1) Family socioeconomic levels, attitudes, and parenting skills. These factors, when negative, contribute to the learning problem of the child and the adolescent. (2) Psychological maladjustment. The hearing loss may be a contributor to these problems and magnify them because of a constant breakdown of interpersonal communication. (3) General intellectual endowment. Both motor and intellectual retardation have the effect of increasing the hearing handicap for the individual. Success for the hearing handicapped is increased by superior intellect.

From the above, it becomes clear that persons with hearing loss are not a homogeneous group for whom generalizations applicable to all may be made. Rather, they are affected by additional variables and distribute themselves on a continuum from mild to profound handicap.

Principal Causes and Medical Treatments for Hearing Loss

The following are seen to be the major categories of causes of hearing loss with descriptions of the ear pathology, the current medical treatment, and the degree of handicap in audiometric terms. For more detailed information, the reader is referred to standard textbooks in otolaryngology such as Ballinger's *Diseases of the Nose, Throat and Ear* (1977) or Northern's *Hearing Disorders* (1976). The latter reference is an excellent source for current information on hearing loss causes and treatments and is organized and written in very readable form without sacrifice of accuracy or important detail.

The ten described causes of hearing loss are organized in the following manner: The first three (otitis media, middle ear infusion, and congenital) are conditions which appear in early life; the second three (otosclerosis, Ménière's Syndrome, and acoustic nerve tumors) represent conditions appearing mostly during adult life; the next two (noise-induced and drug-induced) are the result of environmental conditions; the last grouping (presbycusis and tinnitus) constitutes a miscellaneous category.

Otitis Media. This is one of the most common ear problems seen by the primary care physician as well as by the otolaryngologist. The highest rate of incidence for the disorder is in infancy and preschool years. Otitis media is a condition in which the air-filled middle ear space becomes fluid-filled. The presence of middle ear fluid decreases the

TABLE I
Effective Handicap of Hearing Loss by Decibel Range[a]

Average hearing frequencies 500–2,000 db	Description	Condition	Sounds heard without amplification	Degree of handicap (if not treated in first year of life)
0–15 db	Normal range	Serous, otitis, perforation, monomeric membrane, tympanosclerosis	All speech sounds	None
15–25 db	Slight hearing loss	Serous otitis, perforation, monomeric membrane, sensorineural loss, tympanosclerosis	Vowel sounds heard clearly; may miss unvoiced consonant sounds	Mild auditory dysfunction in language learning
25–40 db	Mild hearing loss	Serous otitis, perforation, tympanosclerosis, monomeric membrane, sensorineural loss	Hears only some louder-voiced speech sounds	Auditory learning dysfunction, mild language retardation, mild speech problems, inattention

40–65 db	Moderate hearing loss	Chronic otitis, middle ear anomaly, sensorineural loss	Misses most speech sounds at normal conversation level	Severe speech problems, language retardation, learning dysfunction, inattention
65–95 db	Severe hearing loss	Sensorineural or mixed loss due to sensorineural loss plus middle-ear disease	Hears no speech sounds of normal conversation	Severe speech problems, language retardation, learning dysfunction, inattention
95 db or more	Profound hearing loss	Sensorineural or mixed loss	Hears no speech or other sounds	Severe speech problems, language retardation, learning dysfunction, inattention

[a] Adapted from Downs, 1976.

efficiency of the middle ear sound transmission system, resulting in hearing losses ranging from borderline (15–20 db) to moderately severe losses (50–60 db). There are two basic types of otitis media defined in terms of the physical findings, type of pathology, and duration of the disease: acute suppurative otitis media and chronic suppurative otitis media.

Acute suppurative otitis media is an acute middle ear infection with rapid onset and resolution. Microorganisms usually carried by the bloodstream build up and may rupture the ear drum. The treatment is often by myringotomies (surgical incision of the ear drum) and antibiotic therapy. The hearing loss is mild to moderate in degree and confined to the period of acute disease.

Chronic suppurative otitis media is the same disease as acute otitis media, but the symptoms extend over long periods of time, during which infection is intermittently present in the middle ear spaces. The danger of chronic ear disease is the possible destruction of bone and surrounding tissues and permanent hearing loss up to the moderately severe range. Since modern medication and treatment have been developed, chronic middle ear disease is usually indicative of neglect or lack of available medical care.

Middle Ear Effusion. The air-filled middle ear spaces are replaced by serum without cells or bacteria. The pathogenesis of this condition is still a matter of conjecture. The result is a mechanical problem caused by eustachian tube dysfunction leading to the development of a partial vacuum in the middle ears. The negative pressure results in a gradual accumulation of noninfectious serous material resulting in a reduction of middle ear function and hearing loss. The problem is resolved surgically by myringotomies (opening the ear drum), suctioning off the fluid, and placement of transtympanic tubes which equalize the air pressure and provide middle ear ventilation. Hearing levels return to normal and are maintained as long as the tubes stay in place or until recovery of normal eustachian tube functions. Northern and Downs (1978) estimate that the untreated problem is present in 10% of the population between birth and age 11, creating language, speech, and learning delays.

Congenital Deafness

Malformations and Craniofacial Disorders. Malformations of the pinna (outer ear) and abnormalities or absence of normal ear canals are associated with conductive hearing loss. Severe conditions such as microtia (malformed or absent outer ear) and atresia (absent or incomplete ear canals) gives rise to maximal conductive hearing losses of 60–70 db. Low-set ears and cup-ear deformity are also associated with hearing loss.

Cleft lip and palate, which are very common congenital malformations, occur approximately once in 900 newborns. A muscular incompetence results in eustachian tube malfunction and recurrent conductive hearing loss with a great majority of these individuals, especially as children, but permanent middle ear problems persisting into adulthood may also result. Not only facial clefts, but also short palates or palatopharyngeal paralyses result in middle ear problems and hearing difficulties.

Heritable Conditions. The prevalence of congenital deafness or prelingual hearing loss is estimated at 1 in 1,000 to 2,000 live births. Nance (1975) estimates that 50% of severe to profound hearing loss present at birth is genetic in cause. Forty percent of this type of hearing loss follows a recessive pattern of inheritance in which deaf babies are born to normal hearing parents. The pattern may skip generations so that there is no apparent family history of hearing loss. Hearing may be normal at birth and then show a progressive decline in the first few years of life. The remaining genetic hearing losses are composed of sex-linked (3%) and dominant inheritance patterns (10%). Family pedigrees must be taken whenever the causes of a hearing loss in a child is unknown; the results may be used to counsel the parents regarding possible recurrence of deafness in future children.

According to Nance (1975), 47% of congenital deafness is due to environmental causes. The most prominent of these are intrauterine viral infections such as maternal rubella and cytomegalic inclusion disease, which damage the fetus. When contracted early in pregnancy, these infections have a more devastating effect on the fetus and may result in additional problems such as impaired vision, congenital heart disorders, failure to thrive, and cerebral palsy. Other prominent causes of congenital deafness are prematurity, oxygen deprivation at birth and craniofacial anomalies.

Otosclerosis. Otosclerosis is a treatable ear disease caused by the laying down of abnormal bone in the middle ear, which results in less efficient transmission of sound to the inner ear. The cause is as yet unknown. It produces a gradually progressive hearing loss almost exclusively limited to the white population, with a 2 to 1 ratio in favor of females. The disease starts in late childhood or early adolescence and may possibly invade the inner ear, causing a sensory hearing loss as well. Hearing loss may be as great as 50 to 70 db. The treatment is by surgical intervention called *stapedectomy*, in which an artificial strut is placed to carry the sound waves more efficiently. A resumption of middle ear function may be achieved, and often very serviceable hearing is obtained in the treated ear.

Ménière's Disease. This is entirely a disease of adulthood, classically described as tinnitus (ringing or roaring sounds in the ears or head), vertigo (dizziness), and fluctuating sensorineural hearing loss. The symptoms are caused by increased inner ear fluid pressure. While medical treatment may relieve some of the symptoms, it is not entirely satisfactory, and many individuals will undergo surgical destruction of auditory and vestibular structures for relief of the distressing symptoms.

Acoustic Nerve Tumors. These tumors are classified as noninvasive and usually originate within the internal auditory meatus; as they grow, they exert pressure on vestibular, cochlear, and facial nerves. They are rare, and typically are identified in early middle age. If untreated, they continue to grow slowly between ages 50 and 70. While rare in children, some cases have been reported.

The hearing loss is often unilateral with poorer speech discrimination than one would expect from the audiometric configuration. Identification from audiometry alone is not conclusive, according to Weaver and Northern (1976). Brain stem-evoked response audiometry, a new electrophysiologic audiometric approach discussed under the section "Trends and Needs," appears to hold much promise for identification of small early tumors. A posterior fossa myelogram involving a contrast X-ray is stated by Weaver and Northern (1976) to be the only definitive test for acoustic nerve tumors.

Since these tumors do not respond to X-ray treatment, surgery is the only procedure available. Surgical intervention can lead to increased hearing loss and possible facial nerve paralysis; therefore, its benefit is weighed against such factors as the stage of the problem or the patient's age.

Noise-Induced Hearing Loss. Acoustic trauma which is the result of prolonged exposure to noise, is an unfortunate by-product of an industrialized society. The situation is one in which the exposed worker experiences a bilateral, temporary decrease in hearing during each working day with *nearly* complete recovery during off work hours, only to return again to the exposure. This results in a gradual reduction of hearing sensitivity over the years. The loss is usually confined to an audiometric loss at 4,000 Hz, which becomes deeper, resulting in speech discrimination difficulty. It also may be accompanied in the older worker by presbycusis, which affects all high frequencies. Individuals show considerable variability in susceptibility to noise-induced hearing loss.

No medical treatment thus far offers promise. The only avenues of care are reduction of industrial noise by acoustic shielding and other mechanical methods, and protection of the individual worker. This involves preemployment baseline audiometric testing and periodic hearing evaluation, as well as the use of individual ear protection devices. These include ear inserts and muff-type head sets. In addition, there are both federal and state guidelines for the lengths of time a worker may be exposed to various noise levels. Despite these safeguards, industrial noise continues to pose a significant threat to the hearing health of the American worker.

Drug-Induced (Ototoxicity). There is a class of antibiotics known to be ototoxic which are not used indiscriminately by the physician, but only as the drug of last resort for specific diseases and for life-saving purposes. The major offenders known now are streptomycin, dihydrostreptomycin, neomycin, kanamycin, and gentomycin. Other drugs and poisons known to cause hearing loss are aspirin and aspirin compounds, quinine, and arsenic of lead. The effect of these chemicals on the hearing mechanism varies with the dosage, and may be increased by combinations with other drugs or when kidney dysfunction is present. Pre-existing hearing loss and individual susceptibility may also predispose toward ototoxicity. The hearing losses are usually bilateral and due to destruction of neural structures of hearing. The onset of the loss is often rapid and progressive and may range from severe to total loss of hearing. Recovery of useful hearing is unusual.

Presbycusis. This is the hearing loss which accompanies aging. It starts in the high frequencies and over decades moves down into the speech range (250–3,000 Hz) causing increased difficulty for the individual in discriminating speech, particularly where the range of best hearing is masked by ambient noise such as that in the work environment, on the street, or in social settings. The vowel sounds of speech which contain greatest energy are often heard normally, but the weak and high-pitched consonants such as /s/, /th/, /f/, /t/, or /k/ may not be heard, leading to inability to understand speech patterns. This communication breakdown may affect the individuals' personality and vocational productivity.

Tinnitus. While not a cause of hearing loss, tinnitus or noises in the ear is often associated with decreased hearing and causes the possessor a great deal of psychological discomfort. The head or ear noises are variously described as ringing with an identifiable pitch or roaring and hissing sounds. This is especially disturbing in quiet situations, such as at the subject's bedtime, when the masking sounds of everyday environmental noise are absent.

The cause of tinnitus is incompletely understood, but some damage to the auditory pathway is usually indicated. Sataloff (1966) describes the situation in which there is a continuous stream of discharges along the auditory nerve to the brain due to abnormal irritation in the sensorineural pathway. This creates a false sensation of sound for the subject. The most promising noninvasive treatment of tinnitus is described by Vernon and Schleuning (1978). Through the use of a tinnitus masker, an electronic device worn behind the ear, like a hearing aid, a specially designed masking signal is delivered into the ear. The masker renders the tinnitus inaudible for the subject. Sometimes the masker and a hearing aid amplifier are combined for subjects requiring the use of a hearing aid. The acoustic characteristics of the subjects' tinnitus, such as predominant frequencies and range, are predetermined, and the masker is designed to provide optimal masking for the specific type of ear or head noises. Also, any vascular problem such as high blood pressure, which may be associated with the tinnitus, is managed medically.

Problems in Identifying Hearing Impairment

Unlike some other disabilities, hearing loss is an invisible problem. Aside from the ear drum and middle ear structures which are accessible for examination, the principal neural structures of audition lie deep within the temporal bones of the head and can only be partly viewed by X-ray methods. Profoundly nerve-deafened individuals may have perfectly normal ear, nose, and throat findings on visual examination of these structures. Only through behavioral screening or special electrophysiological tests can hearing loss be detected early in life. If identification of significant hearing loss is not made in the first months of life, critical periods for learning to use residual hearing and prelanguage development are lost and usually cannot be regained. Even minimal auditory deprivation has been demonstrated by Webster and Webster (1977) in animal studies to result in reduced brain cell development of the auditory pathways.

Two approaches are currently in use aimed at providing earlier identification of hearing loss, but as yet they have not been applied nationally in an organized way. The first is the use of a high-risk registry in the newborn period which will allow identification of babies at risk for hearing loss who can be referred for in-depth audiological assessment. The criteria for this risk include one or more of the following variables: history of hereditary childhood hearing impairment; rubella or other intrauterine viral infections; defects of the ears, nose, and throat; low birth weight; and neonatal jaundice.

Another method is direct screening of hearing in the newborn nursery by an arousal test. This test uses a prescribed signal level, and the sound stimuli are delivered to sleeping infants. Arousal from sleep revealed by motor activity is the acceptable response.

Screening in infancy is recommended twice in the first year of life; once in the first two to four months and once again between eight and twelve months of age. A number of cautions must be observed. Mild to moderate loss of hearing cannot be ruled out, nor can high-frequency hearing losses, unilateral, or progressive losses. From six months of age, less severe losses may be identified but unilateral or high-frequency losses may go undetected. Judicious use of the high-risk registry and behavioral screening, when combined, remain the best tools for early identification of hearing loss currently in use.

Hearing Aid Amplification

The development of the vacuum tube in the early 1900s and of the transistor in the years immediately following World War II provided the hearing-impaired with the most important assistance short of medical/surgical restoration of hearing, namely, the wearable hearing aid. The technology has undergone tremendous improvement year by year from the early heavy, bulky, body-style amplifiers of poor quality to small, light, battery-efficient behind-the-ear and in-the-ear aids with improved standards and quality control. Hearing aids now possess many features designed to provide the wearer with improved speech reception and comfort. Continuous variation in output (power of the aid), frequency response (pitch emphasis), and methods of limiting the output to protect the wearer from sudden intense sounds are now available.

Recent federal regulations require that all children receive a medical examination and medical approval prior to hearing aid purchase. This is also recommended for adults but may be waived by informed consent. The hearing aid purchaser may buy directly over the counter from the hearing center which will, following the hearing aid selection process, either refer to a specific dealer for a specific aid or dispense the aid in their own program. In addition, these programs offer a full range of auditory training, hearing aid orientation, counseling, and follow-up. While rehabilitative audiology services in speech and hearing programs have been available for many years, direct hearing aid dispensing to the public by certified or licensed audiologists is a relatively new service. In the past, many expensive hearing aids have ended up in dresser drawers because of the failure of the delivery system to provide needed professional guidance.

One final point needs to be stressed. Hearing *aids* are just that. They assist the hearing-impaired by amplifying all environmental sound including speech but do not restore normal hearing or necessarily allow for normal speech reception in all listening situations. As we said earlier, one should never assume when dealing with the hearing aid wearer that his instrument eliminates the handicap.

COMMON PSYCHOLOGICAL CHARACTERISTICS AND PROBLEMS

Overview

Learning is highly dependent on environment; anything which minimizes environmental contact limits learning. The senses are the avenues of contact with environment. Hearing enables contact with a broad spectrum of experience from which knowledge is acquired; this experience accumulates in a vast reservoir from which we may draw to build adjustment patterns for the future.

Think for a moment of a soundless world—a world without soothing sounds from mother, without the explanatory words of teacher, without warning sounds of screeching brakes of an approaching car, without the positive emotional experience of beautiful music, without the casual enjoyment of friendly conversation, without being able to hear or use the telephone, without being able to share feelings and to solve problems through individual or group discussions. A lack of sound greatly shrinks the person's environment and in so doing forces use of uncommon ways of compensation. Sometimes the changes may simply involve greater reliance on the other senses. More frequently, the process of adjustment is complicated by the expansion of trial-and-error experiences into a complex of emotional reactions which make demands not only on the personal resources of the individual but also on the environment, which must provide a continuing and effective training structure.

Family Effects

While birth of a defective child may constitute a threat to any family, to certain families the event may be catastrophic. To other families, it may be seen simply as a problem to be dealt with. With a positive family approach, not only will the deaf child receive the support necessary to perform optimally, but the family may emerge with greater strength and solidarity than before. Hersch and Solomon (1973) stress the importance of marital and family strengths and weaknesses as significant factors relating to adjustment to early hearing loss. They suggest that already developed interactions and problem-solving techniques in the family may predict the family's capacity to integrate a hearing-impaired or, especially, a deaf child. One factor of importance might be the meaning of the hearing handicap to each member of the family. Another factor might be whether the pregnancy was desired; this point may relate to the degree of ambivalence about the child, particularly if the child is deaf. Hopes, dreams, and aspirations of the parents for the child may permit acceptance of a child with limitations or, conversely, lead to defense reactions such as denial, emotional distancing, and even rejection.

As we have noted, it is not always easy to determine the presence of hearing loss early in infancy. The longer the period of time after birth that the loss goes undocumented, the more difficult it is to establish emotional responsiveness, particularly between mother and child. Galenson, Mitler, Kaplan, and Rothstein (1979) go so far as to suggest that early disturbances involving limited or absent specific interactional pathways between mother and child will interfere with all aspects of personality development and will eventually emerge in adult life in the form of psychological characteristics such as passivity and emotional shallowness. Passivity in the adult deaf person may also be due to factors other than the emotional distance between mother and child; one cannot overlook the impact on *both* child and mother of failure of the hearing-impaired or deaf baby to respond as the mother might expect or wish. The mother who has dreamed of receiving emotional satisfactions from her baby but who experiences only lack of responsiveness may not only feel personally hurt but may also defend herself by the dynamic of increasing isolation and withdrawal both from family and from the child, whose sensory inputs are already limited.

Mindel (1971) stresses the importance of the parents' personalities not only in understanding emotional reactions to early diagnosis of deafness but, more importantly, in understanding and influencing crucial decisions parents later make—or fail to make—for their child. The parents who delay recognition or admission of the hearing loss by denial and rationalization beyond optimal time for language learning, may set up an almost irreversible loss. Parents with differing capacities to accept and adapt may, especially when marital discord is present, sabotage each others' attempts to help their child; the result may be increased ambivalence, confusion, and lack of confidence on the part of the hearing-impaired or deaf child. The mother who herself is riddled with the anxiety of coping may project her anxieties to her child. The father who subscribes to the concept of the male as the one who assumes an active and aggressive role in handling problems may reflect disappointment in the passivity of the child who does not hear. The child's behavioral reaction may be increased withdrawal or, conversely, increased retaliatory aggressive behaviors. Parents who pity their hearing-impaired or deaf child may vary their discipline pattern from absolute firmness to liberal permission. This variation is especially important when house rules cannot be verbally communicated. As a result, the child may be perplexed and confused and limit reactions only to those few behaviors which he or she knows to be safe and predictably acceptable to the parents. As a result, both emotional growth and adaptive behavior may suffer.

Just as individuals do not exist in isolation, neither does the immediate family. Families also reflect their ties with the extended family. Mindel (1971) suggests that parents not only are vulnerable to their own ideals about parenthood but also react to deeply imbedded attitudes. Discovery of deafness in their child may not only stimulate feelings of personal failure but also raise questions such as, "What will my own mother think?" If relationships are open and flow naturally, no problems need emerge, and, indeed, the extended family can be a bulwark of support. If, on the other hand, the parents continue to maintain a parent–child relationship with their parents, the process of acceptance and constructive planning can be more stressful than supporting.

Lower socioeconomic classes tend not to stress the importance of language development and may attribute lack of speech in the young child to other causes, such as "not wanting to talk" or "being stubborn." Parental reactions in more educated groups place more importance on articulation, language, and semantic correctness and may thus identify deafness earlier. On the other hand, as Vanden Horst and Kamstra (1979) discovered, the hearing-impaired person living in an upper-class setting may be more handicapped by the linguistic standards which cannot be met than those living in a lower-class milieu, where expectations are not so high and where discrepancies between actual and expected performance are not so great.

Individual Effects

"In the study of the psychological consequences of deafness the two most critical variables are the age of onset and the degree of impairment" (Myklebust, 1960). This simple and direct statement underlies the concept that disruption of normal growth and development at an early stage, when the organism is most helpless and vulnerable and before cognitive processes, language skills, and personality attributes have developed, is most apt to have lasting effects. Add to that the truism that the greater the deprivation (degree of impairment), the greater the negative effect, and the formula expands in complexity. Thus, one can set up a severity-of-reaction continuum ranging from total deafness at birth to moderate hearing loss developing in the later years of life.

The above should not imply, however, that the same psychological characteristics and problems exist at all ages or that the only difference is a matter of degree. Time of onset of deafness is equally important.

Some effects resulting from deafness early in life, such as speech and language processing, do not occur to any appreciable degree if the hearing loss occurs later in life; conversely, some problems, such as necessity for vocational changes, do not apply to young children who have not established vocational positions. Psychological defenses such as denial and cover-up are most apt to occur for those who have had adequate hearing only to lose it during adolescent or adult life. Comparably, adults with previous ability to hear are more apt to react with anxiety, feelings of insecurity, and depressive periods which, in the extreme, may result in social isolation and withdrawal from communicative effort.

Effects on Cognition. Years ago Galton observed people with above average intellectual ability and found them to have good ability to see and hear. He then assumed that if one has good senses, one has good intellect. Some, through lack of information, have been inclined to believe not only Galton's assumption but also the reverse: "If one has bad senses [e.g., cannot hear well], one has bad intellect." This assumption, by itself and without elaboration, is invalid. Studies relating to cognitive or intellectual functioning in the deaf and hard-of-hearing (Blair, 1957; Lavos, 1950; Murphy, 1957), have consistently demonstrated that deaf and hard-of-hearing children, *in general,* show ability within the normal range but with differences between subtests measuring different types of mental processes. Murphy (1957), using the Wechsler Intelligence Scale for Children (Wechsler, 1974) with deaf children in a residential institution, found a mean verbal IQ score of 65.5 (mild mental retardation) while the performance IQ score was found to be 101.8 (normal). Boyd (1975), using the Arthur Adaptation of the Leiter International Intelligence Scale (Arthur, 1952), a scale requiring no hearing or speech, found a mean IQ score of 100.01 in children with hearing loss resulting from maternal intrauterine rubella. It would appear from these, and other, studies that the major problem emerges when the deaf person is asked to perform tasks with which he or she is not familiar, particularly those tasks requiring verbal symbolism. It would also appear that those tasks requiring aural input (such as general information and social knowledge) may show lower scores early in life but improve to an average or near average level by adult life (assuming good learning opportunities).

Since the history of intelligence testing is rooted in academic prediction, and since most academic learning is based on the types of tasks required in the verbal subtests of the Wechsler scales, it is not surprising to find generally bleak academic achievement scores in spite of measures of normal or near normal IQ scores based on tasks not requiring aural input. It has been the experience of the authors that deaf children, even in optimal academic training programs, lag behind their hearing peers by one to two grade levels; to the extent that this may be true, it is important *not* to perceive such a child as showing a pathological deficit of intelligence.

Tomlinson-Keasy and Kelly (1978) suggest that the discrepancy between actual achievement indices and predictions of academic success based on assumed cognitive potential may be due to lack of exposure to sound symbols, especially during preschool years, which is more than a quantitative difference due to lack of hearing alone. They suggest that lack of exposure to sound symbols produces a *different* information processing system which affects language. It may well be that the deaf or hard-of-hearing child does not think much in terms of oral language symbols. In confirmation of this assumption, Beratis, Rubin, Miller, Galenson, and Rothstein (1979) report observation of behavior of an infant with transient moderate to severe hearing loss; this infant was found to utilize vision much more than audition when audition was poor (movement of people, lights, etc.) but to show less dependence on visual stimuli as auditory reception improved. Streff, Barefoot, Walter, and Crandall (1978) report no significant difference between hearing and nonhearing groups on various measures of perceptual and memory abilities. The evidence appears clear: Loss of hearing significantly affects those cognitive functions requiring audition for reception and processing but does *not* significantly effect those cognitive functions which depend on other senses, primarily vision, for reception and processing.

Effects on Personality. In spite of multiple problems of measurement (see section on Evaluating the Deaf and Hard of Hearing), many have attempted to describe and document personality differences or problems in the deaf and hard-of-hearing. In addition to some research findings, considerable descriptive lore has emerged, part of which has held up with time and research review, the rest of which has not. Some have suggested that those who are deaf tend to be suspicious and paranoid. Educators have suggested that those deaf from early infancy are better adjusted because they have no awareness of what it means to hear. Similarly, some have posited that those who became hard-of-hearing late in life have the greatest emotional disturbance because of their changing status and their ambiguous position of being neither deaf nor capable of normal hearing.

Myklebust (1960), studying deaf and hard-of-hearing adults, used both descriptive and autobiographical information as well as psychological tests to explore emotional effects of hearing loss. Results should be considered only as reflective of attitudes and reactions at the time the study was done, with full awareness that differences could result from improved treatment or changing social demands and expectations. The results suggested that hearing-impaired persons tend to be more dependent than do normal persons (a reflection not only on the hard-of-hearing person but also the perception of the society in which he or she lives). For those who become hard-of-hearing or deaf later in life, there appeared to be greater need to shift social contacts and affiliation with very few maintaining primary identification with the majority group of hearing people. The hearing-impaired also reflected a degree of social withdrawal, perhaps realistically based, as it became more difficult for the hearing-impaired to keep up, especially with group social interactions. This may be, however, a transitory condition, dependent on whether treatment—such as amplification—is or is not successful. Harris (1980) describes this transition state most lucidly: "I recall vividly my feelings when told I had a hearing loss that might be progressive in nature. After a period of brooding, listening to melancholy music and feeling very alone, I began to struggle more adaptively with a fundamental vocational decision of whether I could still become a clinical psychologist." Harris later points out that after receiving bilateral hearing aids she felt herself no more "handicapped" than colleagues who "put on glasses in the morning"; she adds, "It was easy to forget how hard I used to work. But I am given a gentle reminder each time a battery runs down."

One author of this chapter, working with adults who had recently become deaf or hearing-impaired, found that a frequent emotional and behavioral reaction was denial and cover-up, especially when some degree of hearing remained. A too-easy reaction on the patient's part was to assume that the entire message was heard and to react in those terms, leading to miscommunication and misinterpretation, especially when the responses by the person with the hearing loss were inappropriate. This failure to clarify the message and respond appropriately frequently led to suspicion, sometimes described as paranoia. It was not always easy to convince the hard-of-hearing person that it might be to his or her advantage to admit the loss and request restatement and clarification.

Those who are deaf have different characteristics not only from the normal but also from the hard-of-hearing. Myklebust (1960) found deaf adults to show on psychological tests greater emotional disturbance than the hard-of-hearing but at the same time to be largely unaware of deafness as a handicap, probably because, never having heard, they did not have a negative point of comparison. The characteristic personality pattern was lack of apprehension, worry, or concern with oneself and "manifestation of obliviousness in regard to the true circumstances."

Deaf children, according to Hirshoren and Schnittjer (1979), in addition to showing varying degrees of the same personality factors as the normal on a behavior problem checklist, show one additional factor of passivity–inferiority, characterized by crying over minor hurts, shyness, easy confusion, hypersensitivity, lack of confidence, and passivity. This personality factor was thought to be specifically related to deafness (although it may also characterize reactions of children to many handicapping conditions). Altshuler (1971) describes among common characteristics of the deaf a lack of insight and empathy specifically regarding the effect of their behavior on others.

Interest patterns as related to occupational choices may also be viewed as personality characteristics. Problems occur when disparity exists between vocational goals, usually based on interests which may or may not be known and understood, and the skills and abilities needed for success in a given vocation. To avoid some of these potential problems the career counselor must have a good understanding of hearing-impaired persons, including their interests and abilities. Myklebust (1960) studied interest patterns of adult deaf using the Kuder Preference Record (Kuder, 1953). He reported significantly low interest scores in those areas requiring hearing, verbal language and social interchange, such as persuasive and musical, for both men and women. The three areas of greatest interest for males were literary, clerical and social service, while the women in his sample preferred computational, scientific and mechanical. Myklebust further suggested that a possible implication of these results was that deaf males may find it more difficult to identify with the so-called more masculine activities, while deaf women found it more difficult to identify with more feminine activities. A more recent study by Murphy, Jacobs, and Conklin, possibly reflecting changing concepts about masculine and feminine roles, reported that deaf students, both men and women, more frequently choose undergraduate majors to prepare them to teach or train the deaf and that graduate students tend to enroll almost exclusively in the field of education. These findings should not be construed as suggesting that the deaf *should* enter the field of education, especially without considering and carefully evaluating all necessary skills for whatever occupational direction is under consideration.

EVALUATING THE HEARING-IMPAIRED PERSON

General Problem: Communication

In order to evaluate, one must communicate with the person to be evaluated. If that person has a hearing impairment, one important area of communication is blocked or limited. The degree of limitation of communication will vary extensively from the person with mild hearing impairment, who functions reasonably well in speech comprehension and expression with or without amplification, to the person with prelingual deafness and essential lack of verbal expressive skills who cannot communicate except, possibly, by signing or writing. Prior to attempting communication, one needs as much information as possible regarding the nature and degree of hearing loss, information which usually can be acquired from the audiometric report.

For those with relatively little hearing loss and with satisfactory language skills, only general precautions need to be taken. These normal precautions include quiet surroundings, good visibility, and slow and clear speech while avoiding shouting and exaggerated speech.

For those with special problems of hearing, such as high-frequency losses, one can, at the least, be aware of the problems and adapt to them as much as possible. For example, the person with a high-frequency loss may be able to communicate better with a man whose speech sounds are in a lower register. Even then, or even with an appropriate hearing aid, certain sounds may not be heard and comprehension may be reduced to as little as 50% of spoken words in context. Not only may there be a problem of the client's *hearing*, there may also be a problem of the evaluator's *understanding* what has been said because of sound distortions or omissions producing lowered intelligibility in the speech of the hearing-impaired person.

In dealing with more severe hearing impairments, particularly the totally deaf and those with no speech, greater problems arise, calling for more sophisticated adaptations. These will be discussed later in the section on the evaluation interview.

Evaluating Cognitive Ability

Selection of psychological tests of intellectual ability should depend on the questions being asked and the use to be made of the results. This is particularly true when dealing with those who have a hearing deficit. If one wishes to measure so-called intellectual ability as it might be required in an average class of normal children in an average school, any generally used test of intelligence which demonstrates acceptable measures of reliability and validity may be used. If one wishes to measure intellectual ability separate from verbal and language facility, only certain tests will qualify. If one wishes to measure intellectual ability as compared only with others who are deaf, tests which have deaf norms should be selected.

With children below two to three years of age, only a small number of tests which purport to measure intelligence are available, and even these depend in part on verbal instructions. Further, these tests for the most part measure motor skills which will not necessarily predict later cognitive skills well. Probably the best test at this age level is the Bayley Scales of Infant Development (1969), which have separate measures for motor and mental development. One might also use, as a screening test, either the Denver Developmental Screening Test (Frankenberg, Dodds, and Fandal, 1970), which measures fine and gross motor skills, personal–social skills, and language, or the Boyd Developmental Progress Scale (1974), which measures motor skills, communication skills, and self-sufficiency skills. In the case of a child with suspected or documented hearing deficiency, however, the results should be considered only as tentative baseline data for later comparison and should be tempered by careful clinical judgment.

For preschool, primary, and intermediate school ages, several tests may be suggested, including the Wechsler Intelligence Scale for Children—Revised (1974), which measures both verbal and performance skills; the Nebraska Test of Learning Aptitude (Hiskey, 1955), which has norms for deaf children; the Arthur Adaptation of the Leiter International Performance Scale, which does not require the child taking the test to hear or speak; and the Raven Progressive Matrices (1938), which depend only minimally on language.

Each of these tests has its strengths and weaknesses. The WISC–R used below age seven or eight may produce valid IQ scores, but subtest scores based on such small samples of behavior may well not be predictive. The Wechsler verbal IQ score does not have good face validity for use with the deaf because of its verbal emphasis, and its use is criticized as not reflecting the general cognitive ability of the deaf child. The performance IQ is sometimes criticized as not valid because the standardization did not include deaf children, but research by Hirshoren, Hurley, and Kavale (1979) found it to be a valid measure of intelligence on the basis of their finding that its results were in close agreement with the Nebraska Test of Learning Aptitude (Hiskey, 1955), which was standardized on deaf children. One should keep in mind, however, that the performance IQ score, by itself, does not predict scholastic success well.

The Nebraska Test of Learning Aptitude (Hiskey, 1955) may not be as pure a test of nonlanguage cognitive skills as assumed on the basis of research by Wilson, Rapin, Wilson, and Van Denburg (1975) showing that the test is, in truth, a combination of language *and* nonlanguage materials. The test has also received some criticism on the basis of its age and the fact that norms based on deaf children are not realistic if one expects that deaf persons will live and compete with hearing persons in real life.

The Arthur Adaptation of the Leiter International Performance Scale is an updating of norms for ages two through ten of the original Leiter International Performance Scale (Leiter, 1940). This updating, in effect, lowered the raw score necessary for a given mental age; thus the score that originally gave the subject a mental age of two years, with the Arthur adaptation gave the subject a mental age of 2½ years. This augmentation does not necessarily meet typical expectations as reflected by the 1972 renorming of the Stanford–Binet (Terman & Merrill, 1972), which showed that considerably stronger skills were required to fit the concept of the average child in 1972 as compared with 1960. For this reason, the authors of this chapter believe that one can better defend the use of the original Leiter norms (Leiter, 1940) at this time rather than the Arthur adaptation, especially since, in our experience, the Arthur test results tend not to hold up when compared with other tests at older ages.

The Raven Progressive Matrices (1938) have consistently been criticized on two counts: (1) lack of clear understanding of what is functionally being measured and (2) essential absence of norms for a representative sample of children in the United States.

Measurement of Personality

If one assumes adequate ability to read, most objective personality tests can be used for the deaf and hard-of-hearing population. Garrison, Tesch, and Decaro (1978) found, however, that the Tennessee Self Concept Scale (Fitts, 1965) resulted in relatively low retest reliability measures when used with deaf students. On examining the reason for this through follow-up interviews, they found that the deaf students' low score in self-esteem was largely a function of "peculiar interpretation" of test items as a result of lowered reading comprehension and that responses, therefore, varied.

One may also need to evaluate test items to determine which items may be inappropriate or meaningless because of deafness. Myklebust (1960) found certain items of the Minnesota Multiphasic Personality Inventory (Hathaway & McKinley, 1948) to be "loaded" for the deaf, such as "My hearing is apparently as good as most people's," or "At times I hear so well it bothers me," or "I find it hard to make talk when I meet new people." If one takes these possibly loaded questions into account and corrects for them, the scale may still be a useful instrument.

Other instruments which might be used to describe personality and emotional reactions include projective techniques such as, when the subject can speak sufficiently well, the Rorschach (1948), the Thematic Apperception Test (Murray, 1943), or a sentence-completion test such as the Rotter Incomplete Sentences Blank (1950); or, when speech is not easily understood, drawing tests such as the Draw-a-Person (Machover, 1949) or the Bender–Gestalt (Bender, 1946; Fisher & Cleveland, 1958). One can also construct one's own scale following the format suggested by Osgood, Suci, and Tannenbaum (1957) in the Semantic Differential described in Chapter 9. This technique, utilizing paired adjectives scaled on a seven-point scale, exposes the hearing-impaired person's perception of himself (as a deaf or hard-of-hearing person) and the extent to which this condition is perceived as a problem in contrast with other kinds of handicapping conditions.

One of the authors of this chapter found, in a clinical setting with adult deaf and hard-of-hearing patients, considerable value from the use of a self-made hearing attitude scale made up of a number of sentences descriptive of feelings about the hearing loss and divided into categories such as self-appraisal, depression, overoptimism, tension, job worry, sensitivity, cover-up, and withdrawal. The test sentences were originally collected from statements made by adults with hearing deficits. Although this technique was never standardized and does not produce a numerical score, the scale was of value in eliciting not only overall reaction to the loss but, dependent on the number of statements with which the person agreed, the area of greatest concern. Although this instrument is no longer available, a comparable and up-to-date instrument could easily be developed. Such information could then be used in follow-up exploratory interviews and therapeutic counseling.

Evaluation Interview

Whenever one has to deal with a specific problem area, rather than more general personality exploration, the interview becomes increasingly important, although, especially when one is dealing with limited hearing, it may also bring problems. The problems are twofold: how to increase communication with a deaf person and what sort of information to elicit.

Obviously, one would expect that if the interviewer has developed signing skills communication with a deaf person who also signs would be enhanced, and in most instances it is. Yet signing does not ensure improved communication unless the interviewer and interviewee have familiarity with each other's techniques of signing. Sendelbaugh (1978) found that deaf and hard-of-hearing adolescents watching television preferred captions rather than a separate signing person because of the speed of the signer or the use of different signs or sign techniques. Some of these problems, especially differences in signs or sign techniques, might hamper good communication in the exploratory interview in which rapport and understanding nuances of meaning are so important.

If signing is not possible for whatever reason, but if the deaf person can read and write, communication through written language may be necessary. Because of the language poverty of the deaf, communication by writing will seldom suffice. Myklebust (1960) demonstrated that the reading skills and vocabulary of deaf adolescents were seven to eight years behind those of their hearing peers. Similarly, the writing skills of the deaf, as revealed by sentence length, structure, and correctness, are significantly poorer.

Another suggested resolution of the basic communication problem with the deaf is the use of an interpreter. One would think that an interpreter, especially one who might have familiarity and previous experience with the deaf person, would help solve some of the problems, and under good conditions he may. However, in the experience of these authors the interpreter does not always reflect what the interviewer wishes, especially if the interpreter is an ego-involved parent. One author has found this to be particularly true in administering tests which ask short precise questions only to have the interpreter "ask" the question in a complicated and extended manner including additional "clues" to the correct answer. Gerber (1979) in a letter printed in the *American Journal of Psychiatry* refers to "interpreter-related distortions of clinical material." We suggest that if a signing interpreter is used, he or she should undergo a period of training to stress the importance of reflecting—and rechecking—what is being asked, as well as what is being reflected, by the deaf person. Additionally, there should be some period of free communication prior to the evaluation interview to establish familiarity and better understanding of each person's techniques.

If the deaf person does not sign but relies on speech-reading or lipreading and/or partial hearing, the interviewer must always face the deaf person so that full view of the lips is possible. In fact, if one suspects a hearing loss, an initial check can be made by turning away or casually covering the lips to see if communication is lost. Care also must be taken that the interviewer does not speak so slowly or with such exaggerated lip movements as to confuse the person being interviewed. Markides (1979) describes the speaker and learner variables necessary for the deaf person to utilize speech-reading well. Speaker variables include visibility, rate of speech, and lip movement; and learner variables include visual acuity, motivation, age, intelligence, and training.

A technique useful in interviews between two normal hearing persons is even more important when hearing is limited: the art of reflecting what has been received (understood) by the interviewer. This technique has value not only to clarify understanding but also frequently to bring forth additional and expanded explanation from the person being interviewed.

Assuming that good communication techniques are established, one still is left with questions as to what information is important and what is asked. If one operates on the assumption that one needs to know where a person has been (past) and where he or she is now (present) in order to understand where he or she is going (future), questions of value will seek answers to the past, the present, and the future. These questions may seek knowledge relating to actual experiences in which present feelings may have had their origin, what the person perceives as his or her immediate situation, and what plans or coping mechanisms are in mind. Myklebust (1960), studying two groups of adults, one hard-of-hearing and one deaf, used a set of autobiographical questions to which the respondents could write answers. These questions covered family experiences and reactions to the hearing deficit, experiences with friends, and experiences with employer and working associates. The subjects were also asked to tell how their hearing loss changed their lives and how they currently felt about their hearing loss. Additional focus might center on specific ways of dealing with immediate situations, such as "What do you do now when———?" or "When you find yourself in a crowd of people and unable to hear well, what do you do?" Finally, one might lead into discussion of ways of coping with difficult situations in the future with such questions as "What works well for you now when———?" or "What problems does your current method of handling difficult hearing situations bring?" or "What other ways of handling the situation have you thought of?"

Up to this point we have focused on patient reactions and behavior as perceived by the hearing-impaired person. These reactions, as with any person, may be colored to some extent by underlying feelings of fear or hope and may, therefore, not be accurate appraisals of the true behavioral reactions, especially in stressful or threatening situations. Withdrawal may be more frequent than described; anger may be more intense than stated; bluffing may be the typical reaction but not admitted. This is not to say that one should not seek self-perceived reactions but to suggest that further evaluation through observation of the deaf person's actual behavior in contrived, or, better yet, natural situations is necessary to round out the evaluation process. This may immediately complicate the situation if a discrepancy is found between self-perceived and true behavior. To ignore the discrepancy may be even worse. Defense of self-perceptions may sabotage or block therapeutic reactions and positive change. Knowledge of discrepancies at least gives a more complete definition of the problem to be solved, keeps the therapeutic process on a more stable reality base, and leads to better adjustment reactions and behaviors.

INTERVENTION METHODS

The Multidiscipline Approach

Because of the complexities involved in hearing impairment it is essential that any handicaps in addition to hearing loss be identified and remedied to the fullest extent. A multidiscipline approach is needed in order to develop appropriate medical, audiological, psychological, and educational treatment plans. This is especially crucial for the young hearing-impaired child but is also of help for the adolescents, whose strengths and weaknesses must be identified as they relate to vocational planning and training.

The following specialties can make important contributions to the process: (a) The pediatrician or family practitioner. This physician is responsible for the general health care of the individual and for diagnosis of primary or secondary handicaps. Some physicians play a primary coordinating role which involves family education and counseling. (b) The otolaryngologist: The ear-nose-throat physician performs the medical diagnosis of hearing loss, may determine the site of the auditory lesion, and will provide any possible medical or surgical intervention aimed at improving or restoring hearing function. (c) The audiologist: This specialist provides the audiological assessment which delineates the degree and nature of hearing loss, tolerance for amplified sound, selection of optimal amplification in the form of hearing aids and counseling of parents with regard to the educational needs of the individual. (d) The psychologist: This individual is responsible for assessing developmental levels in the young child and general intelligence with standardized tests. This person will identify special aptitudes or disabilities important for educational planning and may play an important role in assisting parents with child management and handling special behavioral or emotional problems which hearing loss can create. (e) Teacher of the hearing-impaired: This educator has specialized in planning and carrying out programs of academic training and language and speech education consistent with the child's capabilities. The teacher is the implementor as well as a skilled observer of individual differences. Remedial programs can better be tailored for the child with information provided by the various specialists. The key to effective team work lies in good communication and good understanding of each other's vocabularies and roles, while still maintaining an individual function and area of expertise.

Other specialists from time to time may be drawn on for additional assessment and input. These specialties may include social work, psychiatry, ophthalmology, neurology, occupational and physical therapy, orthopedics, nursing, and genetics.

Only with a smoothly functioning multi- (and inter-) disciplinary approach can the gamut of psychosocial, as well as medical and social factors, be adequately evaluated. Such comprehensive procedures may enable more realistic, and yet hopeful, rehabilitation, going beyond medical treatment to personal, interpersonal, and vocational treatment.

Intervention with the Family

As we mentioned earlier in this chapter, interruption of early childhood family interactions can have lasting negative effects. In order to exert the greatest positive influence on the hard-of-hearing or deaf person, the process of treatment should be started as early in life as possible. For the child born deaf or for the child whose hearing loss comes early in life the process should logically include the family.

Parent Counseling. The goal of parent counseling is to help parents become more effective in their interactions with their children (McWilliams, 1976). Although this may not always be easy, even when the children are normal, special problems may occur when the child is handicapped by a hearing deficit. Counselors must take into consideration in the therapeutic process not only the child's handicap but also the living patterns of the family with which they are working and carefully avoid imposing set standards or procedures on the child's family simply because those standards have worked for the counselors in other situations. Counselors must avoid classifying families as *good* or *bad*, although some will be *different* and will require some adaptive approaches. McWilliams (1976), for example, speaks of the nonevolved grandmother who essentially takes over for the mother who relinquishes her maternal role; it is suggested that this situation may constitute a problem in the average suburban family but represent a positive arrangement in families from subcultures which have strong matriarchal structures.

Parental needs are often reflected in their children. To understand the current situation in a family with a handicapped child, one may need to examine these needs as they relate to all of the children in the family—age expectations, hopes, fears, dreams—in order better to understand limitations or breadth of responsive acceptance or rejection. This understanding on the part of the counselor may also help avoid the danger of making the nonhandicapped members of the family become victims of the handicapped.

Care should be taken to establish and continue positive and useful parent contacts; when bad news must be given—such as telling parents about their child's handicap (whether that handicap involves deafness, cerebral palsy, blindness, or some other disability)—one must realize that little of what is said at first is understood, remembered, or even heard because of the initial shock. In good counseling, the counselor, not the patient or family, takes the lead in setting a second appointment. The counselor's awareness of the family's vulnerability may make it easier for family members to recognize and deal with the many feelings which can positively or negatively affect the rehabilitation process.

But there is a danger. Some counselors actually stop at this first stage of acceptance of feelings, thus blocking parents' achievement of the goal of effective interaction especially crucial in the case of a child who has the handicap of deafness or significant hearing loss. The counselor must be sensitive to the clients' readiness to progress to more practical and realistic problems: specifically, how to help the child learn to cope with real life situations. This represents an often repeated phenomenon in good counseling situations: movement from rather complete dependency on the counselor to shared responsibility and eventually to the point at which the parent has learned to cope and no longer needs the counselor.

Once the process toward lesser dependency on the counselor has begun, a useful added technique is to involve the parents in parent groups in which more sharing and reality-testing can take place. McWilliams (1976) suggests that parent groups tend to work better, however, when they are more broadly based and deal more generally with parental concerns rather than when limited to more specific diagnoses, such as parents of deaf children. But other parents of deaf children can be most useful, especially for comparing notes on an informal basis.

As the child becomes older, counseling needs may change. Moores (1978) stresses that attention must be given to the plight of the parents as well as that of the child when the hearing-impaired child is about to enter the first grade and again at adolescence. At each point, parental needs (expectations) may be reactivated in such a way as to produce positive (or negative) interactions and positive (or negative) coping.

Entering school represents a time of new and different decision-making on the part of the parents—decisions regarding regular or residential school placement, integrated or segregated classrooms, oral training or total communication. If progress is not what everyone has hoped, parents may need counseling support to avoid feelings of guilt and recrimination.

Entering adolescence represents another period of potential problems. At this time the parents must face the chronicity of their child's hearing loss and some of their dreams and hopes for normality are bound to be crushed. Also at this time the gap between hearing and deaf or hearing-impaired children tends to widen, when the deaf or hearing-impaired child more obviously has a smaller number of hearing friends, when boy–girl relationships develop with more restriction, and when the deaf or hearing-impaired child begins to seek out friends with a comparable disability, both of the same and opposite sex. When these emerging patterns become more apparent, the family may again need supportive counseling.

Parent–Infant Training Programs. Identification of hearing loss in the first year of life leads logically to the development of parent–infant training programs which can provide guidance in the early critical months and years of the hearing-impaired child's prelanguage and early language development. Sitnick, Rushmer, and Arpan (1977), at Good Samaritan Hospital in Portland, Oregon, have developed a very successful program of clinic and home training called Infant Hearing Resource, which has been adopted by a number of private and public programs nationwide. Encompassing a birth to four-year age span, the program trains the parent to be a stimulator and reinforcer of auditory listening skills and sequential language development. The program is based on the premise that, in order to acquire language, hearing-impaired infants must move through both prelanguage and language sequences in keeping with that of the normal hearing infant. The materials are categorized and graded under headings of Receptive Language, Expressive Language, Auditory Training, and Total Communication. An eclectic approach is utilized in which some infants follow an aural-oral method (without manual signing) and others follow a total communication language development process which combines both aural-oral and manual signing. The success of this early language and auditory program is documented by the fact that numbers of severely hearing-impaired children are being successfully integrated at preschool and kindergarten age with their hearing peers.

Educational Methods

The teacher of the deaf faces the monumental task of teaching language, speech, and academic skills to individuals whose very handicap has its greatest impact on ability to acquire these skills. Normal hearing allows for the development of an extensive language comprehension and language expression base in the infant and preschool years which the deaf child, even with optimal training, may not develop. But given identification of hearing loss in the first year, maximal use of residual hearing through hearing aids, and a tailored program, the child may be able to enter school at a level near his hearing peers and compete successfully.

A detailed description of the various educational approaches for the deaf and hearing-impaired is beyond the scope of this chapter. However, because of the long history of controversy as to methods of deaf education the reader should be aware of the two principal training approaches in use today.

The *aural-oral method* stresses maximal use of residual hearing, speech-reading, and intensive language and speech training. Advocates of this approach discourage the use of manual signing, insisting that the child learn to communicate through oral speech. Historically, many students in many residential and day schools for the deaf have been taught by this method at least in the early years. For some children, intelligible speech and language skills are unattainable, and insistence on strict oralism in education prevented them from learning signing skills for parent and peer interaction. This resulted in social isolation and family disturbances as well as school failure due to lack of communication abilities. The aural-oral method has not lived up to its expectations.

A relatively recent method is termed *total communication*. Rather than a method, this is more a philosophy that seeks to teach the child to communicate by every means possible: American sign language, finger spelling, natural gestures, facial expressions, and accompanying development of speech patterns. It is hoped that by using all methods a sense of communicating will be given the child which will be reinforced by interactions with his teachers, parents, and classmates. The teacher will note which technique works best for developing language, and that method can be continued for the child in the ensuing school years. Too little time has lapsed to determine the value of total communication for the deaf. Critics are concerned that teachers will unconsciously stress one method or another, depending on their particular bias, and fail to make the program *total*. However, the concept of teaching enough techniques so that one or more will be effective for the given child recognizes the individual differences in type and degree of hearing handicap and appears to have promise. Above all, the child who fails with an oral approach will not be denied the power of communication.

Another current trend in education which was formerly called integration is now called *mainstreaming*. Mainstreaming is well established in the United States and requires that the handicapped child and his teacher be provided with outside support so that the child can be educated in the regular classroom with normal hearing peers for most of his career. This concept, which also applies to other handicapping conditions, is further discussed in Chapter 1.

Personal Counseling

As adulthood approaches, the need for personal counseling may increase for the person with a hearing deficit. Even though the hearing-impaired person may have received training in communication in school, even though he or she may have had the benefit of special education techniques in classes, and even though the family may have maintained a positive and supporting climate, growing up can be traumatic. Society expects more independence. Career decisions must be made. Long-term life choices are pending. At this time parents frequently become more overprotective and the deaf children more dependent.

Although parents may need some help at this time, it is the young person who most needs assistance in sorting out his priorities, establishing a positive identity, and beginning to make life (vocational and family) choices. If his or her reaction to emerging life problems is overwhelming, personal counseling may be needed, preferably with a professional who is trained not only in the needs of the hearing-impaired but also in the method of communication used by that particular person, whether it is signing, lip-reading, or some combination of the two. It is most advantageous when the helping person can be someone already known to the deaf person, such as a special teacher—a person who is already established as acceptable and helpful. If the reaction is not as severe, or if emerging questions focus on such areas as career planning, and especially if the degree of loss is not extreme, less intensive counseling may be sufficient. Psychological tests of interest and aptitude can help sort out strengths and weaknesses and possible motivating activities, which can then be discussed. Additional opportunities can be arranged so that the client can test new activities to help make wiser choices.

Almost everything up to this point in our discussion has focused on the person who sustained a hearing loss early in life. What about the adult who grew up as a normal person only to sustain a hearing loss later in life?

One author of this chapter had the opportunity to work for several years with soldiers who had, for various reasons, become deaf or hard-of-hearing while in the armed services and who were to return to civilian life. The goal was to return them with the least possible reduction in productivity, both in terms of their social interactions and job security. Initially, attempts were made to counsel them by giving them good advice on what they might encounter and how they might most meaningfully react to or cope with these new situations. Results were far from acceptable: when told what they might experience, they retaliated with denial; when advised how to cope with situations, they responded with statements such as "You don't know what you're talking about, you're not hard-of-hearing." We soon came to the conclusion that we were dealing with people who were experiencing a kind of psychological shock and who needed to deny and defend themselves.

We decided to modify our approach in several ways. First of all, we brought patients together into groups. Second, we dropped the explanation and advice. Third, we involved several group members in psychodramatic situations in which a person was subjected to an embarrassing social situation or job interview in front of the entire group, with the counselor taking the role of a hearing person. The hearing-deficient person was exposed to shouting, avoidance, "charitable" job offers and the like, and his reactions were observed by all. The end result was consistently positive. At the end of the psychodramatic situation, a statement of denial was made by the group leader, such as, "Of course, that would never happen in real life." The reaction usually was a statement by someone in the group such as, "The hell it wouldn't; it happened to me only last week." When the question was raised by the counselor as to what would be done about it (or sometimes even before the question), participants began to contribute by saying "I think he should have ―――――" or "That never would have happened if―――――." The rest of the discussion usually stressed positive coping behaviors, representing the first steps toward behavioral change.

This approach, involving a degree of countershock to combat typical denial, represents, of course, only one technique. One certainly must not infer that the ultimate goal was immediately reached. Additional counseling was necessary. Individual counseling was essential when reactions were severe, such as depression and withdrawal. Supportive counseling over time was necessary to establish realistic behavior reactions, such as admitting the hearing loss and achieving, by that admission, better communication; it was sometimes difficult to bring the person to the point at which he could say, "I'm sorry, I didn't understand what you said; I have a hearing problem." Considerable follow-up interviewing was done to focus on vocational plans; tests were taken and discussed; a careful work history was taken to discover possible work skills not requiring excellent hearing; lectures were given on work situations which might be particularly difficult or which might bring further damage to the ears; written material was made available regarding various occupations and their requirements; and job familiarization opportunities were made available whenever possible.

Psychological intervention is not always easy and does not always fit one simple or precise formula. To accomplish their goal, counselors must be willing to work with the family, the school, the employer, and the community, as well as with their hearing impaired clients.

TRENDS AND NEEDS

Electrical Stimulation of the Auditory Nerve

Sensorineural hearing loss historically has not been amenable to either surgical or medical treatment either to improve or restore hearing except in rare instances. Research in the area of direct electrical stimulation of the auditory nerve is promising to the degree that the decade of the 1980s may mark the beginning of major breakthroughs for the nerve-deafened. Brackmann and House (1976) describe the history and clinical experience with several varieties of electrode implants into the inner ear and auditory nerve. This method has been conducted on human subjects who have total or nearly total hearing losses. The subjects report some degree of pitch perception and reception of rhythm patterns of speech, although discrimination of speech itself has not been possible. The engineering capability for sophisticated inner ear prostheses has been developed, but it remains for further research to develop the type of implant which is capable of carrying sufficient information to permit speech discrimination.

Electrophysiological Audiometry

Highly valuable new methods and approaches have been developed recently aimed at identification of hearing loss in infancy and diagnosis of the site of the lesion in the auditory system. This approach is called *evoked response audiometry* (ERA). It requires the use of the electroencephalograph and a special purpose computer which permits measures of the electrical activity of the brain and auditory nervous system as they are stimulated by repeated auditory signals. Audiometry using waves generated in the brain stem correlates very closely with behavioral audiometry and has the marked advantage of requiring no behavioral response on the part of the subject. The test is well validated, and, although standardization has not been completed, it is currently the best means of measuring hearing in infants, multiply impaired children, and uncooperative subjects.

With standardization and engineering improvements, hearing may be routinely screened in the newborn period with resulting earlier identification and earlier treatment possibilities.

Regional Resource Centers

The development of Regional Resource Centers for the Deaf is a recent federally funded service program available in a number of regions nationally. These programs are supported by the Rehabilitation Services Administration of the Department of Health, Education, and Welfare. They include publication of a directory of services and specialists available for assistance to the deaf such as audiologists, counselors, interpreters, lawyers, physicians, optometrists, psychologists, religious workers, and social workers. In addition, these directories list associations and programs which offer services for the hearing-impaired and the deaf. Also a part of the resource center function is the development of training programs to assist in the preparation of teachers of deaf students. This development, if continued, will go a long way toward improving services for the hearing-handicapped population.

Public Attitude

While recent social emphasis has improved employment opportunities for handicapped people in general, there continues to be need for follow-up studies resulting in dissemination of informaion to potential employers which will not stress the idea of charity in employing a handicapped individual, whatever the handicap may be, but which will stress the specific advantages to the employer as well as to the employee from appropriately placing the handicapped person in a position which will utilize his skills and possibly bring about better production than would be obtainable from his normal peer.

Prevention Procedures

In order to prevent a sensory limitation such as deafness or hearing impairment from becoming a greater handicap than it needs to be, a multifaceted approach is necessary. As we noted before, early identification and available medical treatment are of major importance, as is availability of educational procedures which adapt to the needs of the handicapped person. Help to assimilate the deaf (and other handicapped) into productive employment may help ease some of the economic and social pressures.

But another more basic preventive procedure may have to emerge. This chapter began with the statement that hearing impairment "is a concomitant of our industrialized society and its increasing urban noise." Thus, anything which reduces the environmental pollution from excessive industrial noise and street noise may reduce the frequency of noise-induced hearing losses. It appears that some progress has been made, but more will be necessary.

APPENDIX: SOURCES OF INFORMATION

Organizations:

Alexander Graham Bell Association for the Deaf, Inc.
3417 Volta Place, N.W.
Washington, DC 20007

American Speech-Language-Hearing Association
10801 Rockville Pike
Rockville, MD 20852

American Deafness and Rehabilitation Association
814 Thayer Avenue
Silver Spring, MD 20910

Conference of American Instructors of the Deaf
5034 Wisconsin Avenue, N.W.
Washington, DC 20016

Deafness Research and Training Center
New York University
80 Washington Square East
New York, NY 10003

Gallaudet College
Kendall Green
Washington, DC 20002

National Association of the Deaf
814 Thayer Avenue
Silver Spring, MD 20910

National Technical Institute for the Deaf
1 Lamb Memorial Drive
Rochester, NY 14623

Office of Deafness and Communicative Disorders
Rehabilitation Services Administration
Mary E. Switzer Memorial Building
330 C Street, SW, Room 3414
Washington, DC 20201

Books and Periodicals:

Myklebust, H. R. *The Psychology of Deafness*. New York: Grune & Stratton, 1960.

Pollack, M. C. (Ed.). *Amplification for the Hearing Impaired*. New York: Grune & Stratton, 1975.

Davis, H., & Silverman, S. (Eds). *Hearing and Deafness*. New York: Holt, Rinehart, and Winston, 1960.

Volta Review. Washington, DC: Alexander Graham Bell Association for the Deaf.

Journal of Speech, Language and Hearing Disorders. Rockville, Md.: American Speech-Language-Hearing Association.

REFERENCES

Altshuler, K. Studies of the deaf. *American Journal of Psychiatry*, 1971, *127*, 1521–1532.

Arthur, G. *The Arthur adaptation of the Leiter scale*. Washington, D.C.: The Psychological Service Center Press, 1952.

Ballinger, J., *Diseases of the nose, throat and ear* (12th ed.). Philadelphia: Lea & Febriger, 1977.

Bayley, N. *Bayley scales of infant development*. New York: The Psychological Corporation, 1969.

Bender, L. *Visual motor gestalt test*. New York: American Orthopsychiatric Association, 1946.

Beratis, S., Rubin, M., Miller, R., Galenson, E., & Rothstein, A. Developmental aspects of an infant with transient moderate to severe hearing impairment. *Pediatrics*, 1979, *63*, 153–155.

Binnie, C. Relevant aural rehabilitation. In J. Northern (Ed.), *Hearing disorders*. Boston: Little, Brown, 1976.

Blair, F. A study of the visual memory of deaf and hearing children. *American Annals of the Deaf,* 1957, *102,* 254.
Boyd, R. *Boyd developmental progress scale.* San Bernardino, Calif.: Inland Counties Regional Center, 1974.
Boyd, R. Intrauterine rubella and intelligence. In L. Milgrim & R. McCartin (Eds.), *The Deaf blind child: Determining a direction.* Seattle: University of Washington, 1975.
Brackmann, D., & House, W. Direct stimulation of the auditory nerve in hearing disorders. In J. Northern (Ed.), *Hearing disorders.* Boston: Little, Brown, 1976.
Carhart, R. (Ed.). *Human communication and its disorders—An overview.* Bethesda, Md.: National Institute on Neurological Diseases and Stroke, U.S. Department of Health, Education and Welfare, 1967–68.
Chalfant, J., & Scheffelin, M. *Central processing dysfunction in children.* Bethesda, Md.: U.S. Department of Health, Education, and Welfare, 1969.
Downs, M. The handicap of deafness. In J. Northern (Ed.), *Hearing disorders.* Boston: Little, Brown, 1976.
Fisher, S., & Cleveland, S. *Body image and Personality.* Princeton: D. Van Nostrand, 1958.
Fitts, W. H. *Tennessee self concept scale.* Nashville, Tenn.: Counselor Recordings and Tests, 1965.
Frankenburg, W., Dodds, J., & Fandal, A. *Developmental Denver Screening Test.* Denver: University of Colorado Medical Center, 1970.
Galenson, E., Mitler, R., Kaplan, E., & Rothstein, A. Assessment of development in the deaf child. *Journal of American Academy of Child Psychiatry,* 1979, *18,* 128–142.
Garrison, W., Tesch, S., & Decaro, P. An assessment of self concept labels among post secondary deaf adolescents. *American Annals of the Deaf,* 1978, *123,* 968–975.
Gerber, B. M. Interpreter effects with deaf patients (letter). *American Journal of Psychiatry,* 1979, *7,* 990.
Harris, S. A letter from the editor on living with impairments. *The Clinical Psychologist,* 1980, *33,* 3.
Hathaway, S., & McKinley, J. *Minnesota multiphasic personality inventory.* New York: The Psychological Corporation, 1948.
Hersch, L., & Solomon, M. A comprehensive approach to understanding deafness. *American Annals of the Deaf,* 1973, *118,* 34–36.
Hirshoren, A., Hurley, O., Kavale, K. Psychometric characteristics of the WISC-R Performance Scale with deaf children. *Journal of Speech and Hearing Disorders,* 1979, *44,* 73–79.
Hirshoren, A., & Schnittjer, C. Dimensions of problem behavior in deaf children. *Journal of Abnormal Child Psychology,* 1979, *7,* 221–228.
Hiskey, M. *Nebraska test of learning aptitude for young deaf children.* Lincoln: University of Nebraska, 1955.
Kuder, G. *Kuder preference record, vocational: Manual.* Chicago: Science Research Associates, 1953.
Lavos, G. The Chicago Non-verbal Examination: A study in retest characteristics. *American Annals of the Deaf,* 1950, *95,* 379.
Leiter, R. G. *Leiter international performance scale.* Santa Barbara, Calif.: Santa Barbara State College Press, 1940.
Machover, K. *Personality projection in the drawing of the human figure.* Springfield, Ill.: Charles C Thomas, 1949.
Markides, A. Speechreading (lipreading). *Child Care, Health and Development,* 1979, *5,* 93–101.
McWilliams, B. Various aspects of parent counseling. In E. Webster (Ed.), *Professional approaches with parents of handicapped children.* Springfield, Ill.: Charles C Thomas, 1976.

Mindel, E. *They grow in silence.* Mt. Vernon, N.Y.: National Association for the Deaf, 1971.
Moores, D. *Educating the deaf: Psychological principles and practices.* Boston: Houghton Mifflin, 1978.
Murphy, H., Jacobs, L., & Conklin, P. The majors of handicapped students at California State University, Northridge. *College-Student Journal,* 1978, *12,* 26–30.
Murphy, K. Tests of abilities and attainments. In A. Ewing (Ed.), *Educational guidance and the deaf child.* Washington, D.C.: The Volta Bureau, 1957.
Murray, H. *Thematic apperception test.* Boston: Harvard University Press, 1943.
Myklebust, H. *The psychology of deafness.* New York: Grune & Stratton, 1960.
Nance, W. *Heredity and deafness.* Washington, D.C.: Public Service Programs, Gallaudet College, 1975.
Northern, J. (Ed.). *Hearing disorders.* Boston: Little, Brown, 1976.
Northern, J., & Downs, M. *Hearing in children* (2nd ed.). Baltimore, Md.: Williams & Wilkins, 1978.
Osgood, C., Suci, G., & Tannenbaum, P. *The measurement of meaning.* Urbana: University of Illinois Press, 1957.
Raven, J. *Guide to using the progressive matrices.* London: H. K. Lewis, 1938.
Rorschach, H. *Rorschach psychodiagnostics.* New York: Grune & Stratton, 1948.
Rotter, J. B. *The Rotter incomplete sentences blank.* New York: The Psychological Corporation, 1950.
Sataloff, J. *Hearing loss.* Philadelphia: J. B. Lippincott Co., 1966.
Sendelbaugh, J. Television viewing habits of hearing-impaired teenagers in the Chicago metropolitan area. *American Annals of the Deaf,* 1978, *123,* 536–54.
Shein, J., & Delk, M. *The deaf population of the United States.* Silver Spring, Md.: National Association of the Deaf, 1974.
Simmons, F., & Russ, F. Automated newborn hearing screening, the Crib-o-gram. *Archives of Otolaryngology,* 1974, *100,* 1–7.
Sitnick, V., Rushmer, N., & Arpan, R. *Parent-infant communication: A program of clinical and home training for parents and hearing impaired infants.* Beaverton, Oregon: Dormac, Inc., 1977.
Streff, M., Barefoot, S., Walter, G., & Crandall, K. A comparative study of hearing-impaired and normal-hearing young adults—verbal and nonverbal abilities. *Journal of Communication Disorders,* 1978, *11,* 489–498.
Terman, L., & Merrill, M. *Stanford-Binet Intelligence Scale, Form L–M.* Boston: Houghton Mifflin, 1972.
Tomlinson-Keasey, C., & Kelly, R. The deaf child's symbolic world. *American Annals of the Deaf,* 1978, *123,* 452–459.
Vanden Horst, A., & Kamstra, O. Social class, defective hearing and language. *Journal of Communication Disorders,* 1979, *12,* 217–228.
Vernon, J., & Schleuning, A. Tinnitus: A new management. *Laryngoscope,* 1978, *88,* 413–419.
Weaver, M., & Northern, J. The acoustic nerve tumor. In J. Northern (Ed.), *Hearing disorders.* Boston: Little, Brown, 1976.
Webster, D., & Webster, M. Brain stem auditory nuclei after sound deprivation. *Archives of Otolaryngology,* 1977, *103,* 392–396.
Wechsler, D. *Wechsler intelligence scale for children—Revised.* New York: The Psychological Corporation, 1974.
Wilson, J., Rapin, I., Wilson, B., & Van Denburg, F. Neuropsychologic function of children with severe hearing impairment. *Journal of Speech and Hearing Research,* 1975, *18,* 634–651.

Index

Absences (petit mal), 148–149, 171–172
Acoustic nerve tumors, 382
Acyanotic heart diseases, 305
   and intellectual development, 309
Adaptation stage, after spinal cord
      injury, 223
   to physical disability, 4
Adaptive behavior measures, 30
   mental retardation and, 181, 197–198
     AAMD Adaptive Behavior Scale
       (ABS), 198–199
     guideline for relevance, 203–205
Adjustment, 190
   to blindness, 350–351, 354
   to chronic disability, 4–5
   coping skills, 5, 47
   coronary patients, 325
   diabetic families, 47
   hemophiliacs, 27–28
     employment and, 29
   in progressive muscle disorders, 286
   to traumatic injury, stages of, 3–4, 221–223
Adolescents
   blind, 342, 364
   cerebral-palsied, 127
   diabetic, 47–48
     psychological evaluation, 50, 57
     self-concept, 49, 50
   effect of disability on parents, 232
   hearing-impaired, 396–397, 402
     counseling for, 404

Adolescents (*cont.*)
   hemophilic, 32–33
   with Klinefelter's Syndrome, 93–94
   mentally retarded, 192
   with myelomeningocele, 252, 253–254, 255
     counseling, 267
     interviewing, 259
   skills for, 15–16
   with Turner's Syndrome, 86, 89
Adult-onset diabetes, 40
Agressive behavior
   in adolescence, 5
   in congenital heart disease, 307
   in hemophilia, 28
Akinetic seizures, 150
Alcoholism and epilepsy, 152
American Association on Mental
      Deficiency (AAMD)
   Adaptive Behavior Scale (ABS), 134, 198–199
   Manual, 180
American Diabetes Association (ADA), 40, 44
   on employment of diabetics, 48–49
   as information source, 60, 63
Amyotrophic lateral sclerosis (ALS), 277–278
   independence, aids to, 297
   psychological characteristics, 293
Anger, injury and, 4, 222–223
Angina pectoris, 319

Anterior horn cell disease
  amyotrophic lateral sclerosis, 277–278, 293, 297
  Kugelberg-Welander Disease, 277
  Werdnig-Hoffman Disease, 276–277, 284, 287
Antibiotics, ototoxic, 383
Anticonvulsant medications, 155
  list, 159–161
  and pregnancy, 158
Aortic defects, 303
Arthur adaptation of Leiter scale, 389, 395
Aspiration level, and physical disability, 8–9
Atherosclerosis, 317
Audiologist, role of, 399
Audiometry
  for acoustic nerve tumors, 382
  electrophysiological, 406–407
Auditory nerve, electrical stimulation of, 406
Aura before seizure, 157
Aural-oral method of deaf education, 403
Autosomal dominant disorders, 72
  Huntington's disease as, 96
  muscular, 278, 281–282
Autosomal recessive disorders, 71–72
  muscular, 276, 277, 281
  PKU as, 75
Autosomes, 70

Becker-type muscular dystrophy, 281
Behavior modification
  for cerebral-palsied, 140–141
    possibilities, 142
  for coronary-prone behavior, question of, 329–330, 331
Bicuspid aortic valve, 303
Biological risk factors, 185–187
  and intervention, 209–210
Biopsies
  muscle, 275–276
  nerve, 276
Blandness, in the lives of the physically disabled, 9
Blindness. See Visual handicaps
Blood coagulation defects in newborns, 158

Blood products for hemophilic patients, 23
Blood sugar level in diabetics, 43
  and psychological characteristics, 50–51, 52, 55–56, 57
Body image of diabetics, 49
Bowel/bladder functioning in myelomeningocele child, 247, 253, 263–264, 266
Braille, 365–366
Brain stem-evoked response audiometry, 407
Brain surgery for epilepsy, 158

Callier-Azuza Scale, 358
Camps
  for cerebral-palsied, 137–138
  for diabetics, 60
  for hemophiliacs, 32
Canes for blind persons, 365
Car, driving of, disabilities and, 16
  epilepsy, 165–166
  myelomeningocele, 255
  Turner's Syndrome, 87
Cardiac surgery. See Surgery: cardiac
Cardiovascular disorders
  muscle disease and, 284
  rheumatic, 304
  See also Congenital heart defects; Coronary heart disease
Career. See Vocation
Carriers, genetic, 71
  of Duchenne dystrophy, 280
  of hemophilia, 22
Cataracts, 337
Cerebral palsy, 117–143
  definition, 117
  evaluation of persons with
    interview, 129–130
    testing, 125–126, 131–135, 140
  hearing loss, 121
  incidence/prevalence, 118–120
  information sources, 142–143
  and intelligence, 122
    testing, 125–126, 131–135
    interventions, psychosocial, 136–141
    possibilities for, 142
  motor symptoms, 118
    treatment, 120
    prospects, 142

INDEX

Cerebral palsy (*cont.*)
  psychological characteristics/problems in, 123–129
  seizures, 122–123
  severity levels, 118–119
  speech problems, 121, 126–127
    and interview, 129–130
  treatment, 120–121
  types, 118, 119
  vision, defects of, 122
Cerebrospinal fluid in myelomeningocele patients, 244, 246
Charcot-Marie-Tooth disease, 278
Chromosomes, 70
  and disorders, 72–73
    congenital heart defect with, 304–305
    Down's Syndrome, 183–184
    Klinefelter's Syndrome, 90–91
    Turner's Syndrome, 82–83
Cleft lip/palate, 380–381
Coarctation of aorta, 303
Cognitive functioning. *See* Intelligence levels
Comic books, stereotyping in, 2
Complex partial (psychomotor) seizures, 150
  and psychopathology, 167–168
Congenital defects
  deafness, 380–381
  visual, 336
  See also Congenital heart defects; Genetic disorders
Congenital heart defects, 301–314
  diagnosis, 305–306
  evaluation of persons with, 310–311
  incidence, 302, 303, 304
  information sources, 314
  interventions, psychosocial, 311–313
  kinds, 303
    acyanotic versus cyanotic, 305
    manifestations, physiological, 305
  needs concerning, 313–314
  pathological conditions associated with, 305
    Down's Syndrome, 184, 304
  psychological characteristics/problems in, 306–310
  surgery, 184, 304, 306, 310
    indications for, 303

Congenital myotonic dystrophy, 283
Coping skills, 5
  diabetic families, 47
Coronary heart disease, 317–331
  diagnosis, 320
  evaluation of persons with, 326–327
  incidence, 318
  information sources, 331
  interventions, psychosocial, 327–331
  needs concerning, 331
  psychological characteristics/problems in
    post-coronary, 323–326
    Type A personality, 321–323, 327, 329
  risk factors, 318–319
    See also Type A personality
  treatment, 320–321
  types, 317–318, 319–320
Creatine phosphokinase (CPK) and muscular dystrophies, 275, 280, 281
Cumulative risk index, 187
Cyanotic heart diseases, 305
  and intellectual development, 309

Dancing eyes syndrome, 150
Deafness. *See* Hearing loss
Death counseling, 297–298
Decibel range and severity of hearing loss, 378–379
Dejerine-Sottas disease, 278
Demyelinating neuropathies, 278
Denial mechanism, 3–4, 190
  hearing-impaired, 391
  hemophiliacs, 27–28
  muscle disease patients, families of, 287
  after spinal cord injury, 222, 231
Dependence versus independence, 5, 10
  in blind, 347, 348, 353, 354
  in diabetics, 48
    and symptomatology, 51–52
  in muscle disease patients, 285
  in spinal cord injured, 232–233
Depression, 4
  blindness and, 350–351, 367
  child's mother, 342
  diabetics, 50, 55
  after spinal cord injury, 223
Detached retina, 337–338

Developmental inventories, 133, 195–196, 394
  for blind children, 357, 358
  guideline for relevance, 203–205
  for myelomeningocele child, 260
Diabetes mellitus, 39–64
  complications, 45, 338
  control
    and familial coping, 47
    rating of adult patients, 53–54
    variation in concept, 43–44
  and development, 44–45
  evaluation of persons with, 54–58
    cognitive functioning, 56–57
    emotional status, 50, 57–58
  genetic factors, 41
  information
    and body image, 49
    and control, 53–54
    in intervention, 59
    interviewer, requirement for, 55
    sources, 63–64
    tests, 53, 56–57
  interventions, psychosocial, 58–61
  prevalence, 40–41
  psychological characteristics/problems in
    common to chronic illnesses, 46–50
    unique to diabetes, 50–54, 55–56
  research prospects, 62–63
  symptoms, 42
  treatment, 43–44
    future prospects, 61
    patient responsibility for, 43, 52–54
  types, 40
Diabetic retinopathy, 45, 338
Diet for PKU persons, 76, 77, 78
  evaluation, clinical, 80, 81
  parents' role, 76–77, 79, 80
Disabling conditions, acceptability of, 2–3
Disorder/disability, Colenbrander's concepts of, 340, 341
Dogs for blind persons, 365
Dominant gene disorders, 72
  Huntington's Disease as, 96
  muscular, 278, 281–282
Down, J. H. Langdon, 183
Down's Syndrome, 183–185
  congenital heart defect and, 184, 304

Drawings, use of, for evaluating muscle disorder patients, 295–296
Driving of car, disabilities and, 16
  epilepsy, 165–166
  myelomeningocele, 255
  Turner's Syndrome, 87
Drugs
  abuse by hemophiliacs, 27, 33
  anticonvulsant, 155
    list, 159–161
    and pregnancy, 158
  for muscle disorders, 284–285, 292–293
  ototoxic, 383
Duchenne muscular dystrophy, 280–281
  enzyme testing, 275
  psychological characteristics/problems in, 287–289
    intelligence, 289–290, 298
  treatment, 284

Education. *See* Schooling
Electrocardiogram (ECG or EKG), 320
Electroencephalogram (EEG), petit mal seizures and, 171–172
Electromyography (EMG), 275
Electrophysiological audiometry, 406–407
Emotional adjustment. *See* Adjustment
Emotional neutrality, question of, 10–11
Emotional release in cerebral palsy, 126
Employment. *See* Vocation
Environmental risk factors, 187–189
  and intervention, 210
Enzyme testing for muscular dystrophies, 275
Epilepsy, 147–176
  classification of seizures, 148–151
  etiology, 152–153
    determination of, 154
  evaluation of persons with, 168–174
    employment-related issues, 173–174
    intellectual/cognitive, 172–173
    interview, 168–171
    neuropsychological, 173
    petit mal seizures, behavior during, 171–172
    standards for, 156
  information sources, 176
  interventions, psychosocial, 174–175

INDEX

Epilepsy (cont.)
  needs concerning, 176
  prevalence, 151
  psychological characteristics/problems in, 162–168
    behavioral problems, 169–170
    treatment, 153–161
      anticonvulsant medication, 155, 158, 159–161
      standards of medical care, 154, 156–157
Estrogen for Turner's Syndrome, 85
Evoked response audiometry (ERA), 407
Expedience, attitude of, toward disabled, 6

Facioscapulohumeral muscular dystrophy, 281–282
Factor replacement for hemophiliacs, 23
Families
  adjustment process, 4–5, 190
  of blind children, 341–343, 344, 345
    evaluation, 354–356
    intervention with, 362–363
  of cerebral-palsied children, 123–124
    intervention with, 136, 137
  of congenital heart patients, 308–309
    intervention with, 312, 313
  coronary patients, spouses of, 323–324
    intervention with, 328, 330
  of diabetics, 46–47, 52, 58–59
  of epileptics, 162–164, 165
    intervention with, 174, 175
    interview with, 169, 170–171
  of hearing-impaired, 386–388
    intervention with, 400–402
  of hemophiliacs, 25–26, 30–31
  Huntington's Disease in, 100, 104–105, 106
    diagnosis, disclosure of, 101, 107–108
  of Klinefelter's Syndrome males, 93, 94
  of mentally retarded
    altered feedback and, 191–192, 200
    interaction, observation of, 191–192, 199–202
    and interventions, 208–210
    reaction to diagnosis, 189

Families (cont.)
  risk factors, mother and, 184, 186, 188–189, 209
  and special considerations in assessment, 206, 207
  of muscle disorder patients, 286, 287–289
    intervention with, 296
  of myelomeningocele children, 248–250, 252
    evaluation of, 257–258
    intervention with, 261–263
    treatment decision, role in, 246, 262
  of PKU children, 76–77, 79–80
    intervention with, 82
  Questionnaire on Resources and Stress for, 295
  of spinal cord injured, 232
  of Turner's Syndrome girls, 86, 87, 89
Fathers
  of diabetics, 53
  of hemophiliacs, 26
Febrile convulsions, 151
Feedback
  to disabled, 7–9
    cerebral-palsied, behavior modification for, 140–141
  to parent, alteration of, 191–192, 200
Framingham study, 318, 319
  Type A personality in, 321
Free play situation, parent–child interaction in, 191–192, 201

Gehrig, Lou, 277
Gender role identity
  in Klinefelter's Syndrome, 92
  in Turner's Syndrome, 85–86
Generalized seizures, kinds of, 148–150
Genes, 70–71
  and disorders, 71, 72
Genetic counseling, 73–74
Genetic disorders, 69–110
  chromosomal abnormalities, 72–73
  congenital heart defect and, 304–305
  in Down's Syndrome, 183–184
  in Klinefelter's Syndrome, 90–91
  in Turner's Syndrome, 82–83
  counseling about, 73–74
  diabetes as, 41

Genetic disorders (cont.)
  diagnosis, 69–70
    Huntington's disease, 96–97
    Klinefelter's Syndrome, 91
    PKU, 75
    Turner's Syndrome, 83–84
  dominant, autosomal, 72
    Huntington's Disease as, 96
    muscular, 278, 281–282
  hearing loss, 381
  hemophilia as, 22
  Huntington's Disease, 95–109
  information sources, 110
  Klinefelter's Syndrome, 90–95
  muscular, 274
    muscular dystrophies, 280, 281–282
    peripheral neuropathies, 278
    spinal muscular atrophies, 276, 277
  myelomeningocele as, 245
  needs concerning, 108–110
  phenylketonuria (PKU), 74–82
  recessive, autosomal and X-linked, 71–72
    hemophilia as, 22
    muscular, 276, 277, 280, 281
    PKU as, 75
  Turner's Syndrome, 82–90
Gestational diabetes mellitus, 44
Glaucoma, 337
Grand mal, 149–150
Group approaches
  diabetes, 59, 60
  hearing impairment, 405
  for parents, 401
  hemophilia, 32
  myelomeningocele, 263
  Turner's Syndrome, 89
Growth hormones for Turner's Syndrome, 84–85
Guide dogs, 365
Guthrie, Marjorie, 97–98, 107

Halstead-Reitan battery, 173
Handicap, visible, in social interaction, 2
Haptic Intelligence Scale (HIS) for Adult Blind, 359
Hayes-Binet test, 357
Head trauma and epilepsy, 152–153
Headstart programs, 210
Hearing aids, 385

Hearing loss, 375–409
  amplification for, 385
  in cerebral palsy, 121
  conditions causing, 377, 380–384
    and severity, 378–379
  developments in field, 406–407
  evaluation of persons with, 392–399
  identification, 384–385
  impact
    by decibel range, 378–379
    economic, 375–376
    variables affecting, 376
  incidence, 375
    congenital, 381
  information sources, 408–409
  interventions, psychosocial
    educational methods, 403–404
    with family, 400–402
    multidisciplinary approach, 399–400
    personal counseling, 404–406
  needs concerning, 407–408
  psychological characteristics/problems in, 386–392
Heart
  disorders
    muscle disease and, 284
    rheumatic, 304
    See also Congenital heart defects; Coronary heart disease
  working of, 301–302
Hemophilia, 21–35
  emotional factors and bleeding, relationship of, 28, 34–35
  evaluation of persons with, 29–30
  incidence, 21
  information sources, 35
  interventions, psychosocial, 30–34
  manifestations, physical, 22
  psychological characteristics/problems in, 24–29
  treatment, 22–23
    changes in, 35
  types, 21–22
Hereditary disorders. *See* Genetic disorders
Hereditary motor and sensory neuropathy (HMSN), 278
High blood pressure (hypertension), 319
Histochemical stains, use of, 275–276

INDEX

Home infusion for hemophiliacs, 24, 32
Hope, and realistic self-appraisal, 8–9, 10
Hormone therapy
  Klinefelter's Syndrome, 91, 95
  Turner's Syndrome, 84–85
Huntington, George, 97
Huntington's Disease, 95–109
  at-risk individuals
    counseling for, 108
    parenthood decision, 100–101, 108
    psychological characteristics/problems, 99–100
  diagnosis of, 96–97, 101
  disclosure, 101, 107–108
  evaluation of persons with, 105–106
    testing, 102–104, 105
  genetic factors, 96
  history of, 97–98
  interventions, 107–109
  psychological characteristics/problems in
    at-risk individuals, 99–101
    diagnostic confirmation and, 101
    of family, 104–105
    symptomatic, 102–104
  symptoms
    cognitive, 102–104
    emotional, 102
    motor, 98
  treatment, 98–99
Hyalene membrane disease, 185
Hydrocephalus, myelomeningocele and, 244, 246
  intelligence, effect on, 247, 250–251
Hypertension, 319
Hypertrophic peripheral neuropathies, 278

Identification with other handicapped persons, 9
Ignorance toward disabled, 6
Impairment, Colenbrander's concept of, 340, 341
Impotence in diabetics, 44–45
Incontinence, myelomeningocele and, 247, 253
Independence versus dependence. *See* Dependence versus independence
Industrial visual efficiency, measurement of, 339

Inertia of emotional arousal in Turner's Syndrome, 86
Infant Hearing Resource program, 402
Infantile spasms, 150
Infantile spinal muscular atrophy (Werdnig-Hoffman Disease), 276–277
  parental reaction, 287
  treatment, 284
Institutionalization of mentally retarded, 211–212
Instructional aids
  diabetes, 59
  hemophilia, 31–32
  Turner's Syndrome, 89
Insulin-dependent diabetes mellitus (IDDM), 40
  symptoms, 42
Intelligence levels
  of blind, measurement of, 357–359
  of cerebral-palsied, 122
    testing of, 125–126, 131–135
  congenital heart patients, 309–310
    research need, 314
  of deaf, measurement of, 389–390, 393–395
  diabetics, 56
    adult changes, possibility of, 57
  epileptics, 166
    assessment, 172–173
    parental fears, 164
  hemophiliacs, 26
  in Huntington's Disease, measurement of, 102–104
  in Klinefelter's Syndrome, 93
  maternal attitudes and, 188–189
  in mental retardation
    severity classification, 180–181
    testing, 196–197
  in muscular dystrophies, 289–290, 291, 298
  myelomeningocele and, 247, 250–251
    and adjustment, 253
    evaluation, 260–261
  in PKU, 74, 78
  in Turner's Syndrome, 86–87
  and vocation, 17
International Classification of Epileptic Seizures, 148, 149

Interpersonal Cognitive Problem Solving approach, 368
Interpreters, use of, in evaluation of deaf, 397
Ischemia, defined, 317

Jacksonian seizures, 150
Jenkins Activity Survey, 327
Juvenile diabetes, 40

Kinetic Family Drawing technique, 295
Klinefelter's Syndrome, 90–95
  evaluation of persons with, 93–94
  genetic factors, 90–91
  interventions, psychosocial, 94–95
  manifestations, clinical, 91
  psychological characteristics/problems in, 92–93
  treatment, 91–92
Kugelberg-Welander Disease, 277

Labeling of disabled, 14
  mentally retarded, 181
Language
  development
    by blind child, 345–346
    importance in socioeconomic group, 388
  problems in cerebral palsy, 121
Legal blindness, 338–339, 340
Leiter International Performance Scale, adaptations of, 358, 389, 395
Limb-girdle type of muscular dystrophy, 281
Lipodystrophy in diabetics, 45
Lipreading by deaf, 397
Little, William J., 117
"Lou Gehrig's disease," 277
Low-vision aids, 362
Lower motor neuron disease. *See* Anterior horn cell disease

Macular degeneration, 338
Mainstreaming/normalization, 14–15
  of blind, 364
  of hearing-impaired, 404
Marriage
  coronary patients, spouses of, 323–324
    intervention with, 328, 330
  effect of diabetic child on, 47

Marriage (*cont.*)
  effect of epileptic child on, 170–171
  effect of Huntington's Disease on, 104–105
  effect of myelomeningocele child on, 249
  hemophiliacs, 28
  Klinefelter's Syndrome males, 92
  spinal cord injured persons, 227, 235
Maxfield-Fjeld scale, 357
Medications. *See* Drugs
Memory, Huntington's Disease and, 103
Ménière's disease, 381–382
Meningomyelocele. *See* Myelomeningocele
Menstruation in Turner's Syndrome female, 85
Mental health problems, 12
  criteria for referral, 13
  diabetics, 50
  epileptics, 167–168
  hemophiliacs, 33–34
  Huntington's Disease patients, 99, 102
  spinal cord injured, 223
    psychotherapy for, 233–234
  suicide, thoughts of. *See* Suicidal ideation
Mental retardation, 179–213
  definition, 180
  etiology, 182–183
    biological risk factors, 185–187, 209
    environmental risk, 187–189, 210
    intervention based on, 207–210
    medical disorders with known risk, 183–185, 208
  evaluation of persons with, 193–207
    adaptive behavior measurements, 197–199
    developmental screening instruments, 195–196
    intelligence testing, 196–197
    issues in, 193–194, 203–205
    parent-child interaction, 191–192, 199–202
    risk indices, 194–195
    selection of procedure, 202–206
  information sources, 212–213
  intervention
    etiology as basis of, 207–210
    focus of, and assessment procedure, 203–205

Mental retardation (*cont.*)
 intervention (*cont.*)
  interdisciplinary approach, 210–211
  residential, 211–212
 in Klinefelter's Syndrome, 93
 myelomeningocele and, 247
 and adjustment, 253
 needs concerning, 212
 PKU and, 74
 prevalence, 182
 psychological characteristics/problems in, 189–193
  in parent-child interactions, 191–192, 200–202
  as "reversible," 181
 severity classification, 180–181
Metabolic disorders
 screening for, 195
 See also Phenylketonuria
Middle ear disorders, 381
 fluid-caused, 377, 380
Minnesota Multiphasic Personality Inventory (MMPI), use of, 135, 230
 for deaf, 395
 for diabetics, 57, 58
 for Huntington's Disease patients, 102
 for muscle disorder patients, 293, 295
Mobility training for blind, 365
Mothers
 age of, and Down's Syndrome, 184
 and biological risk factor, 186, 209
 of blind children, 341, 342, 343, 345, 362–363
 of cerebral-palsied children, 124
 of diabetics, 46–47
 and environmental risk factor, 188–189
 of hearing-impaired children, 387
 of hemophiliacs, 25–26
 mentally retarded child, interaction with, 191, 200, 201
 of muscle disorder patients, 286, 296
 of myelomeningocele children, 249–250, 262
 of Turner's Syndrome daughters, 87
Motor function, impairment of
 cerebral palsy, 118
  treatment, 120
 Huntington's Disease, 98
 myelomeningocele, 247, 251
  evaluation, 260

Motor function (*cont.*)
 See also Progressive muscle disorders; Spinal cord injury
Motor neuron diseases. *See* Anterior horn cell disease
Motor unit, 273, 274
Muscle biopsies, 275–276
Muscles
 reflexes, in spinal cord injured, 220
 See also Progressive muscle disorders
Muscular dystrophies, 279–283
 enzyme testing for, 275
 psychological characteristics/problems in, 287–291
  intelligence, 289–290, 291, 298
 treatment, 284
Myasthenia gravis, 278–279
 interventions, 297
 psychological characteristics, 291–293
 treatment, 284–285
Myelomeningocele, 243–268
 definition, 243–244
 etiology, theories of, 245
 evaluation of persons with, 256–261
 incidence, 245
 information sources, 268
 interventions, psychosocial
  goals of, 261
  with parents, 261–263
  with patient, 266–268
  with school, 263–265
 physical problems related to, 244, 246–248
 psychological characteristics/problems in, 248–256
 training of personnel, need for, 268
 treatment decision, 245–246, 262
Myocardial infarction, 318, 319–320
 patients. *See* Coronary heart disease
Myoclonic seizures, 150
Myopathies. *See* Muscular dystrophies
Myotonic dystrophy, 282–283
 psychological characteristics, 290–291
 treatment, 284

Nebraska Test of Learning Aptitude, 394–395
Nerve biopsy, 276
Nerve conduction studies, 275
Nerve deafness, electrical stimulation for, 406
Nerve tumors and hearing loss, 382

Nervous system
  motor unit, 273, 274
  muscle disorders, kinds of, 276–279
Neurological examination, 275
Neuropathies
  in diabetics, 45
  kinds of, 276–278
Neuropsychological assessment of epileptics, 175
Neurosurgery for epilepsy, 158
Noise-induced hearing loss, 382–393
  need for prevention, 408
Non-insulin-dependent diabetes mellitus (NIDDM), 40
  development, 42
Normalization. *See* Mainstreaming

Obesity and diabetes, 42
Optic atrophy, 338
Oralism in deaf education, 403
Organ transplants for diabetics, prospect of, 62
Otitis media, 377, 380
Otolaryngologist, role of, 399
Otosclerosis, 381
Ototoxicity, 383
Outer ear malformations, 380
"Outhouse syndrome" in myelomeningocele, 247, 253, 264
Overprotection of disabled, 6
  cerebral-palsied, 124
  Duchenne's boys, 288–289

Paraplegia, traumatic. *See* Spinal cord injury
Parents. *See* Families
Partial seizures, epileptic, 150
Patent ductus arteriosis, 303
Peabody tests, 229
Perceptual-motor problems in myelomeningocele, 251
  evaluation, 260
Peripheral neuropathies, 278
Perkins-Binet test, 358
Peroneal muscular atrophy, 278
Petit mal, 148–149, 171–172
Phenylalanine (PA) in PKU, 74
  and classification, 75, 76
  dietary control, 76, 77
  evaluation, 81

Phenylketonuria (PKU), 74–82
  classification of severity and type, 75–76
  diagnosis, 75
  evaluation of persons with, 79–81
  genetic factors, 75
  and metabolic clinic, 211
  psychological characteristics/problems in, 78–79
    interventions for, 82
  treatment, 76–78
    parents' role, 76–77, 79–80
Physical therapy for cerebral palsy, 120
Physically disabled
  acceptability ranking of, 2–3
  adjustment process, 3–5
  development, psychological problems in, 5–10
  helping relationships with, 10–13
  labeling of, 14
  mainstreaming/normalization, 14–15
  milestones in progress, 15–18
  stigma attached to, 1–2
  See also names of individual disabilities
Piaget, Jean, 197
PKU. *See* Phenylketonuria
Postural drainage for muscle disorders, 284
Pregnancy
  in diabetics, 44
  epilepsy and, 158
  infections during, 381
Prematurity in infants, 185, 186
Presbycusis, 383
Productivity factors in spinal cord injured, 225–226
Progressive muscle disorders, 273–299
  diagnosis, 274–276
    myasthenia gravis, 279
  evaluation of persons with, 293–296
  information sources, 299
  interventions, psychosocial, 296–298
  kinds
    peripheral neuropathies, 278
    See also Anterior horn cell disease; Muscular dystrophies; Myasthenia gravis
  needs concerning, 298
  psychological characteristics/problems in, 285–293

INDEX

Progressive muscle disorders (*cont.*)
   with adolescent/early adult onset, 290–291
   with adult onset, 291–293
   with childhood onset, 287–290
   treatment, 283–285
Pseudohypertrophy in muscular dystrophy, 280
Psychodrama for hearing-impaired, 405
Psychological/intelligence testing
   blindness and, 357–361
   of parents, 355
   in studies, 348, 350
   cerebral-palsied persons, 125–126, 131–135, 140
   congenital heart patients, 311
     intellectual-development studies, 309–310
   coronary patients, 327
   deaf persons, 389, 393–396
     interest patterns, 392
   diabetics, 50, 56, 57–58
   epileptics, 166, 173
   hemophiliacs, 30
   Huntington's Disease individuals, 102–104, 105
   Klinefelter's Syndrome males, 93
   mentally retarded
     adaptive behavior measures, 197–199
     developmental screening procedures, 195–196
     intelligence tests, 196–197
     selection, guideline for, 203–205
   muscle disorder patients, 289–290, 294–296
   myelomeningocele and, 259–261
   parents of patient, 257
   spinal cord injured, 228–230
   Turner's Syndrome females, 86–87
Psychological self-protection, 6–7
Psychomotor seizures, 150
   and psychopathology, 167–168
Psychosocial retardation, 187–189, 210
Psychotherapy
   for myocardial patients, 329
   for spinal cord injured, 233–234
Public Law 94-142, 14, 137
Pulmonary stenosis, 303

Quadriplegia, traumatic. *See* Spinal cord injury
Questionnaire on Resources and Stress, 295

Raven Progressive Matrices, 395
Recessive disorders, 71–72
   diabetes as, 41
   hemophilia as, 22
   muscular, 276, 277, 280, 281
   PKU as, 75
Regional Resource Centers for the Deaf, 407
Repetitive behavior in blind children, 347–348
Residential treatment of mentally retarded, 211–212
Resource centers for deaf, 407
Respirators for muscle disease, 284
Response Class Matrix, 201
Retinal disorders, 45, 337–338
Reversibility of mental retardation, concept of, 181
Rheumatic heart disease, 304
Right-to-treatment movement, 211
Risk indices, 194–195
   cumulative risk index, 187
   guideline for relevance, 203–205

Schedule of Recent Events, 52
Schooling
   of blind, 364
   of cerebral-palsied, 125, 137
   diabetics, 59–60
   Duchenne's boys, 289
   epileptics, 170
     interview about, 169
     petit mal seizures and, 172
   of hearing-impaired, 403–404
     and parents, 402
     teacher, 399–400, 403
   hemophiliacs, 31
     achievement, 27
   of mentally retarded
     intelligence testing before, 197
     issues, 193
   myelomeningocele children, 250, 251–252
     intervention methods, 263–265

Schooling (*cont.*)
  preschool, 192
  Turner's Syndrome girls, 87, 89–90
Screening procedures, 195
  developmental assessment, 195–196, 260, 357, 394
  for hearing, 384–385
  for PKU, 75
Seeing-eye dogs, 365
Seizures
  in cerebral palsy, 122–123
  See also Epilepsy
Self-help skills, 15–16
Self-protection, psychological, 6–7
Semantic differential scales, 257, 327, 396
Septal defects of heart, 303
Sex chromosomes, 70
  and disorders, 72
    Klinefelter's Syndrome, 90–91
    Turner's Syndrome, 82–83
Sex hormones
  for Klinefelter's Syndrome, 91, 95
  for Turner's Syndrome, 84–85
Sex-linked inheritance, 72
  in Duchenne muscular dystrophy, 280
  in hemophilia, 22
Sexual activity, disabilities and, 18
  cerebral palsy, 138
  coronary patients, 325–326
    counseling, 330
  Klinefelter's Syndrome, 92
  myelomeningocele, 247, 255
    counseling, 267
  spinal cord injury, 226–227
    counseling, 228, 234–235
Sexual development/function
  in diabetes, 44–45
  in myelomeningocele, 248
  in Turner's Syndrome, 85
Shock reaction after traumatic injury, 221
Shunt insertion for myelomeningocele patients, 246
  and intelligence, 250–251
Siblings
  of cardiac children, 309
  of dystrophic boys, 288
Sick role, 1
Sight impairment. *See* Visual handicaps

Signing for deaf, 396–397
  versus oralism, 403
Situational press, blind persons and, 348
Social-cultural mental retardation, 187–189, 210
Social Maturity Scale for Blind Pre-School Children, 357
Social Situation Questionnaire for spinal cord injured, 224–225
Spasticity, 118
Speech problems
  in cerebral palsy, 121, 126–127, 129–130
  and interview, 11, 129–130
Speech-reading by deaf, 397
Spina bifida. *See* Myelomeningocele
Spinal cord, disabilities involving. *See* Myelomeningocele; Spinal cord injury
Spinal cord injury, 217–239
  care of patient
    acute, 218
    rehabilitative, 219–220
  evaluation of persons with
    interview, 227–228
    psychological testing, 228–230
  incidence, 217
  information sources, 238–239
  interventions, psychosocial, 231–236
  level of, 218, 219
  physical problems related to, 220, 221
  psychological characteristics/problems in
    personality patterns, 223–224
    reaction, stages of, 3–4, 221–223
    social/sexual adjustment, 224–227
  trends, 238
  vocation after, 235–236, 237
    interest testing and, 230
Spinal muscular atrophies. *See* Anterior horn cell disease
Spread, Wright's concept of, 2, 162, 253
Stanford-Binet Intelligence Scales
  for blind, 357–358
  for cerebral-palsied, 133, 135
Status epilepticus, 151, 154
Steinert's disease. *See* Myotonic dystrophy
Stenosis, kinds of, 303

INDEX

Stress
  and coronary risk, 323
  and diabetic physiology, 51
Structured Interview, 327
Suicidal ideation, 12–13
  hemophiliacs, 34
  Huntington's Disease and, 100, 101, 106
  spinal cord injured persons, 234
Surgery
  brain, for epilepsy, 158
  cardiac, 304, 306, 310, 320–321
    for Down's Syndrome children, 184
    indications for, 303
    preparation of patient, 328
  for cerebral palsy, 120
  for ear disorders, 380, 381, 382
  shunt insertion for myelomeningocele patient, 246
  for visual defects, 337–338
Sympathy, unsophisticated, toward disabled, 7

Teaching aids. *See* Instructional aids
Team approach
  for hearing-impaired, 399–400
  hemophilia treatment, 23, 24
  mentally retarded, care of, 210–211
Teenagers. *See* Adolescents
Tennessee Self Concept Scale, 395
Testing. *See* Psychological/intelligence testing
Testosterone for Klinefelter's Syndrome, 95
Tetralogy of Fallot, 303, 304, 305
Tinnitus, 383–384
Tonic-clonic seizures (grand mal), 149–150
Total communication in deaf education, 403–404
Transplants for diabetics, prospect of, 62
Transposition of great arteries, 303
Traumatic injury. *See* Spinal cord injury
Trisomy, 73, 183–184
Tumors and hearing loss, 382
Turner's Syndrome, 82–90
  diagnosis, 83–84
  evaluation of persons with, 87–88
    intelligence, 86–87

Turner's Syndrome (*cont.*)
  genetic factors, 82–83
  interventions, psychosocial, 89–90
  manifestations, clinical, 83–84
  psychological characteristics/problems in, 85–87
  treatment, 84–85
Type A personality, 321–323
  measures of, 327
  modification, issue of, 329–330, 331

Unsophisticated benevolence toward disabled, 7
Urine management
  for myelomeningocele, 247, 253, 263–264, 266
  for spinal cord injury, 219–220
Uzgiris-Hunt ordinal scales, 197

Verbalism in blind persons, 346
Visual handicaps, 335–371
  in cerebral palsy, 122
  and definitions of acuity, 338–340
    functional, 340, 341
  development of child with, 342–346
  evaluation, 356–357, 358
  diabetes and, 45, 338
  evaluation of persons with, 354–361
  incidence, 335–336
  information sources, 369–371
  interventions
    aids, 362, 365–366
    medical, 337–338, 361–362
    with parents, 362–363
    rehabilitative/therapeutic, 366–368
    training, 363–365
  needs concerning, 369
  psychological characteristics/problems in, 341–354
  types causing blindness, 336–338
Vocation, 16–17
  behaviors, necessary, 17–18
  blind persons
    interest testing, 360–361
    and personality, 349
    planning, 367–368
  cerebral-palsied persons, 128, 129, 139–140
  congenital heart patients, 313

Vocation (*cont.*)
  coronary patients' return to, 324–325, 326
    counseling, 330
  diabetics, 48–49
  epileptics, 165, 173–174
  hearing loss and
    counseling for, 406
    interest patterns, 392
    noise as cause, 382–383
    public attitude and, 407
  hemophiliacs, 29, 33
    evaluation for, 30
  mentally retarded, 192–193
  myelomeningocele and, 255–256, 267–268
    interest testing for, 261
  requirements for, minimum, 17
  skills preceding, 15–16
  spinal cord injured, 235–236, 237
    interest testing and, 230

Wechsler intelligence scales, use of
  with blindness, 358–359
  with cerebral palsy, 133, 134–135

Wechsler (*cont.*)
  with deafness, 389, 394
  with Huntington's Disease, 102–104
  with Klinefelter's Syndrome, 93
  with muscle disorders, 295
  with myelomeningocele, 260–261
  with Turner's Syndrome, 86–87
Werdnig-Hoffman Disease, 276–277
  parental reaction, 287
  treatment, 284
Wheelchairs for progressive muscle disorders
  Duchenne dystrophy, 281, 289
  motorized, 283–284
  as turning point, 286
Willis, Thomas, 39
Wohlfart-Kugelberg-Welander Disease, 277

X-linked inheritance, 72
  in Duchenne muscular dystrophy, 280
  in hemophilia, 22